NOT A
CONSPIRACY
THEORY

NOT A CONSPIRACY THEORY

How Business Propaganda HIJACKS Democracy

DONALD GUTSTEIN

KEY PORTER BOOKS

Library and Archives Canada Cataloguing in Publication

Gutstein, Donald, 1938-
    Not a conspiracy theory : how business propaganda hijacks democracy / Donald Gutstein.

ISBN 978-1-55470-191-9

    1. Corporations--Canada--Political activity. 2. Corporations--United States--Political activity. 3. Propaganda, Canadian. 4. Propaganda, American. 5. Democracy--Canada. 6. Democracy--United States. I. Title.

HD3616.N672G88 2009   303.3'75   C2009-902050-5

The publisher gratefully acknowledges the support of the Canada Council for the Arts and the Ontario Arts Council for its publishing program. We acknowledge the support of the Government of Ontario through the Ontario Media Development Corporation's Ontario Book Initiative.

We acknowledge the financial support of the Government of Canada through the Book Publishing Industry Development Program (BPIDP) for our publishing activities.

Key Porter Books Limited
Six Adelaide Street East, Tenth Floor
Toronto, Ontario
Canada M5C 1H6

www.keyporter.com

Text design and electronic formatting: Alison Carr

Distributed in Canada by H.B. Fenn and Company, Ltd.
Printed and bound in Canada

09 10 11 12 13 5 4 3 2 1

Dedication

For Mae, Josh and Niki

Acknowledgments

Alex Carey, the Australian sociologist, first alerted me to the corporate-sponsored propaganda machine in his posthumous book, *Taking the Risk Out of Democracy*. While I was writing the book, Charlie Smith of the *Georgia Straight* and David Beers of The Tyee published my stories, many on themes being developed for the book. Shane Gunster and Murray Dobbin provided helpful comments on draft chapters. Jim Turk of the Canadian Association of University Teachers invited me to present my ideas at the 2007 Universities at Risk Conference. Simon Fraser University School of Communication graduate students and colleagues, and the Council of Canadians gave me opportunities to present my arguments. I want to thank to Bob Hackett for his collegiality and work on Project Censored Canada and NewsWatch Canada. Several web sites should be recognized for their invaluable information on business sponsored propaganda: Media Transparency, for its articles on conservatives and database of conservative funders and recipients; and SourceWatch, for its profiles of public-relations and think-tank issues and personnel. Thanks also: to Barbara Pulling for her early encouragement and assistance in framing the book's argument; my agent Robert Mackwood, for seeing the potential in the proposal; Liba Berry for her impeccable editing skills; and my sincerest thanks to Jonathan Schmidt, my editor at Key Porter, who helped transform the manuscript from a litany of accusations into a clear exposition of the corporate propaganda process. Finally I want to acknowledge my partner Mae Burrows for her always helpful comments, critical reading and unconditional support during the five years I was writing this book.

Table of Contents

Introduction

All week long the media world waited for the showdown between the two cable-TV giants.

In March 2009, Jim Cramer, stock-picker extraordinaire and host of CNBC's *Mad Money*, was set to square off against Jon Stewart of Comedy Central's *The Daily Show*. Stewart had been outraged by the reporting and commentary about the financial meltdown provided by CNBC, the leading business cable channel. He aired a hilarious eight-minute thrashing of CNBC, highlighting the misreporting of its commentators. Cramer was invited onto the show and, perhaps unwisely, he accepted. Sniping at each other during the week had created an aura of great expectation. *USA Today* ran a front-page banner story touting the confrontation.

Despite the segment's title—"Brawl Street"—Stewart's sights were set not so much on Cramer as on the financial press for not alerting investors about the market's highly leveraged structure. Stewart blasted the channel for cheerleading Wall Street in the run-up to the worst economic collapse since the Depression.

"You knew what the banks were doing," Stewart charged, "and yet you were touting it for months and months. The entire network was. And so now to pretend this was some sort of crazy, once-in-a-lifetime tsunami that nobody could have seen coming is disingenuous at best and criminal at worst."

"I had a lot of CEOs lie to me on the show," Cramer said in his defence. "It's very painful. I don't have subpoena power . . . But Dick Fuld who ran Lehman Brothers called me in when the stock was forty dollars because I was saying I thought that the stock was wrong, it was the wrong place to be.... Brings me in, lies to me, lies to me, lies to me. I've known him for twenty years."

Feigning disbelief, Stewart exclaimed: "The CEO of a company lied to you?"

With a smile on his face, Cramer countered: "Shocker. Stop trading."

Stewart asked why his network didn't act like real journalists and check their claims. They simply repeated the lies, Stewart said. Instead of doing tough investigative journalism to expose the lies, the network did PR for Wall Street. It was too cozy with the corporations it covered, he charged.

We can thank Jon Stewart for blowing the whistle on CNBC for its having neglected to give its viewers the straight goods on market machinations. But that's just the tip of an iceberg. CNBC and the rest of the mainstream media didn't report an even bigger story: the prolonged and highly sophisticated propaganda campaigns mounted by business to change our minds on fundamental issues of social and political life. For thirty-five years, dozens of business-backed think-tanks in the United States, Canada and most other countries have been beating the drum for deregulated markets, lower taxes for the wealthy and for weak, ineffective government. It requires no genius to realize that an unregulated market coupled with a government with no appetite for oversight except to enforce rules that protect the unregulated market is of great advantage to business. It's not about what is right for consumers, it's all about ever-increasing return to shareholders. Profit, in other words. Regulation that protects consumers, human health and the environment, in contrast, might limit corporate profits.

That effective regulation and enforcement could have prevented the market meltdown is not part of the profit-at-any-cost business agenda. Think-tanks have evolved into an especially effective mechanism for publicizing and promoting the profit-at-any-cost message that what is good for business is good for the consumer.

This massive anti-government, anti-regulation exercise in corporate propaganda worked because the media didn't report the story. The media treated—and continue to treat—think-tanks as if they are independent, scientifically qualified and even scholarly, when in fact think-tanks are simply agents of their corporate sponsors. Just as Cramer and company failed to reveal the incestuous relationship between media and business—never hinting that supposedly unbiased market reporting was in fact being spoon-fed to them by financially interested parties—the mainstream media have rarely exposed the just-as-questionable links between think-tanks and the gigantic corporations that sponsor them.

The economic crisis seemed to tear through the market like a sudden storm. How could this have happened? we wondered in disbelief. We now better understand, however, that a source of our confusion could be laid at the feet of a media that for months and months merely parroted the "All is Well" message of Wall Street and its big-business cronies. We didn't get the real facts we needed to navigate the perilous shoals. In what had become a virtually unregulated market open to the wildest and most dangerous speculation, we had little idea just how vulnerable we had become. By the time the truth emerged, it was too late.

Because of our disastrous experience we need to ask the following questions. First: what does democracy mean in a world of instant, biased and manipulated information? Investors misled by Cramer and his cohorts lost huge amounts of money. As painful as that might be, as citizens who were—and are—continually misled by the mainstream media, we risk losing a lot more: our ability and obligation to govern ourselves. We require accurate and adequate information to make responsible decisions about who should govern us and what policies we should implement. If we don't get the information, or if we're not able to evaluate the information because we don't know who paid for it, we're likely to make bad decisions. Perhaps the meltdown could have been avoided, or at least reduced in severity, if we had known what was going on between business, the media and the think-tanks.

Second: Why is this kind of business propaganda a threat to democracy? It's not because business propaganda is worse than other kinds of propaganda—all propaganda damages democracy—but because it has been infinitely more successful than progressive or oppositional propaganda in changing our attitudes and beliefs. It has deeper pockets, has benefited from long-term, coordinated effort, has the ear of commercial media, as Jon Stewart noted, and has significant influence over government. Because of the success of corporate propaganda, business is no longer just one voice, albeit an important one, in the democratic debate. It controls the debate. Society would be better served if all propaganda was banished, but, like global warming, massive societal effort will be required to make propaganda go away. For twenty years corporate-sponsored propaganda was successful in casting doubt about the existence of human-caused global warming by discrediting climate scientists and preventing action. When the evidence became incontrovertible that global warming was occurring and posed a dire threat to the planet, it was almost too late to stop it. Attention turned to an inadequate Plan B: accommodating global warming, an outcome that would have less impact on the corporate bottom line.

Democratic debate has been hijacked by corporate propaganda. Wealthy businessmen created conservative think-tanks which dominate public policy discussions, but are never identified as agents of corporate power. Because of the media's unwillingness to "follow the money," Canadians and Americans know little about these developments. Business has captured the upper hand thanks to a coordinated, well-funded, prolonged effort.

The Canadian financial and economic crises were not as severe as those in the U.S. Canada didn't experience the flood of home foreclosures, and our banks remained in healthier shape because of more effective regulation and less opportunity for the banks to invest in toxic mortgages. But we were as badly duped by our own corporate-sponsored think-tanks. Canadian media did as poor a job as the Americans in tracing the financial sources of think-tank messaging that advocated for lower taxes, deregulation and ineffective government. And if Canada's think-tanks have their way, Canada will become even more closely tied to the U.S., with less room for independent economic and political action.

Come the next financial crisis, we may be right down there with the Yanks.

CHAPTER 1

Integration ...
Even Though We Don't Want It

If sovereignty does not appear to have produced
superior economic outcomes, of what value is it?
—Fred Lazar, "No national vision, no national currency," *Financial Post*

No small country can depend for its existence on the loyalty of its capitalists.
—George Grant, "Lament for a Nation"

The 2001 *Maclean's*–CBC News year-end survey of the Canadian people revealed a nation adjusting well to the post–September 11 world.[1] Canadians rushed to New York to assist with rescue operations and comfort the survivors—more than forty Canadians died in the terrorist attacks on the World Trade Towers. They headed to the mall to spend, spend, spend and save the economy at the behest of George W. Bush. They agreed to go along with Bush's harsh security measures and were prepared to support a larger, more aggressive role for the Canadian military. But by December, the initial shock and horror of September 11 had receded and Canadians returned to their traditional ambivalence towards the United States. They sympathized with their neighbours, but didn't want to be Americans. In the *Maclean's* survey, only 25 percent answered "yes" to the question "If you had an opportunity to become a citizen of the U.S. and live and work there, would you?" Nor did they feel like bosom buddies: 47 percent said Canadians were "friends but not especially close" to the Americans, while only 23 percent said the two peoples were "the best of friends." Other responses were "cordial but distant" (18 percent) and "like family" (10 percent). Relations with the Americans was not high on their list of priorities. When asked "What is the most important issue facing Canada today?" most respondents answered health and education (29 percent) or unemployment and the economy (25 percent). The September 11 attacks were a distant third with 11 percent. At the very bottom of the list was Canada–U.S. relations, cited by just 1 percent of respondents.

These were the wrong answers, at least according to big business. The correct answer is that Canada–U.S. relations must be number one in Canadian thinking. Just two weeks before the *Maclean's* survey was released, Canadian National Railway (CNR) president Paul Tellier announced that integration of the two economies "will continue, it is inevitable, it is irreversible and it is taking place faster than any of us expected."[2] Forget health care, education and jobs. Canadians must start an urgent debate about integration, Tellier warned.

Why was Tellier raising the alarm about integration so soon after September 11? He said Canadians need to debate the issue, but what's to debate if integration is inevitable, even if Canadians didn't appear to want it? Did he want a debate or was he preparing public opinion for the inevitability of increased U.S. integration?

Tellier delivered his speech to the Railway Club of Canada just four weeks before an important event in the corporate world, the annual general meeting of the Canadian Council of Chief Executives (CCCE), where Tellier was a vice-chair. He had just been appointed co-chair of a CEO Council North American policy committee to address Canada–U.S. economic interdependence, integration and security. The CCCE is the most influential business organization in Canada, comprising the chief executives of 150 of the country's largest companies. These chief executives weren't interested in debating integration; they were already at work on strategies to deepen it. The debate would be for ordinary Canadians who needed to change their attitudes and bring them in line with what business wanted.

The timing of Tellier's railway club speech, coming just before the CEO Council meeting, helped bring the chief executives together on the issue. The CCCE used this tactic—placing a chief executive in the public eye without emphasizing the link to the organization—in an effective campaign in 1999 to convince the federal government to cut taxes. Nortel Networks CEO (and the then CCCE vice-chair) John Roth threatened to pull his company out of Canada if the government didn't cut business and personal taxes. The Chrétien government complied, but Nortel went down the tubes anyway. Roth and his CEOs got their cuts, leaving them with more money and government with less ability to provide social programs.

Integration remained largely off the public radar until September 11 provided a "powerful catalyst" to business efforts, CCCE president Tom d'Aquino reported to the January 2002 chief executives meeting. The CEOs agreed that "redefining Canada's role and responsibilities in North America was the country's most urgent priority." Homeland and economic security leaped to the top of the business agenda.[3] D'Aquino worried that the "bilateral trade, investment, regulatory, security and institutional relationship did not reflect the advanced level of integration between the two countries."[4] The CEOs agreed to a twelve-month research-and-analysis program to develop an integration strategy. Their vision may have been expressed by RBC vice-chairman and CCCE member Chuck Winograd, in describing the bank's investment banking business: "What I think it's heading for is a North American business with very pronounced regional strength, that region being Canada."[5] In this world, Canada is no longer a distinct nation, but merely an economic region in a North American market, about the same size as California, but, unlike citizens in that state, without the right to vote in American elections where the big decisions are made.

Journalist Lawrence Martin reports a comment that then Liberal leader John Turner made to Liberal MP Lloyd Axworthy in the run-up to the historic 1988 free trade election. Turner had gone on vacation to Georgian Bay with some of his business friends after Brian Mulroney "signed a trade agreement he thought terribly one-sided." This action ignited Turner's nationalistic fervour and he discussed the future of the nation with his friends, expecting a similar reaction. "To his astonishment he found out differently," Martin reports. "Turner met with . . . Axworthy afterward and said something Axworthy would not forget. 'Jesus, Lloyd,' Turner told him. 'I've just come back from Collingwood. They don't believe in Canada any more.'" Turner wanted to talk to them about the country, Martin notes wryly. "What big business cared about, however, was first-quarter profits."[6] And first-quarter profits depend on access to the American market.

Turner should not have been surprised by what he heard in cottage country. Continentalism is an old story in Canada, going back to the pre-Confederation era. It gathered strength after the Second World War when, led by the Liberal government of William Lyon Mackenzie King and C.D. Howe, who was called the CEO of corporate Canada, the U.S. replaced Britain as Canada's most important business and financial partner. In his pessimistic 1965 essay "Lament for a Nation," George Grant excoriated the Canadian business class for throwing its lot in with the Americans and turning its back on Canada. Grant's thesis was that Liberal policies since the Second World War led to the impossibility of any alternative to the American Empire. The thrust of these policies was to turn Canada into a branch-plant society of the U.S., dependent on American finance and industry. Long before the so-called free trade agreements, the industrial heartland of Ontario was being integrated with Michigan and New York. Investment and profit would come from those centres, not Montreal or Calgary. About the Mulroney government's free trade "sellout" of Canada with the enthusiastic support of big business, Grant would have declared: "The wealthy rarely maintain their nationalism when it is in conflict with the economic drive of the day."[7] They embraced their American business partners and customers and turned their backs on the Canadian people, whose outmoded notions of nationalism would have to be managed so that they would not interfere with the business agenda of an integrated North American market.

The problem with the all-your-eggs-in-one-basket approach to economic development did not become apparent until the 2008 financial meltdown. By then Canada had largely lost the ability to manage its own economy. Stephen Harper's 2009 budget contained a package of stimulus measures that was supposed to boost Canada's economic output. But economist Dale Orr, whose work had been used by the Department of Finance for eleven years, doubted the stimulus would have any effect. He argued that "the power to revive economic growth is out of Ottawa's hands because Canada is utterly dependent on sales to the recession-ridden United States . . . [which] buys 80 per cent of this country's exports."[8]

Alex Carey, the Australian sociologist, explains in *Taking the Risk Out of Democracy*, how business manipulates the public to go along with policies the public actually opposes. He identifies three developments of "great political importance" in the twentieth century: "the growth of democracy, the growth of corporate power, and the growth of corporate propaganda as a means of protecting corporate power against democracy."[9] By the growth of democracy he means the expansion of voting rights and the right of workers to organize in unions in the early part of the century, and the establishment of social and economic rights after the Second World War. Corporate power is self-explanatory: the rapid growth of multinational corporations, many of which are larger and more powerful than nation-states and can influence governments to act on their behalf rather than for the public good. Corporations use their power to get tax cuts for the rich, weaken consumer, worker and environmental regulations, divert spending to weapons and the military and away from social programs, and undermine policies to control global warming. None of these actions would likely be endorsed by the voting public. So business must obscure the extent to which corporate power is anti-democratic, resulting in a crucial need for corporate-sponsored propaganda. Public opinion must be managed to prevent it from becoming hostile to corporations, even though there are good reasons for rolling back corporate power. The purpose of corporate propaganda is to "take the risk out of democracy." A democratically elected government with a mandate from voters to protect jobs, regulate environmentally destructive industry and ensure business pays its fair share of taxes, presents great risks to business, limiting a company's ability to produce ever-increasing profits for its shareholders.

In a word, the risk to business is that in a democracy the public will engage in healthy, critical discussion, which will conclude that business is too power-ful and needs to be reined in. The purpose of corporate propaganda is to ensure that these ideas don't arise. When such ideas emerge in Third World countries, a different technique is used, Carey notes: brutal military suppression, the method of choice in countries like Iran (1953), Guatemala (1954) and Chile (1973). In Canada, the U.S. and other developed democracies, business prefers propaganda, which Carey defines as "communications where the form and content is selected with the single-minded purpose of bringing some target audience to adopt attitudes and beliefs chosen in advance by the sponsors of the communications."[10] There must be identifiable messages, target audiences and sponsors to qualify as propaganda. Successfully selling NAFTA as a free trade agreement beneficial to the nation, when it is, in fact, a charter of rights for corporations that undermines the people's right to determine their future, Carey would argue, is a major victory by corporate propaganda over democ-racy. Convincing us that economic and social integration are inevitable, as Paul Tellier claims, would be another triumph.

We're not usually aware of the existence of such propaganda. "The success of business propaganda in persuading us, for so long, that we are free from propaganda is one of the most significant propaganda achievements of the twentieth century," Carey writes.[11] The reason for this triumph is that business interests are never identified as special interests. We rarely acknowledge that the business elite is concerned with preserving wealth and privilege and not creating jobs, although that's what it always says. Rather, corporate propaganda has been successful in merging the national interest with business interests. We are told—and we accept without blinking an eye—for instance, that we need to promote our information technology *industry* by giving it subsidies and tax breaks—directed increasingly at U.S.-controlled firms because of free trade—so that *Canada* can survive in the global age. In this formulation, Canada and industry are cleverly joined together as one: what's good for Microsoft and IBM is good for the country. In a propaganda-free society we would ask first what's good for the Canadian people and then decide how best to achieve this.

We often observe business power at work, but rarely do we see the rationale for it. We can catch a glimpse of this in a paper by two economists from the business-sponsored C.D. Howe Institute, which provides a classic defence of wealth against democracy. David Laidler and William Robson argue that the Bank of Canada's pursuit of zero inflation in the late eighties—which benefited the wealthy, but was sold as being necessary for the country—should be "insulated" from parliamentary democracy and electoral politics because interest groups might exert inflationary pressure on those who run the government's monetary institutions.[12] They don't say that democracy should be abandoned to maintain a low-inflationary environment, but they do argue for a system that prevents governments from enacting policies that might benefit workers and the poor, and which might result in higher inflation and lower returns for lenders and bondholders. Such a dire consequence is based on their belief that "inflation distorts the actual and the apparent pattern of profitability both within and across firms and industries."[13]

Carey identifies two forms of propaganda in the modern democratic state under capitalism. An earlier form was created by communications experts recruited by U.S. president Woodrow Wilson to win public support for American participation in the First World War and it spread from government to business after the war. Carey calls this "grassroots propaganda" because its purpose is to reach as vast a number of people as possible in order to change public opinion so that it is sympathetic to business interests. This is the propaganda practiced by advertisers, public relations practitioners, and government and corporate media consultants. The campaign by business to create an aura of inevitability for free trade is an example of successful grassroots propaganda.

A new form of business propaganda was created in the U.S. in the early 1970s in response to the threat of reinvigorated citizen activism in civil, human and consumer rights, environmental protection and the movement to control and regulate business. Carey calls this "treetops propaganda." It is directed at influencing a select group of lawmakers, bureaucrats, newspaper editors, prominent columnists and TV commentators who, in turn, can influence policy. Business set up treetops organizations in the mid-seventies in the United States, Canada, Australia and Europe to counter the advances in political, social and economic rights of the previous half-century. The Business Council on National Issues (BCNI), the original name of the CCCE, was modelled after the Business Roundtable in the U.S. The idea was to bring together corporate chief executives who could quickly commit their companies' financial and political resources to the goals and actions developed by the council. At the same time, seemingly arm's-length, but industry-backed think-tanks—such as the Howe and Fraser institutes—were set up. Following the American model, they were a necessary adjunct to the overtly pro-business BCNI, providing a scholarly, or at least independent, patina to the propaganda efforts.

Dual grassroots and treetops propaganda is not new. Its antecedents lie in Marxist theory in the terms "propaganda" and "agitation" first used by Georgy Plekhanov and later elaborated by Lenin in his 1902 pamphlet, *What is to be Done?* Lenin defined propaganda as the reasoned use of historical and scientific arguments to indoctrinate the educated and enlightened (treetops propaganda); agitation was the use of slogans, parables and half-truths to exploit the grievances of the uneducated and the unreasonable (grassroots propaganda). Lenin regarded both strategies as indispensable to political victory and he twinned them in the term "agitprop."[14] Business doesn't call what it does agitprop, preferring the neutral terms "persuasion" and "education," which mask agitprop.

The purpose of treetops propaganda is to set the terms of debate, to determine the kinds of questions that will dominate public discussion; to set the political agenda in ways that are favourable to corporate interests. If treetops propaganda is successful, grassroots efforts become less necessary. Public discussion will no longer assume, for instance, that affluent countries like Canada have a responsibility to provide jobs for everyone who wants one. Instead, the debate is about whether 6 or 10 percent unemployment is a "natural" and therefore acceptable, level. And, as a result of the free trade agreements, the question is no longer asked about how far and in what areas government should be involved in the economy, but focuses instead on arguments for how far and fast government involvement should be reduced.[15] And when government intervention becomes indispensable, as it did in countries around the world after the 2008 financial meltdown, debate, in the U.S. at least, was not about renewed and invigorated government participation in the economy, but about how quickly government could help turn things around and then get out.

A third illustration of successful treetops propaganda is the removal of the option of increasing taxes on the wealthy as a way to finance social programs. This policy is rarely discussed seriously in the corporate media. President Barack Obama's proposal in his 2010 budget to hike the highest tax rate from 35 to 39.5 percent to fund his health-care plans provoked near hysteria by many media outlets. Commentators were outraged that the increases were a sign that "class warfare" had been declared by the Obama administration.[16] Perhaps the most egregious response came from commentators with the CNBC cable channel who called Obama a "Bolshevik" intent on "rampant wealth destruction."[17] In fact, Obama was simply allowing the George W. Bush tax cuts to expire in 2010.

Paul Tellier's claim that integration is inevitable is ironic given that he was one of a small group of powerful people around Brian Mulroney who made integration "inevitable." As Ottawa's chief bureaucrat—clerk to the Privy Council and secretary to the cabinet—Tellier was central to the free trade negotiations, which set Canada on the road to economic and social integration.[18] His role was to ensure that government officials were onside with the big-business game plan. Of course, back then Mulroney government officials denied that integration was inevitable and irreversible. Free trade, they argued, was definitely not the first domino on the road to total integration. This claim was probably a falsehood. Economic integration would lead inevitably to more economic integration as well as integration in other areas. Early on, business knew that increased trade and investment would result in the need for monetary and customs unions. So much of Canada's economy would be tied to the U.S. that it would make sense for the two countries to form a monetary union; a common currency would make doing business so much easier, Tom d'Aquino told Lawrence Martin over lunch in a posh Washington hotel.[19] It would also make sense for the two countries to harmonize their trade policies vis-à-vis the rest of the world. U.S. president Ronald Reagan was right when he mused that free trade was not just a trade deal, but "a new economic constitution" for North America.[20]

Few companies benefited more from the new economic constitution than Canadian National. CN's whirlwind ride from Crown corporation to American-dominated agent of continental integration took less than ten years. As a government enterprise, it was accountable to the Canadian people; privatized, it was accountable to its mainly American shareholders and customers. Mulroney chose Paul Tellier to lead the railway's transformation, appointing him president in 1992. Tellier took CN private three years later, with the Liberals at the helm. American investors liked what they saw and snapped up the shares, generating proceeds of CAN$2.2 billion for the government. Investors knew this was a good deal. The company was undervalued so that the shares would go up, not down. Shareholders would thus reap the benefits, the company would earn a glowing review and taxpayers would shoulder the subsidy to the new owners. In fact, the shares more than doubled in the first year and the new shareholders pocketed their profits, while thousands of workers lost their jobs.

At the time of privatization, 39 percent of revenues were earned in the U.S. In 2001, the year Tellier proclaimed integration to be inevitable, for the first time more than half of CN's revenues were generated either inside the U.S. or from transborder operations, and just over half the company's assets resided south of the border. On any given day, at least half the trading in CN's shares takes place on the New York Stock Exchange. Tellier claimed he had turned Canadian National into a "Canadian-based North American business." The reality, however, was that aside from its historic name and Montreal office, Canadian National was American. In 2006, for the first time, CN held its shareholders' meeting outside Canada, in Memphis, Tennessee. This was done to make the point that CN was better described as a North American railway and Memphis a major operations hub.[21] The point was reinforced several years later, after American managers removed two large Canadian flags from the Transcona works yards in Winnipeg, Manitoba, where about five hundred are employed. In response, the workers put Maple Leaf stickers on their hats and overalls. "The American influence is pretty strong," one employee said, but didn't want to be named for fear of reprisal.[22]

It's not difficult to understand why Canada's bankers and business leaders want integration with the U.S. The more integrated the economy, the more money they will make—because of lower wages paid to their employees and less stringent regulations applied to their operations—and the more they will be able to keep—because of lower taxes. Their companies will grow; they will earn greater revenues; and shareholders will benefit from greater returns on their investments. Integration is certainly good for railway company executives. As Ottawa's chief bureaucrat in the early nineties, Paul Tellier earned

$165,000 a year, placing him in the top 1 percent of Canadian earners. In 2000, with CN fully integrated into the North American rail system, Tellier took home $2.28 million, boosting him to the top 0.01 percent of Canadian wage earners.[23] And he wasn't alone. The same year, chief executives in Canada received a stunning 43 percent median pay increase. Nortel Networks' John Roth led the pack with total direct compensation of $70.8 million, a 91 percent increase over his 1999 pay.[24] Nor was this an isolated situation. Emmanuel Saez and Michael Veall, researchers at the University of California and McMaster University in Hamilton, found that the ratio of compensation paid to the top ten Canadian CEOs compared to average wage income was about 40 to 1 in 1978 and almost 1000 to 1 in 2000.[25] (Management guru Peter Drucker says the ratio should be no more than 20 to 1.)

Saez and Veall studied the tax returns of Canada's highest-income earners and discovered that "over the last 20 years, top income shares in Canada have increased dramatically."[26] Their studies show that the top income share in Canada fell sharply during the Second World War and did not recover during the next three decades. These were the years in which Canada's social programs (unemployment insurance, public housing, health care, social assistance) and strong regulatory regimes were in place. But the income share of top earners shot up dramatically after the free trade agreement was implemented. Such figures are usually obscured by economists, who compare the top and bottom 20 percent and conclude that income inequality changed very little over those years.[27] But when the researchers looked at the very wealthy, a different picture emerged. There is a gap, and the higher on the income scale, the more pronounced the gap. In 1980, the top 0.1 percent of income earners captured 2 percent of total income. In 2000, their average income was $923,000 and they had more than doubled their share of total income to over 5 percent.[28] And these astounding gains occurred before the wealthy finally got their tax cut, thanks to John Roth and the Canadian Council of Chief Executives.

These results puzzled Saez and Veall because they parallel closely those of top earners in the U.S. Skyrocketing income for wealthy Americans is understood as a direct consequence of tax cuts for the wealthy since Ronald Reagan's day. But tax cuts for wealthy Canadians were modest and recent. In 1997, American families in the highest tax bracket paid about five percentage points less of their total income in income taxes than did comparable Canadian families.[29] So why did Canadians do so well? Because, conclude Saez and Veall, the Americans did so well. Top Canadian earners can command unprecedented pay because they can find jobs in the United States with relative ease via the brain drain (talented individuals emigrating to the U.S.). Canadian firms attempt to retain their best-paid employees by increasing their salaries.[30] As George Grant warned forty years ago, the fortunes of wealthy Canadians largely depend on the success of their American partners, employers and customers and hardly on the performance of the Canadian economy. In a post-mortem after the 2008 financial meltdown, the *Globe and Mail*'s Jeffrey Simpson asked, "[In] corporate Canada, how many times did we see U.S. remuneration used to explain and justify huge salaries in this country?"[31]

Wealthy Canadians don't care about medicare because they pay private clinics and American hospitals to jump the queue in Canada. They don't worry about public education because they send their children to private schools and colleges. They see social programs as being of use only for the poor and unemployed, few of whom they know. Nor do they care about Canada's vaunted quality of life. They can buy safety and security in the U.S. with their inflated incomes. Their vacation homes are in secure compounds in Florida, Colorado and Arizona, not Saskatchewan, Manitoba and Newfoundland. Even before his company merged with Coors in 2004, Molson CEO Dan O'Neill built an 8000-square-foot "hideaway" on a US$1.6-million lot in Beaver Creek, Colorado. Brian and Mila Mulroney publicized the wealthy Canadian penchant for Florida real estate with their 1997 purchase of a new house on Plantation Road near the Palm Beach Country Club in Florida for US$1.45 million. Their neighbours include Canadian business tycoons Paul Desmarais (Power Corp.), Charles and Edgar Bronfman (formerly Seagrams), Frank Stronach (Magna) and George Cohon (McDonald's), and used to include Conrad Black. Bakery billionaire Galen Weston, who finances the Fraser Institute's school report cards and other education studies, built his own gated community on a lush barrier island 8 miles north of Vero Beach, where houses sold—only to those acceptable to the Westons—for up to $8 million.

The benefits of integration for the majority of Canadians are buried in the barrage of claims that we need deeper integration if we are to keep what we won in NAFTA, masking the fact that Canadian working people won very little in that deal. Free trade propaganda trumpets the phenomenal increase in trade between the two countries as incontrovertible evidence that the deals were a great success. And it's true that between 1989 and 2002, when Tellier mused about the inevitability of integration, Canadian exports to the U.S. rose by 221 percent, while imports from the U.S. went up by 162 percent. But those increases did not translate into benefits for working people. Over the free trade period, Canada's gross domestic product (GDP) rose an average of 1.6 percent per capita per year. But in the eight years before free trade, GDP rose an average of 1.9 percent a year, meaning that free trade led to a decrease of about 15 percent in the GDP growth rate.[32] This downward trend was reflected in people's incomes. Average total family income rose about 2 percent a year in the six years before free trade and about 0.7 percent a year after free trade.[33] Between 1990 and 2002, the share of the income pie earned by the top 10 percent of Canadian earners rose from 31.7 to 35.7 percent. This is an increase of four percentage points but an actual gain of 12.5 percent. Meanwhile, the share of income earned by the bottom half of the population fell from 19.0 to 16.9 percent, which is a drop of 11 percent. The intermediate 40 percent of income earners experienced a drop in income share from 49.3 percent to 47.4 percent.[34] Only the very well off gained from free trade. No wonder most Canadians are not enamoured of it.

Integration benefits mainly the wealthy, but must be sold as good for everyone. A 2003 study of public attitudes about integration by the C.D. Howe Institute prescribes the recipe for manipulating the public: "Political leaders will have to educate and persuade the public of the merits of a renewed or augmented relationship with the United States if they decide that it is essential to negotiate closer economic and political ties," Alan Alexandroff, of the University of Toronto, and Don Guy, a senior vice-president of public opinion research firm Pollara, recommend.[35] Here's how it works. Business leaders want closer economic and political ties because they and their friends will make more money. They tell political leaders that business needs these closer ties. Political leaders "decide" it is essential for the country to have these ties. They then set out to "educate and persuade" the public of the merits of closer ties, with the help of the Howe and other think-tanks. The public has no real input into the decision to form closer ties.

The job of the propagandist is rarely easy, since he must manipulate people's deeply held beliefs. Alexandroff and Guy discovered that Canadians were expressing a "growing skepticism over the benefits of free trade," which would be expected, given how poorly most Canadians fared from it. They also found that the public did not favour any policy described as "economic integration with the United States." If most Canadians are skeptical about free trade and don't favour economic integration, shouldn't their political leaders reject further moves in that direction? But because business wants it, the public must be "educated and persuaded" about the merits of integration. Just don't call it integration, the authors caution, because "how matters are labelled can, in fact, have an impact on whether Canadians initially approve or disapprove of an initiative." Call it, they suggest, "a renewed or augmented relationship with the United States" and not economic integration, even if that's what it is.[36]

The Howe study is not recommending swaying public opinion through persuasion and education, even though that's what it says. Persuasion is communication that attempts to influence an audience to accept or adopt a new response in a voluntary fashion. A positive response might be, "I never thought of it that way, but I do now," or "I never did that before, but now I intend to."[37] To achieve his or her purpose, the persuader must pay attention to fulfilling the needs of the audience. Persuader and audience depend on one another to have their needs met. "If you workers get more jobs and improved health-and-safety standards, then we bosses are entitled to higher compensation," might be one persuasive bargain. In contrast, the purpose of propaganda is to promote *not* mutual understanding and satisfaction but the propagandist's veiled objectives. "We'll get our pay hikes and you'll lose your jobs, but we'll hide those facts from you."[38] For psychologists Anthony Pratkanis and Elliot Aronson, persuasion "could take the form of an argument, a debate, a discussion, or just a well-argued speech presenting the case for or against a given proposition." Propaganda, in contrast, is the "communication of a point of view with the ultimate goal of having the recipient of the appeal come to 'voluntarily' accept this position as if it were his or her own," they explain.[39] To the persuader we are intelligent, informed and thoughtful. Give us the information and we can make an informed decision about integration. To the propagandist, we are an irrational mob that must be manipulated into supporting his or her objective even though that objective counters—or even undermines—our own interests.

Nor, as Alex Carey observes, are the Howe authors describing education, where "the purpose is to encourage critical enquiry and to open minds to arguments for and against any particular conclusion, rather than close them to the possibility of any conclusion but one."[40] Education and propaganda, in truth, are not mutually exclusive. There is not so much a fine line between the two as a broad overlapping territory. An intention to engage in propaganda—a desire to manipulate—must be present at least some of the time in the minds of those teaching subjects like politics, history, economics and the social sciences. But they are no less educators because they use the techniques of the propagandist. The crucial difference is that "the propagandist does not seek to influence attitudes or opinions as an end in itself . . . [but] . . . to translate belief into action."[41] For continental integration, the educator wants his audience to come to an informed opinion; the propagandist works to ensure that the audience will support it at any cost.

For propaganda to succeed, the propagandist must create a crisis, or at least the perception of a crisis. If the public perceives that a crisis is, in fact, merely a problem, it won't support a radical solution. But if the projected scenario is perceived as a true crisis, the desired action is virtually ensured. Enormous effort goes into campaigns to convince us that one situation or another is a crisis and not merely a problem. Business worked for a decade to convince Canadians that the country was about to crash into a debt wall unless they agreed to cut spending on social programs. Linda McQuaig documents the campaign to lower Canadian expectations about what a society can do for its citizens, to turn them away from "the notion of government as a provider and equalizer, and re-establish the discipline of the marketplace."[42] We are living beyond our means, it was claimed, racking up deficits and debts that will push us over the cliff and into ruin. This message was generated by the Business Council on National Issues and the Fraser and Howe institutes and communicated continually by the corporate media. The term "debt crisis," for instance, peaked in the news media between 1991 and 1994, tailing off after the Paul Martin budget slashed spending on social programs.

September 11, 2001, proved too good to be true for propagandists of integration: it was a ready-made crisis. The endlessly repeated footage of planes crashing into the World Trade Towers and similar footage of trucks lined up for miles at Windsor's Ambassador Bridge after the shutdown of the U.S. border, screamed crisis. The propaganda apparatus swung into high gear.

Work on deeper integration was underway before September 11, but didn't grab public attention. A flurry of activity occurred in June 2001, when David Zussman gave a speech titled "What's after NAFTA," at a conference in Calgary sponsored by Industry Canada, signifying some sort of government recognition. Zussman headed the Public Policy Forum, a think-tank situated among business, government and the voluntary sector in Ottawa. He was a well-known adviser to Jean Chrétien and headed Chrétien's 1993 transition team. Zussman called for a "debate over new ideas, which, until a few years ago, were completely taboo in respectable Canadian society."[43] These were issues like dollarization (the two countries would adopt a common currency), a common perimeter (once goods entered Canada or the U.S. they could move freely between the two countries) and harmonization of standards (Canada and the U.S. would have the same regulations governing goods and services). The next day, Paul Cellucci, the new U.S. ambassador to Canada, suggested that borders between Canada, the United States and Mexico be dismantled to more fully integrate the North American economy. Zussman went further in a front-page *National Post* story several days later under the headline "Union with U.S. on table: PM's advisor." The story led with the statement that "Canadians need to debate the possibility of a North American political and economic union with the United States and Mexico." The *Post* billed the speech as "the first occasion where a senior public-policy figure has broached economic and political union of the continent."[44] Zussman went still further in a pro-integration feature by columnist Drew Fagan in the *Globe and Mail* several months after the terrorist attacks. "This is the issue of our generation," Zussman warned. "I suspect we will continue to see further integration of our economies and therefore of our societies, unless Canadians eventually decide otherwise," as if most Canadians would have any meaningful say in the matter.[45]

Just six days before September 11, a group of influential business people, lobbyists and politicians quietly assembled in the appropriately named Intercontinental Hotel on Toronto's tony Bloor Street for an invitation-only confab on relations between Canada and the United States under a Bush administration. Titled the "Canada–U.S. Executive Summit," the gathering featured Brian Mulroney, grandiosely billed as the person whose warm friend-ships with former president George H.W. Bush, Vice-President Dick Cheney and Secretary of State Colin Powell gave him "unique insights" into the Bush administration's approach to continental trade.[46] Then came September 11 and discussions about continental integration moved from the shadows of the Intercontinental Hotel into the limelight.

It doesn't require a conspiracy theory to account for the outpouring of business-backed studies, reports, conferences and newspaper opinion pieces arguing for deeper continental integration in the months following September 11. Thanks to the efforts of Paul Tellier and the Canadian Council of Chief Executives, a consensus was forming among the business elite and it was expressed through all available channels. Every business think-tank and lobby group in the country was part of the action, each providing its own recipe for how to fix what ails us. The problems were obvious, at least to the cognoscenti. Border lineups cost us billions in lost exports. Our military was weak and not shouldering its fair share of the burden of defending freedom and democracy. We were presumably too anti-American. Our dollar was too weak, then too strong. Productivity was declining. In ten years we would be earning half of what the average American would earn. We were on crisis alert, but was there a crisis?

York University political economist Stephen Clarkson was one of those with an opinion on Canada–U.S. relations who was actually an expert on the subject, having studied the political economy of Canada's integration in the American system since the late sixties. He called the phenomenon a "massing of elite brain power," and worried about "the bias built into this work, which is not just designed to investigate but explicitly to promote an enhanced degree of North American integration." He didn't speculate as to why the bias existed.[47] Nonetheless, the combined effect of the studies, reports and conferences was to create an echo chamber that amplified the integration message beyond the individual contributions.

Over the span of thirty years, the CCCE has perfected its methods of pushing Canadian public policy in directions desired by business. As the Business Council on National Issues, the organization masterminded the free trade campaign. The council changed its name in 2001 to better reflect its international interests and consign the word "national" to the dustbin of history. In his analysis of corporate rule, *The Myth of the Good Corporate Citizen*, Murray Dobbin provides a checklist of the business council's successes over those years. As well as forcing through the free trade agreement in 1988, the council was successful in: defeating Liberal finance minister Allan MacEachern's 1981 budget, which would have closed 165 corporate tax loopholes; deregulating Canadian oil and gas prices, allowing them to rise (1984); removing the teeth from anti-combines legislation, encouraging corporate mergers and takeovers (1981); introducing and promoting the Goods and Services Tax (GST), transferring $18 billion in taxes from corporations to individuals; and convincing the Liberals to abandon their Red Book of enhanced social programs and focus instead on slaying the deficit (1993).[48] To find out what the federal government plans for tomorrow, it has been said, look at what the CCCE advocates today. The Jean Chrétien Liberals promised to split budget surpluses fifty-fifty between new spending and tax cuts and debt repayment. Then CCCE went into action, urging (ordering?) Chrétien to forget new spending. Chrétien complied and Tom d'Aquino applauded this dramatic change in Liberal policy. The CC-CE's clout is evident in its ability to frame public debate. Spending on social programs is called "new spending" when in fact it's old spending that needs to be restored.

While the CCCE has the word "Canadian" in its name, the list of U.S.- and foreign-owned companies in the organization is long. It includes CVRD, Cargill, Daimler Chrysler Canada. Dow Chemical Canada, DuPont Canada, Ericsson Canada, General Electric Canada and many others. The council includes nominally Canadian companies like Nova Chemicals, Ipsco, Thomson Reuter Corp. and Nortel Networks, which have moved their executive offices to the U.S. Even Hunter Harrison, the American president of American-controlled Canadian National, who took over the reins of power from Paul Tellier, is a member. And while none of the American-controlled companies was represented on the powerful executive committee at that time, some people who were close to Brian Mulroney when his government pushed through the Free Trade Agreement (FTA) led the council: Paul Tellier, who left CN to become chief executive of Bombardier, and Derek Burney, who figured centrally in the birth of the new continentalism, according to Chrétien biographer Lawrence Martin: "Burney was the man most intimately involved in the free trade story from beginning to end—in its formative stages as a member of the civil service, in its introduction as Mulroney's chief of staff and in its execution as ambassador in Washington."[9] And of course Tom d'Aquino, who directed the Canadian negotiating team with his black binders filled with business proposals, still leads the council.

Under d'Aquino's leadership, the organization has cultivated what David Langille, director of the Toronto-based Centre for Social Justice, calls a non-adversarial, non-confrontational style.[50] It conveys the impression that it always seeks what is best for the country. It works in partnership with the federal government whenever it can to ensure that what government thinks is possible will converge with what business wants, resulting in the ultimate treetops success—call it collaborative pre-emption. It was at work in the highly publicized 1991 study of the Canadian economy by Michael Porter of Harvard University. In "Canada at the Crossroads," Porter diagnosed Canada's performance and confirmed the CCCE view that even though Canada had some "strikingly different traditions, . . . to advance and prosper in the modern world, Canada would have to follow the corporate agenda and go forth and globalize like everyone else," Lawrence Martin noted wryly.[51] Such an approach is designed to "gain the edge" in policy-making, defining the issues in its own terms and upstaging other players—including the Ottawa bureaucrats—with a complete package of analysis and recommendations.[52] After the Porter study made the rounds of senior officials, the corporate agenda became the government agenda. This is the route the CCCE took after it decided to move ahead with an integration strategy in January 2002.

To ensure that federal mandarins and politicians would pay careful attention to its proposals, the CCCE hired an important person in their world, the recently retired assistant deputy minister for the Americas in the Department of Foreign Affairs and International Trade. (Earlier the CCCE hired Industry Canada's director of policy analysis and integration to be its vice-president of policy and research.) George Haynal was Canada's chief adviser on border issues. He retired in 2001, received a year's paid sabbatical at Harvard University and then became senior vice-president at the CCCE. Haynal was valuable to the chief executives because for him the question was "less whether we need to negotiate new instruments to further the process, but whether the public realm is capable of keeping up with emerging forces pushing us into deeper integration."[53] Once again, the problem was not one of involving Canadians in deciding their future direction, but of managing public opinion. During his eighteen-month stint at the council, Haynal helped craft the document called the "North American Security and Prosperity Initiative" (NASPI), and then helped sell it to senior government officials and political leaders. The name stuck. Canadians wanted prosperity, Americans security. The initiative tied them together and created an air of inevitability. Haynal left in 2003, following Paul Tellier to Bombardier, where he was appointed vice-president of public policy and chief government lobbyist. Foreign Affairs was one of his targets,[54] but this wasn't a conflict of interest according to government rules because it was more than a year since he left government service.

NASPI was launched at the next CEO Council's annual meeting in January 2003. It was framed as a blueprint for where Canada needs to go next in its relationship in North America. Even the title speaks of carefully crafted messaging, tying security to prosperity: our security depends on the U.S., therefore our prosperity does too. In fact, in this strategy Canada is submerged within North America. The five principles of NASPI are infused with doublespeak and bafflegab.[55] Principle Number One, "Reinventing the border," proposes eliminating the border and creating a common continental perimeter in which rules most likely will be set by Americans. It also masks a proposal for a customs initiative, to eliminate "burdensome requirements" on most goods entering the common North American space. Is the customs initiative actually a customs union? That isn't clear.

Principle Number Two, "Maximizing economic efficiencies," will further integrate already highly integrated Canada–U.S. markets. The proposal mentions areas such as food safety where common standards and regulations can be applied. Would this principle sanction Health Canada's 2004 plan to loosen the rules governing what vitamins and minerals may be added to foods? The new rules would allow manufacturers to add virtually any vitamins or minerals they choose. The consequence, warned Bill Jeffery, national coordinator of the Ottawa-based advocacy group Centre for Science in the Public Interest, would be that "they'll be able to take a nutritional train wreck like a chocolate bar, add some vitamins and minerals to it and represent it on the label as if it's a nutritional superstar." This is not a move desired by consumers, Jeffery said. The government caved in to the demands of Canada's powerful food industry, which had been lobbying for parity with the U.S., where there are very few rules dictating which nutrients may be added to foods.[56]

The other principles were similarly deceptive: negotiating a comprehensive resource security pact (ceding control over Canada's gas and oil resources to the U.S.), rebuilding Canada's military capability (sending our troops to locations where the Americans wanted them) and creating a new institutional framework for North America (removing decision making from the hands of elected representatives).

Canadians could have obtained a rare glimpse of d'Aquino's tactics when he presented NASPI to the Senate Standing Committee on Foreign Affairs a month after its launch. (He was accompanied by George Haynal.) A customs union is a development that business dearly wants, but was not included in NASPI, he informed the senators. In a customs union, participating countries adopt a common tariff or external trade policy towards the rest of the world, allowing free circulation of goods and services within the common area. Even its strongest advocates agree that this move would mean giving up Canada's remaining economic sovereignty. A common trade policy negotiated between the Canadian mouse and the American elephant would clearly be the American trade policy. "Why is [a customs union] not in your strategy?" one senator asked. He "strongly favour[ed]" a customs union and believed it to be "realistic and doable," d'Aquino replied, but he wasn't advocating it because many powerful business people in the U.S. were opposed. They didn't believe the

U.S. Congress would approve such a proposal. So the CEO Council dropped the idea, at least in name because it wasn't "tactically desirable." But the senators need not worry. D'Aquino reassured them that "if we move ahead in all the areas [of NASPI], we will achieve a *de facto* situation that will equate to a customs union." He continued: "We are talking within our family here, although I know it is part of the public record," suspecting perhaps that hardly anyone reads Senate committee proceedings. "We are trying to achieve, via the backdoor, what we do not think we could achieve via the front."[57] The chief executives wouldn't tarnish their standing with the Americans and could still get what they want. Let the customs union be put forward by somebody else.

As the ultimate treetops functionary, the council's target audience is narrow: the prime minister and cabinet, senior government officials, the business elite and leading media pundits. It's not interested in obtaining broad media coverage of its proposals, which is just as well, since "many Canadians' natural reaction is to immediately distrust the concerns raised by the [council.]" That observation originated, not with a left-wing critic, but, perhaps surprisingly, with then C.D. Howe Institute president Jack Mintz. Canadians perceive the CCCE as the "fat cats" who are "pressing their agenda for tax cuts on high-income earners and businesses," Mintz wrote in *Canadian Business Economics*.[58] The professor of taxation at the Rotman School of Management at the University of Toronto finds much of the debate "rather sterile." It shouldn't be about tax cuts yes, or tax cuts no, but about the "optimal" size of government. Then, in a deft piece of intellectual footwork, he concludes that government is too big because it spends too much on "wasteful programs" and requires "too much tax revenue." Because government is too big it needs to be downsized through tax cuts. The C.D. Howe president reaches the same conclusion as the CEOs. However, this is no longer the fat cats saying they need tax cuts, but an "independent and reasoned"—the Howe's motto—academic.

Because its self-interest is transparent, the business elite requires the support of academics and professionals who tacitly assume the same goal as business: take the risk out of democracy by assisting in the management of public opinion in the interests of business. They are the "organic intellectuals of the ruling class" identified by Antonio Gramsci in his *Prison Notebooks*. This role in the propaganda system is filled by think-tanks and research institutes like the Howe and Fraser institutes, the Public Policy Forum and the Institute for Research on Public Policy. Business provides about $25 million a year to these organizations in Canada so they can hire and commission sympathetic academics to produce studies and reports compatible with the business agenda, and market the reports through books, conferences and media. Think-tanks work because we see them to be at a distance from direct corporate influence even though they are largely funded by business, and their boards are dominated by corporate executives.

Of course, progressives have their own think-tanks, which are funded largely by trade unions and progressive individuals, non-governmental organizations (NGOs) and foundations. And they advocate for improved social programs, stronger, more effective regulations, less free—and more fair—trade and more national sovereignty. But they have significantly less impact on public policy than the corporate-sponsored think-tanks. Business has simply been more effective than NGOs with its propaganda efforts. It is more effective because it has greater financial resources. Business-sponsored think-tanks can hire more staff, fund more scholars, cover a wider range of topics and produce more studies and reports. They are also more effective because they have the ear of a sympathetic corporate media far more frequently than progressive think-tanks. The Howe and Fraser institutes receive far more coverage—and far more favourable coverage—than the progressive think-tanks. Just as important, business often receives a sympathetic hearing from Liberal and Conservative governments, which are usually on the same side of the political spectrum. At best, progressive think-tanks play a counter-propaganda role, providing alternative perspectives on policy issues.

The Howe Institute says it is independent, but its links to the CCCE are extensive. In 2002, sixteen CCCE member companies were represented on the Howe board. Some companies represented on the board were already well integrated with the U.S. economy. Ipsco and Nova Chemicals had moved their executive offices to the U.S. to be closer to their customers and investors, while Cargill Canada was a subsidiary of a U.S.-based multinational. The board was dominated by representatives from banks, financial institutions and the oil and gas sector. There were no labour leaders or representatives from civil society on the board that year, nor have there been any since. And only one university professor was a director, although many universities were members, raising the question about the intellectual independence of the universities. So were major news organizations like CanWest Global Communications, Rogers Communications, and even the liberal Torstar.[59] Perhaps that explains why Howe studies are well reported by the media.

There is no question that the integrationist voice is well represented on the Howe board. And this view is overwhelmingly reflected in the Howe's work. This is not to suggest that the institute's academics write what the board tells them. But it does mean that academics are selected whose views coincide with those of business and who are willing to lend their work to the corporate propaganda effort.

Howe grabbed public leadership of integration propaganda (or perhaps it was bestowed by the CCCE) with a well-funded and highly publicized series of reports and a brand, the Border Papers, three months after the chief executives moved integration to the top of their agenda. The campaign led off with what Howe called a framework paper, by economist Wendy Dobson, a colleague of Jack Mintz at the Rotman School of Management. Canada cannot solve its economic problems with the U.S. on an issue-by-issue basis, Dobson argued in her paper, "Shaping the future of the North American economic space." It will take a big idea such as a customs union to catch the attention and interest of U.S. power brokers. Tom d'Aquino couldn't have said it better, but then he didn't have to.

The series was guided by an advisory group with Dobson as chair. It included many of the same players from the 1988 BCNI-backed free trade campaign. Nearly $200,000 was provided by the Donner Canadian Foundation, which was funding many conservative projects during this period.[60] Donner was chaired by Allan Gotlieb, Brian Mulroney's ambassador to the U.S. and a chief functionary in pushing through free trade, along with Derek Burney and Paul Tellier.

Canada fell behind the U.S. in the nineties following the implementation of NAFTA, Dobson wrote, posing a puzzle she chose not to address, since she argued back then that free trade would boost the Canadian economy. Our standard of living lagged behind that of the United States, our real exchange rate declined and our share of foreign direct investment fell. The one absolute in all of this change must be that "we" (read: Canadian-located businesses) must maintain easy and assured access to the U.S. market. September 11 made access to it less assured, Dobson explained. A narrow window of opportunity had opened because the U.S. became more receptive to its friends and neighbours. Because power is so dispersed in the U.S. system and because the Bush administration is so preoccupied with security and defence, Dobson said, only a big idea will succeed in catching the administration's attention. The big idea must address U.S. and Canadian objectives. Dobson calls it a "strategic bargain," proposing three big ideas. In the first, Canada should unilaterally launch strategic initiatives in areas of interest to the U.S.—border security, immigration, defence and energy security—and in exchange, seek deepening economic integration. A customs union is the second big idea, while the third, a common market, goes further by freeing up the movement of people and flows of capital and technology, with common institutions administering common standards and regulations and harmonized policies.[61] In this partnership of unequals, harmonized policies likely will be those of the Americans, a conclusion Dobson avoids. But other observers filled in the gaps. A customs union would establish common external tariff rates. Canadian policy "would have to change so that its Most Favoured Nation trading provisions were kept in line with those of the United States," wrote University of Toronto geographer Emily Gilbert, who studied the rhetoric around deep integration.[62] Canada's relations with Cuba would be in jeopardy, for instance.

All three big ideas would likely lead to loss of Canadian sovereignty, a concern of critics of deep integration. Sovereignty, Dobson wrote, is "a country's determination of key policies and national control of decisions affecting its governance." Most critics of integration would agree with this definition. And they must certainly recognize that Canada has never been truly sovereign, first as a colony under British rule, and then as a small presence on the North American continent. As Canadian prime minister Pierre Elliot Trudeau once declared about Canada–U.S. relations, "living next to you is in some ways like sleeping with an elephant. No matter how friendly and even-tempered is the beast, if I can call it that, one is affected by every twitch and grunt." Canadians are well aware they are the mouse in the relationship, and to survive—and retain their sovereignty—they've tried to keep their distance. In addition, Canada has given up sovereignty to international organizations like the World Trade Organization (WTO) and the Kyoto Accord of the United Nations Conference on Environment and Development. It has agreed to be bound by the conventions of these organizations, but, in exchange, gained some influence in the setting of their policies and standards. These organizations are governed by rules that all member nations helped establish. But when the mouse cedes sovereignty to the elephant, the outcomes are established by might, not rules. Who knows what the elephant will want next? Canadians can't know in advance what they might have to give up to retain favour with the Americans. Clearly, though, increased economic integration with the U.S. will lead to national policies that mirror those of the U.S. and lose their traditional Canadian nature.

Dobson seemed to recognize this situation when she argues that "sovereignty is not just about what a country gives up but also about what it gains in more efficient production, larger markets, freer flow of investment, swift resolution of disputes, and greater protection of intellectual property, to name a few of the benefits."[63] The problem with this argument is that these benefits accrue to business owners and investors, and not to Canadian workers, who will have less ability to control their destiny. Veering close to propaganda, Dobson confounds the narrow business interest with the broader public interest.

After the release of her study in 2002, Dobson repeated her big-idea arguments in many prestigious forums the same year, including the Asia-Pacific Summit in Vancouver and the North American Committee in Ottawa. Perhaps her most noteworthy presentation was to the North American regional meeting in Toronto of the Trilateral Commission, of which she was a member. For generations of progressives, the Trilateral Commission is the organization that runs the world. It was established in 1973 by David Rockefeller, then head of Chase Manhattan Bank, and Columbia University professor Zbigniew Brzezinski, who became President Jimmy Carter's national security adviser. Their goal was to create an international forum to foster closer cooperation among the core industrialized democracies of Europe, North America and Japan. It included 250 members of the financial, industrial, political, bureaucratic and media elites, carefully selected and screened by Rockefeller.

When Rockefeller set up the commission, the business priority was to guide national economies towards an international marketplace. Such a reorientation of economic priorities would require dramatic changes in governmental policies in most industrialized nations. But before this could happen, a serious problem would have to be dealt with. The problem was an "excess of democracy," and was the subject of the commission's first book.[64] In the book's analysis, "special interests," such as environmentalists, social justice advocates and equal rights organizations, an overemphasis on social welfare programs, a "bloated" bureaucracy, and too much emphasis on protection for workers and national economies, all combined to bog government down in ineffectuality. The solution the book offered was that government must become stronger to resist the demands of citizens, except of course those citizens who were business executives. In this case, government must become weaker. Wendy Dobson's "big idea" is in the Trilateralist tradition: weaken democratic institutions to facilitate the business agenda. She was the only woman and the only academic in the Canadian delegation, which was headed by the Donner Foundation's Allan Gotlieb. Perhaps Dobson and Gotlieb devised the Border Papers when they met at a commission meeting after September 11. Gotlieb had his own version of the big idea, which he calls a "community of law," emphasizing legally binding institutions. It is similar to Dobson's proposal in that it includes elements of a customs union and a common market, and seems to exclude democratic governance.[65]

About six Border Papers were pumped out each year until 2005, when the output was cut in half. Dobson's paper, and the entire Border Papers series, received prominent media exposure. The big idea worked its way from the corporate agenda onto the public agenda, thanks to positive and widespread media attention. The *National Post* provided a front-page story and an excerpt from the paper on the op-ed page the day Dobson's paper was released. The same day, she had an op-ed piece in the *Globe and Mail* and her study was lauded in a column in the *Report on Business*. The *Globe* followed with a favourable editorial several days later. The study was also reported positively in many CanWest papers. With a few exceptions the *Toronto Star* and some *Globe* opinion pieces—economic integration became an instant media darling.[66]

The *National Post* is best positioned as an instrument of business propaganda. The paper was created by Conrad Black to bring a more conservative, business-friendly voice into the Canadian news media system. The torch was passed to the Asper family, which espouses similar goals. Izzy Asper was a long-time member of the Business Council on National Issues. As well, the Aspers have expressed a desire to sell at least part of their holdings to foreign interests, so they would have a vested interest in deeper integration because that would open the Canadian media market to more foreign investment. The *Post* struck a deal with the Howe Institute to publish exclusive commentaries on the series. *Post* editor Ken Whyte was a director of the Donner Canadian Foundation along with Allan Gotlieb, and therefore an insider in funding the Border Paper series. What better way to ensure its success than by publicizing it?

Prolonged and extensive coverage of integration in the news pages creates an impression that this is an important issue, a crisis in need of immediate attention. The multiplicity of think-tanks producing reports, studies and conferences creates a ready-made supply of news stories. The impression of urgency is reinforced by the musings of the pundits, those journalists who make their living by commenting on, rather than reporting, the news. Pundits also include academics who write frequent opinion pieces. Long-time University of Toronto historian Michael Bliss wrote many pro-integration columns in the *National Post* during this period. He wrote his most incendiary piece—with front-page positioning—just two weeks after September 11. He accused Canadians of contributing nothing more than the "chanting of camp songs" and "mantras about sovereignty," and predicted that Canada was "heading toward some kind of greater North American union." This will occur, Bliss claimed, because we have already "accepted the continentalization of North American defence and the economy." But this argument, like Dobson's, confounds "we," the business and political leaders who do embrace integration, with "we," the Canadian people who are doubtful, but have little say in the matter. Similarly, Bliss claimed that "when a nationalist prime minister, John Diefenbaker, balked at the closeness of defence integration during the early 1960s, Canadians replaced him with a Liberal government committed to even closer co-operation."[67] But this is a disputed interpretation. George Grant argued it wasn't the Canadian people who replaced Diefenbaker; the Toronto business elite, the Canadian military and the U.S. government did the dirty work behind the scenes to replace Diefenbaker and presented it to Canadians as a *fait accompli*.[68]

Another Bliss piece is titled "Is Canada a nation in decline?" The answer he provided, not surprisingly, was an unqualified yes. And he had little confidence that Canadians would change. We will continue to "drift from season to season, riding American coattails, adjusting policies occasionally to keep Washington happy," he predicted, and relying on them "for our security and economic well-being." We are hypocrites, Bliss charged, who "still mouth the platitudes about our achievements and importance and sovereignty . . ."[69] Strong words from this academic, and in the pages of the *National Post*, unchallenged.

The *Globe and Mail* provided at least some critical viewpoints on integration. The paper gave extensive space to the opinions of York University political economist Stephen Clarkson, who, along with writers at the *Toronto Star*, created a small ripple against the deep-integration tsunami. Clarkson's views were never found in the *Post*. He wrote a half-dozen pieces in the *Globe* pointing out problems with integration. In one, Clarkson argued that Canadians were fooled into thinking that NAFTA was about the economy when it was "an external, if virtually secret, constitution for Canada."[70] Future politicians "who might be elected on the strength of having more activist ideas about using the state to achieve social justice or economic growth" will be frustrated in achieving these goals because of NAFTA, which they will not be able to reverse. In another piece he claimed that NAFTA increased the power asymmetries between North America's central and peripheral states, a significant point that the CCCE and C.D. Howe Institute rarely raised. Nor did they ask the question "What does Uncle Sam want from Canada?" At the top of the U.S. wish list,

Clarkson suggested, was access to Canada's water through environmentally disastrous diversion projects. Second would be a Washington demand to resolve a number of "irritants": terminating egg, milk and poultry supply-management systems; privatizing the Canadian Wheat Board; opening up the health care system to U.S. investment; and neutering Ottawa's cultural policies.[71] Clarkson concludes that what Uncle Sam wants "will be good for American corporate interests." And for Canadian corporate interests too, he might have added.

Clarkson's few columns criticizing integration, however, were overwhelmed by those of Drew Fagan, the *Globe*'s Washington bureau chief during the nineties and senior Ottawa political correspondent. Fagan was a reliable cheerleader for integration and helped business disseminate its propaganda messages. Fagan wrote a pre–9/11 piece with the provocative headline "Is it time for Canadians to think the unthinkable?"[72] Once Paul Tellier and the CEO Council put integration into play, Fagan wrote more than two dozen columns promoting business goals, and he wasn't even a business reporter. In one piece he argued that Canada needs to cut business taxes even more than the Americans—it wasn't enough to merely keep up. As the smaller rival, Canada needed to do more and faster. His sole authority here was C.D. Howe president Jack Mintz, who never met a tax he didn't want to cut. Fagan spent not one sentence on the consequences of tax cuts, such as reduced social programs.[73] This was followed by a column in which he argued that the free trade pact was growing more dated every day. His sole source in this piece was Bill Dymond of the Centre for Trade Policy and Law at Carleton University, a former trade official and an influential lobbyist for increased integration.[74] Then in March, Fagan wrote a 3000-word feature with the provocative title "It's the year 2025. There is no U.S. border. Has Canada become the 51st state?" The trade deal, he wrote, "has been credited with pressing Canadian businesses to modernize, raising living standards, boosting employment, as well as turning the border into Canada's lifeline." His sources were seven "forward-thinking Canadians," but they all wondered if we even need a border. One was Public Policy Forum president David Zussman, who suspected Canada would see further integration of its economy and society, while another, George Haynal, lectured Canadians to get over the word "border." Fagan favourites Bill Dymond and Wendy Dobson were also quoted. (This was a month before Dobson's Border Paper was released.) Dobson said there needs to be a "seamless border." In the world according to Drew Fagan, no one opposes deeper integration.[75]

He next wrote an adoring column on Dobson's paper[76] and followed with a piece on the Canada–U.S. Smart Border Declaration, a thirty-point plan signed in December 2001, aimed at improving joint efforts to facilitate trade and fight terrorism. This column illustrates Fagan's valuable role in the corporate propaganda machine. Deputy Prime Minister John Manley makes a special background point that "most of the declaration was written in Ottawa. The U.S. government questioned some details up until the last hour, but signed on to largely a Canadian vision of how the border could operate in each country's interests." The message conveyed is that this is a Canadian—not American— initiative. Following the Ronald Reagan–Brian Mulroney strategy of pretending the U.S. was not directing the free trade negotiations, Fagan made the point that Canada's sovereignty was not further threatened. "The border declaration is replete with efforts to jointly develop new programs, from biometric identifiers to overseas visa approvals," he wrote. "That makes some Canadian nationalists nervous on grounds that sovereignty is being undermined. But by taking the lead in proposing border solutions, Ottawa has started to exercise its sovereignty adroitly—harmonization is hardly a dirty word if it is clearly in the Canadian interest."[77] But was it?

Fagan's supportive work must have impressed the CEO Council and the Liberal government, because no sooner was the 2004 election over than the government hired him. He went to work in the Economic Policy Branch of Foreign Affairs and International Trade, George Haynal's old department. (Two years later he was appointed assistant deputy minister for Strategic Policy and Planning.) *National Post* political columnist Don Martin, a competitor, groused that Fagan's news coverage had served "as the government's official trial balloon." Martin questioned the practice of reporters going into government because, in Fagan's case at least, he must have known he was being considered for a job while he was still reporting and commenting on his future employer.[78] How could he give his readers the unvarnished truth? But Martin didn't ask the question of whether the government's official trial balloons had been inflated by Tom d'Aquino.

Since Paul Tellier's musings on the inevitability of deeper integration several months post 9/11, Tom d'Aquino worked hard to make deeper integration inevitable. He first created a consensus among the Canadian business elite, then sold it to leading political and business figures in the NAFTA countries, and finally moved it onto official government agendas, all within the space of three years. He didn't want integration to become an issue during elections the way free trade did in 1988. Such a debate could spiral out of control, as it did then. Even though *Financial Post* editor Terence Corcoran smelled "an ugly replay of the free-trade election of 1988," it didn't happen, in 2004, 2006 or 2008. His nose for news let him down.[79] None of the parties made integration a major issue and the media seemed content to downplay d'Aquino's backroom machinations. The elections were framed around issues like government accountability, health care and the financial meltdown in 2008. Integration barely flickered across the election screen.

Several months before the 2004 election was called, the chief executives quietly released a discussion paper called "New Frontiers: Building a 21st Century Canada-United States Partnership in North America." This paper wasn't to be thought of as an ad hoc, weak-kneed assemblage of stale ideas, but a "comprehensive strategy" that was "ambitious" and "bold," these words being used many times in the document.[80] These terms must have been intended as a warning for the elite audience. To say your proposals are ambitious and bold is to suggest you don't expect them to be fully accepted. They go further than the audience may be prepared to. But the more ambitious your claims, the further you will likely move your agenda.

"North American economic integration is now well advanced and irreversible," the preface states, "and in the face of global terrorism, the economic and physical security of the continent have become indivisible."[81] This document resorts to a rhetoric of inevitability, a theme that will be addressed shortly. The direction is not open for discussion, only the details. And the direction is the one outlined in the CCCE's original NASPI document. To promote its ideas to American movers and shakers, the CCCE held its annual spring members' meeting in Washington, D.C. The Canadian public seemed irrelevant in moving these proposals forward. The meeting, which was closed to media and the public, was timed to occur a few weeks before Prime Minister Paul Martin met with George W. Bush at the end of April, and was intended to influence the leaders' discussions.[82]

Over the next year, d'Aquino worked the backrooms of Ottawa, Washington and Mexico City to move the chief executives' strategy onto official government agendas. He was instrumental in organizing an independent task force on continental integration sponsored by the Washington-based Council on Foreign Relations. D'Aquino was Canadian vice-chair while John Manley was chair. Was Manley the puppet and d'Aquino the puppet-master? This body added its weight to the CEO proposals. It issued an interim report ten days before Martin met with Bush and Mexico's president, Vicente Fox, in Waco, Texas, in what was billed as the "Three Amigos" meeting.[83]

At this meeting, the leaders launched a new agreement named, significantly, the Security and Prosperity Partnership of North America (SPP). The title echoed CEO Council rhetoric that safety and economic well-being were Siamese twins that could not be separated. D'Aquino proudly pointed out that the five goals—"pillars," he now called them—of his "New Frontiers" document were reflected in the leaders' agenda: eliminate the border, deregulate the economy, lock Canada's energy resources into American needs, fashion a unified defence force and create a new institutional framework for North America.[84]

The Three Amigos met again the following March in Cancún, Mexico. Paul Martin was out and Stephen Harper—clearly more of an amigo to Bush—was in. While the mainstream media obsessed over Harper's wardrobe—he wore a short-sleeve blue shirt and olive-coloured hunting vest—the three governments were on the verge of taking a giant step towards continental integration. The ploy seemed to have worked, since the Security and Prosperity Partnership went largely unreported. The *Globe*'s Margaret Wente wrote a column about Harper's attire and paunch, without mentioning the reason for his visit.[85]

Over the previous year, government and business leaders from the three countries met privately to organize an agenda for the SPP. A meeting in Washington, D.C., just two weeks before the Cancún summit, focused on the creation of a North American Competitiveness Council (NACC), which could be the foundation for the "new institutional framework" for North America, as recommended by the CEO Council.[86] The rationale for the SPP was that cross-border economic activity had largely outgrown the legal and regulatory framework and physical infrastructure on which it depends. The SPP was framed less as a process of rationalizing the integration that had already taken place. Key to this task is the NACC, which would offer ideas on how business could promote competitiveness.[87] But it's not competitiveness as is commonly understood—providing better products and services at lower prices. In this Orwellian world, competitiveness means "regulatory cooperation," or deregulation, a move to limit further the role of government in the economy. The NACC seems designed to reduce public oversight of the economy.

Stephen Harper was onside with the CEO agenda. The CCCE's April, 2004

"New Frontiers" document notes with approval that Harper, as the new leader of the Conservative Party, had already called for a "continental 'strategic partnership,' one that would link freer flows of goods, services, labour, capital and technology with improvements in continental security."[88] Now he was prime minister and he appointed Canada's representatives to the Competitiveness Council. All ten were CCCE members. They included Richard George, head of oil sands giant Suncor Energy and CCCE chair, plus two more members of CCCE's powerful executive committee, and three more CCCE directors. Hunter Harrison, head of the integrated CN, was an appointee, which raises the question of whether he represents Canada or the U.S. Or perhaps it didn't matter any more.

The Competitiveness Council deals directly with government ministers in the U.S., Canada and Mexico. Harper appointed his public safety, industry and foreign affairs ministers to meet with the council three times a year. "The guidance from the ministers was 'tell us what we need to do and we'll make it happen,'" Lockheed Martin president Ron Corvais, who chairs the American section of the council, and is a former Pentagon adviser to Dick Cheney, candidly told *Maclean's* reporter Luiza Savage several months after the council was created. "We've decided not to recommend any things that would require legislative changes," Corvais said, "because we won't get anywhere."[89] The North American political economy would be shaped by executive order. This approach was probably a wise one, since most Canadians were not enamoured of the SPP. A survey of Canadians by Environics Research Group for the Council of Canadians in 2008 found that 87 percent of respondents strongly or somewhat agreed with the statement that "Canada should maintain the ability to set its own independent environmental, health and safety standards, even if this might reduce cross-border trade opportunities with the United States." The survey also found that 89 percent agreed with the statement that "Canada should establish an energy policy that provides reliable supplies of oil, gas and electricity at stable prices and protects the environment, even if this means placing restrictions on exports and foreign ownership of Canadian supplies." And, significantly, 86 percent want the Security and Prosperity Partnership to be debated and submitted to a vote in Parliament, something that was not going to be allowed to happen, according to Ron Corvais.[90]

Underlying these rapid moves towards deeper integration, despite public opposition, is a rhetoric of inevitability. Paul Tellier said it first: integration of the two economies "will continue, it is inevitable, it is irreversible and it is tak-ing place faster than any of us expected." Tom d'Aquino's 2004 "New Frontiers" discussion paper begins with this statement: "North American economic inte-gration is now well advanced and irreversible." University of Toronto geogra-pher Emily Gilbert studied the rhetoric about the inevitability of integration.[91] She assembled a list of statements by business leaders, think-tank experts, academics and government officials. Typical were those by Sherry Cooper, vice-president and chief economist at BMO Nesbitt Burns ("indeed the inte-gration is inevitable"), Perrin Beatty, CEO of the Canadian Manufacturers and Exporters ("a new North American partnership is inevitable"), historian Michael Bliss ("we are heading toward some kind of greater North American union"), professor Louis Balthazar of Laval University ("a customs union with the United States is eventually inevitable") and Liberal MP Jacques Saada, Canadian chair of the Canadian–U.S. Permanent Joint Board on Defence ("greater integration is unavoidable, inevitable, and necessary"). John Manley didn't use the word "inevitable" but that's what he meant: "I don't think there's a policy choice here."[92]

Gilbert argues that the claim that integration is inevitable was consciously deployed to encourage acceptance of the business agenda and limit alterna-tives. One alternative rudely elbowed out was a proposal for public debate on integration and the creation of a strategy based on what the public might pre-fer, as evidenced by the 2008 Council of Canadians survey. Since integration is inevitable, what the public might want—perhaps stronger government regu-lation of business—is irrelevant. The only item up for discussion is what kind of deal the Canadian government can make in the face of inevitability.[93]

The business agenda, as Alex Carey noted two decades earlier, is to take the risk out of democracy, to reduce the ability of democratically elected gov-ernments to rein in corporate power and prerogative. Wendy Dobson's new economic space, which she outlined in her framework Howe Border Paper, is fundamental. To the uninformed, a new economic space seems simply to be North America with the border between the countries drawn with a thinner pencil. But as the border fades into insignificance in this vision of the future, so do the governments to the territories straddling the border.[94] The New Economic Space would be governed, not by traditionally elected governments, but by the North American Competitiveness Council acting on behalf of "mar-ket forces." Citizenship in this space would be a mere shadow of the tradi-tional concept of the role of citizens in a democracy.

Regulatory cooperation is one critical development for deeper integration. There cannot be a single economic space if the various regions of North America operate under different rules mandated by the voters of the regions. In a 2006 Howe Border Paper commentary titled "Steer or Drift?," former Canadian trade official Michael Hart, who became an effective polemicist for integration, writes that the problem faced by Canada and the U.S. may be called "the tyranny of small differences," silly differences, in fact. In Canada, cheese-flavoured popcorn must contain no more that 49 percent real cheese, whereas in the U.S., the same product must contain no less than 53 percent real cheese. In Canada, fortified orange juice is classified as a drug; in the U.S., it is a food. These are indeed on the level of silly differences. Surely both economies—but especially the smaller Canadian market—would benefit from one standard, Hart suggests.[95]

In the real world of politics, the small, silly differences outlined in Hart's paper are replaced by major threats to health, safety and environmental protection. A key proposal is a "tested-once" policy for biotechnology and pharmaceuticals. If this policy had been in effect in the nineties, Canada would have been required to accept the use of Monsanto's bovine growth hormone (BGH) because it was approved for use in the United States. BGH was suspected of being linked to cancer and was ultimately rejected by Health Canada, partly as a result of public pressure.

The problem with Hart's approach was that regulatory cooperation was taking place during the presidency of George W. Bush, the most deregulation-minded president since Ronald Reagan. And Stephen Harper, another deregulation-minded leader, was still the Canadian prime minister. That the Obama administration might follow the same deregulation agenda was evidenced by Obama's nomination of legal scholar Cass Sunstein as head of the White House Office of Information and Regulatory Affairs, which oversees regulations throughout the government. Sunstein has argued that all proposed regulations should be subjected to cost-benefit analysis. Critics of this approach say it was used by the Reagan and Bush administrations to weaken regulations. Supporters say that if properly applied, cost-benefit analysis can "be a neutral tool for sound policy making . . . while promoting a strong regulatory agenda in a time of crisis."[96]

A decision by the Pest Management Regulatory Agency (PMRA), which sets Canada's pesticide rules, to raise its limits on pesticide residues on fruit and vegetables for hundreds of products could be seen as a consequence of the regulatory harmonization effort. Differences in residue limits posed a potential "trade irritant," PMRA chief registrar Richard Aucoin explained. Canada would relax its rules only "where this poses no risks," he stressed. But critics were not convinced.[97]

Underneath the rhetoric of inevitability is a blueprint for a deregulated economy. In the Dobson-CCCE plan, the Canadian government's last act as an independent political entity may be to take a "bold and ambitious step" and sign on to the full corporate agenda. And Stephen Harper is there for the signing. The softwood lumber pact, concluded several months after he took office, may indicate Harper's route to deeper integration. Harper and Bush were feted by trade officials for pushing through the agreement to end American duties on Canadian lumber and return to Canadian producers 80 percent of the $5.3 billion collected. Little mentioned was a clause that requires U.S. government approval of any provincial forest policy changes. This may be a significant retreat from sovereignty. This provision will ensure Canadian forest policy changes in one direction only: towards industry-controlled timber pricing.[98] Harper's deal would hobble the ability of provincial governments to tie timber supply and pricing, for instance, to community economic development and job creation and retention.

The North American Competitiveness Council may do for the rest of the economy what the softwood lumber agreement did in one industry if it survives. Robert Pastor, the American academic who rivals Tom d'Aquino in his zeal for deeper integration, cautions that the Obama administration will likely take a different tack than George W. Bush. In Pastor's view, the SPP approach failed. "The strategy of acting on technical issues in an incremental, bureaucratic way and of keeping the issues away from the public view, has generated more suspicion than accomplishments. The new president will probably discard the SPP," he wrote several months before the U.S. presidential election. Instead of a NACC made up only of CEOs, he proposed a commission "composed of independent and distinguished leaders from academia, civil society, business, labor and agriculture and with an independent research capacity." But the goal remains the same: deepen economic integration by negotiating a customs union and by fashioning common North American standards for transportation, infrastructure, energy, environment and labour.[99]

For his part, Tom d'Aquino didn't miss a beat. When U.S. president Barack Obama visited Ottawa in February 2009, the CEO Council urged the two nations to work together to speed economic recovery. The council stressed the need to reduce the cost of doing business across the border by harmonizing regulations. It also proposed launching a bilateral energy and environment initiative and enhancing joint management of North American defence and security.[100] But it wouldn't be through the Security and Prosperity Partnership. A week after Obama's visit, d'Aquino told the House of Commons Foreign Affairs Committee that "the SPP is probably dead . . . because under President Obama we will see something else . . . Something will replace it."[101]

And several weeks later, d'Aquino organized a special summit of Canadian and American business leaders and policy-makers in Washington. As well as senior officials from the Obama administration, participants included the presidents of the three major American business lobbies—the Business Roundtable, the United States Chamber of Commerce and the National Association of Manufacturers (NAM).[102] Whatever the shape of future integration efforts, d'Aquino was going all out to ensure he and his organization would be at the table.

Analyzing the Deep-Integration Campaign

It's not easy to analyze propaganda. One problem is that propaganda campaigns often take place over extended periods, so their progress must be studied. As well, because the sponsors have a specific intent in mind, considerable investigation is required to determine the propagandist's purpose. Despite these difficulties, propaganda scholars Garth Jowett and Victoria O'Donnell have developed a ten-step plan of propaganda analysis. They caution that the unit of analysis must be an entire propaganda campaign and not an individual report, conference or propaganda message.[1] The campaign to make Canadians more accepting of deep economic and social integration with the United States began in the early 1980s with the first attempts to fashion a free trade deal between the two countries. The campaign analyzed in Chapter 1 is more specific: the seven-year period that began just after September 11, 2001, and ended on November 4, 2008, with the election of Barack Obama. But deep integration is far from over. A new approach would be forthcoming under the new administration, integration strategists assured their constituencies.

Step 1: *The ideology and purpose of the propaganda campaign*
The first step in propaganda analysis, Jowett and O'Donnell suggest, is to examine

the prevailing ideology underlying the propaganda campaign. The propagandist must be keenly aware of a target audience's ideology. This is a people's common-sense view of the world that helps it delineate what is good and bad, right and wrong, and which arguments will be well received. So the propagandist can never lose sight of the fact that a key element in Canadian ideology is its ambivalence towards the United States, Canadians want the benefits of being close; but they also want to maintain their distance and sovereignty. Integrationists want Canada to be understood as a nation in North America, whose destiny is intertwined with that of the U.S. But political scientist Philip Resnick argues that to understand the Canadian identity, we need to recognize the nation's European roots. True, Resnick concedes, Canada *is* a North American state sharing the northern part of the continent with its powerful neighbour. But, he claims, through origins and sensibility, Canada is very similar to Europe. Citing British journalist Will Hutton, Resnick argues that what is central to the European state tradition, are "beliefs about the obligations of the propertied to society, about the need for a social contract, and about the centrality of a public realm and government to a happy community."[2] Canadians, Resnick claims, are akin to Europeans when they come to think about these questions. They "seek to find a balance between the extremes of the marketplace and the state, between individual liberties and group rights." They do not distrust government in the way the Americans instinctively do, nor are they as blindly enamoured of the spirit of unbridled capitalism. As Peter Jennings, the Toronto-born ABC News broadcaster, once observed, "Canada, as it is with some of the European countries, is trying to balance some of the market forces with public policy, which is not as apparent in the United States, where the pursuit of happiness and individualism are very much alive."[3]

The purpose of the deep-integration campaign is to promote the interests of the business and professional classes by tying the Canadian economy and social structure more tightly to the U.S. The propaganda goal is to stress the inevitability of integration. It's inevitable, the propagandist argues, because Canadians have already made the decision about free trade and this is simply the necessary next step for maintaining our standard of living. As John Manley said, "I don't think there's a policy choice here."

Step 2: *The context in which the propaganda occurs*
Successful propaganda relates to the prevailing mood or climate of the times, Jowett and O'Donnell say. Fifteen years of free trade have passed, with

dwindling support among the majority of Canadians. This reality must be interpreted by the propagandist to fit with campaign messages. The terrorist attacks of September 11, 2001, provided a unique opportunity to create effective messages that played on people's fears about their security and future. The propagandist must recognize Canadian ambivalence towards the United States, fearing social and political integration, while favouring the economic benefits. And there are additional obstacles to overcome. The growing resistance to free trade discovered by the Guy-Alexandroff study for the C.D. Howe Institute required the propagandists to take a different approach and develop the rhetoric of inevitability. Deeper integration was further hampered by three Canadian government decisions: Jean Chrétien's insistence on ratifying the Kyoto Accord in the face of American rejection; Chrétien's refusal to join George Bush in the U.S. invasion of Iraq; and Paul Martin's refusal to join the American continental missile defence shield.

Step 3: *Identification of the propagandist*
The sponsors of propaganda are almost always organizations or institutions rather than individuals. Academics or think-tank employees who write pro-integration papers are not propagandists. Rather, we need to look at the organizational context within which these studies and reports were produced. Sometimes the organizational sponsor is masked, as when a company or industry sets up a front group or Astroturf organization to promote a hidden message. In the deep-integration campaign, the sponsor appears to be the C.D. Howe Institute, with its $200,000 in Donner Foundation funding. But if we ask who has the most to gain from successful deep-integration propaganda, the answer must be the members of the CEO Council and the corporations they represent. The many links between the CEOs and the Howe Institute provide evidence of the centrality of Tom d'Aquino's organization. And further confirmation that the CEO Council is the propagandist can be obtained by examining the recent history of integration. The CEO Council—then the Business Council on National Issues—was the main pro-integration proponent in the 1987–88 free trade debate.

Step 4: *The structure of the propaganda organization*
The propaganda analyst wants to know if the Canadian Council of Chief Executives, C.D. Howe Institute and other business organizations worked well together during the campaign. Possible rifts within the business community

could occur between western resource industries and eastern manufacturing, big business and small- and medium-sized enterprise, or conservative and moderate business factions. In this case, though, the propaganda campaign benefited from a highly structured organization centred on the CEO Council and its executive committee. Arrayed around the operational nucleus were overlapping interest groups: the board of directors and researchers at C.D. Howe, the bureaucrats from the Mulroney-era government, other pro-American conservative academics and sympathetic media columnists.

In examining the structure of a propaganda campaign, Jowett and O'Donnell recommend, how well its goals are articulated should also be considered. York University's Stephen Clarkson's comment about the "massing of elite brain power" to describe the outpouring of reports and studies after 9/11 is relevant here. Clarkson noted "the bias built into the work, which is not just designed to investigate but explicitly to promote an enhanced degree of North American integration." There wasn't much debate about radical proposals such as a customs union. Rather, most discussion was about how best to achieve it. In the end, though, this proposal went nowhere.

Step 5: *The target audience*
A target audience is selected by a propagandist for its potential effectiveness in advancing the message, Jowett and O'Donnell advise. Which audience, they ask, will be most useful to the propagandist if it responds favourably? There were several target audiences. Paul Tellier was after the narrowest—the 150 CEOs in the Canadian Council of Chief Executives and other senior business leaders. Once these core leaders were on board, communication was designed to reach a larger treetops audience of opinion leaders: government bureaucrats, cabinet ministers, policy-makers and prominent columnists. At a crucial time, the CEO Council hired George Haynal, Canada's chief adviser on border issues in the Department of Foreign Affairs and International Trade (DFAIT). Haynal's task was to help craft the council's prosperity and security initiative and sell it to federal government bureaucrats, a key target audience. The Canadian public was a secondary audience for much of the campaign. If the elites were onside, the public was largely irrelevant. It was more important to reach one journalist than ten housewives, a United State Information Agency once declared in a report about shaping opinion.[4] In fact, once the elites were onside, a cone of silence was dropped over the activities of the Security and Prosperity Partnership.

Canada's national dailies, the *National Post* and *Globe and Mail*, were important channels for reaching business and political audiences. The deal struck between the C.D. Howe Institute and the *National Post* to publish excerpts from, and report on, Howe Border Papers helped to advance the propaganda message.

Step 6: *Media-utilization techniques*
Several communication forms predominated: academic studies was the primary form, while interviews given by key actors and conferences designed to attract academics, politicians and researchers were others. Think-tanks have used these forms of communication for thirty years because they work. They maintain a high degree of credibility with target audiences and they attract media attention. The combined weight of all the reports crowding into the public space within a short time period signalled a crisis in the making, a crisis that would require strong measures by government. Another technique was to flood the public sphere with polls tracking Canadian attitudes to the United States and its current administration. Even if some polls indicated a coolness by Canadians towards their neighbour to the south, the sheer volume of polls sent a message to Canadians that how they felt about the States required careful consideration. Why? Because we're moving closer to the U.S. and integration is inevitable.

Step 7: *Special techniques to maximize effect*
Many special techniques were developed to maximize the effects of propaganda. Perhaps the most important is ensuring the credibility of sources. If Canadian National says we need deeper integration, it is not credible. But if academics say we need deeper integration, we are more likely to believe them, even if the organization that recruited them is sponsored by CN. Source credibility is the key to business's success in propelling its agenda. The C.D. Howe Institute may be sponsored by big business, but its messages are accepted as if they originate from independent sources. This is not to say that Howe academics are paid by business to write their papers, but business money allows the Howe to exist, enabling Howe organizers to recruit sympathetic academics to write papers that promote the goals desired by business.

As John Burton, professor of economics at the University of Birmingham in the U.K., told the 1983 regional meeting of the libertarian Mont Pèlerin Society in Vancouver, "The more authoritative the source involved, the greater the impact, all other things the same, on audience acceptance." Burton suggested that over recent decades, "classical liberal" or libertarian economists have successfully marketed the ideas of a free society and now they need to maintain the forward momentum on the high ground of the debate "where intellectual authority is determined."[5] Along with source credibility, Burton offered, must go endless repetition. The reason is that "audiences tend to return to their earlier opinion after a period of time, even if the source is rated of high credibility." Burton's authority for this observation is "that past master of the technique of political propaganda, Adolph Hitler . . . [who said] . . . only constant repetition will finally succeed in imprinting an idea on the memory of the crowd."[6] By publishing six papers a year in its Border Papers series promoting deeper integration, Howe worked to ensure that the repetition of the message would maximize its impact.

Another effective technique was the use of a subtext of inevitability. Canadians may not be kindly disposed towards the Americans, especially under George W. Bush, but since integration is inevitable, the task is for Canadians to make the best deal they can. The change in language between the first (1985–88) and second (2002–08) integration campaigns indicates a shift in the propagandist's techniques. In the eighties, the struggle was over free trade, the word "free" being a powerful propaganda "glitter" word. But, as Alexandroff and Guy noted, free trade was losing its lustre. Time for a new term: partnership, tied to security and prosperity.

Step 8: *Audience reaction to various effects*
If the target audience is, as Chapter 1 claims, business, political, bureaucratic and media elites, then the campaign was successful. The target audience adopted the propaganda frame, that integration is inevitable and good for the country. There was little public dissension among this key group. With the exception of the *Toronto Star*, no journalists offered critical rejection of deep integration. When a major counterpropaganda report was released by the Canadian Centre for Policy Alternatives,[7] the only media response was a critical column by the *Vancouver Sun*'s Barbara Yaffe.[8] The media were largely unanimous in their support for deeper integration, thanks, perhaps, to the work of the CEO Council in bringing leading media commentators into the consensus. The only messages the public received were framed around the inevitability and desirability of deeper integration. The public came to accept two conflicting beliefs: they wanted to maintain their distance from the Americans, but also realized that, despite their wishes, they were being drawn closer.

Step 9: *Counterpropaganda*
Normally, in a free society, we can expect the occurrence of counterpropaganda
in response to a propaganda campaign. The *Globe and Mail* (but not the
National Post) occasionally presented the anti-integration views of University
of Toronto political economist Stephen Clarkson and Vancouver writer Murray
Dobbin. Counterpropaganda organizations such as the Council of Canadians
and the Canadian Centre for Policy Alternatives were blanked from the pages
of the *National Post* and obtained only sporadic access from the *Globe and
Mail* and the CanWest newspapers. The major channels of communication for
counterpropaganda organizations are through their web sites and print publications, which communicate with associated organizations such as trade unions
and other non-governmental organizations, but have less impact on the general public. In contrast to the freewheeling debate that occurred during the
1988 free trade election, this time the corporate propagandists were largely successful in keeping the debate out of the election arena, denying opponents of
deep integration a forum.

Step 10: *Effects and evaluation*
The Security and Prosperity Partnership phase of deep integration came to a
close with the change of administration in Washington at the end of 2008.
Over the course of seven years, the CEO Council did achieve some goals, but
nothing of the magnitude of the original free trade agreement: economic sectors
like food and pharmaceuticals were further harmonized; the oil and gas industry was more fully integrated into a North American market; and additional,
but not major, cooperation on security matters was achieved. This doesn't
mean that Canadians are becoming fonder of Americans. Just the opposite. A
CTV/*Globe and Mail* poll released on the eve of Stephen Harper's meeting with
George Bush in March 2006 indicates that most Canadians held a negative
view of both Bush and the U.S.[9] Such an attitude is long-standing and will not
prevent Canadian and American elites from moving the deep-integration
agenda forward.

CHAPTER 2

The Propaganda Century

A subject moves in a direction you desire for reasons he believes to be his own.
—CIA instruction manual

So how can the ordinary newspaper reader and television viewer distinguish the news from the propaganda? The answer is that he cannot.
—Philip Knightley, quoted in *War and the Media: Propaganda and Persuasion in the Gulf War*

In 1949, British sociologist T. H. Marshall delivered a famous lecture on the development of citizenship in the West. Citizenship consists of three dimensions, he told his audience: civil, political and social. Western nations, he explained, adopted one dimension after another in succeeding centuries. In the eighteenth century, the struggle was for civil citizenship, which means freedom of speech, thought and religion and the right to a fair trial. In the nineteenth century, the focus was political citizenship, the right to participate in the exercise of power as exemplified by the right of citizens to vote and of workers to join a union. In the twentieth century, social and economic citizenship came to the fore. This, Marshall understood as the right to basic levels of education, health, economic well-being and security.[1]

It was a grand scheme and made sense. When Marshall presented his lecture, the Second World War was only recently over, the Labour Party was in power and the battle for social and economic rights was off to a rousing start. But Marshall was overly optimistic. The road to the welfare state made an unexpected U-turn. Thirty years after his lecture, Margaret Thatcher was elected prime minister and undid many Labour achievements. In the U.S., the Reagan administration rolled back many gains of Franklin Delano Roosevelt's

New Deal; by the end of the century, the movement for social and economic rights was in tatters. Marshall was also wrong about civil and political rights, counters Albert Hirschman, a prominent economist. They were not gained smoothly either, he writes in his seminal book *The Rhetoric of Reaction*. "[E]ach and every one of Marshall's three progressive thrusts has been followed by ideological counterthrusts of extraordinary force," Hirschman argues. Each counterthrust was sponsored by the entrenched interests of the day, fighting to protect their privilege and wealth, block progress towards a more just, equal and enlightened society, and undo the reforms already achieved. Each counterthrust led to "convulsive social and political struggles often leading to setbacks for the intended progressive programs as well as to much human suffering and misery," Hirschman wrote forty years after Marshall's lecture.[2] Each counterthrust comprised a mixture of physical violence and propaganda (intellectual violence), with the physical component decreasing as propaganda techniques became more effective.

The French Revolution (1789–99) overthrew the monarchy, executed the royal family, terminated the privileged position of the nobility and established new institutions based on popular sovereignty and democratic rights. The counterthrust was led by Napoleon Bonaparte, the French military hero who helped engineer a coup d'état ten years after the revolution, when Napoleon was named First Consul and virtual dictator. By this time, revolutionary gains had largely been extinguished by Robespierre's Reign of Terror. Over the next four years Napoleon re-established much of the old order, reinstituting Catholicism as the religion of France and welcoming back "the old landowners and aristocrats who had been driven into exile by the Revolution and whom he wanted back to provide further legitimacy to his regime."[3] In 1804, he declared himself emperor.

Napoleon used both military power and propaganda to achieve his goals. Like others of the day, he was an accomplished master of propaganda. The Jacobin clubs, which supported the Reign of Terror, "were nerve centers for the diffusion of news and propaganda," until they were shut down after Robespierre's execution.[4] And on the right, supporters of the Crown published *Ami du Roi*, a counter-revolutionary daily newspaper until 1792.[5] Napoleon simply had more resources at his disposal than anyone else, to ensure his version of events was the one received by his countrymen. He created favourable public opinion using theatre, painting, medallions and newspapers. He influenced news dispatches, wrote his own, censored news stories he didn't like and even took over six newspapers to spread the good news. In 1800 he ordered the suppression of sixty of the seventy-three newspapers then published in France. "Three hostile newspapers," he declared, "are more to be feared than a thousand bayonets."[6] He utilized virtually his entire government organization to promote his propaganda, attacking the enemy, whomever it happened to be at the time, and reinforcing the confidence the people of France had in their government, which was personified by Napoleon.[7]

In the nineteenth century, when the movement for political rights was in full flower, business was the new establishment. The business elite joined European and American aristocracies to face the challenges to their rule. The Paris Commune of 1870 and the spread of socialist ideas among the Parisian working class terrified the elites. Hirschman notes that "Europe had long been a stratified society with the lower classes being held in the utmost contempt by both the upper and the middle classes."[8] Mass participation in politics was abhorrent and potentially disastrous. Business did resort to armed force to beat back attempts by workers to organize into unions, but newly emerging propaganda techniques dramatically improved the effectiveness of reaction. Operating through capitalist-controlled media, advertising and public relations blunted the drives for more political freedom that followed the First and Second World Wars.

Demands for social and economic rights—the third dimension to citizenship—emerged as a political force during the Great Depression and after the Second World War, when Marshall delivered his lecture. At first, the advertising–public relations machine was adequate to contain them and direct them towards policies that didn't challenge the status quo. After the Second World War, for instance, big business—the National Association of Manufacturers, the U.S. Chamber of Commerce, the largest firms in the United States and the American Advertising Council—launched a propaganda campaign of massive proportions to "drench the country with anti-communist, anti-socialist, anti-union and anti-New Deal propaganda," writes Alex Carey.[9] This assault on public opinion was designed to turn the public against the Democratic administrations of FDR and Harry Truman and their liberal supporters, Carey notes. It was accomplished with the election of Dwight D. Eisenhower in 1952 and the inauguration of the McCarthy era.[10]

Business signed on to the welfare state because it feared working-class activism and a return to Depression-era conditions. It supported, albeit half-heartedly, nearly full employment for males, expanded trade union rights and the construction of a social safety net, which was financed by economic growth.

But in the 1970s the good times ended—profits declined and inflation rose due to oil price hikes, and competition from Japan and the newly industrializing countries. As well, the excesses of rapid economic growth led to consumer, trade union and environmental activism and a burgeoning citizen-participation movement. Vietnam and then Watergate produced a collapse in public regard for many institutions, especially business. A 1976 poll found that 82 percent of Americans believed that big business had "too much power," reports business historian David Vogel, making business the least trusted of the twenty-four groups about which the public was questioned.[11] Many business leaders concluded that it was time to end the three-decade-long experiment in Keynesian economics and launched a new counterthrust, turning their attention once again to managing democracy and rolling back the gains of those years. In 1976, the American Advertising Council initiated a national program of conservative "economic education" on a scale similar to one it had implemented after the Second World War. According to *Fortune* magazine, it was a study in gigantism, saturating the media and reaching practically everybody. By 1978, American business was spending $1 billion a year on grassroots propaganda aimed at promoting free enterprise by persuading the American public that its interests were the same as business interests.[12]

Unlike the campaigns after the First and Second World Wars, this time business felt the need to go further in its propaganda efforts. In his famous memo to the U.S. Chamber of Commerce, Lewis Powell, who was soon to be elevated to the U.S. Supreme Court, provided a blueprint for a new treetops propaganda system. Train a generation of conservative ideologues who will develop critiques of the welfare state, set up institutes to disseminate anti-progressive propaganda, and monitor the media and push their reporting and commentary to the right. Eliminate public sentiment that favours social and economic rights. Ensure these ideas never again arise. In short, create a right-wing information infrastructure to beat back the newly acquired rights.[13] Think-tanks had existed for many decades, largely to provide objective analyses of military and industrial problems. The conservative think-tank was a mutation, designed to advocate for business goals. From its first establishment in the early seventies, this propaganda machine, copiously funded by business and conservative foundations, together with the ongoing grassroots advertising and public relations efforts, was astonishingly successful in reversing the gains of the welfare state. In less than a decade of massive grassroots propaganda by the Advertising Council and the rapid deployment of treetops think-tanks,

Margaret Thatcher was ensconced at 10 Downing Street and Ronald Reagan was in the White House. To be sure, factors other than mere propaganda efforts were involved in the tectonic political shifts of the seventies and eighties. Double-digit inflation undermined the middle class's confidence in the future and turned many Americans away from trusting government and government regulation, and towards tax cuts and deregulation. Ronald Reagan was there to capitalize on these developments and business lined up behind him. T. H. Marshall would surely be crestfallen to discover the sorry state of social and economic citizenship today. Worse, due to the successes of the third counter-thrust, even hard-won civil and political rights have come under fierce attack.

We all have a good idea what propaganda means. Stanley Cunningham provides one list in his important study, *The Idea of Propaganda*: "self-serving reports; lies, distortions, fabrications, and exaggerations; disinformation, selective disclosures and censorship; 'spin,' hype, mass persuasion, manipulation, mind control, brainwashing, psychological warfare, public relations, advertising, election campaign rhetoric, rumours and gossip."[14] In Chapter 1 we saw Alex Carey's definition of propaganda: "communication where the form and content is selected with the purpose of bringing some target audience to adopt attitudes and beliefs chosen in advance by the sponsors of the communication."[15] Other authors have put forward similar definitions. Garth Jowett and Victoria O'Donnell, who developed the ten-step method of propaganda analysis described earlier, define propaganda as "the deliberate, systematic attempt to shape perceptions, manipulate cognitions, and direct behavior to achieve a response that furthers the desired intent of the propagandist."[16] Terence Qualter, who studied the use of propaganda in democracies, defines propaganda more simply as "the deliberate attempt by the few to influence the attitudes and behaviour of the many by the manipulation of symbolic communication."[17] For George Lakoff, a professor of linguistics at the University of California, propaganda is "an attempt to get the public to adopt a frame"—a mental structure that shapes the way we see the world—"that is not true and is known not to be true, for the purpose of gaining or maintaining political control."[18]

The word "propaganda" originated with an edict of Pope Gregory xv. In 1622 he established the Sacra Congregatio de Propaganda Fide (Congregation for the Propagation of the Faith). In Latin, "propaganda" means propagate, sow, multiply or breed. Until this time, the church had engaged in mostly unsuccessful holy wars against the Reformation to re-establish the Catholic faith by force of arms. Gregory realized this was a losing effort and established the Sacra Congregatio as a department of the Roman Catholic Curia to coordinate efforts to bring men and women to accept church doctrine voluntarily, rather than by coercion. It was also used to carry the faith to the New World. Propaganda had negative connotations in northern Protestant and English-speaking countries where the church was extending its influence, and not in Catholic ones, where it had the positive connotation of education or preaching.[19]

The roots of propaganda lie in classical Greece. Plato was probably the first thinker to describe a theory of rhetoric or persuasive speech in a series of dialogues between Socrates, who was a seeker of truth, and a sophist, who was concerned with the appearance, rather than the reality, of truth. "Plato saw the sophist position as dangerous because they used word tricks to win their arguments."[20] In the sixteenth century Niccolò Machiavelli advised leaders to conceal their true intention and manipulate appearances: "A prince, therefore, need not necessarily have all the good qualities I mentioned above, but he should certainly appear to have them . . . He should appear to be compassionate, faithful to his word, kind, guileless and devout . . . But his disposition should be such that, if he needs to be the opposite, he knows how."[21] Machiavelli cautioned though that if the populace could not be persuaded to believe, "they can be made to believe by force."[22] Propaganda analysts see this advice as the mindset of the successful propagandist. We can also see the concerns of the ruling elite in pre-Revolutionary France in harnessing public opinion. But Stanley Cunningham cautions us not to go too far with these parallels. Propaganda should be seen as a phenomenon of modern, mass media–sated society, he wrote, sponsored by an organization such as a corporation, government or church.[23] Propaganda in Western democracies has become so effective that coercion as an alternative is rarely necessary. There are exceptions though, such as the police crackdowns against public demonstrations protesting the deliberations of the World Trade Organization in Seattle in 1999 and in other locations such as Genoa, Italy (G8 Summit), Berne, Switzerland (World Economic Forum) and London, England (G20 Summit) over the ensuing years.

In one theory of the democratic state, citizens select the policies they want their governments to implement by electing the parties that most closely reflect their views of what should be done. Such a concept of democracy requires rational public discourse. Individual members of the public make decisions based on the availability of accurate and relevant information they receive from the mass media. This theory of democracy derives from eighteenth-century Enlightenment philosophy—the spark for the French Revolution—which presumed "a rational process of judgement and decision-making on the basis of freely available information and effective communication."[24] The emergence of mass media enhanced ideas of a public as an audience for communication and of public opinion as a political force.[25]

Organized public opinion that could challenge the status quo was a frightening concept for the elites: they might lose power. This could not be allowed to happen. No sooner did mass media make popular decision making possible through their ability to connect people widely separated in time and space, than the ensuing reaction set out to cast doubt on the ability of citizens to make sound and responsible decisions. The newly emerging social sciences were pressed into service to provide reasons why democracy would never work and strategies for ensuring it never could. Studies began to suggest that human behaviour was motivated less by rational thought than by irrational forces, undermining the reliability of public opinion.[26] Perhaps the most effective argument against democracy was made by Gustave Le Bon in his best-selling book, *The Crowd: A Study of the Popular Mind*, which was first published in 1895. What applied to the rational and calculating individual, he argued, did not apply to the group or the crowd, which was irrational and easily swayed. The franchise was spreading across Europe and Le Bon's irrational crowds were threatening to take charge.[27] Rule by universal suffrage, Le Bon wrote, "amount[s] to nothing less than a determination to destroy utterly society as it now exists, with a view to making it hark back to that primitive communism which was the normal condition of all human groups before the dawn of civilization."[28] Le Bon's work became a tool by which "a technocratic elite could help serve the interests of vested power," Stuart Ewen noted in his groundbreaking book, *PR! A Social History of Spin*.[29]

Le Bon provided a theoretical justification for social control by vested power. But how to achieve this? The answer, for Ewen, was provided by fellow Frenchman and friend Gabriele Tarde, who changed the focus from "the crowd" to "the public." The crowd represents the past, Tarde wrote, when face-to-face communication predominated. The future belongs to the public and the media, he presciently claimed.[30] Modern mass media—newspapers, magazines and transoceanic telegraph wires—were creating far-reaching networks of physically separated individuals who were beginning to think along the same lines. Tarde foresaw a future in which the mass media would provide channels which, if properly employed by experts, could manage consciousness and bring order to a chaotic world. But in his view, and in the view of those who followed him, "order" meant elite control and "chaotic world," democracy.[31] As Ewen saw it, the rise of public relations was necessary so that institutions of vested power could justify and package their interests in terms of the common good.[32] Public relations would be the propaganda instrument of the second counterthrust. Such propaganda is primarily an American creation resulting from that nation's entry into the Great War in 1917. The American public originally opposed entering the war, which it saw as a foreign, European-only affair. That sentiment changed dramatically because of a telegram. A coded telegram from German foreign minister Arthur Zimmermann to the president of Mexico, via the German ambassador in Washington, caused public outrage when its contents were published in American newspapers on March 1, 1917. The German High Command had decided on a policy of all-out submarine warfare, which would inevitably cause American civilian casualties, threatening to draw the U.S. into the war. In the telegram, Zimmermann proposed to the Mexicans that if the United States entered the war, Germany would support a Mexican invasion of the States and help the Mexicans reclaim Texas, New Mexico and Arizona. Five weeks later, the U.S. declared war on Germany. (Obviously, Mexico never did invade.)[33]

Within a week of declaring war, Woodrow Wilson set up the Committee on Public Information (CPI) to sell his Crusade for the American Way. The committee was led by George Creel, a small-circulation newspaper publisher and writer. By the end of the war, Creel and his phalanx of journalists, publicists, advertising executives, novelists, historians and muckrakers, using every available medium of communication and targeting every identifiable segment of the American people, turned the CPI into an effective organ for shaping public opinion.[34]

The CPI enlisted scholars to write pamphlets, which it distributed in the tens of millions, organized and coordinated a national network of tens of thousands of speakers, prepared and placed advertisements in hundreds of newspapers and magazines, distributed untold posters, produced its own film documentaries, published a daily newspaper, and ghostwrote newspaper stories, magazine articles and books for government officials to put their names to. The

CPI perfected the short news release, a story in newspaper style and format suitable for immediate use by editors. The organization churned out an average of ten news releases a day, seven days a week, for the duration of the war. Not only did Creel have the resources to flood the U.S. (and abroad) with his propaganda messages, under the Espionage Act he could censor those who would "threaten national solidarity." As chief propagandist and censor, Creel dominated the media, ensuring that the war reported to the American people was the war the CPI wanted them to see. In 1920, Creel set down his accomplishments in a book titled *How We Advertised America*.[35] He proudly recounted how he and his committee used advertising principles to convince Americans to go to war. Echoing Le Bon's work, Creel justified the need to manipulate the public by claiming that citizens were often irrational and poor judges of their own interests, making decisions based on whim, emotion and tradition. He believed that he had demonstrated that people need guidance in making good decisions. The mass media, which made public opinion possible, would be used to direct it.

After the First World War, many Creel operatives turned their efforts to a new crusade: making the world safe for business. They applied the lessons they'd learned in wartime to the marketplace and the domestic political arena. This cynical approach to democratic governance was justified in the twenties by journalist Walter Lippmann, who argued that "the problems that vex democracy seem to be unmanageable by democratic means."[36] Citizens, he wrote, were not competent to deal with the growing complexity of society. Consequently, public relations would play a "vital role" in the "management of public opinion and the engineering of democratic consent."[37] Creel alumnus Ivy Ledbetter Lee was one of the first great PR men who taught business how to use the press to its advantage. He established his reputation by helping John D. Rockefeller clean up his image, no mean feat given Rockefeller's brutal treatment of workers in the Ludlow, Colorado, massacre and a coal miners' strike in West Virginia, as well as his ruthless crushing of competitors. It was a pioneer exercise in "damage control."[38]

Joseph Goebbels and Adolf Hitler were much impressed by the Creel Committee's propaganda successes, and sought to ensure that the Nazi regime followed the principles Creel established. Hitler's *Mein Kampf*, published in German in 1926, described how effective Allied propaganda had been in contrast to that of Germany, which, Hitler believed, contributed to the demoralization of German soldiers and the country's eventual defeat. *Mein Kampf* outlined the

Nazis' basic propaganda principles: appeal to emotion, not reason; repeat a few ideas constantly; use stereotyped phrases; put forward one side of the story only. Hitler's checklist is an accurate description of public relations and advertising. In 1933, through German chemical industry conglomerate I.G. Farben, the Nazis invited Ivy Lee to meet with Hitler and Goebbels and provide PR advice. Farben retained Lee to help improve Germany's image in the U.S., a task that provoked an enormous American backlash when it became known.[39]

Edward Bernays was another Creel graduate, who had been in charge of news for Latin America. Bernays, rather than Lee, is considered to be the father of modern public relations because he was concerned about the broader role of PR in a democracy. Our society is too complex for us to make decisions, Bernays wrote, so we must leave them to "trained professionals who can deal with increasingly difficult problems of adjustment, interpretation and persuasion."[40] Experts guided by rational thought will engineer a democratic society. Was the public relations industry a vehicle for propaganda dissemination? Bernays certainly thought so. He titled his 1928 book on public relations *Propaganda*. "The new propagandists," he wrote, "are public relations counsel. . . . Propaganda is necessary in political life" and it is "the modern instrument of intelligent men."[41]

Bernays earned his place in PR annals for his ability to create news. He would place self-serving stories favourable to his clients' interests in the news media without indicating the origins of the stories. It's a tribute to Bernays's genius at media manipulation that even today studies estimate that 60 percent of news stories originate with corporate and PR sources. Bernays was a master at creating pseudo-environments—"pictures in the minds of millions"—by staging what seemed to be spontaneous events that would influence the public into comprehending a situation in a desired way.[42] Because recent psycho-analytical research indicated that some women regarded cigarettes, usually equated with men, as symbols of freedom, Bernays, who was Sigmund Freud's nephew, came up with a legendary publicity stunt that is still referenced in PR schools. As John Stauber and Sheldon Rampton report in their eye-opening exposé of the PR industry, *Toxic Sludge Is Good for You*, Bernays recruited attractive young women to march in New York City's Easter Parade. Each debutante waved a lit cigarette and proclaimed it a "torch of liberty." Bernays distributed publicity photos of the event around the world.[43]

When Bernays wrote his books, *Crystallizing Public Opinion* (1923) and *Propaganda* (1928), he saw a society in which the masses were increasingly bold and threatening the established order. There is, he wrote, an "increased readiness of the public, due to the spread of literacy and democratic forms of government, to feel that it is entitled to its voice in the conduct" of all facets of social life. To maintain social order in the face of challenges from below, Bernays argued, it had become necessary to shape and direct public opinion. The "future of civilization," he claimed, would rest on the ability of the elites to manoeuvre public opinion into the direction they desired.[44] He saw the new profession of public relations as an instrument to regiment the public mind. He dubbed himself a "counsel on public relations," or an "invisible wire-puller" who would successfully reconcile the aimlessness of popular desires with the realities of elite control.[45]

Bernays expressed concern with democracy, but he was no democrat. He believed in a division between the intelligent few, like himself, and the ill-schooled mass, like the rest of society. An article Bernays wrote in 1947 offered a rationale for the use of propaganda in a democracy. It claimed that "the engineering of consent" is "the very essence of the democratic process, the freedom to persuade and suggest."[46] The elite (a highly educated class of opinion-moulding tacticians) analyzes the social terrain and adjusts the mental scenery from which the public mind, with its limited intellect, derives its opinions. Bernays's article became a bible for corporate interests. The same year, *Fortune* magazine made a similar argument that, "it is as impossible to imagine a genuine democracy without the science of persuasion as it is to think of a totalitarian state without coercion."[47] By the 1950s, the belief that democracy was not possible without public relations—propaganda—was firmly held, at least by business and public relations consultants.

The public relations industry claims it operates on the basis of a "two-way symmetric" model of PR that emphasizes "balanced and dialogic communication between organizations and [the] public," writes Margaret Duffy, a former PR practitioner who teaches at Austin Peay State University in Tennessee.[48] To test this claim, Duffy examined five leading textbooks used in post-secondary public relations programs. The textbooks all take as given an equal partnership between organizations and publics, but not one presents any evidence or insight into how this balance and dialogue are to occur. Instead, Duffy finds, the books are filled with strategies for how to influence and persuade audiences in order to achieve organizational goals.[49] Duffy concludes that public relations practices look and function a lot more like propaganda than like socially responsible, two-way communication.[50]

The Second World War was a draw between Allies and Germans on the propaganda front, if not on the battlefield, as both sides furiously applied the principles developed by the Committee on Public Information as refined by Bernays and Lee. After the war, veterans began to question the economic and social system to which they were returning. With the hard times of the Great Depression still fresh in their minds, they were not kindly disposed to business and looked to government to protect their interests. John W. Hill, a co-founder of the public relations firm Hill and Knowlton, worried about the "deep divide" separating corporate management from workers and the public. The mission of big business, he instructed in 1946, was to gain workers' trust, convert them "to a belief in the private enterprise system" and thus regain control over the direction of American society.[51] The Advertising Council and the PR industry mounted massive pro-capitalism grassroots campaigns between 1945 and 1950 and largely brought the American public back to the belief that democracy depends on capitalism.

Stuart Ewen recounts how, in 1949, the conservative American Medical Association (AMA) used a vast and costly PR campaign to defeat attempts to create universal, federally insured health care. These developments threatened to undermine doctors' traditional powers, and doctors went to extraordinary lengths to ensure that public health insurance never happened. Their PR team designed an aggressive smear attack linking national health insurance with communism, a threat which was on everybody's mind. People's health care needs were pushed into the background, while the evils of government intervention were thrust into the spotlight. The message was conveyed—and received—that national health insurance reflected an un-American way of life.[52] In less than a year, national health insurance was dead. In its place, doctors helped create a system of private, employer-sponsored plans under which they could earn more money than under a national, government-sponsored plan. One consequence of this propaganda triumph is that sixty years later the U.S. suffers from the highest health care costs—and has some of the wealthiest doctors—in the world.

Almost from the beginning, propagandists and PR practitioners, whatever they called themselves, realized that using factual information strategically, rather than merely disseminating lies and crude caricatures, could create more credible, and consequently more effective, messages. Propagandists would use the truth, not because it is always good to tell the truth, but because it would suit their own ends. Even when a propaganda message is truthful, we must remember that truth is being debased to serve the propagandist's ends. Philip Katz notes that during the Second World War, accurate information used by the Germans about the accomplishments of their v-1 rockets was more successful in demoralizing the British than dubious messages about capitalists or Jewish plots.[53]

The propagandist makes selective and manipulative use of the truth. Stanley Cunningham writes that truth has long been cherished as the supreme value of the human intellect.[54] French philosopher Jacques Ellul argued that propaganda could not succeed without a patina of truth. As Machiavelli commented nearly five hundred years ago, the prince (propagandist?) must provide at least the appearance of a commitment to the truth. Modern propaganda relies on facts—propositions, portrayals or descriptions which truthfully accord with reality. Ellul pointed out that Hitler's minister of propaganda, Joseph Goebbels, commonly associated with the "Big Lie," urged the use of truth—selectively—as much as possible. If the facts are true, then it is possible to believe the interpretation.[55]

Garth Jowett and Victoria O'Donnell call truthful propaganda white propaganda, which "comes from a source that is identified correctly, and the information in the message tends to be accurate." It is "presented in a manner that . . . attempts to build credibility with the audience, for this could have usefulness at some point in the future."[56] Black propaganda, in contrast, occurs "when the source is concealed or credited to a false authority and spreads lies, fabrications, and deceptions."[57] Black propaganda can succeed when the audience is willing to accept the source's credibility and the message's content. For this to occur, sources and messages need to be placed within the target audience's social, cultural and political framework. An example might be an actor dressed like a scientist who peers into a microscope and then tells viewers that genetically modified foods will help feed the world's hungry. In between lies the vast realm of gray propaganda, in which the "source may or may not be correctly identified and when the accuracy of information is uncertain."[58]

A common technique to legitimize propaganda is to promote the theme of public debate, which can be defined as "a regulated discussion of a proposition between two matched sides." Often the purpose of a debate is to discover persuasive solutions to complex problems. Propaganda, of course, has a different purpose: to achieve a response from the audience that furthers the propagandist's intent. An effective propaganda campaign using the guise of debate creates an appearance that the propagandist has the audience's best interest at heart. A recent example of this technique from the business-sponsored campaign to undermine medicare is a *Globe and Mail* editorial titled "Hey, a health debate!"[59] The *Globe* comments favourably on a report produced by former Reform Party leader Preston Manning and former Ontario premier Mike Harris, and published by the Fraser Institute. The report recommends ending medicare and turning health care over to the provinces, which could allow any combination they wish of private, for-profit and public health care provision. The *Globe* allows that "some of the Manning-Harris ideas will go too far for many Canadians." But that's OK because "we need . . . a free-wheeling national debate." The paper applauds Harris and Manning for starting it. But where is the debate, which requires two matched sides? The pro-medicare side is largely absent.

A classic example of this tactic was a series of ads by the R. J. Reynolds Tobacco Co. in the 1980s that was analyzed by Stanley Cunningham. The ads appeared in major U.S. mass-circulation magazines, such as *People, Time*, the *New York Times Magazine* and *Seventeen*. They were designed to deflect public anger about second-hand smoke towards smokers and away from the tobacco company. They look like public service ads; they are anything but. The first ad in the series asks "Can we have an open debate about smoking?"[60] It emphasizes that there are "lots of questions," "no simple answer," "more than one side" and the need for "open debate." The tobacco company is speaking out to "discuss" and "explore" several important issues. This ad and others in the series emphasize the theme of controversy and open-ended debate. They deflect attention from the known harm suffered by smokers.

Cunningham calls the second ad a "tour de force" because its theme, in both the ad's layout and its message, is unresolved debate. The ad is structured as a dialogue between smokers and non-smokers. One side is titled "A message from those who do to those who don't" and the other side, "A message from those who don't to those who do." The arguments and the number of words given to each side are identical, conveying the impression that the two messages pose "as a serious dialogue between two equally defensible points of view," Cunningham says. The smokers' messages are on the right half of the ad, meaning they will be read after the non-smokers' messages and act as an effective rebuttal. The debate "is calculated to remain just where it began," Cunningham notes, "in a state of open and unresolved controversy."[61] Meanwhile, the tobacco company has disappeared from the debate.

"Because RJR appears open to reason and science," Cunningham concludes, "anxious to discuss and debate, ready to provide alternative evidence . . . we, the reading public, are encouraged to believe that we are party to informative discussion with reasonable spokespersons."[62] But there's a hidden propaganda message beneath the veneer of reason and dialogue, whose purpose is to turn our attention away from the known facts about smoking and to prolong discussion interminably. The goal is to reduce public anxiety about smoking and boost the tobacco industry's image.

Most communication researchers spent the war years engaged in government and quasi-government-funded research on U.S. and foreign propaganda. Allied troop morale, public opinion, clandestine Office of Strategic Services (oss) operations, and newspaper, magazine and radio-broadcast analysis were some of the subjects they studied.[63] After the war these researchers turned away from propaganda analysis because of its association with critical and rhetorical (i.e., non-scientific) method and with a left-wing political stance. There was no longer government or corporate money for critical propaganda research, but an abundance to study how to persuade people and shape public opinion, following a more "objective" social-scientific method for analyzing problems of communication.[64] Communication research became the more accepted term for social science researchers and their funders.[65] How do you persuade someone to buy your beer, vote for your candidate or support your brand of capitalism? Edward Bernays was not afraid to call what he did propaganda. A 1998 biography of him, however, was titled *The Father of Spin*,[66] and a review of the book in *BusinessWeek* was headlined "The High Priest of Hype."[67] Propaganda had disappeared from the discussion and was replaced by hype and spin. But, as we've seen, hype and spin are code words for propaganda. "Spin" refers to "a coordinated strategy to minimize negative information and present in a favorable light a story that could be damaging."[68] It is often used in reference to the manipulation of political information. Press secretaries and public relations officers are referred to as "spin doctors" when they attempt to launder the news. The word "propaganda," as applied to Western democracies, was being consigned to the dustbin of history.

But not for long. In the mid-eighties, Garth Jowett and Victoria O'Donnell broke a generation's silence on propaganda studies with the first edition of their comprehensive text, *Propaganda and Persuasion*.[69] And propaganda was brought into the public realm by Noam Chomsky, Edward Herman and Alex Carey, whose work is central to our understanding of corporate propaganda. Chomsky and Herman published their landmark study, *Manufacturing Consent*, the year Carey died, and they dedicate the book to his memory. In that perennially popular book they analyzed media coverage of U.S. interventions in Cambodia, the Dominican Republic, El Salvador and Nicaragua, and outlined a propaganda model in which prevailing power elites co-opt intellectuals and large media companies and transform them into instruments for shaping public opinion.[70] The model is based on five filters through which raw news must pass before it is considered appropriate for distribution to audiences.

The first filter is corporate ownership, which rests on the undisputed fact that media corporations are firmly embedded in the market economy. They are profit-seeking businesses owned by very wealthy families or by other companies. Owners are generally very conservative politically and favour the dominant North American private enterprise ideology.[71] They are funded largely by advertisers who are also profit-seeking entities and who want their ads to appear in a supportive selling environment. The interests of advertisers constitute the second filter. By advertising in one news outlet and not in another, advertisers in effect bestow a licence to do business on a news organization. In a system that depends on advertising revenues, withdrawal of advertising can lead to a news organization's demise.

The third filter is an overwhelming dependence on information from official—mainly government and corporate—sources. These organizations spend heavily on media and public relations, subsidizing news organizations by making it cheap and easy to collect information for stories from them. News organizations marshal their resources at locations where "news" is likely to occur: city hall, the legislatures, Wall Street and Bay Street, and the courthouse. Information from non-official and alternative sources is less likely to make it through this filter.

The fourth filter they call flak—criticism and negative responses to media statements generated by powerful news sources and by organizations set up primarily to attack the media and push their reporting further to the right. Organizations like Accuracy in Media and Brent Bozell's Media Research Center, had an inestimable effect in forcing all media reporting to the right. Writing in 1988, Herman and Chomsky's fifth filter was the ideology of anti-communism, shared by media, political and corporate elites. Today, the fifth filter is probably the ideology of anti-terrorism, although some argue it is the ideology of neoliberal global capitalism.[72]

Herman and Chomsky were excoriated by conservative and liberal critics alike for suggesting that the news system was central to a society dominated by propaganda. But the two were simply restating what Edward Bernays said half a century earlier. A key concern among the critics is the role of journalists within the propaganda model. For British sociologist Stuart Allan, the model turns journalists into puppets whose strings are pulled by forces they don't comprehend. "Journalists are not propagandists," Allan wrote. We need to take into account "the everyday practices journalists engage in when constructing news accounts as truthful 'reflections' of reality."[73]

This is a fair point which, for many, renders the model useless. But Colin Sparks, another British scholar, has proposed modifications that may help revive the critique. The model, he suggests, works best for senior journalists who do identify with media owners and the political and corporate elites. They are highly paid, have worked their way up through the organization, indicating they have been embraced by media managers and owners, and have links to other members of the elite through many channels.[74] *Washington Post* media columnist Howard Kurtz said something very similar: "Most big-city journalists earn considerably more money and enjoy more privileges than the great majority of people who buy their newspapers and watch their newscasts," he wrote in the *Columbia Journalism Review*. "Gradually, almost imperceptibly, this sort of high-level schmoozing and socializing can change one's outlook."[75]

Most journalists, Sparks continues, operate within a very different situation. They are "subordinates in a hierarchical division of labour and their activities are directed by their superiors." As Kurtz describes the situation in his newsroom, "many people come from modest backgrounds, attended public colleges and worked their way up from small papers." Frequently, Sparks notes, their interests don't coincide with those of their managers and employers. He proposes that the difference in interests between employer and employee is epitomized by journalists' insistence that they must be guided by professional standards and autonomy, and not by management dictates. At the very least, they must be able to select relevant sources and provide an account of a situation that is comprehensible to their audience. But whether journalists can actualize these goals depends on their power in the newsroom, which depends on being represented by a trade union. "The isolated journalist, however professional and however courageous, is an easy target for an employer anxious to assert control over their [sic] property. The organized journalist," Sparks concludes, "at least has a chance of surviving and perhaps winning."[76]

Writing in 1996, Herman applied the propaganda model to a new case study: media treatment of the North American Free Trade Agreement (NAFTA). As with deep integration ten years later, there was a rift between the desires of most citizens and those of business and political elites. News coverage and the selection of experts and opinion writers, Herman observed, were skewed sharply in favour of NAFTA, lauding its benefits and attacking the "special interests" who were opposed. Herman noted the "pro-corporate and anti-labor bias of the mainstream media" in the "editorial denunciations . . . of labor's attempt to influence votes on NAFTA, with no comparable criticism of corporate or governmental . . . lobbying and PR."[77] Byron Dorgan, a Democratic senator from North Dakota and a NAFTA opponent, complained that the mainstream media accused him and other opponents of being "hysterical alarmists."[78] Herman's view was supported by Howard Kurtz, who noted "the cultural gap between elite journalists and working-class Americans" in media coverage of NAFTA, which was "warmly embraced by the American punditocracy, from both the right and the left."[79] And Herman's interpretation was buttressed by an analysis of more than three hundred articles about NAFTA in the *New York Times* from 1993. This study demonstrated "how the private sector's and Clinton government's emphatic support for the agreement was regularly insinuated into *The Times*'s coverage." Despite "legitimate controversy" that surrounded NAFTA, *The Times*'s sourcing patterns distinctly shaded toward pro-NAFTA sources. . . . Conversely, *The Times*'s treatment of NAFTA opposition (most particularly, the opposition of unions and Ross Perot) was harsh and encased within personalized narratives that skirted away from substantive analysis.[80]

Instead of reporting a genuine debate, the media targeted the labour movement, which had a well-thought-out position. Instead of allowing labour to voice its position, the media simply attacked unions, using a long line of curse words such as "crude, tough, blundering and old-fashioned."[81] Few business bosses were guilty of these sins.

Other critical thinkers worked at the margins of American social science, analyzing propaganda. Sut Jhally, a media scholar at the University of Massachusetts, claims provocatively that "20th century advertising is the most powerful and sustained system of propaganda in human history."[82] Advertising, he argues, is central to the modern capitalist system as an essential part of the production system. There's no point producing cars or iPods if no one buys them. "More thought, effort, creativity, time and attention to detail has gone into the selling of the immense collection of commodities than any other campaign in human history to change public consciousness," writes Jhally. In the U.S. in a typical recent year, he estimates, over $175 billion was spent to sell goods and services to Americans. Add that amount again for the rest of the world and the figure exceeds a third of a trillion dollars. Little of this frenetic activity actually goes into selling products, Jhally cautions. Car ads never provide objective information on the quality of the cars. Instead, they sell happiness and satisfaction. Buying these commodities will make consumers happy is the implicit message of most ads.

Much of this advertising activity is directed at private consumption and not public opinion. True, the torrent of advertising does raise significant public policy questions. To what extent should we allow advertising to target children? What is the impact of unbridled consumption on the health of the planet? And some advertising is directed at manipulating public opinion. The R.J. Reynolds ads calling for a debate on second-hand smoke is a particularly mendacious example. Ads claiming the oil giants are environmental stewards arc no better. Each fossil fuel company has its motto: Chevron's "People Do" campaign; Exxon's "Save the Tiger Fund," which associates its logo with the endangered tiger; Mobil's op-ed page ads every Thursday in the *New York Times*.[83] Royal Dutch Shell's "Profits or Principles" campaign is designed to convince us it does not need to choose between these because it can satisfy everyone. As the Sixth UN Conference on Climate Change got underway in 2000 in The Hague, Netherlands, Shell published a particularly interesting ad. It asked, "Is the burning of fossil fuels and increased concentration of carbon dioxide in the air a serious threat or just a lot of hot air?"[84] Shell's ad is an example of greenwash, or environmental whitewash. According to Corpwatch, a watchdog group that monitors corporate activity, greenwash is "the phenomenon of socially and environmentally destructive corporations attempting to preserve and expand their markets by posing as friends of the environment and leaders in the struggle to eradicate poverty."[85]

Perhaps the most famous greenwash advertising campaign in recent years is British Petroleum's (BP) "Beyond Petroleum," in which chairman John Browne endorsed the precautionary principle and recognized that BP needs to take into account the views of the society in which it operates. He bragged loudly and widely about the fact that BP bought a company called Solarex for $45 million, making the oil giant the largest solar energy company in the world. But $45 million for solar energy is less than one-five-hundredth of the amount the company spent the same year to purchase Arco—$26.5 billion—a year after merging with Amoco in a deal worth an additional $52 billion. These acquisitions were not trumpeted in the popular press. They strengthened BP's marketing position in the U.S. and gave it control over Alaskan oil exploration, where the company is spending $5 billion over five years on oil exploration and production. In contrast to its words, BP's actions indicate that it is committed to continued reliance on oil and gas, such as its manoeuvres to gain access to the oil fields of Iran, which will likely lead to catastrophic climate change.[86] It's not "Beyond Petroleum" but "Blatant Propaganda."

Alex Carey tells us that "the success of business propaganda in persuading us, for so long, that we are free from propaganda is one of the most significant propaganda achievements of the twentieth century."[87] Two axioms underscore business's propaganda triumph. First, the free enterprise system, which sponsors corporate propaganda to manipulate and control democracy, is a bulwark and guarantor of a democratic society. We can't have democracy, it is claimed, without free enterprise. The second axiom is to admit that propaganda exists, but only in regimes hostile to democracy.

Following the Herman-Chomsky propaganda model, we can expect corporate news media to be central in disseminating these messages. Just as the R. J. Reynolds ads were designed to divert attention from the tobacco company and onto smokers, corporate news media's contribution is to focus public attention away from corporate propaganda and onto the corporation's opponents: interventionist governments, enemies of the U.S., trade unions and special interests. In Canada, the *National Post* is the most unabashedly pro-business, anti-government news outlet. It enforces the core messages that business is free of propaganda and only capitalism's enemies engage in this nasty business.

The *Post*'s use of the word "propaganda" hasn't received much attention. The year 2004 is a typical year in which the word "propaganda" appeared in 210 opinion pieces, editorials and news stories in the paper. (The pattern is similar for the years between 2000 and 2008.) You can expect to find the word "propaganda" in the *Post* once every other day. About three-quarters of the word's use was in reference to the U.S.'s international enemies. Nearly half of these were in relation to the Middle East: Iraq and Iraq militants (17), Islamic militants (7), Palestine Liberation Organization (6), Al-Jazeera (5), Iran (4) and al Qaeda (2) were mentioned as sources of propaganda. Only one article mentioned Israel as a possible propaganda source and this was a hypothetical situation at the UN International Court of Justice in The Hague. The court agreed to hear a complaint from the Palestine Liberation Organization (PLO) about Israel's national security wall. If the case went ahead, the *Post* reported, senior Israeli officials might boycott it and "mount a propaganda campaign outside the court."[88] The *Post* was similarly vexed by propaganda it saw emanating from China (13 mentions), North Korea (6) and Russia and the former Soviet Union (5), but did not detect any propaganda from American friends like the United Kingdom, Hong Kong, Singapore, Taiwan, Japan or Australia.

The paper's editorials were hot on the propaganda trail. Over the year 2004, *National Post* editorials made the following claims: all Iraq papers under Saddam Hussein were propaganda organs (February 4); British Muslims' claims of torture were motivated by propaganda (March 15); Shiite cleric Moqtada al-Sadr controlled vicious propaganda and an army of murderous thugs (April 15); the Greek Cypriot state broadcaster barraged voters with propaganda (April 28); the movie *The Day After Tomorrow* was a dose of left-wing propaganda (May 20); loonie-left representative Ralph Nader's advice to not support the Conservatives was paternalistic propaganda (June 26); the film *Fahrenheit 9/11* was a masterful, if specious, piece of political propaganda (September 18); Hamas-operated community services helped spread propaganda (October 5); Yasser Arafat could deliver propaganda victories only (November 8); the Ukrainian regime operated an extensive propaganda machinery (November 25); Baghdad Bob [Iraqi Information Minister Mohammed Said al-Sahaf] was everyone's favourite Iraqi propaganda master (December 3); young Palestinians were fed a steady diet of hateful propaganda (December 13); and, two days before Christmas, the *Post* claimed that Cuban authorities had beefed up their anti-American propaganda (December 23).

Most occurrences of the word "propaganda" in a Canadian or American context were in relation to critics of corporate power or the actions of interventionist governments: Kyoto Protocol (9), Michael Moore (5), *The Corporation* (4), the Liberal election campaign (4) and the CBC (2). Ralph Nader, anti-fat crusaders, feminists, Canadian nationalists, Quebec separatists, the federal government, the New Democratic Party (NDP) and multiculturalists were all disseminators of propaganda.

No surprise, business was not a source of propaganda in the *National Post* in 2004. A company was mentioned in only one column. This was a David and Goliath story by *Financial Post* editor Terence Corcoran, who wrote frequently about propaganda. In a column titled "An epic struggle of good and evil," Corcoran recounts the (unsuccessful) attempt by the United Food and

Commercial Workers Union to organize Wal-Mart stores in Saskatchewan. In the real world, Wal-Mart is the largest company on the planet with more than $375 billion in sales and two million employees. In Corcoran's mind, the union is Goliath and Wal-Mart David, which "may succeed in warding off an oppressor that gets its power from warped labour laws and massive anti-corporate propaganda." Wal-Mart, the 97-pound weakling kicked around by the union bullies.[89]

Any attack on business that receives widespread public discussion is turned back by the *Post*. In 2004, the movie *The Corporation* was all the rage and led to four nasty and vindictive attacks by *Post* columnists. Peter Foster's column in April was a whine about how democracy is no friend to business. All democratic governments promote negative and false ideas about business, he complained. The more successful governments are at attacking business, the more power they will be able to grab for themselves. Foster then alleges that the Canadian government is unlikely to "level hate crime charges against the producers of ... *The Corporation*, even though that film uses Nazi propaganda techniques to demonize one of the most useful institutions in history."[90] Foster doesn't explain how the film uses these techniques or even what they are.

Terence Corcoran dismisses the film as a "145-minute anti-corporate screed ... an evil, ugly and dishonest pack of lies." Producers Mark Achbar and Joel Bakan "set new standards," he claims, "for inconsistency, misrepresentation, distortion and twisted logic, even for radical leftists, engaging in traditional propagandist name-calling." Before assailing the movie, he asks his readers a question: "Why would Canada's governments and taxpayers give a pair of anarcho-socialists more than a million dollars to create a piece of Marxist propaganda?"[91] Two weeks later, the *Post* published Achbar's response, but instead of giving Achbar a respectful right of reply, Corcoran used the opportunity to repeat his accusations. "I didn't know anarcho-socialist-capitalists were so touchy about Marx. ... That people can make money off of Marxist propaganda isn't new. Noam Chomsky must be a millionaire many times over by now."[92]

Editorials editor Jonathan Kay weighs in with a column claiming that Michael Moore had invented a new artistic genre: "the post-communist left-wing propaganda film." *The Corporation*'s producers, he writes, are "Moore's leading Canadian acolytes," the use of this word seeming to imply some kind of secret left-wing sect. What drives the film, he asserts—without evidence— is "blind anti-capitalist hate." The film can't bring itself to credit the many good things companies do, he writes gushingly, such as, "feeding the world, giving jobs to billions of people, inventing medicines, creating wealth, making stuff people want." He ends his homage to corporate propaganda in a fit of name-calling: capitalism is "the most successful economic ideology in history," and it's "*The Corporation*'s brain trust . . . that's psychopathic."[93]

Gillian Cosgrove was the *Post*'s society columnist in 2004. She contributed five columns with the word "propaganda" that year, before she was fired for writing a column about Governor General Adrienne Clarkson which, in the *Post*'s own words, contained "fundamental errors and intentional misrepresentation." Several of her columns were about the CBC. "The CBC has scored a huge propaganda victory by somehow getting the four federal political parties and the private networks to make CBC lefty, Anna Maria Tremonti, the moderator of the English leaders debate" during the 2004 federal election. Tremonti's crime is that she hosts a taxpayer-supported "coast-to-coast daily diatribe against everyone to the right of Fidel Castro on CBC Radio."[94] Earlier in the year Cosgrove complained about CBC anchor Peter Mansbridge's Afghanistan mission, which was "yet another costly CBC propaganda stunt . . . in pursuit of rating points." The private networks didn't engage in propaganda stunts like this, she wrote. They stayed home in Canada, where the big stories are.[95] Another plausible reason why the private broadcasters didn't send correspondents overseas was to cut newsgathering costs and return a larger portion of revenues to the shareholders, even if one result could be a decline in the quality of foreign-news coverage.

Cosgrove's other three columns about propaganda related to the 2004 federal election. Two were about the Liberals and her concern that $12 million would be spent on "Grit propaganda" (May 14, June 18). Finally, Cosgrove reported how "members of the federal NDP caucus were using their free mail privileges to blanket the [Toronto-Danforth] riding with Jack Layton propaganda." (June 4). In the *Post*'s world, the Conservatives and business were never guilty of blanketing anything with propaganda.

Writing on the *Financial Post* editorial page, Corcoran and fellow libertarian Peter Foster led in the use of the word "propaganda," accounting for sixteen out of the sixty-eight columns written by *Post* columnists and guest opinion writers during the year. According to this duo, the forces behind the Kyoto Protocol were the worst propagandists in the country. In April, Corcoran warned readers about a "government-funded propaganda television series called the Great Warming." He knows it's propaganda because of the "weird, ominous-sounding music and industrial-type noise [rattling] in the background." Its other crime is that the show doesn't "bother with the details of the science" in the style of "thousands of propaganda makers."[96] Three weeks later, Corcoran reported on a conference to be held in Toronto sponsored by a British organization called the Climate Group, which Corcoran labelled a "major corporatist propaganda mill designed to bolster the flagging campaign to reduce emissions of greenhouse gases."[97]

In July, Corcoran wrote that "[O]ne of the great propaganda icons of the United Nations climate-change machine [the hockey stick] is about to get swept away as a piece of junk science," summarily dismissing the work of thousands of climate scientists. The perpetrator was the UN's Intergovernmental Panel on Climate Change (IPCC) which, the *Post* consistently alleges, uses the hockey stick as a central propaganda tool.[98] In November, he wrote that the Arctic Council, comprising Canadian and other governments, released a report that collected all the information about rising temperatures in the Arctic. Corcoran called this report "a propaganda blast from Ottawa . . . full of gloss and glitz [containing] no scientific reports."[99] In December, he complained that the Liberal government's One-Tonne Challenge, which urges Canadians "to do their bit to cut down on energy use," was filled with "cheap marketing tricks and propaganda."[100]

For his part, Peter Foster argued in June that Canadians support Kyoto because they "have little or no idea about the science of climate change." Foster apparently does, although he never reveals any knowledge about climate change in his columns. And we have been misled by the Liberal government's $3.7-billion "campaign of propaganda, misinformation and barmy Stakhanovite [see below] schemes such as the 'One-Tonne Challenge.'"[101] Foster repeats this charge two months later. "The fundamental lunacy [of Kyoto] is why so little has actually been done in the past seven years, except for spending literally billions on propaganda and Stakhanovite try-harder schemes such as the 'One Tonne Challenge.'"[102] Foster is correct that very little had been accomplished since the Kyoto Protocol was approved by 154 countries in 1997. He's wrong about the reason, though. The "fundamental lunacy" of Kyoto wasn't at fault. The culprit was the vast, well-financed corporate propaganda messages that were disseminated faithfully by corporate media, like the *National Post*, to sow doubt and confusion in the public mind. Oil giants like ExxonMobil seemed more concerned about short-term return to shareholders than about the long-term survival of the planet. Former *Boston Globe* reporter Ross Gelbspan, who wrote two books about the politics of global warming (*The Heat Is On* and *Boiling Point*), called the oil companies and their think-tank and public relations propagandists "criminals against humanity."[103] This is a charge that would never be expressed in the pages of the *Post*.

Foster's use of the term "Stakhanovite" is interesting. Alexei Stakhanov was a Ukrainian miner who, in 1935, "devised a system of increasing his output by the skilled organization of a group of subordinate workers." They were the official heroes of Soviet labour and were paid higher wages. The word was extended to mean anyone putting in particularly effective and energetic work in any field.[104] This word creates a fallacious link between the Chrétien government and the Soviet Union in the 1930s, an interesting propaganda technique in itself.

In the years since 2004, Corcoran and Foster stood fast against Marxists, leftists, Liberals and bureaucrats who persist in their attempts to spread their propaganda among the masses. Corcoran continued to obsess about the hockey stick as an icon of climate-change propaganda, which, he alleged, had been exposed as uncertain and possibly unsupportable, a statement that would come as news to the world's climate scientists. In one notable flight of rhetoric, Corcoran claimed that "never in world history, outside the collective insanity marshalled behind Marxism" had a political movement (i.e., climate change) required such "an unrelenting flood of propaganda and media manipulation to stay afloat."[105] But be forewarned, climate-change propagandists, Corcoran warned them in one column. Despite the billions in government propaganda spending, Canadians are not that caught up in the global warming scare, a claim that is at odds with many public opinion polls taken over the past decade, which show consistent support for strong action on global warming.

Corcoran found other targets to vent his spleen on as well. He was troubled by David Suzuki's two-part "propaganda homage" to the greatness of Cuba's agricultural economy, which ran on the CBC's *The Nature of Things*. For Suzuki, the Cuban food supply system is "the largest program of organic and sustainable agriculture ever undertaken"; for Corcoran, it's just "messed up" and "reminiscent of Canadian farming, circa 1870."[106] Corcoran informs readers that the ethanol industry exists solely on "the backs of taxpayers snookered by governments hooked on farm votes and green propaganda." He took up the cudgels again for Wal-Mart and its ongoing struggle against the union bully, applauding the workers who resisted the union crew "sipping coffee in your kitchen and filling the air with propaganda and promises of big improvements under union protection."[107] And he chastised "the fanatics and raging leftists" engaged in a propaganda push against urban sprawl.[108]

Corcoran's references to propaganda tailed off in 2007, but the gap was filled by Foster, who increased his output of columns defending business from alleged propaganda attacks. In one, he warned Canadians not to blame business for the continuing existence of slavery in the world. "The notion that capitalism is some kind of inverted pyramid balancing on the backs of Amazonian slaves—or that markets promote slavery or even 'exploit' labour—is pure propaganda," he barked.[109] And if corporations were blameless, the same could not be said about unions. The Canadian Union of Public Employees (CUPE), he determined, was guilty of disseminating anti-privatization propaganda in Canada by claiming that the Walkerton tragedy—in which seven died and thousands were made ill by tainted water—arose from privatization. "Nothing could be farther from the truth," he reassured readers.[110] He went after Al Gore's *An Inconvenient Truth* twice, calling it an "extraordinary propaganda coup" and "a propaganda masterpiece." Nor did he let Fidel Castro off the hook. He claimed that "Cuban education amounts to indoctrination; the best medical care is restricted to Castro's Communist Party apparatchiks and foreigners who pay high fees (or who come on a propaganda medical tour with Michael Moore)."[111]

Business faces a fundamental problem in its struggles to limit democracy. Despite the effectiveness of corporate propaganda, the modern age—from the eighteenth century onward—overall has been a progressive one. Most people believe, along with T. H. Marshall, that the acquisition of civil, political and social rights is inherently a good thing. Business-backed conservatives cannot claim outright that people shouldn't have these rights. They would be dismissed out of hand if they did. They can't say that the poor are shiftless and lazy and don't deserve a penny of taxpayers' money—let them starve! Instead, Albert Hirschman explains in *The Rhetoric of Reaction*, conservatives will endorse the change, "sincerely or otherwise, but then attempt to demonstrate that the action proposed or undertaken" is "ill conceived" and will produce, "via a chain of unintended consequences, the *exact contrary* of the objective being proclaimed and pursued."[112] Welfare to help the poor improve their lot will create more poor, conservatives claim. Society will achieve the opposite of what it says is its putative objective. Hirschman calls this argument "the thesis of the perverse effect." Any initiative to direct society to adopt progressive policies will result in a move in the opposite direction. A push towards a just society will result in dictatorship. A minimum-wage law will lead to lower employment and thus lower wages. Being "simple, intriguing, and devastating (if true)," Hirschman notes, "the argument has proven popular with generations of 'reactionaries,' as well as fairly effective with the public at large."[113]

Hirschman's study of modern history found that this propaganda device was utilized in all three reactions to progressive advances. It was first put forward in the aftermath of the French Revolution. In this context it was a no-brainer. "As Liberté, Egalité, Fraternité turned into the dictatorship of the Comite de Salut Public (and later into that of Bonaparte)," writes Hirschman, "the thought that certain attempts to reach for liberty are bound to lead to tyranny instead almost forced itself upon one's mind."[114] The leading advocate for the perverse effect during the French Revolution was Edmund Burke, considered the father of modern conservatism, who accurately predicted that the French democracy would degenerate into terror. "Massacre, torture, hanging! These are your rights of men!" he wrote in his *Reflections on the Revolution in France* in 1790.[115]

The thesis of the perverse effect reappeared in the nineteenth century with the broadening of the franchise. The new business elite and the old aristocracy obsessed over the prospect of the unworthy herd ruling over the worthy few. They turned to the emerging social sciences and especially the work of Gustave Le Bon, discussed earlier in this chapter, for new reasons to affirm the "inevitability of a perverse outcome." An argument was soon fashioned that mass participation in politics and the advance of democracy would inevitably turn into the rule of bureaucracy through the many laws and regulations that would be passed in the illusion that such laws can safeguard equality and liberty. As a result, democracy would be diminished.[116]

The perverse effect achieved its most widespread and damaging use during the third counterthrust, commencing in the 1970s, in an all-out effort to reverse the social and economic gains of the previous half-century. In its broadest meaning, "unintended consequences" refers to outcomes of any kind from policies or actions that were not originally intended. "Unintended consequences" can be positive or may even go unnoticed. But the unintended consequence has come to be epitomized by the perverse or negative effect. Key was to link perversity to the alleged superiority of free markets in solving social and economic problems. The extraordinary influence of the free market–perversity duopoly may be due to the enormous investments by business and conservative think-tanks to propagate these ideas through think-tanks, journals and policy networks over the decades.[117]

In its modern iteration, the perversity thesis holds that any public policy that interferes with the workings of the free market will fail because it upsets the market's internal regulating mechanisms. This argument leads to two conclusions: all dimensions of social life should be organized according to market principles; and government has almost no role in the economy or, indeed, in social life. At its very best, the argument suggests, government policy may be "well intentioned but misguided" and this theme is widely repeated. The Fraser Institute's annual report, for instance, explains each year that the "fundamental objective of all Institute research programs is to show the benefits of market-based alternatives to *well-intentioned but misguided* and conventional views about appropriate roles of government."[118]

How real is the perverse effect? Are all government actions well intentioned but misguided? Certainly, because human society is so complex, human actions may have unintended consequences of considerable magnitude. Building a new bridge to alleviate traffic congestion may lead to the perverse effect of greater congestion. But governments have built enough bridges to anticipate such consequences and correct their policies accordingly. A rapid-transit line should be built at the same time as the bridge, encouraging more people to travel by public transit, thus helping society achieve the desired outcome of alleviating congestion. And there could be unanticipated but serendipitous outcomes such as reduced urban sprawl and carbon dioxide (CO_2) emissions. It is also known that some unintended effects of government policies are welcomed and not perverse. Hirschman cites the positive effects on literacy of universal military service and the ability of many women to take on employment as a result of compulsory public education.

One example of an unintended but serendipitous effect is the decline in American crime rates in the 1990s that likely resulted from legalizing abortion in the 1970s. A 2001 study calculated that legalized abortion accounted for up to 50 percent of the drop in crime rates. Crime began to fall roughly eighteen years after abortion was legalized, the study found, and crime fell earlier in states that allowed abortion before the 1973 *Roe v. Wade* decision that made abortion legal throughout the U.S.[119]

And sometimes the claim that a perverse effect exists may be based on erroneous, or at least contested, research. Conservative economists have long claimed that the imposition of a minimum-wage law will mean less labour will be hired and the income of workers will fall, rather than rise. But, says Hirschman, "there is actually nothing certain about these perverse effects."

Minimum-wage laws could just as readily lead to higher productivity and employment.[120] The Fraser Institute and other pro-market think-tanks have so often repeated the claim that raising the minimum wage will lead to increased unemployment among the young workers the increase was designed to help, that it verges on being accepted as common sense. But recent research may be changing the views of some economists about the minimum wage and employment. Studies published by Princeton University economists David Card and Alan Krueger found that increasing the minimum wage had no effect on employment and, in some cases, resulted in job growth.[121]

Card and Krueger's work was attacked by conservative economists like Harvard's Greg Markiw, who chaired George W. Bush's Council of Economic Advisers and is a visiting fellow at the American Enterprise Institute (AEI). But it was supported by liberal economists and Nobel Prize winners Paul Krugman and Joseph Stiglitz.[122] The Fraser Institute ignored this debate in a 2009 study of the economic effects of increasing British Columbia's minimum wage. The institute once again played the perverse-effect card when it discussed "the tension between well-intentioned efforts to increase incomes for lower-income workers and the significant negative economic costs associated with increasing minimum wages." In a footnote, the report lists studies that attacked Card and Krueger's work, but did not cite studies that supported it.[123]

The perversity thesis was used in the U.S. to greatest effect in the decades-long campaign to end welfare. Eliminating this key entitlement would signify a major defeat for the welfare state. Lyndon B. Johnson's Great Society reforms, which saw welfare rolls expand dramatically during the 1960s, had never been fully explained or justified to the American people, making the welfare program vulnerable to free-market attack. Such an attack was coordinated and backed by a network of conservative scholars, think-tanks and foundations. Martin Anderson, an economist at the Hoover Institution at Stanford University and an adviser to Ronald Reagan, revived the perversity thesis in a 1978 book about welfare reform titled *Welfare: The Political Economy of Welfare Reform In the United States*.[124] Most credit for bringing down welfare, however, must go to political scientist Charles Murray. He first wrote a monograph in 1982 arguing that Lyndon Johnson's massive spending on welfare had not helped the poor any more than President Dwight Eisenhower's laissez-faire policies. This work so impressed the Manhattan Institute for Public Policy, a fledgling libertarian think-tank in New York, that it offered Murray an annual stipend of $35,000 ($79,000 in 2009 dollars) to expand it into a book. The resulting publication, widely promoted by the institute, *Losing Ground: American Social Policy, 1950–1980,* was a best-seller and received highly favourable media treatment. The book became a cornerstone of Ronald Reagan's domestic policy.

In this critique of the social programs of the Great Society, Murray utilized the perversity thesis to argue that poverty had been made worse by welfare programs. "We tried to provide more for the poor and produced more poor instead. We tried to remove the barriers to escape from poverty and inadvertently built a trap," Murray provocatively wrote.[125] As sociologists Margaret Somers and Fred Block point out, "the logic behind the rhetoric is impeccable—if assistance is actually hurting the poor by creating dependence, then denying it is not cruel but compassionate"[126]—shades of George W. Bush's compassionate conservatism.

Regardless of the merits of his work—and it has been widely praised and widely condemned—Murray, with the support of two think-tanks and one foundation, played a leading role in the success of the third counterthrust. He remained a senior fellow at the Manhattan Institute until 1990, with an increased stipend of $90,000 ($168,000 in 2007 dollars). In 1990, Murray moved to the American Enterprise Institute as a resident scholar. Over two decades at the AEI, Murray received over $3 million from the Lynde and Harry Bradley Foundation of Milwaukee, Wisconsin. Bradley, as the next chapter will explain, is one of the five foundations that provided the greatest support for the counterthrust.

A 1994 public opinion survey of the American public indicated the success of the anti-welfare campaign. It found that 71 percent of respondents agreed with the statement "The welfare system does more harm than good, because it encourages the breakup of the family and discourages the work ethic." Surveys in earlier years did not ask this question, Somers and Block note, but respondents had been far less inclined to blame government programs for worsening the conditions of the poor.[127]

The free market–perversity campaign achieved its long-sought victory with the 1996 Personal Responsibility and Work Opportunity Reconciliation Act. After signing the legislation, President Bill Clinton declared, "We have ended welfare as we know it." A long-established welfare regime, with roots going back to FDR's New Deal, had been overturned by a market-driven one, which proclaimed itself the solution to welfare dependency. Under the new law, welfare—cash assistance for single mothers and their children—would no longer be an entitlement. Stiff new work requirements were imposed on the mothers. Temporary assistance was available, but a cumulative lifetime limit of five years was placed on receipt of aid. This dramatic U-turn in social policy was swaddled in rhetoric. As Clinton said in a Thanksgiving radio address after he signed the law, "Now that we have ended welfare as we know it, let the change not be to have even more children in more abject poverty, but to move people who can work into jobs."[128]

But behind Clinton's challenging words lay the law's harsh reality. Getting people off welfare was certainly successful. The average number of monthly recipients of cash benefits dropped from 12.3 million in 1996, the last year of the welfare program, to 3.9 million in 2007.[129] Yet while the welfare rolls were slashed, there was only a slight reduction in poverty over the decade. In 1996, the overall poverty rate for the U.S. was 13.7 percent; in 2007, the rate was 12.5 percent.[130] The figures also indicate that the poverty rate was declining for four years before the end of welfare, so the connection between welfare and poverty is hard to show. As for former welfare recipients, they were condemned to "low-wage, part-time, insecure, boring and dead-end jobs," writes James Mulvale in a review of geographer Jamie Peck's book *Workfare States*.[131] The new system created a large pool of low-wage labour, depressed the wages of existing workers and increased profits for employers. Those at the bottom of the income scale saw their share of both income and wealth drop. A study of changes in distribution of wealth of American families over this period showed that wealth not only became more concentrated at the top, but that the wealth share of the bottom half of the population fell from 3.6 percent of total wealth in 1995 to 2.5 percent in 2004.[132] And the income share of the bottom 20 percent of the population dropped too, from 4.6 percent in 1996 to 4 percent in 2005.[133] Little discussion about the plight of former welfare recipients took place in the public realm and, as a result, the conclusion took hold that the poor were actually better off without welfare. Free markets and the perversity thesis could chalk up one big victory. The third wave of citizenship had received a near-fatal blow. Free market solutions to social problems, which were seen as too extreme in 1968, had become mainstream in 1996. And in between was Ronald Reagan.

CHAPTER 3

American Roots: the Rise of the Corporate Propaganda System

Government is not the solution to our problems; government *is* the problem.
— Ronald Reagan

Ronald Reagan's television appearances have faded from memory, but they were a phenomenon during his presidency. Here's Reagan on the six o'clock news accepting the Olympic torch from a young disabled athlete and then passing it on to another disabled athlete. He shakes hands exuberantly with both of them. The scene cuts to the athletes, some in wheelchairs, marching past. Reagan is saluting, creating an image that he has great respect for these brave young people. Or here's Reagan cutting a ribbon and beaming as he shakes hands with some older people. A sign behind him says, "Neighbors helping neighbors, Santa Maria Towers, Buffalo, New York." The camera cuts back to show an enthusiastic crowd clapping and then pans up the building.[1]

Looking at these news clips of Reagan beaming, shaking hands and saluting, the viewer has no way of knowing Reagan tried to cut the budgets for the disabled and for federally subsidized housing for the elderly. As Reagan media handler Michael Deaver explained to Bill Moyers in his 1994 documentary, *Illusions of News*, "The aim of the pictures was to erase the negatives of an unpopular issue with a carefully chosen backdrop that actually contradicts the president's policy." On the day Reagan cut the corporate tax rate (meaning that ordinary Americans would have to shoulder more of the tax burden), the evening news led off, not with this item, but with what Deaver calls the "compensating image": Reagan "downing a pint of ale in a local pub with the ordinary folk." "Ronald Reagan," Moyers remarks, "just one of the boys."

For Reagan, as for no president before him, the television image *was* reality. It mattered little what he actually did, such as reduce taxes for the wealthy or cut government spending on programs for the poor, the elderly and the disabled. What he said, how he looked on television, his Marlboro Man walk, were what counted for Americans. He often adopted the persona of the battling crusader, even though he was nothing of the sort. Historian Gerard De Groot surmises that "as an actor he knew how to strike just the right authoritative pose and to deliver the appropriate stern warning. His voice and facial gestures suggested courage and determination," De Groot writes, but these were two qualities he never actually exhibited.[2] His hero was Franklin Delano Roosevelt, not because of FDR's progressive policies or political vision, but for his "uncanny magnetism." Reagan found FDR's "empathetic and strikingly accessible presence electrifying," Stuart Ewen reports in his landmark study of the public relations industry.[3] What FDR achieved with radio, Reagan trumped with television, using it to create the role of an affable grandfather who spoke simple truths. But behind the facade lurked a consummate corporate propagandist who, for thirty years, promoted the interests of business and the wealthy by attacking democratic institutions and government itself. Ronald Reagan epitomizes the corporate reaction to the democratic advances of the 1960s and '70s, bringing together for the first time grassroots and treetops propaganda. Public relations specialists shaped him, put him in the White House and kept him there, while conservative think-tanks such as the Heritage Foundation supplied the scripts for cutting government and social programs he and his handlers sold so convincingly.

When public concern about the poor quality of American education increased, Deaver sent Reagan on an orchestrated tour featuring the president in classrooms, eating with teachers and using his acting talents to express "concern" over education. He didn't propose new programs, nor did he reverse his administration's massive cuts in education spending. The campaign successfully swayed public opinion, and that "solved" the problem. Deaver told NBC's Chris Wallace, "You can say whatever you want, but the viewer sees Ronald Reagan out there in a classroom talking to teachers and kids, and what he takes from that is the impression that Ronald Reagan is concerned about education."[4]

Reagan's metamorphosis from Hollywood actor into president is well known. Less well known is the fact that the entire voyage was charted by corporate public relations specialists. As official spokesperson for General Electric and cheerleader for private enterprise in the 1950s, and as the genial grandfather in the White House in the eighties, he combined the image of the ordinary person with policies that served the corporate elite. Reagan's talent, and his incalculable value to business, was his ability to encourage white, middle-class Americans to imagine that, through him, they had "actually assumed power." And while he was hoodwinking ordinary working people, he promoted policies that served the elite's interests: providing subsidies for business and tax cuts for the rich, boosting high-profit military production, loosening environmental regulations, cutting the rights of workers, deregulating business and dismantling "New Deal-inspired social guarantees."[5]

Reagan began his propaganda work in 1954, when he left a collapsing film career to begin an eight-year stint as an official spokesperson for the General Electric Co., at an enormous salary. The idea for a program hosted by Reagan was sold to GE by its advertising agency. As a major advertiser, GE needed to reach the rapidly growing television audience, which skyrocketed from four million households with television sets in 1950 to nearly forty-six million ten years later. Reagan was already doubling as a spokesperson for the movie industry, acting as toastmaster at banquets, giving speeches, pleading for a tax break for actors and promoting Hollywood. His success convinced the booking agency that he was the ideal person for the job—he could act, introduce and sell GE products and make a decent speech.[6] Reagan's job was to humanize the industrial giant and spread the gospel of free enterprise the corporation was promoting.[7]

Over the years he developed what he called "The Speech," sometimes titled "Encroaching Control," and sometimes "Our Eroding Freedoms." This was his main lecture on the horrors of the welfare state. Government—staffed by professional politicians and career bureaucrats—is by nature more wasteful than most human institutions and should be reduced to the barest minimum. The speech was rabidly anti-communist. He declared that the "Communist party has ordered once again the infiltration of the picture business as well as the theater and television. They are crawling out from under the rocks . . . the ideological struggle with Russia is the number one problem in the world . . ." He called the communists "the most dangerous enemy ever known to man," whose advance guard inside America was FDR's welfare state. Business leaders, Reagan claimed, were the dam restraining the collective tide, despite the burdens of high taxes, government regulation and social security imposed by the liberals. His message always sounded upbeat and inspirational rather than a prediction of doom.[8]

Reagan gave this speech again in 1964, two years after he was dropped by GE because *Bonanza*, a show on a competing network, was achieving higher ratings. Reagan was unemployed, but the resourceful former actor soon had a job as salesman for the emerging conservative-ideas industry. He kicked off his new career with a nationally televised speech in support of the faltering 1964 presidential campaign of Arizona senator Barry Goldwater. Reagan called the speech "A Time for Choosing" and incorporated many of the themes he used in his GE "Encroaching Control" speech. Reagan recounted "the relentless expansion of the federal government, the proliferation of government bureaucrats who were taking control of American business . . . the liberal Democrats [who were] taking the country down the road to socialism . . ." He gave this speech more grandeur by adding phrases like "You and I have a rendezvous with destiny," without informing the audience he had cribbed this and other phrases from FDR. Reagan the actor had played this role hundreds of times before. This time he attracted the attention of the newly emerging reactionary movement and a group of wealthy Californians who agreed to back him politically. Two years later, by then a wealthy, conservative Republican himself, Reagan was elected governor of California. His success was due, in part, to strong public relations guidance. Reagan's backers arranged for a political consultant and a team of media specialists to "program him." They sought to "goof-proof" the candidate by limiting his appearances to short presentations in front of friendly audiences, with little opportunity for spontaneous questions from the press. They provided information on the issues he was to address on easily handled five-by-eight cards. They recognized Reagan as a master of electronic media and worked to confine his campaign as far as possible to television.[9]

Whether unbelievable moron, as many insiders perceived him, or pathological liar, according to some, Reagan executed his mission flawlessly. He spent eight years in the California governor's mansion, and eight in the White House, where he introduced much legislation desired by business and the wealthy. He was labelled the "Teflon president" because, like the Teflon-coated frying pan, nothing stuck to him. He always came away smelling clean and sweet. The media attributed this phenomenon to his innate ability to portray Mr. Nice Guy. How could anyone hate this man who smiled so convincingly and was positively upbeat (even as he screwed millions)? But the real reason he was beyond criticism was that his administration gave huge benefits to the media, allowing large media corporations to become even larger. In return, they gave him a free ride. And if that didn't work, Michael Deaver could manipulate the media into reporting the message the White House wanted.

In his final *Economic Report* before leaving office, Reagan claimed that his administration had reversed a fifty-year liberal trend of turning to government for solutions to problems. He had turned back the clock. The poor were thrown into the streets to fend for themselves, and the wealthy were cracking open the champagne after he cut their taxes by two-thirds.

Twenty-four years earlier, despite Reagan's efforts to prop up Barry Goldwater's presidential campaign, liberal Democrats, led by Lyndon B. Johnson, swept both houses of Congress for the first time since the Second World War.[10] At first, the wave of policy liberalization in the quest to create Johnson's Great Society did not directly affect business, as the lawmakers dealt with pressing issues of civil rights, poverty, minority employment, housing and education. But Congress and the president soon turned their legislative attention to consumer and environmental issues. The new or strengthened laws they passed did have a major impact on business, forcing it to absorb some of the costs previously externalized onto other sectors of society. In just three years, Congress enacted the National Traffic and Motor Vehicle Safety Act, the Fair Packaging and Labeling Act, the Federal Hazardous Substances Act, the Federal Meat Inspection Act, the National Gas Pipeline Safety Act, the Truth in Lending Act, the Flammable Fabrics Act and the Child Protection Act. "Such an outpouring of consumer legislation by the federal government," comments business historian David Vogel, "was unprecedented in the history of business-government relations in the United States."[11] And threats to business profitability continued even under a Republican president. During Richard Nixon's first term of office, Vogel writes in his history of business and political power, "Congress enacted a significant tax-reform bill, four major environmental laws, an occupational safety and health act, and a series of additional consumer-protection statutes."[12] In addition, Vogel notes, the government created new regulatory agencies with broad powers over business activity. These included the Environmental

Protection Agency, the Occupational Safety and Health Administration and the Consumer Products Safety Commission.

No individual epitomized the threat to business dominance of American society more than Ralph Nader who, with his activist band of "Nader's Raiders," championed the cause of consumer rights. Traffic deaths rose sharply during the sixties, largely because automobile manufacturers spent too little on automobile safety. They didn't have to because few regulations required them to do so. Then, in 1965, Nader published his exposé, *Unsafe at Any Speed: The Designed-in Dangers in the American Automobile*. He argued that auto injuries were caused, not so much by the collision of the car with another car or object, but by the subsequent collision of the passenger with the interior of the car. And that situation was due to faulty design by manufacturers. Nader's book and the publicity it garnered resulted in the passage of the National Traffic and Motor Vehicle Safety Act.[13]

It didn't take long for Nader to become an object of revulsion to big business. *Fortune* magazine demonized him in a 1971 profile:

> The passion that rules in him—and he is a passionate man—is aimed at smashing utterly the target of his hatred, which is corporate power. He thinks, and says quite bluntly, that a great many corporate executives belong in prison—for defrauding the consumer with shoddy merchandise, poisoning the food supply with chemical additives, and wilfully manufacturing unsafe products that will maim or kill the buyer ... He emphasizes that he is talking not just about "fly-by-night hucksters" but the top management of "blue-chip business firms."[14]

Many Americans probably agreed with Nader's claim that some corporate executives did belong in prison. But business had other worries besides Nader. The economic boom of the sixties pushed unemployment to low levels, while strengthened social programs provided workers with a greater cushion if they lost their jobs.[15] These developments weakened employers' leverage over their workers. Two consequences of this were a resurgence of rank-and-file worker militancy and a sharp fall in corporate profit rates, which remained stagnant during the seventies. Steep hikes in oil prices caused by the actions of the Organization of Petroleum Exporting Countries (OPEC), after two decades of low prices, increased the cost of doing business. Worse, American companies faced growing competition both abroad and in home markets. Arms spending on the Vietnam War became a significant drain on the economy. The 1974–75 recession proved to be the most severe downturn since the thirties, leading to several years of stagnation.

Companies sought to cut their labour costs by relocating plants in the union-free Deep South and by attacking unions. They pressed for reduced government regulation and for further cuts in corporate taxes, which were already falling steadily. Business had been fractured over these issues since the New Deal. Moderates went along with FDR, while conservatives staunchly opposed him. Given the tougher climate, business was able to reach consensus on core goals: "to crank up the cold war and military spending; to dismantle social programs, environmental legislation, and other government regulations on industry; to roll back what remained of labor union power; and to cut taxes," independent scholar Matthew Lyons observes.[16]

Business had successfully employed grassroots techniques on a large scale after the Second World War, writes Alex Carey, to "drench the country in anti-communist, anti-socialist, anti-union and anti–New Deal propaganda."[17] The Advertising Council and the National Association of Manufacturers (NAM) were the leading grassroots propaganda organizations. Carey reports that NAM used all channels through which the public may be reached to beat back support for unions and to replace "bureaucratic control with free competition." Following the formula created by the Creel Committee, the business effort included full-page ads in thousands of newspapers, millions of booklets and pamphlets, special articles in magazines and business publications, thousands of news releases, stories delivered to seven hundred radio commentators and thirteen hundred editorialists and columnists.[18] When television became important, NAM produced weekly films for television that were shown nationally.

The Advertising Council represents large corporate advertisers and advertising agencies. In 1947 alone it spent over $100 million to "sell" the American people on the wonders of the American economic system. The campaign, which continued into the 1950s, had two aims: to re-win the loyalty of workers who had switched to the union; and to halt "creeping socialism" (i.e., the New Deal).[19] A General Electric print ad, which was part of the Advertising Council campaign, appeared in Harper's Weekly in 1956, while Ronald Reagan was stumping the country for GE and capitalism. The ad contains a photograph of a shareholders' meeting, which it claims was the largest shareholders' meeting in history. Titled "People's Capitalism—What Makes It Work for You?," the ad presents the claim that "our American brand of capitalism is distinctive and unusually successful because it is a 'people's capitalism': *all* the people share in its responsibilities and benefits." The ad concludes by claiming that "the more the principles of America's distinctive brand of capitalism become known and understood, the more certain everyone can be of continued progress— progress which is shared by consumers, employees, share owners, all business- es—large and small, and the nation. Progress is Our Most Important Product. General Electric."[20]

To meet the threats posed by liberal legislation and citizen activism, business at first resorted to the advertising and PR tactics that worked two decades ear- lier. In addition, many businesses established public affairs departments inside their organizations, increased funding and staffing of those departments, and indicated their importance to the corporate mission by allocating executives at senior-vice-president level. They turned to public relations consultants like Hill and Knowlton for help on specific projects and engaged in grassroots organizing, coalition building, telephone and letter-writing campaigns, using the media, writing research reports and testifying at hearings. They sent in- creased numbers of lobbyists to Washington, and trade associations moved their head offices to Washington, if they weren't already there.[21]

In 1975 the Advertising Council and NAM launched a massive national campaign of conservative "economic education," in an effort to regain public trust in corporate responsibility and consequent freedom from government regulation. By 1978, according to an expert witness before a congressional in- quiry, American business was spending a billion dollars a year on grassroots advertising propaganda, persuading the American people that their interests were the same as those of business.[22]

In the midst of the anti-corporate turmoil of the early seventies, business created a new organization to lobby government and change the views of opinion leaders. The Business Roundtable was established in 1972 and con- sisted of the chief executive officers of 194 of the largest corporations in the United States, representing about half the country's economic output. Only active CEOs could be members, a strategy aimed at solving a problem faced by traditional business lobby groups, whose staff and spokespeople could not make decisions quickly. Because they could not speak for their corporations without referring questions back to them, a consensus among corporations and rapid action was difficult, if not impossible, to achieve.[23] The Roundtable is a prototypical treetops propaganda and lobbying organization with a dual purpose: to produce favourable research on public policy issues that affect business; and to encourage the organization's prestigious members to speak out on these issues to government, unions and the community. The Roundtable maintains fifteen "task forces" which produce "position papers" on issues, these terms being utilized to provide a veneer of objectivity and the appearance of a desire for dialogue when, of course, the efforts are self-serving. The organization was an instant success, in part because of its rich endowment from corporate members. Officially the Roundtable did not engage in grassroots propaganda, preferring to pressure Congress, but covertly it worked closely with grassroots propagandists NAM and the U.S. Chamber of Commerce. Within four years, the Roundtable became the voice of big business in Washington, eclipsing NAM and the Chamber.[24]

Like the Canadian Council of Chief Executives, the Business Roundtable is limited in the claims it can make because it is clearly a voice of big business. The business interest has to be masked. So business created a more sophisticated form of treetops propaganda, establishing a network of well-funded conservative think-tanks that could promote the objectives of business without being seen as tied to business. It is unlikely that pro-business conservative ideology would have swept the U.S. so quickly without the network of right-wing think-tanks and the billions of dollars behind it. And conservatives would have remained on the fringe of the Republican Party as they were in the 1950s. At that time, they included Robert Welch, founder of the extremist John Birch Society, and William F. Buckley, who established the influential conservative journal *National Review*. Buckley famously proclaimed in the first issue that conservatives were a "minority standing athwart history and yelling, Stop!" They might have remained a minority yelling Stop! if they had not formulated a new strategy by forging an alliance between business (supplying the money) and intellectuals (supplying the ideas) within a think-tank context (marketing the product). Using this structure, they created the New Right, but, as Albert Hirschman argues, was the counterthrust mounted by the business elite to resist the movement for social and economic rights and to hold on to its power and privilege. They succeeded famously. A 1964 public opinion poll found that 76 percent of Americans trusted government to do what is right always or most of the time; by 1994, the number had dwindled to 21 percent. It's not possible to determine if the dramatic decline in government trust would have occurred without the conservative propaganda system. To what extent did the Vietnam War, Watergate, rampant inflation and economic stagnation sap public trust in government? But the surveys did find that very few respondents blamed government employees for what was wrong with government, while the two top groups blamed for government's problems were special interest groups and the media.[25]

A key figure in establishing the organized counterthrust to the third wave of citizenship was Lewis Powell, a corporate lawyer in Richmond, Virginia, who in 1971 was about to begin a fifteen year stint as a justice of the U.S. Supreme Court. Like his business colleagues—he was a member of eleven corporate boards, including the Phillip Morris Tobacco Co.—Powell loathed the progressive advances. He was convinced that Ralph Nader and the anti-business rebellion had to be defeated. Powell commiserated with friend and neighbour Eugene Sydnor, a department store owner. Sydnor was chairman of the education committee of the U.S. Chamber of Commerce, which was already working with NAM and the Advertising Council on grassroots campaigns. Powell and Sydnor agreed that a new type of national campaign was necessary, and Sydnor invited Powell to outline his ideas about the direction the project should take. The result was the so-called Powell Manifesto, which Powell turned over to Sydnor two months before he was nominated to the bench by Richard Nixon.[26]

The Chamber circulated the five-thousand-word document confidentially to members and it had an enormous impact. Titled "Attack of American Free Enterprise System," it began by claiming that "no thoughtful person can question that the American economic system is under broad attack." Powell had read the *Fortune* hatchet job on Ralph Nader, published just three months earlier, and referred to it in his memorandum. Powell's analysis of why the system was under attack and, more important, his recommendations to turn the situation around, became a blueprint for the backlash of the next thirty years. Powell laid responsibility for the dismal situation at the feet of businessmen, who must "confront this problem as a primary responsibility of corporate management." Managers must concern themselves with "protecting and preserving the system itself" as well as with the next quarter's profits. Business must go far beyond its traditional public relations activities; individual corporate action would not suffice. Phillip Morris, acting alone, will get nowhere. "Strength lies in organization, in careful long-range planning and implementation, in consistency of action over an indefinite period of years, in the scale of financing available only through joint effort, and in the political power available only through united action and national organizations," Powell wrote. The U.S. Chamber of Commerce should be the coordinating body, he argued. This did not happen. Chamber members decided against leading the reaction because they thought Powell's ideas were too ambitious and costly. But within a year the Business Roundtable was formed and this organization did meet Powell's criteria for a coordinating body.

Powell recommended action on four fronts: the media; politics; the courts; and institutions of higher learning. In the battle for public opinion, business needed to monitor television, radio and newspapers for content hostile to the free enterprise system and demand equal time when appropriate. Soon, organizations with names like Accuracy in Media and Center for Media and Public Affairs were created to accuse media of being too liberal and demand equal time. It was successful in pressuring media commentary and reporting to be more business friendly.

On the second front, Powell urged business to cultivate and use without reluctance political power, "aggressively and with determination." Electoral success came quickly: the defeat of five targeted liberal Democratic senators in 1978, the election of Ronald Reagan in 1980, a Republican Congress in 1994, George W. Bush and a Republican Congress in 2000 and their re-election in 2004, and the transformation of the Republican Party from moderate to right. The Republican-controlled Congress began to undo many of the regulations from the sixties that were designed to curb business power. And the centrist Obama administration, which took office in 2009, was unlikely to re-establish the strong environmental social and consumer laws of the Johnson and first Nixon administrations.

In the legal arena, Powell recommended that business fund a staff of lawyers to appear in court to protect the business viewpoint. His recommendations inspired a thirty-year campaign to change the face of American law. Business and foundation money created law firms to advance the business agenda in the courts, law schools and government agencies. Through its legal think-tank, the Federalist Society, business successfully installed ideologically friendly faculty in law schools, rewarded students who held the "correct" views with scholarships and clerkships under conservative judges and placed hundreds of conservative lawyers and judges on the bench.[27]

Powell's most far-reaching recommendations were on the battleground of post-secondary education. As he saw it, academia was infected by liberals, socialists and Marxists, who were poisoning the minds of their students against capitalism. Business needed to establish a staff of "highly qualified scholars in the social sciences who do believe in the system." They would counter the critics, evaluate social science textbooks, write scholarly and popular books and articles, demand equal time for guest lectures and ensure balanced faculty appointments. These eminent scholars "will do the thinking, the analysis, the writing and the speaking for the business community." Powell recommended that these scholars be on the staff of the Chamber. Instead, business adapted for its own use a model originated by its mortal enemy, Ralph Nader.

Three years after steering automobile-safety legislation through Congress, Nader sought to increase his influence in Washington by establishing a think-tank called the Center for the Study of Responsive Law. Relying on a small, full-time staff and hundreds of student summer volunteers (Nader's Raiders), the centre published many books documenting the failure of regulatory agencies to protect public health and safety. Nader established eight more centres to force government to strengthen its regulatory activities and increase its protection of the public. By the mid-seventies, these organizations employed about seventy-five full-time lawyers and had a budget of over a million dollars. The money came from Nader's speaking fees, book royalties and direct-mail fundraising.[28]

Nader's success convinced business it could exploit his techniques using interrelated think-tanks for research and promotion. The term "think-tank" described contract-research organizations, such as the RAND Corporation, which were set up by the military. Thanks to Nader's efforts, "think-tank" entered the popular lexicon. It is an imprecise term that can refer to all kinds of private research groups, but, as used by conservatives, its meaning is clear. Wealthy businessmen and their charitable foundations provide ample and ongoing support to tax-exempt think-tanks run by aggressive policy entrepreneurs, who locate and support sympathetic scholars to write reports, books and op-ed pieces, which the entrepreneur then promotes widely through the media and other channels of communication. Alex Carey saw this as an "elite version of the factory system," in which sympathetic intellectuals convert "millions of corporate dollars into up-market propaganda for corporate interests."[29] It was Powell's proposal except that the Chamber was replaced by a network of seemingly independent, dispersed think-tanks, each with a slightly different emphasis, but making extensive use of each other's work. Like the Business Roundtable itself, the model was an instant success.

Many business-backed think-tanks call themselves "research institutes," but do not mean research in the traditional scientific sense of systematic, peer-reviewed work employing a replicable methodology. They don't use these established procedures because their purpose is not to advance the state of knowledge, but to promote their radical-conservative ideas and undo support for progressive laws and programs. Heritage Foundation senior vice-president Burton Pines once called his think-tank the "intellectual shock troops of the conservative revolution."[30] It is engaged in a war of ideas, not in a search for truth.

Joseph Coors, head of the largest brewery west of the Mississippi River, was "stirred up" after reading the Powell memorandum. Like Powell, he was convinced that American business was "ignoring a crisis" and invested $250,000 to fund the Heritage Foundation, a new policy research institute sponsored by conservative Republicans in Congress and members of their legislative staff. Conservative billionaire Richard Mellon Scaife kicked in another $900,000 over the first three years and became Heritage's largest supporter for the next three decades.[31] Heritage joined two existing conservative think-tanks. The Hoover Institution on War, Peace and Revolution on the campus of Stanford University in California was established in 1919 with a $50,000 gift ($610,000 in 2009 dollars) from Herbert Hoover to develop anti-Bolshevik propaganda. The American Enterprise Institute (AEI) was founded in 1943 by industrialist Lewis Brown, who hoped to create a conservative organization that could rival the influence of Robert S. Brookings of the liberal Brookings Institution. A young AEI scholar, Karl Hess, wrote the notorious acceptance speech given by Barry Goldwater at the 1964 Republican convention where he proclaimed that "extremism in the defence of liberty is no vice; moderation in the pursuit of justice is no virtue."[32] Within a decade of Goldwater's ill-fated campaign, "a tidal wave of money, ideas and self-promotion . . . carried the Reaganites to power" and unravelled many social and economic gains of the past half-century, *Nation* media columnist Eric Alterman observes.[33] And the tidal wave swept across the industrialized world.

Business supported both libertarian and neoconservative think-tanks, these being the ideologies most capable of being exploited for business purposes. Libertarian think-tanks, such as the Cato, Reason and Fraser institutes, are based on the ideas of European émigrés Ludwig von Mies and Friedrich Hayek, and the American-born Milton Friedman. They are called variously classical liberals, neoliberals or libertarians. Hayek and Friedman argued that individual freedom and liberty are the highest achievements of civilization, higher than the collective accomplishments of civilization itself. Freedom and liberty are to be achieved and protected by a system of strong private-property rights, free markets and free trade, goals that coincide with those of business. The state should not be involved in the economy except to use its power to preserve private-property rights and market institutions. The belief that markets can solve most of society's problems can become so exaggerated and irrational that progressive scholars have dubbed it "market fundamentalism."[34] This is an effort to compare libertarians with Christian, Jewish and Islamic fundamen talists, who see everything in black and white. For the libertarian variety, the market (God) is good, government (the devil) is evil.

Market fundamentalism's roots lie with its eighteenth-century apostles Adam Smith and John Locke. It was known then simply as liberalism. Neoliberalism is the late-nineteenth- and early-twentieth-century revival of liberalism. In 1947, just as movements to establish social and economic rights were gathering momentum, Hayek formed the Mont Pèlerin Society, to keep classical liberal ideas alive during the looming "dark age" of the welfare state. Like the early Christians in the caves of Rome, they kept the faith alive and out of sight of the prevailing orthodoxy. They feared state intervention in the economy because Hayek prophesied it would lead inevitably to slavery and serfdom. It wasn't just fascism and communism that troubled them, though. The welfare state itself, and indeed any government intervention in the market, would be oppressive, Hayek taught.

Based on the extremist idea that the market can solve all our problems, market fundamentalism should have remained a fringe movement. But it provided the intellectual veneer the corporate elite needed to justify its economic goals for lower taxes, less regulation and smaller and less effective government. As Marxist scholar David Harvey points out in his history of neoliberalism, "It was a minor society but got a lot of support from wealthy contributors and corporations to polemicize on the ideas it held."[35] The expenses of the ten Americans who attended the first meeting at the fashionable resort at Mont Pèlerin, Switzerland, were paid by the William Volker Fund, whose financial resources derived from a Kansas City household-furnishings multimillionaire. This fund "enabled extreme market ideologues . . . to come together to plot change," writes Australian environmentalist Sharon Beder. It also provided financial support for market-fundamentalist economists who couldn't obtain positions at American universities, and sponsored lectures by Milton and Rose Friedman.[36]

When corporate profits declined and democracy threatened to become "excessive" (as *The Crisis of Democracy*, the first book published by the Trilateral Commission, worried), market-fundamentalist high priest Milton Friedman and his disciples were handed a golden opportunity to bring the religion down from the mountain (Mont Pèlerin) to the plains below. Within a few years, market fundamentalists grabbed control of economic policy in many Western nations. But one obstacle to greater acceptance of their ideology they could never overcome was that their only full-blown success occurred in Chile under brutal dictator Augusto Pinochet, and that was for a few years only.

Several years after his 1973 bloody coup against the democratically elected government of Salvadore Allende, Pinochet asked his business backers for ideas on how to fix the sputtering economy. Chile's business leaders had established relationships with Chilean economists who were trained in Chicago under Friedman. According to Latin-American scholar Greg Grandin, the University of Chicago's Economics Department "had turned itself into [a] free-market madrassa that indoctrinated a generation of Latin American economists to spearhead an international capitalist insurgency."[37] Under the guidance of these economists—the Chicago Boys—Chile was transformed from a mixed economy into a fundamentalist market state.

Friedman paid a six-day visit to Chile in 1975, at the behest of the Chicago Boys. He recommended "shock treatment" to the economy, a concept Pinochet could readily understand, since he was already applying such treatment to thousands of Chilean citizens. A month after Friedman's visit, the junta cut spending, virtually stopped printing money, deregulated interest rates, removed all restrictions on foreign investment and auctioned off over four hundred state enterprises to the private sector, causing thousands of workers to lose their jobs. All labour laws were repealed. Health care, education and the public pension fund were privatized.[38] Despite the shock treatment, the economy continued to sink for several more years, rebounding briefly and finally flaming out in 1982. After that, the junta had to undo much of Friedman's work, devaluing the country's principal monetary unit, the escudo, renationalizing the banking system and reimposing controls on finance, industry, prices and wages. The brief experiment in market fundamentalism was over. But the revolution continued to be a success, at least for the wealthy. The share of national income going to the richest 10 percent of the population rose between

1980 and 1989 from 36.5 percent to 46.8 percent. And the share going to the poorest 50 percent declined from 20.4 to 16.8 percent.[39]

Was the market fundamentalism advocated by Friedman and the Chicago Boys possible only through Pinochet-style repression? The prevailing notion during the welfare state era was that political freedom could be achieved only when social and economic disparities were reduced. Friedman turned this thinking on its head. In a deft Orwellian move, he claimed that economic freedom had to come first, before political freedom could be achieved. He thus equated capitalism and freedom, a theme fundamental to the corporate counterthrust. It's the free market and not democracy, Friedman argued, that leads to freedom. Dictatorship (and torture) may be necessary to remove democracy's false trappings and begin the trek to true freedom. Shades of the Reign of Terror!

But there is, in fact, little connection between democracy and capitalism. The Economic Freedom of the World project, which was devised by Friedman and Michael Walker of the Fraser Institute, proves this point. The project ostensibly measures "the extent to which one can pursue economic activity without interference from government." It has mushroomed into a joint venture of dozens of market-fundamentalist think-tanks around the world. The two highest-scoring countries on the list are regularly the city-states of Hong Kong and Singapore, states that do not spring to mind when thinking of countries with strong democracies.[40] But they do boast large and growing income disparities between rich and poor. Hong Kong, for instance, has more billionaires per capita—twenty-two in all—than any other jurisdiction.

Friedman received the grief for his dalliance with the Chilean dictator, but the real brains behind the experiment was Hayek. He visited Pinochet's Chile several times and thought so highly of developments in that brutalized country, he held a meeting of his Mont Pèlerin Society there several years after he helped establish the Fraser Institute in Canada. He recommended Chile to Margaret Thatcher as a model to complete her free market revolution. Thatcher was certainly an outspoken devotee of Hayek's work. In one famous incident, after she became Conservative Party leader, she slammed Hayek's *The Constitution of Liberty* on the table at a party meeting and proclaimed, "This is what we believe."[41] The prime minister, at the nadir of Chile's 1982 financial collapse, agreed that Chile represented a "remarkable success," but admitted Britain's "democratic institutions and the need for a high degree of consent"—the propaganda approach—made "some of the measures" taken by Pinochet "unacceptable."[42]

Did Hayek understand Thatcher's objection to Pinochet's shock treatment? He believed that Pinochet would rule as a dictator only for a "transitional period," until decades of state regulation could be reversed. "My personal preference," he told an interviewer, "leans toward a liberal dictatorship rather than toward a democratic government devoid of liberalism." For Hayek, Allende's democratically elected government was little more than a way station on the road from the welfare state to serfdom. The junta's terror was needed, Greg Grandin observes, "not only to prevent Chile from turning into a Stalinist gulag but to sweep away fifty years of tariffs, subsidies, capital controls, labor legislation, and social-welfare provisions."[43]

Chile's Chicago Boys liked Hayek's approach so much they named their country's new constitution after *The Constitution of Liberty*. In this world, economic liberty and political authoritarianism were peas in a pod. The dictator would allow "the jungle . . . of economic life" to take hold in the Chilean mind, which had become too used to being swaddled by the nanny state. Chile would become "a jungle of savage beasts, where he who can kill the one next to him, kills him," as Admiral José Toribio Merino, who was responsible for economic policy in the military junta, starkly framed his government's experiment in market fundamentalism.[44]

A key figure in spreading libertarian-style think-tanks to countries not ruled by dictators was British industrialist Antony Fisher, who met Hayek after the war. Fisher was inspired by Hayek's *The Road to Serfdom* and wanted to go into politics to defeat the Labour government. Instead, Hayek counselled him to change the prevailing climate of ideas. Following this advice, in 1955 Fisher set up the Institute of Economic Affairs in London, one of the world's first libertarian think-tanks. Fifteen years later, when Lewis Powell's memo was circulating among the business elite, Fisher helped establish three more think-tanks, the Manhattan in New York, the Fraser in Vancouver and the Pacific Research Institute in San Francisco, choosing geographical names to blur their ideological purpose.

Fisher received requests from business people around the world to help them set up similar think-tanks in their own countries to bring democracy to heel. In 1981, he established the Atlas Economic Research Foundation to automate the process of establishing and running think-tanks. Atlas is based in Arlington, Virginia, and is named after Ayn Rand's libertarian screed *Atlas*

Shrugged. Today it works with more than two hundred market-fundamentalist—Atlas calls them "market-oriented"—think-tanks around the world.[45]

Some libertarian think-tanks were not established by Fisher. The Cato Institute, which prefers the label "market-liberal" to market-fundamentalist, was set up in 1977 by Wichita-based oil billionaires David and Charles Koch, with a gift of $500,000. They continue to provide about a million dollars a year to the organization for general support. This institute was first based in San Francisco and moved to Washington when Ronald Reagan became president. It is named after *Cato's Letters,* a series of essays written by two Englishmen, John Trenchard and Thomas Gordon, that promote eighteenth-century liberal ideology. To enhance individual liberty, Cato proposes *abolishing* (not just reducing) welfare, affirmative action programs, income tax and all regulations on business and industry, legalizing drugs, cutting the defence budget and restraining the authority of law enforcement. Supreme Court Justice Clarence Thomas was a frequent writer and speaker at Cato, where he regularly blasted affirmative action and school busing as meeting the demands of groups rather than protecting the rights of individuals.[46]

Business also supported a network of neoconservative think-tanks. Unlike libertarian, or market-fundamentalist, institutes which emphasize the market and small government, neoconservative think-tanks delve into social and defence policy and international affairs, as well as economic policy. They are based on the ideas of another European émigré, Leo Strauss, as translated by former Trotskyists like Irving Kristol, who moved to the right in the 1950s.

Leo Strauss was a German-Jewish philosopher who fled Nazi Germany in 1938 and taught at the University of Chicago—Milton Friedman's home base—for several decades. He developed a following of students and disciples who achieved enormous influence in academia and government. Strauss died in 1973, two years after Lewis Powell delivered his manifesto to the U.S. Chamber of Commerce. So he did not participate in setting up the first neoconservative think-tanks, as Hayek did with the libertarian ones. Nor would he likely have agreed to this project, given his preoccupation with secrecy. But some of his followers exploited his ideas for their own ends and pressed them into the service of the business elite. Inspired by Strauss's idea of the "noble lie," they aggressively promoted a reactionary agenda at home and abroad.

Strauss's teachings grabbed public attention after the United States invaded

Iraq. The U.S. had to go into Iraq, the Bush administration told the people, because Iraq had weapons of mass destruction (WMDs). Strauss student Abram Shulsky, the director of the Office of Special Plans in the Department of Defense, "was responsible for finding intelligence that would help to make the case for the war on Iraq," writes Strauss's foremost Canadian critic, Shadia Drury, in her landmark critique *The Political Ideas of Leo Strauss*.[47]

When no such weapons were found, the American government said instead it had to go to war to depose a ruthless dictator and bring democracy and freedom to the Iraqi people. It was also discovered that the Bush administration knew all along that Saddam Hussein had no WMDs. Many Americans concluded that their leaders had lied. Thanks to Strauss, though, these lies were no longer to be thought of as miserable, cheap, crooked, self-serving lies, but noble ones. They were noble because the Straussians in the Bush administration knew that gaining control of Iraq's oil fields and privatizing the Iraqi economy were in the best interests of American business. But the American people would never agree to invade Iraq merely to enrich corporate coffers. Lies were no longer just a regrettable part of political life, but instead "virtuous and noble instruments of wise policy," Earl Shorris explains in *Harper's Magazine*.[48]

Strauss believed in the inherent inequality of humanity. He agreed with Edward Bernays, the founder of public relations, that most people are too ill educated to make informed decisions about their political affairs. Allowing people to govern themselves will lead inevitably to terror and tyranny, in the same way that Germany's Weimar Republic succumbed to Nazi dictatorship, an event Strauss witnessed first-hand. According to Strauss, a ruling elite of political philosophers must make decisions about governance because it is the only group knowledgeable enough; it must resort to deception to protect citizens from themselves. The "superior few"—Strauss's students—must rule over the ordinary people, "not honestly or with candid veracity," Drury wryly observes, "but by duping, deceiving and manipulating them."[49]

Strauss's critics argue that his goal was to found an aristocracy within a mass democracy. Rule by the wise, as understood by Strauss, meant tyranny: rule in the absence of law or rule by those who were above the law. But Strauss believed "the superior few" would not abuse their power and would give the people just what was commensurate with their needs and capacities. To Strauss, liberal secular society was untenable because it led to the "isms"—individualism, liberalism and relativism, traits that encourage dissent, which in turn could weaken society's ability to cope with external threats. What the people needed most, Strauss believed, were religion and perpetual war. Strauss regarded religion as a political tool intended for the masses, but not for the superior few. He agreed with Marx that religion is the opiate of the masses, but, unlike Marx, believed that the people need their opium.[50] Religion was necessary to provide society with moral order and stability. Strauss's followers concluded that the centuries-old principle of the separation of church and state had to be revoked, a process that was underway during the George W. Bush administration.

Strauss taught further that a political order can be stable only if it is united by an external threat. Following Machiavelli, he maintained that if no external threat exists, one has to be manufactured. "You have to fight all the time [to survive]," explains Drury. "Peace leads to decadence. Perpetual war, not perpetual peace, is what Straussians believe in." Such a view inevitably leads to an "aggressive, belligerent foreign policy," Drury adds.[51] Had Strauss lived to see the collapse of the Soviet Union he might have been troubled, because the collapse of the "evil empire" posed a threat to America's inner stability. For a decade Straussians worked quietly to replace the Soviet Union with Islamic terrorism. Perpetual war would continue.

Neoconservatives and libertarians are far apart on some issues. For libertarians, small government means no welfare state and no foreign military adventurism. They opposed George Bush's foreign policies and the neocons who promoted it. Neoconservatives, in contrast, "want a strong state and one that will put its strength to use," writes ex-Straussian Anne Norton.[52] And they want the strong state to "ally itself with—and empower—corporations, with tax cuts targeted to stimulate the economy." They appeal to the concerns of small business, small property owners and working people, but they ensure that the benefits go to the wealthy and big corporations. They combine populist rhetoric with a corporatist strategy, a program that would be reflected a decade later by Preston Manning and the Reform Party in Alberta.

Libertarians are advocates for human rights and reject gay bashing, once again putting them at odds with neoconservatives, who have allied themselves with the religious right to promote a traditional religious agenda. Neoconservatives "encourage family values and the praise of older forms of family life, where women occupy themselves with children, cooking and the church and men take on the burden of manliness," Norton writes.[53]

Strauss's students carried on his work, teaching Strauss to their own students and creating a growing network of Straussians in American and Canadian colleges and universities, and in government. During the Reagan years (1981–89) they grabbed ownership of social policy and pushed it to the right; during the George W. Bush years (2001–09), foreign and defence policy became their field of operation. In Canada, they exerted influence on government through the Calgary School and the Reform Party. Libertarians took over economics departments and gained considerable influence over economic policy. At the turn of the twenty-first century, Straussians and libertarians were the most powerful, most organized and best-funded scholars in the United States. They had the ear of the White House, at least until Barack Obama took office. They controlled major market-liberal and neoconservative think-tanks and foundations. And for much of that they could thank Irving Kristol.

Irving Kristol was the first intellectual to call himself a neoconservative. He was an entrepreneur of ideas who operationalized the Powell memorandum, bringing together money and intellectuals in the new think-tanks. "I raise money for conservative think-tanks," Kristol explained. "I am a liaison to some degree between intellectuals and the business community."[54] Kristol's teachers were Leo Strauss and Donald Kagan, a Yale historian who wasn't a Straussian, but who moved sharply to the right with them in the early seventies. Kristol is widely recognized as "the Godfather" of neoconservatism.[55] He went to City College of New York in the 1930s. This institution was a hotbed of radical politics, where the mostly Jewish student population fiercely debated Marxism. Kristol joined a small Trotskyist group. The common element among participants was their anti-Stalinism.[56] After the war he became a strident anti-communist because of revelations about Soviet liquidations, purges and massacres. He turned against the liberals, too, because they weren't doing enough to condemn the Soviet Union. He came to believe they were dupes defending the civil liberties of communists.

The term "neoconservative" was coined by American socialist leader and *Dissent* magazine editor Michael Harrington, to describe his former comrades who became first liberals and then reactionaries. Long-time student of neoconservatism Gary Dorrien defines it "as an intellectual movement originated by former leftists that promotes militant anticommunism, capitalist economics, a minimal welfare state, the rule of traditional elites, and a return to traditional cultural values."[57] But this is a misnomer. There is nothing traditional about the movement inspired by Leo Strauss and implemented by Irving

Kristol. It is radical and reactionary, a corporate-financed project that seems to want to return Western society to a pre-welfare, pre-democratic era.

Kristol was one of the first neoconservatives to join the Republican Party, and became an unofficial adviser to the Nixon administration in the early seventies. Corporate executives were soon seeking his advice. He grabbed their attention on the editorial page of the *Wall Street Journal* through his association with Robert Bartley, *Journal* editorial page editor and ardent supporter of the Straussians. Kristol and Bartley attacked the Soviet Union and the New Class—"scientists, teachers, and educational administrators, journalists and others"—both of which they accused of launching an attack on American society and business. The *Journal* editorial pages became a hotbed of neo-conservative counter-revolution, with Kristol a regular contributor, Eric Alterman writes. Following Lewis Powell's advice, Kristol told businessmen they needed to "defund" socialist and Marxist academics and recruit their own intellectuals.[58] Kristol complained that business executives on college and university boards were raising money to finance "left-wing humanities and social sciences departments, 'women's studies' programs that are candid proselytizers for lesbianism, programs in 'safe sex' that promote homosexuality, 'environmental studies' that are, at bottom, anti-capitalist propaganda, and other such activities of which they surely disapprove."[59] These trustees, he complained, tried to be non-ideological and avoid confrontation, but they were contributing to America's subversion. Business needed to defend its interests by subsidizing the work and careers of ideologically sympathetic intellectuals who believe in the preservation of a strong private sector.[60] With Kristol's encouragement, business and conservative foundations snatched the American Enterprise Institute from middle-of-the-road obscurity and transformed it into a smoothly functioning vehicle for corporate propaganda. The AEI grew from twelve resident "thinkers" in the mid-seventies into a sophisticated, well-funded organization with 145 resident scholars, 80 adjunct scholars and a large supporting staff. Kristol was AEI's star scholar for more than twenty-five years. He helped the institute's operating budget mushroom from $1 million in 1970 to $10 million in 1981 and $31.3 million in 2007,[61] before declining the following year as a result of the financial meltdown.[62]

President George W. Bush spoke at the American Enterprise Institute's annual dinner in February 2003, at which AEI's new highest honour, the Kristol Award, was bestowed. Having commended the institute for representing "some of the finest minds in our nation," Bush added, "You do such good work that my administration has borrowed twenty such minds."[63] AEI operatives were clustered in government positions that resembled a Straussian strategy primer. The necessity for perpetual war? AEI resident fellow Richard Perle was chairman of the Defense Policy Board Advisory Committee; AEI vice-president John Bolton was undersecretary of state for arms control and international security affairs; and another AEI research fellow was Bolton's special assistant. Religious domination and traditional values? AEI senior scholar Lynne Cheney wasn't a Bush appointee, but the Second Lady and a long-time cultural warrior who attacked multiculturalism and feminism and promoted school prayer; a senior policy analyst from AEI's ethics and public policy centre was Vice-President Cheney's deputy assistant for domestic policy; and two AEI senior scholars were chairman and member of the President's Council on Bioethics (stem-cell research); the editor-in-chief of AEI's *American Enterprise* magazine became Bush's top domestic policy adviser. Advocates for the free market? A visiting AEI scholar was chairman of the President's Council of Economic Advisers; a resident scholar was assistant to the president for economic policy; and AEI trustee Paul O'Neill was Bush's secretary of the treasury.[64] It was an instructive display of political and ideological power.

The outing of star *New York Times* reporter Judith Miller reveals how neoconservatives at the AEI used the media to implement a Straussian agenda and conceal the truth from the public.[65] For Straussians, as previously mentioned, telling Americans that Saddam didn't have weapons of mass destruction and had nothing to do with al Qaeda, but we need to take him out for geopolitical and ideological reasons you can't comprehend, was a non-starter. The people wouldn't get it. Time for a whopper. Miller was responsible for pushing into the *Times* the key neocon (noble) lie that Saddam was busy stockpiling WMDs. This deception helped build support among Americans for the invasion of Iraq. Miller was no independent journalist seeking the truth, nor a victim of neocon duplicity, as she claimed. She worked closely with Lewis "Scooter" Libby, who was Cheney's chief of staff and the person responsible for coordinating Iraq intelligence and communications strategy. Libby is a Straussian who studied under Paul Wolfowitz, then deputy secretary of defense, where he led the "Invade Iraq" lobby. Wolfowitz had studied under Strauss and Strauss's star student, Allan Bloom.

Miller cultivated close links to the neocons in the administration and at the AEI, which played a key role outside government in fabricating intelligence to make the case for invading Iraq. Richard Perle coordinated AEI's efforts. Inside government, John Bolton was part of the team of heavy hitters. Earlier, Miller co-wrote a book about Iraq with AEI scholar Laurie Mylroie. Rather than being a victim of government manipulation, as she portrayed herself, Miller was a willing conduit between the neocons and the American public. As a result of her reporting, many Americans came to believe that Saddam had the weapons. War and regime change followed. Credit Strauss's noble lie as implemented by Wolfowitz, Libby, Miller and the AEI.

In 2005, the same year Miller left the *Times*, Bush promoted Wolfowitz to head the World Bank. Two years later, Wolfowitz resigned before the World Bank's executive board could reprimand him for breaking ethical rules in awarding a substantial pay raise for his girlfriend, which would be a serious breach of conduct for a member of Strauss's ruling elite. Wolfowitz returned as a visiting scholar at the AEI where he could still "have the President's ear" on national security issues.[66] In January 2007, a report written by AEI resident scholar Frederick Kagan (son of Donald, Irving Kristol's teacher) became the basis for the Bush administration's "surge strategy" in Iraq. The report was produced with the help of an AEI study group called the Iraq Planning Group.[67] Miller resurfaced in 2007 as an adjunct fellow, not at the AEI, but at the libertarian Manhattan Institute, hired as a contributing editor to the think-tank's *City Journal* publication. And in 2008 she was hired by Fox News to be an on-air commentator and write stories about the Middle East and terrorism for the Fox web site.

The Heritage Foundation says it is in "the business of changing minds." It was established in 1973 by Republican congressional aides Paul Weyrich and Edwin Feulner. Money flowed into the organization's coffers from wealthy conservative business people, such as Joseph Coors and Richard Mellon Scaife, and from direct-mail fundraising. Heritage quickly became, and continues to be, the largest and best-funded think-tank in the world, with 2006 expenditures of $40.5 million and a staff of two hundred. The secret to Heritage's success is what founder and president Edwin Feulner calls "the four Ms: mission, money, management and marketing."[68] Heritage produces conservative books, monographs, newsletters, policy papers and reviews of domestic and foreign issues. Two-fifths of its budget is directed at public relations, lobbying and education, making these activities a top priority. Its short papers are marketed expertly to their target audience: 8,000 political decision makers, including every member of Congress, 1,200 congressional staffers (sorted by expertise), 900 members of the executive branch and 3,500 journalists. These papers must meet the "brief-case test." They must be succinct enough to be read in the time it takes for someone to be driven from Washington National Airport to a congressional committee hearing on Capitol Hill—about twenty minutes.[69] Heritage sends condensed versions of its views to 95 percent of the nation's daily and weekly newspapers, many of which buy the full versions. The authors of the papers are encouraged to turn them into op-ed articles for major publications like the *New York Times*, the *Washington Post* and the *Wall Street Journal*.[70]

Heritage's finest moment was the Reagan presidency and it provided eleven members of the transition team. Within a week of Reagan's victory, Feulner delivered a thousand-page volume to transition-team head Ed Meese, Reagan's chief of staff (and later Attorney General, and later still, a Heritage senior fellow). Entitled *Mandate for Leadership*, this tome contained two thousand recommendations to serve as a "blueprint for the construction of a conservative government."[71] The publication provided detailed guides on tax and spending cuts and deregulation. By grabbing visible leadership in the war of ideas, Heritage positioned itself as the major player in national policy setting.

The foundation issued a follow-up report entitled *The First Year*, which claimed that about 60 percent of the initial report's recommendations had been implemented, at least in part.[72] Among these was the infamous 1981 tax cut, which introduced the world to supply-side economics and created the greatest deficit of all time, at least until the Obama presidency. Heritage also recommended the Star Wars, spaced-based defence system, which turned out to be a dismal failure. The day after Reagan was re-elected he received *Mandate for Leadership II*, with an additional 1,300 policy recommendations for the continuation of the "Reagan Revolution."

Heritage succeeded because of its big-tent approach to policy. "All kinds of conservatives have a home at The Heritage Foundation," the annual report says. "Traditional conservatives, economic conservatives, fusionists, libertarians, social conservatives, fiscal hawks—all are welcome here."[73] Heritage makes no bones about its mission—to marshal the facts on behalf of the cause. Its function is advocacy and not academic research. After Heritage concluded a successful $30-million-dollar fundraising campaign, Reagan addressed the celebration crowd, praising their efforts as both a reflection and a cause of the "revolution in ideas occurring throughout the world."[74]

No individual understood the inner workings of the reactionary counter-thrust better than William Simon, a long-time Heritage board member. Simon took up the torch from Lewis Powell and became, along with his sometimes partner Irving Kristol, a leading representative of moneyed interests in encouraging business to wage its war of ideas against social and economic citizenship. When he died, Simon was lauded by *National Review Online* as a "hero of the revolution." In an interview with that publication, Heritage president Ed Feulner credits Simon for suggesting Heritage publish its *Mandate for Leadership*, "which," Feulner noted, "really put Heritage on the map."[75] Simon was a partner in the Salomon Brothers Wall Street investment house before going into politics in the early seventies. He was Nixon's energy czar, and then treasury secretary in the Gerald Ford administration. Rather than fight each piece of legislation as it came up, or spend money electing particular candidates, he argued, business should foster a "counterintelligentsia" in the foundations, universities and media that would regain ideological dominance for business.[76] Simon was well placed in the conservative pantheon as a member of the Hoover Institution's board of overseers and Friedrich Hayek's Mont Pèlerin Society, as well as a Heritage board member.

In 1978, Simon teamed up with Irving Kristol to found the Institute for Educational Affairs and actualize the fourth plank in Lewis Powell's program: to recapture institutions of higher learning from the "liberals, socialists and Marxists." The institute accomplished this by linking corporate funders with sympathetic scholars. According to the progressive organization People for the American Way, the institute "sought out promising Ph.D. candidates and undergraduate leaders, [helped] them to establish themselves through grants and fellowships and then [helped] them get jobs with activist organizations, research projects, student publications, federal agencies, or leading periodicals."[77] Two years later, Simon was appointed president of the Olin Foundation, where he could exert more direct influence over the direction of the counter-revolution.

Dozens of think-tanks based on the AEI, Cato and Heritage models were established in the United States during the seventies and eighties, as business took control of the federal agenda. While Washington was being largely pacified, business turned its guns on state and local governments. It needed to change local opinion about issues such as economic and environmental regulation, where the states and even cities play a big role. By the mid-nineties, the country was saturated with business-backed think-tanks, mostly with a libertarian orientation. Most states had one, some states, several. Colorado had the Centre for the New West and the Independence Institute; Illinois, the Rockford Institute and Heartland Institute; New York, the Manhattan Institute and Empire Foundation for Policy Research. These organizations repackage propaganda for local target audiences. They "publish reports advocating deregulation, privatization, property rights, school choice and a few other topics. And each produces reports that sound the same as others," explains Marquette University communication professor Lawrence Soley.[78]

> Between 1994 and 1996, the Washington Institute released *State Government Privatization*, the Mackinac Center released *Privatization Opportunities for States* . . . the Georgia Public Policy Foundation released *Privatization: Dispelling Myths*, the Commonwealth Foundation for Public Policy Alternatives in Pennsylvania released *Privatization of Government Services in Pennsylvania*, and the Wisconsin Policy Research Institute released *The Privatization of Milwaukee County's Airport, Private Tollways for Wisconsin*, and *Privatizing Welfare in Brown County, Wisconsin.*

Each report, Soley notes, "describes the advantages of replacing government-provided services with private enterprise." They are released and promoted as though they are social scientific research, but they have "very little" in common with "real research."[79]

The Heritage Foundation and the rest of the corporate propaganda system require a steady flow of funds to achieve their goals. Most money comes from businesses and conservative philanthropic foundations. In addition, some think-tanks such as Heritage depend on direct-mail donations from thousands of individuals. Nevertheless, a few conservative foundations set the agenda for reactionary propaganda. The National Committee on Responsive Philanthropy (NCRP) examined grants made by conservative foundations to conservative think-tanks between 1999 and 2001. It found that seventy-nine foundations made grants worth $250 million over the three years, but five foundations provided half the funding. These were Sarah Scaife, Lynde and Harry Bradley, John M. Olin (led by William Simon until 2000), Shelby Cullom Davis and Richard and Helen DeVos. They shape policy by financing think-tanks that promote an anti-government, unregulated-market agenda.[80] Political scientist

Anne Norton, a former Straussian, says that some foundations—Olin, Scaife, Bradley and Earhart—prefer students of Strauss in their grant-making.

> They fund fellowships and internships for graduate students, post-doctoral fellowships and fellowships for senior scholars. There are book subsidies, honoraria, fellowships designed to give young conservative scholars time to write, fellowships reserved for conservative scholarship and the advancement of conservative ideas, and subsidies offered to presses—and student newspapers—to represent the "conservative point of view." They provide research funds, book subsidies and money for conferences.[81]

Richard Mellon Scaife led conservative grant-making with $44.8 million donated between 1999 and 2001 through the Sarah Scaife Foundation, plus another $5.8 million through his Carthage Foundation. A *Washington Post* profile of Scaife in 1999 found that he and his charitable foundations had given $340 million to conservative causes and institutions—about $620 million in current dollars, adjusted for inflation.[82] Scaife comes from a fifth-generation Pittsburgh blue-blooded family. His mother, Sarah Mellon Scaife, was judged to be among the eight wealthiest Americans by *Fortune* magazine in 1957. She was a Mellon, whose enormous wealth was based on holdings in Gulf Oil, Alcoa and Mellon Bank. Son Richard administers her foundation as well as his own, plus Carthage. *Forbes* estimated his personal fortune in 2006 at $1.2 billion.

With his aggressive grant-making, Scaife set much of the agenda of political and public debate in the United States and, as an early funder of the Fraser Institute, in Canada, as well. His participation in the discussions that led to the think-tank-foundation-intellectual system is revered by the right. "The victories we're celebrating today didn't begin last Tuesday," Heritage president Ed Feulner told supporters in 1994, after Republicans swept the House of Representatives. "They started more than 20 years ago when Dick Scaife had the vision to see the need for a conservative intellectual movement in America . . . These organizations built the intellectual case that was necessary before political leaders like Newt Gingrich could translate their ideas into practical political alternatives." Gingrich, who would become a senior fellow at the American Enterprise Institute and a visiting fellow at the Hoover Institution, was at the meeting and hailed Scaife as "a good friend and ally for a very long time."[83] Over the years, Scaife donated nearly $20 million to Heritage, more than double the amount he contributed to any other organization. Scaife poured more than $6 million into the shadowy campaign to bring down Bill Clinton, which Hillary Clinton accurately labelled as a "vast right-wing conspiracy."[84]

The Lynde and Harry Bradley Foundation was created after the profitable sale by the Bradley brothers of their Allen-Bradley Co. to Rockwell International in 1985. In the three years of the NCRP study, the foundation gave $35 million to conservative organizations. In its twenty-two years of existence, Bradley gave away $600 million, but in 2006 still had assets of $850 million. Bradley made the support of conservative books a priority, financing more than four hundred, including Charles Murray's controversial best-sellers *Losing Ground* and *The Bell Curve*. Says Bradley president Michael Joyce, who was groomed for his job by William Simon: "We have the conviction that most of the other media are derivative from books. Books are the way that authors put forth more substantial, more coherent arguments. It follows, that if you want to have an influence on the world of ideas, books are where you want to put your money. It is what we are most proud of, of all the things we've done here."[85] Bradley put up $3.5 million to start its own publishing arm to ensure that books with a right-wing slant do get published. It skimps on advances, but spends mightily on publicity. If a book takes off, profits are split, with a high royalty rate for the author and more investment funds for the publishing house.

John Olin's fortune came from his holdings in pharmaceuticals (Olin Chemical) and the Winchester Group, which manufactures rifles and ammunition for the U.S. Department of Defense. William Simon held the post of president until his death in 2000. Simon was a libertarian, but as president of a major grant-making organization, he had to have a broader perspective on the movement. Olin previously directed his foundation's money to anti-union organizations and to educational programs on free enterprise. With Simon running the operation, grant-making was directed towards grantees who could influence debates on national policies.[86] Like Bradley, Olin was a big funder of neoconservative books, such as Abigail and Stephan Thernstrom's anti–affirmative action tome, *America in Black and White: One Nation Indivisible*, and Dinesh D'Souza's best-selling books, *Illiberal Education, The End of Racism* and *Ronald Reagan: How an Ordinary Man Became an Extraordinary Leader*, while he was in residence at the American Enterprise Institute. Olin provided $750,000 to Irving Kristol to start a new neoconservative foreign policy journal, *The National Interest*. Olin supported Straussian scholar Francis Fukuyama's article "The End of History," which was published in *The National Interest* and was later expanded into a well-publicized book.

Over twenty years, Olin handed out $325 million. Its largest think-tank grants went to Heritage ($9 million) and AEI ($7 million), while an even larger amount—$26 million went to conservative scholars at Harvard University (for the Olin Center for Law, Economics and Business, the Institute for Strategic Studies and the Program on Education, Policy and Governance). Another $21 million went to the University of Chicago, where for two decades Olin financed the Center for Inquiry into the Theory and Practice of Democracy.[87] This centre was run by former students of Strauss. One year it made Strauss's book, *Natural Right and History*, a focus of study. The centre closed its doors in 2005. Its final conference considered the question that if the U.S. is becoming a worldwide empire, can it still have freedom at home, a topic of great theoretical and practical interest to the Straussians.[88]

John Olin died in 1982. He wanted to ensure that all the money in the foundation's vault would be spent on conservative causes before the foundation could be taken over by hostile, liberal forces, as he believed the Ford Foundation had been. That day came in 2005, when the trustees—still staunch conservatives—doled out the last $20 million and the Olin Foundation closed its doors. But neoconservatives and libertarians weren't worried. By 2005, dozens of similar foundations had sprung up to continue funding for the reaction. As the National Committee for Responsive Philanthropy's survey discovered, more than forty foundations gave at least a million dollars to conservative causes between 1999 and 2001. Olin is gone, but Scaife, Bradley and the rest continue to provide a steady—and increasing—flow of funds for pro-business propaganda.[89]

The NCRP also examined the sophisticated funding strategy used by these foundations. Most grants had a political purpose, the study found. The foundations single out and support aggressive and entrepreneurial organizations committed to cutting the role of government, privatizing services, deregulating industry and the environment, and devolving authority from the federal to the state level. They bolster the strength of those organizations by providing general operating funds, as well as specific project funding. This allows groups considerable flexibility in attracting, training and keeping talented people, and launching special projects.[90]

The NCRP study observed that the foundations emphasize marketing, funding grant recipients to flood the media and political marketplaces with conservative policy ideas and to communicate with and mobilize their constituency base on behalf of those ideas. They encourage networking with other groups around a common agenda and they make long-term funding commitments, providing large grants over years and even decades. Finally, they concentrate their grants—18 percent of grantees received 75 percent of the funding. The consequence is that some think-tanks became effective in taking the political offensive on key issues over prolonged periods. The Cato Institute started advocating for social security privatization as early as 1983. In 1995, the institute launched its Project on Social Security Privatization and spent millions of dollars on a public relations campaign depicting social security as being in a state of crisis and saying that it could be rescued only by significant reform (privatization). Cato published more than thirty papers on the subject. In 2002, the institute changed the name to Project on Social Security Choice. By altering the name, Cato made an unpopular policy choice—destroying a staple of the New Deal—seem more palatable.[91] Cato received funding over twenty years largely from Bradley and Olin for this work. Finally, social security privatization burst onto the political agenda in the early years of the George W. Bush presidency.[92]

By the turn of the century, Irving Kristol was too old to continue leading the reaction, but his son William stepped ably to the plate. He is a Straussian too, taught by two Straussians. William is editor of Rupert Murdoch's *Weekly Standard*, a basic reference for neoconservatives. He was chairman of the Project for a New American Century, which promoted a program for global U.S. military dominance. William's mother, Gertrude Himmelfarb, is another famous neoconservative, whose studies of Victorian England inspired Bush's "compassionate conservatism," signalling a return to nineteenth-century England.

Thanks to the successes of the corporate propaganda machine, it no longer seems to matter who wins elections. The issues discussed and the range of opinions considered legitimate will be a far cry from the issues on the public agenda in Ralph Nader's heyday. For that, business and the wealthy can thank Lewis Powell for providing a blueprint for regaining control. And it's not over yet. True, the conservatives lost control of the White House and Congress in 2008. And President Barack Obama was taking his advice from the centrist Center for American Progress, headed by John Podesta, former chief of staff to President Bill Clinton, and not from AEI or Heritage. And most think-tanks, of the left, right and centre, took big hits after the financial and economic meltdowns forced foundations and corporations to slow the flow of funds. But the basic structure envisioned by Lewis Powell is still in place. University and college campuses are populated by well-funded Straussian and libertarian academics, with many more on the way. Corporate media have shifted sharply—and perhaps permanently—to the right. The courts are stacked with conservative, business-friendly judges, and a generation of conservative politicians is regrouping to regain control of the levers of power. And as they deployed dozens of conservative think-tanks across the U.S., they spread their efforts to countries around the world. Canada was one of the first to adopt the Powell propaganda approach.

CHAPTER 4

Building the Infrastructure:
the 1970s and 1980s

> The purpose of the conservative movement is to change public opinion
> and public policy, not solely to elect a party to office with a particular name.
> Much has already been achieved and can be advanced further by working on
> public opinion and pressuring the governing Liberal party.
> —Tom Flanagan and Stephen Harper

The Fraser Institute, based in Vancouver, held its thirtieth-anniversary gala celebration in Calgary, signifying the importance over the years of the Alberta oil patch's support. The scene was the glitzy Imperial Ballroom at the Hyatt Regency, where 1,200 adoring libertarians and conservatives paid $275 each—or $600 for a seat at the VIP table—to hear conservative politicians Ralph Klein, Stephen Harper, Mike Harris and Preston Manning pay tribute to the Fraser Institute for its success in pushing Canada's political agenda to the right.

Calgary Herald editorial writer Danielle Smith emceed the evening, introducing Alberta premier Ralph Klein as the Fraser Institute's "teacher's pet," for adopting so many of its ideas.[1] The institute showed its appreciation of his slash-and-burn approach to governance by creating an award for him, the International Fiscal Performance Award and appointing him a senior fellow after his retirement from active politics. Conservative Party leader Stephen Harper was next. He had sent his wife, Laureen Teskey, and Tory MP Peter MacKay to fill in for him, having chosen to remain in Ottawa, opting to convey his remarks by videotape. In his address, Harper showed off his $45 Fraser Institute silk Adam Smith tie and confirmed he was a big fan of the institute.[2]

It's appropriate that Tom Flanagan followed Harper, because he worked behind the scenes to help Harper consolidate his grip on the conservative right. Flanagan is a University of Calgary political scientist and Fraser Institute senior fellow who was Harper's closest adviser at the time. He leads the so-called Calgary School and is best known for his book *First Nations? Second Thoughts.* Then followed tributes from two more Fraser senior fellows, former Reform Party leader Preston Manning and Mike Harris, former premier of Ontario. Manning said he was influenced by the institute when he was building the Reform Party in the 1980s.[3] And Mike Harris concluded the evening with a lamentation that he should have gone further and faster in Ontario with Fraser Institute ideas. Health care should be privatized, he urged his audience. "We waste more money in health care, probably, than the delivery of any other program. It's consuming more and more and more of government dollars, whether they're federal or provincial, and the only reform I've seen is give it more money,"[4] Harris concluded.

The Fraser Institute's achievements were celebrated, not only in the hotel ballroom, but in the pages of the CanWest Global papers owned by the Asper family. David Asper was a Fraser Institute trustee until he took over as publisher of the *National Post.* The *Calgary Herald's* Danielle Smith is a former Fraser Institute intern. In fact, the *Herald* was a sponsor of the event.[5] Several CanWest papers went over the top in lionizing the Fraser. *The Province* proclaimed that "we're all 'right wing' now" and ended by congratulating the institute for "daring to dissent. May it do so for another 30 years."[6] This editorial was picked up by the *Ottawa Citizen* and the *Windsor Star. National Post* columnist Lorne Gunter reported that "the Fraser Institute is so highly regarded that not only was the room chock block full of prominent provincial and national conservative politicians, organizers, consultants, academics and volunteers, it was also full of financiers of conservative parties and causes." Gunter didn't mention their names.[7]

The thirtieth-anniversary bash is a good place to continue an examination of corporate propaganda in Canada because many elements of the system were on display that night. The location is significant, since the American counterthrust to the welfare state spread into Canada mainly through Alberta, which is more like the American Southwest than the rest of Canada. Calgary, Alberta's chief business centre, has a civic culture that seems to derive from Denver or Houston rather than from another Canadian city. And its principal event—the Stampede—is a celebration of the American rural west and its cowboy culture, fertile ground for anti-government, anti–"special interest" crusades.[8]

Policy entrepreneur Michael Walker brings the elements of the propaganda system together, as the speakers at the anniversary celebration remarked. He served notice that since the institute's ideas of no debt and low taxes were considered mainstream, he would next begin pushing free market reforms in education and health care. The fellows and academics who prepare policy positions were there in full force. So were the financial backers, if anonymous. The corporate media, without whose newspapers and television programs disseminating propaganda is not possible, were in attendance. Leaders of the two most successful conservative provincial governments were present, while the triumvirate most responsible for the Reform Party's radical-conservative policies—Stephen Harper, Preston Manning and Tom Flanagan—were featured speakers. True, Reform never captured government, but its electoral successes forced the Chrétien government to move to the right and adopt Fraser Institute policies, changing the climate of political opinion in Canada.

The theme of the night—celebrating success—was a far cry from the situation faced by business thirty years earlier. In 1974, business people in British Columbia were alarmed. The activist Trudeau government in Ottawa was aggressively promoting participatory democracy and a Just Society through worrisome policies like universal health care, regional development, job creation, environmental protection, expanded social programs and independence from U.S. influence. Also of concern was the New Democratic government of Premier Dave Barrett in Victoria, which also had implemented many controversial measures, such as the Land Commission Act, which froze the conversion of agricultural land to urban uses, and the Residential Tenancy Act, which imposed rent controls, along with other constraints, on the unfettered rights of property owners.[9]

Local business leaders began hatching plots to topple Barrett. *Barron's* magazine referred to B.C. as the "Chile of the north," calling to mind clandestine interventions by the CIA and American government into the country three years earlier. But the propaganda approach was soon settled on. Noranda chairman Alf Powis, who helped organize the Business Council on National Issues (BCNI), felt "what was needed was a think-tank that would re-establish the dominance of free enterprise ideas, the values of the market, and property rights."[10] Powis soon became a Fraser Institute trustee.

Patrick Boyle, a vice-president at forestry giant Macmillan Bloedel (MacBlo), took the lead in developing a plan of action. Boyle had been alerted to the "dangers of socialism" by Csaba Hajdu, a refugee from the Soviet Union's 1956 invasion of Hungary. As a graduate student in economics at the University of Western Ontario, Hajdu shared an office with Michael Walker, a friend of the Chicago School's Milton Friedman, who was studying econometrics and monetary policy. Hajdu went to work for MacBlo after graduation and kept in touch with Walker, who worked at the Bank of Canada and the Department of Finance, pushing the bank to adopt Friedman's conservative monetary policies. Walker was on the same page as Hajdu regarding government's role in the economy—it should get out—and met with Hajdu and Boyle in Vancouver to discuss these issues.[11]

Walker's pitch was based on the approach devised by Friedman and Friedrich Hayek, who both won the Nobel Prize in economics around this time, Hayek in 1974 and Friedman in 1976. The "problems" confronting British Columbia's corporate elite, Walker told them, were similar to those faced by business in other countries. They needed an international institute to promote the ideas of Hayek—Margaret Thatcher's hero—and Friedman—Ronald Reagan's inspiration (or at least the inspiration of the people who thought for him).[12] But they would succeed only if they could get access to corporate boardrooms and the $500,000 a year they estimated would be necessary to run the operation. Several senior corporate executives stepped up to the plate: Jack Clyne, head of MacBlo and Boyle's boss (donated $40,000 the first year); Ian Sinclair, head of Canadian Pacific, and Earle McLaughlin, chairman of the Royal Bank of Canada. Funding wasn't a problem. The institute's first-year budget was $420,000 and it hit the $500,000 mark in the third year, by which time corporations were clamouring to get on board.[13]

They found the international connection in Antony Fisher, head of the IEA in London, England, and brought him to Vancouver, to set up a similar organization in Canada. Fisher was just starting his crusade to blanket the world with libertarian think-tanks. He developed a formula for funding, projects, experts and dissemination that he applied in Vancouver. Fisher had been an RAF fighter pilot in the Second World War. After the war he earned his fortune in the U.K. poultry industry, having created the largest poultry-processing plant in Europe. He later sold his interests for $51 million (about $310 million in 2009 dollars). Fisher had read—and embraced—Hayek's *The Road to Serfdom*, in which Hayek urged reducing government intervention in the economy to a bare minimum. Hayek "warned Americans and Britons about the dangers of expecting government to provide a way out of the economic danger." Fisher recounted Hayek's views in his own book, *Must History Repeat Itself?*, where he wrote that "... the decisive influence in the great battles of ideas and policy was wielded by the intellectuals whom he characterized as the second-hand dealers in ideas."[14] Like most rich people, Fisher believed that capitalism produces more wealth and distributes it more fairly than any amount of government intervention can ever achieve. He was so far to the right that he advocated an end to the government monopoly on postal service and government control over interest rates.

Politics, Fisher thought, might be an avenue to promote his ideas. But around the time Hayek was establishing his Mont Pèlerin Society (1947), he advised Fisher instead to set up a scholarly research organization to supply intellectuals in universities, schools, journalism and broadcasting with authoritative studies of free market economics and their application to practical affairs. Fisher liked the idea and obliged by establishing the IEA in Britain in 1955. Fifteen years later, having sold his poultry business, he founded its American twin sister, the International Institute for Economic Research in Los Angeles. Like Irving Kristol and William Simon in the U.S., Fisher saw himself as a catalyst bringing together corporate sponsors and academic spear carriers.

The Fraser Institute founders were determined that their institute be as intellectually respectable as the IEA. It was set up in the same mould; it employed a core group of researchers and engaged like-minded libertarian and conservative academics from Canada and elsewhere to conduct specific studies that would be published in book and report formats, distributed widely and promoted heavily in the media. The institute was named after the nearby Fraser River, aping the New York–based Hudson Institute, another venerable conservative think-tank adjacent to the Hudson River. Fisher set up several other think-tanks at this time, the Manhattan in New York and the Pacific Research Institute in San Francisco.

To further heighten the international and academic cachet of its work, a board of academic advisers was given prominence in institute literature, deliberately overshadowing the board of trustees, which was the real power and the source of the corporate funds behind the organization. With a mandate to oversee the research and editorial activities of the institute, this second publicly visible board consisted of a carefully selected panel of international libertarian and conservative scholars. These included two prominent Canadian economists, Herbert Grubel of Simon Fraser University and Tom Courchene of the

University of Western Ontario. The international scholars included Alan Walters, Margaret Thatcher's economics adviser, and Friedrich Hayek himself. Another adviser was Armen Alchian of the University of California at Los Angeles, who popularized the idea that because humans are rational, self-seeking economic beings, economic principles can be applied to most human activity, appropriate or not. Another scholar on the advisory board was James Buchanan, who founded the public-choice school of economics, which allows little space for government in public affairs.[15]

The Fraser Institute opened its doors in February 1975, with a staff of three economists, including Sally Pipes, formerly with the Council of Forest Industries who later left to head Fisher's Pacific Research Institute. It already had twenty-eight corporate and eight individual members. The members included all five major banks, Canadian Pacific, MacMillan Bloedel, John Labatt and Molson Companies, Jack Poole's Daon Development Corp., Canada Trust, Canada Packers, Kelly Douglas, and Norcen Energy Resources. Two years later corporate memberships had swelled to more than 175, and individual memberships to more than 50. The Fraser made big inroads in the Calgary oil patch, signing up Amoco Canada, Canadian Petroleum Association, Imperial Oil, Oakwood Petroleums, Pacific Petroleums, PanCanadian Petroleum, Ranger Oil, Shell Canada, Siebens Oil and Gas, Texaco Canada, Union Oil and Gas and Voyager Petroleums.[16]

While the Fraser was gearing up to become the first libertarian think-tank north of the Canada–U.S. border, business was establishing additional organizations across the country to address other concerns. Wealthy corporate executives had already established the National Citizens Coalition (NCC) in the late sixties. In Calgary they founded the Canada West Foundation (CWF) to promote western business and financial interests, while Bay Street financiers and CEOs did the same for central Canada by funding the C.D. Howe Institute, which focused on federal government monetary, economic and social policy.

The imposition of wage and price controls in 1975 by the Trudeau government was a powerful signal to business that the decades-long truce with the welfare state was over. Business needed an organization to fight this government intervention in the economy and to take charge of a newly constituted pro-business agenda. The Business Council on National Issues was established within a year. Modelled on the American Business Roundtable, the organization comprised the CEOs of the 150 largest corporations in the country. (A similar organization, the Business Council of Australia, was set up there several years later.) W. O. Twaits, retiring chairman of Imperial Oil, and Noranda president Alf Powis were the first co-chairs. With its deep pockets and political and economic clout, the Business Council on National Issues quickly became Canada's chief treetops organization.[17]

It didn't take long for the Fraser to reach its target budget of $500,000. Most of the money—about 60 percent—came from its corporate members, which were assessed a fee based on the size of their assets, with the largest companies paying up to $15,000 a year. The rest came from conservative American foundations. Early backers included the John M. Olin Foundation and billionaire Richard Mellon Scaife, who was pumping about $10 million a year into reactionary causes in the U.S. Scaife's contributions to the Fraser Institute were not as grandiose as some of his American ones, but they came in the early years, when the Fraser was just getting off the ground.

Michael Walker claimed that the Fraser Institute was outside politics, but observers in Vancouver's business press found it strange that the think-tank's first research projects were hot political issues in B.C.[18] The Fraser's first publication rolled off the press in 1975. It attacked rent controls, with contributions from Walker, Hayek and Friedman. This slim volume was a hasty knock-off of work published earlier by Fisher's IEA, with a new introduction and conclusion by Walker. The second book was to have been a study of the Canadian financial system, focusing on the Barrett government's proposals for a provincially controlled near bank to be called BC Savings and Trust. (It couldn't be a full-fledged bank because it would have to be chartered by the federal government.) Shortly after, the NDP was defeated and the bank study was deep-sixed. It must have been a coincidence that the Fraser tackled issues that would benefit its corporate members, since Walker has steadfastly claimed that the financial backers have no say in determining the institute's research priorities. The institute published about six books on rent controls and land development in the early years of its existence. Its position on rent controls is that they are not needed because there is no housing crisis in Canada. In fact, Canadians are among the best housed people in the world. If some people are poorly housed, the institute argues, there may be a poverty problem (but in other publications the institute claimed there was very little poverty in Canada) and those people should be given a housing subsidy, which would likely go into the landlord's pocket. Coincidentally, it must be assumed, most of the large real estate, land development and construction companies in Canada were members. And regarding the proposed provincial bank book, all Big Five banks (Bank of Montreal, Bank of Nova Scotia, Canadian Imperial Bank of Commerce, Royal Bank of Canada and Toronto-Dominion Bank) were, or soon became, members.

Another part of the formula developed by Fisher was to hold international conferences and publish the papers in book form. Target treetops audiences are academics, policy-makers, elected lawmakers and their advisers, prominent media columnists and business and labour leaders. The electorate, the grassroots target, would find out about the conferences through news reports and book reviews. The institute held its first conference in September 1976. It was part of an audacious scheme by Walker and Simon Fraser University economist Herbert Grubel to undermine government-run employment insurance programs (called "unemployment insurance" until 1996) by claiming they induce unemployment. "Induce" is a slippery word that can range in meaning from "influence" to "cause." Does unemployment insurance cause unemployment or merely influence it? Walker and Grubel didn't say. They revealed the propaganda intent of the conference by writing in the introduction of their book that their goal was to slash unemployment insurance programs. But before that could happen, it was necessary that "the concept of unemployment induced by welfare programs be accepted more widely . . . This book constitutes only an early beginning of this process . . ."[19] The introduction made some astonishing claims. It began by asserting that "in the private insurance industry it has been known for a long time that the incidence of a certain hazard is greater when its victims are insured against losses from it than when they are not."[20] They used the example of restaurant fires and provided a superstructure of graphs, tables and equations, but did not provide the evidence to support their claim that the incidence of restaurant fires increases with increased insurance coverage. In fact, the leading cause of restaurant fires is the ignition of grease or cooking oil. And most restaurant fires result in small or no losses because they are confined to the cooking vessel or extinguished before property damage occurs.[21] Does a restaurant operator let grease build up on her equipment, confident that she can always collect insurance if the place burns down?

Having made the claim that fire insurance leads to more fires, they then applied this principle to what they call "work and leisure trade-offs." They created another superstructure of graphs, tables and equations, basing their work on "casual observation." They equated unemployment with leisure and relied on "stories about 'cheating' by the unemployed," again providing no evidence of such behaviour. They ended up with the dubious concept of "government-induced unemployment," concluding that Canada's unemployment insurance program was too generous and led to inflated jobless rolls.[22]

The conference was sponsored by the Liberty Fund of Indianapolis, Indiana. The goal of this fund, which was established several years earlier by Indianapolis businessman Pierre Goodrich, is to promote individual liberty by sponsoring conferences and publishing books. Presumably, unemployment insurance is an obstacle to the individual's right to be free and self-reliant, just like Goodrich, who happened to inherit a huge fortune (newspapers, telephone and electrical services, banking) from his father and grandfather. The publication of the book resulted in a large number of favourable editorials, columns and reviews. Walker believed the book led to a toughening of unemployment insurance regulations. "The fact that the book was reverberating in all the newspapers across the country must have influenced the government's thinking on unemployment insurance," Walker claimed.[23]

It took several years to iron out the glitches in the formula. On at least one occasion Walker selected academics who submitted articles that weren't pro–free market enough. A book of essays titled *Which Way Ahead? Canada After Wage and Price Controls* was published in response to the federal government's program of wage and price controls and the Anti-Inflation Board. The government had released a document, "The Way Ahead," that outlined the direction it intended to take after the controls ended. In the Fraser book, fourteen of the fifteen economists argued that the government should quickly end general price and income controls, but keep restraints on public sector bargaining. (Keep the wages of public employees tightly controlled, but not those of corporate executives?) The fifteenth economist was James Dean of Simon Fraser University. He called for continued controls on everybody. In his essay, "The case for continued controls (and other heresies)," Dean argued that emergency control programs "have been doomed by their adhoccery and lack of coherence to limited success." What was really needed, he wrote, were controls as part of a "more general framework of governmentally-planned resource allocation."[24] Dean proposed a system of tax-based wage and price controls as the preferred solution to the dual problems of soaring inflation and high unemployment. Unlike the other articles in the book, Dean's was peppered with footnotes from Walker, attacking his arguments. Walker dismissed Dean's proposal as something that was debated in the federal civil service and dropped because it was considered unworkable.[25] But Walker ignored similar proposals made by prominent American economists, such as Walter Heller and James

Tobin—neither neoconservatives nor libertarians—for a tax-based anti-inflationary policy.[26]

Like its libertarian brethren in the U.S., the Fraser Institute relies on the thesis of the perverse effect to attack government programs. As Albert Hirschman explains, reactionaries don't attack a progressive policy head-on. Instead, they endorse the policy and then purport to show the policy will produce, "via a chain of unintended consequences, the exact contrary of the objective being proclaimed and pursued."[27] Employment insurance induces unemployment. Social assistance increases poverty. Rent controls lead to higher housing costs. These actions have the opposite effect to those desired by policy-makers, Fraser economists argue in their many publications attacking social welfare policies. Rent controls restrict the production of new housing, which leads to a deterioration of the existing stock, which leads to less housing being available. Of course, in this case government should step in and build more housing to supplement the controls, but this proposal is not put forward by the evangelists for smaller government.

A 1982 book titled *Discrimination, Affirmative Action, and Equal Opportunity* is a classic exposition of the perverse effect. The preface declares that "... much of the recent 'equal rights' legislation ... while launched in many cases with the best of intentions, will nevertheless create a set of unforeseen consequences which will harm the very minority groups they were designed to help."[28] Hirschman couldn't have said it better. This collection of articles by Walker, Walter Block and other libertarian economists expressed hostility to any type of human rights legislation. Concerns about human rights, the authors argued, should be left to the private sector. The book's unusual thesis was that "the market test of profit and loss ... tends to eliminate from the private sector (through bankruptcy) those who indulge in discriminatory practices."[29] There is nothing wrong with discrimination, Walker and Block claimed. It is "... nothing more than the expression of a preference ... the right to discriminate is a desirable feature of free societies." But this distorts what happens in the workplace, where discrimination can be crucial because employers can profit from discrimination by paying lower wages to women and minorities.[30]

The book did admit that women earn less than men, but claimed this was due to marital status and not sex discrimination. Marriage improves wages for men and reduces them for women, Walker said in an interview on the book's release. "A comparison of the incomes of never-married Canadian men and women reveals that women are paid, on the average, 99.2 per cent of the male salary," he told the *Vancouver Sun*.[31] This claim is misleading, though, because never-married women are older than never-married men and should earn more. When challenged about this distortion of the data, Walker replied, "Sure our statistic was misleading but so are all the others on sexual income inequalities which get thrown around unchallenged, and which is the point we wanted to make."[32] But, confession aside, Walker and Block continued to claim that the difference between male and female incomes was due to marriage and not discrimination. A column they wrote in the *Globe and Mail* in 1985 was headlined "Marriage key to gap in wages."[33] They argued that women earn less, not because of discrimination by employers, but because they chose to get married—individual choice. It was a rare opportunity to observe how "lies, damn lies and statistics" merge in the Fraser's work.

The National Citizens Coalition wasn't on the agenda for the Fraser's thirtieth-anniversary celebration, but its influence was everywhere in the Imperial Ballroom that night. Stephen Harper had been NCC president prior to his return to politics. Klein, Harris, Walker and Harper were all winners of the NCC's Colin M. Brown Freedom Medal that honours individuals who make outstanding contributions to "the advancement or defence of political and economic freedom." Preston Manning hadn't received the award—he would win it in 2008—but his father, Ernest, was an NCC founder and remained on the advisory council for many years. During the 1970s and '80s, the NCC and the Fraser Institute together promoted the corporate agenda and helped propel it to the top of the political agenda.

Colin M. Brown was an insurance salesman who became a millionaire in London, Ontario. He was a long-time Tory, but believed John Diefenbaker and Robert Stanfield were socialists, demonstrating his far-right credentials. Two events occurred in 1967 that sparked Brown into action. Stanfield was elected Tory leader and the federal Liberal government proposed a universal health care service. Brown later said he knew "what would happen to a universal, government-run plan, because I was in the insurance business and I had studied how the plan worked in Britain."[34] He placed a full-page ad in the *Globe and Mail* condemning the government and encouraging people to send in donations for more ads. Brown formed the NCC and went on to fight for the full range of libertarian and social conservative policies under his motto "more freedom through less government." Reform Party historian Trevor Harrison presents one NCC wish list: smaller government, more restrictive immigration laws, reduced social programs like pensions and welfare, balanced budgets, deregulation, right-to-work laws, privatized health care and "an end to public insurance, bilingualism and multiculturalism."[35]

At the urging of Ernest Manning, in 1975. Brown transformed the NCC into a non-profit organization without charitable tax status, funded by unnamed corporate and individual donors. Because the organization wasn't registered as a charity, businesses couldn't write off their contributions as charitable donations, but they could still deduct them as business expenses. Taxpayers ended up subsidizing the organization because fewer tax dollars flowed into government coffers as a result of the deductions. "Businesses are much more able to make their views heard with deductible tax dollars than are individuals," tax lawyer Arthur Drache wrote in the *Financial Post*. This allows lobby groups with purely political aims such as the NCC "to operate on handsome budgets" far beyond the wildest dreams of most charitable organizations, which cannot engage in political activities.[36] Brown said he based the NCC on American organizations such as the Heritage Foundation and the Conservative Opportunities Society, an organization of congressional Republicans founded by Newt Gingrich to topple the Democratic majority. Brown read *Trudeau Revealed*, a so-called exposé of Trudeau's alleged plan to turn Canada into a one-party socialist state, written by former *Toronto Sun* reporter David Somerville. Brown liked it so much he offered Somerville a job as vice-president and chief spokesperson of the NCC. Somerville became the public face of the organization, orchestrating its legal battles.[37] Key was its victory in the 1984 court challenge to government changes to the federal Elections Act to restrict third-party advertising during elections. The NCC spent hundreds of thousands of dollars to influence the outcomes of the 1984 and 1988 elections.

The Fraser Institute and the National Citizens Coalition grew in size and output during the 1970s, but expanding their audience remained a challenge. In 1974 a weekly magazine—the *Alberta Report*—emerged as "chief disseminator of neo-conservative ideology" in western Canada, according to Trevor Harrison.[38] "More than anyone [*Alberta Report*] has amended the views of this province," enthused long-time Conservative political consultant and journalist Ralph Hedlin at the magazine's twenty-fifth anniversary bash held at

Edmonton's Fantasyland Hotel.[39] The *Alberta Report* was the creation of Ted Byfield, who started as a copy boy at the *Washington Post* and became a reporter and editor for the *Ottawa Journal*, *Timmins Daily Press* and *Winnipeg Free Press*. In the late fifties, Byfield and parishioners at St. John's Cathedral in Winnipeg formed St. John's Cathedral Boys' School in Selkirk, Manitoba, for problem boys. The school was conservative and emphasized discipline.

In 1962, Byfield left the newspaper business to become a history teacher at the school. A second school opened in Genesee, Alberta, just west of Edmonton. He was concerned about the feeble attempts of conservative Christian churches to become socially relevant and influence the political agenda. The year before the Fraser Institute was launched, he convinced other members of the Genesee board to begin publishing a weekly newsmagazine, the *St. John's Edmonton Report*, which was modelled on *Time* magazine. This was followed in 1974 by *St. John's Calgary Report*. The two later merged into the *Alberta Report* to save money and to remove the publication from church control. Circulation peaked at 60,000 in 1984, the year of intense western loathing for Trudeau's National Energy Program (NEP), and great triumphs by the Fraser Institute and the NCC. An identical but renamed version of the *Alberta Report*—the *Western Report*—was created for distribution in the other western provinces. This venture failed and was followed by the *BC Report*. Meanwhile, the *Alberta Report* had begun to suffer declining circulation and was placed in receivership. Byfield did find two angels to rescue the magazine: John Scrymgeour, a Fraser Institute trustee and oil patch veteran who had retired to Bermuda, and Don Graves, a Calgary businessman and former oil executive. The three magazines attained a combined paid circulation of about 62,000, but spiralled into another decline and ceased publication in 2003, the year the *Alberta Report* would have celebrated its thirtieth birthday.

The *Alberta Report* "stood firmly for corporal and capital punishment, the teaching of fundamentalist Christian religion in schools, the rights of the family (that is, the parents), and free enterprise," Harrison writes.[40] It opposed the sanctioning of special interests like feminists, homosexuals, unions and human rights commissions. It scorned most government social and cultural programs and agencies, such as the CBC, the Foreign Investment Review Agency (FIRA), the National Energy Program, much of public school curriculum and methods of discipline, and public ownership of anything. It showered contempt on moral "failings" like abortion, divorce and sex education. The business community by and large embraced the *Alberta Report*'s pro-business, anti-government

views, but shied away from supporting Byfield's stultifying moral conservatism. Nonetheless, he was applauded by the conservative establishment on the
twenty-fifth anniversary of the magazine, receiving the NCC's Colin M. Brown
Freedom Medal and congratulations from the likes of Ralph Klein, Preston
Manning and Mike Harris.

Not only did Byfield use his magazine to preach conservative Christian
values across the West, the *Report* served as a training ground for conservative
and libertarian journalists who would later find their way into the corporate
media. Byfield's star graduate is undoubtedly Ken Whyte, whom he hired from
the *Sherwood Park News* and soon promoted to executive editor. Whyte later
joined Conrad Black's *Saturday Night* and became editor there before being
moved by Black to the position of editor-in-chief of Black's new conservative
daily, the *National Post*. Whyte worked there five years, before departing in 2003.
Two years later he caught the eye of conservative billionaire Ted Rogers, who
appointed him editor-in-chief and publisher of *Maclean's*. Other *Report* graduates
include Brian Bergman (*Maclean's*), Dunnery Best (*Financial Times*), Lorne Gunter
(*Edmonton Journal*), John Robson (*Ottawa Citizen*) and Colby Cosh (*National
Post*). *Alberta Report* may be gone, but its influence will live on for years.

When the magazine folded, corporate media were reluctant to criticize this
far-right ideological attack dog. The *Edmonton Journal* called the ending "a little sad." The *Globe and Mail* opined that "at its best, the Report was indeed a
superb preacher. It will be missed." "Nobody who loves democracy . . . will welcome the demise of Alberta Report," wrote the *Vancouver Sun* of a magazine
that was profoundly intolerant. "It's going to be a lot duller around here without that pesky magazine," wrote a former *Alberta Report* editor in the *National
Post*.[41] The dullness lasted less than a year. Into the vacuum stepped Reform
Party stalwart and former Fraser intern Ezra Levant, who launched another
libertarian-neoconservative magazine, the *Western Standard*. This publication
was modelled on the *American Standard*, which was founded by Straussian
William Kristol, but lacked Kristol's intellectual heft. Some *Alberta Report* regu-
lars went to work for Levant and his corporate backers, until this magazine
ceased its print edition in 2007, becoming an online publication only. *Western
Standard* subscribers who lost their subscriptions were given six free issues of
Maclean's, which, under Whyte's tutelage, was becoming just as pesky.

"Despite its increased media prominence, corporate support, and general social respectability, neo-conservative ideology began the 1980s lacking direct access to federal decision-making," Trevor Harrison observes.[42] This would soon change. In British Columbia and Saskatchewan, re-elected conservative governments were advised by the Fraser Institute and its allies to implement wide-ranging libertarian policies in the blitzkrieg fashion advised by Walker's ally Milton Friedman, fresh from his triumph in Pinochet's Chile. Later in the decade, western corporate interests would coalesce around the Canada West Foundation, Preston Manning and his Calgary School advisers to promote neoconservative and libertarian ideas in Ottawa.

In 1979, the B.C. Social Credit Party, led by Bill Bennett, won its second election in a row over Dave Barrett's New Democrats. The province's recession was just underway. Bennett's re-election strategy was based in part on privatizing resource assets previously acquired by the NDP government. He created the B.C. Resources Investment Corp. (BCRIC) and offered five free shares to every resident. In 1977, the Fraser Institute had published *Friedman on Galbraith, and on Curing the British Disease*, a slim volume of essays based on lectures delivered by Friedman in England. Friedman discusses methods for turning over public assets to the private sector. Instead of auctioning them off, he suggests "giving every citizen in the country a share" of the assets.[43] Emboldened by this success, in 1980 the Fraser Institute published another book, *Privatization: Theory and Practice*, which chronicled the BCRIC wheeling and dealing—Howe Street backers of the Bennett government and of the Fraser Institute made millions of dollars from the privatization—and proposed further forays.

As Social Credit (Socred) fortunes waned during the deep recession of the early eighties, Bennett's political advisers decided on a marketing strategy that would present Bennett as a "tough guy" who would straighten out B.C.'s economic problems. Bennett's chief adviser for this campaign was Patrick Kinsella, who came to the province fresh from leading Bill Davis and the Ontario Tories to victory in 1981. The tough-guy image was based on Kinsella's assessment that it would market well with B.C. voters. It would be crucial in justifying the flurry of activity that would follow the anticipated election victory. It would also mirror the tough, take-no-prisoners tactic Reagan used against striking air-traffic controllers. In a talk to university marketing students, Kinsella admitted he was "involved quite a bit with the Republican Party." As an Ontario Conservative official, he "went to candidate schools and candidate colleges . . . that the Republican Party puts on a regular basis," he told the students. "Frankly, I stole all of their ideas. If something works, you steal it and see if you can employ it in your own way, for us."[44]

Bennett positioned himself for the upcoming election by imposing a curb on public sector wages and a freeze on government spending. The economy continued to crumble. The election was set for May 5, 1983. During the campaign, Bennett had promised that, if re-elected, he would be the tough guy who could make the tough decisions the province needed. Kinsella was assisted by pollster Allan Gregg of Decima Research, who claimed his polling techniques could find out, not only what people were thinking, but could also determine under which conditions people would accept change that their values would otherwise cause them to reject. Decima, Kinsella told the students, believes you can take poll results ". . . and we can change your mind. We can move you to do something that you may not have agreed on is a logical thing to do . . . We can move you from one side of the ledger to another."[45]

The tough-guy strategy worked to perfection. Bennett won the election with an increased majority. Three weeks later, the new cabinet met with Michael Walker at a posh lakeside resort in the Okanagan Valley for a crucial strategy session. Walker had been a featured speaker at the 1982 Social Credit convention in Vancouver and had already met with the premier and members of his cabinet about half a dozen times. He brought Milton Friedman with him on one occasion and introduced him to Bennett, just like the Chicago Boys had introduced Friedman to Pinochet a few years earlier. Walker recommended a strategy based on the government selecting a level of service it had provided in a previous year. Government spending was lower in previous years because the population was smaller and inflated dollars worth less, so this would automatically translate into cuts in programs and services for the larger population. The recommendation became the basic formula for the hundreds of programs run by the government. Government administrators were told to "make do" by adhering to a previous year's financing level.[46] Six weeks later, Bennett's government introduced a torrent of legislation proposing to centralize power, slash spending on social and health services and education, lay off thousands of public sector workers and reduce the bargaining rights of those who remained, abolish rent controls and the Human Rights Commission, and introduce many other initiatives whose cumulative goal was to roll back the province's social and economic gains. Directed by Walker and Friedman, the Socreds set about to make British Columbia ground zero for libertarian ideology in Canada.

Bennett and Walker referred to the budget legislation as a blueprint for economic recovery. As *Province* reporter Barbara McLintock noted, however, "the budget was not an economic document at all, but purely a political one."[47] Bennett, she wrote, was "setting out to be Canada's cross between Ronald Reagan and Margaret Thatcher." Bennett was "moving his government as far as possible away from the welfare state and back to a purer era of free-enterprise capitalism." She itemized her charge:

- Public sector employers could lay off workers for any reason at all. Walker called the provision for "termination without cause" a "giant step in government taking charge of its own house." It reminded him of "the kind of single-mindedness Ronald Reagan displayed in dealing with the air traffic controllers."
- Landlords could evict their tenants without any reason and thus without any recourse.
- Regional governments could no longer regulate developers.
- Homosexuals would lose their protection under human rights laws.
- Individuals would be responsible for ensuring their cars were safe.

Public reaction to the budget was immediate. One political analyst commented that "it was remarkable how many different groups the government managed to offend at once."[48] Four days after the legislation was introduced, a coalition of groups—called the Solidarity Coalition—was formed to fight the legislation. Despite several mass demonstrations and escalating job actions by unions, however, the opposition eventually crumbled. "Largely unopposed, Bennett pressed ahead with the agenda set out by the Fraser Institute," wrote Trevor Harrison. "In 1984, more bills were passed that severely restricted union powers and otherwise shifted power away from the socially disadvantaged."[49]

To signal that the counter-revolution had only just begun, Walker told a Toronto meeting of the Fraser Institute that he was disappointed the budget lacked restraint. Government spending, he lamented, had increased by 12 percent because of mandated health and welfare costs. He was exhilarated, however, because the government's tough-guy showdown with the unions proved the pendulum was swinging—finally—back in the direction of the private sector.[50] The same year Walker hosted a regional meeting of Hayek's Mont Pèlerin Society. From their perches in a downtown luxury hotel, hundreds of libertarian economists from around the world who had flocked to the city, heaped withering scorn on the unions and other "special interest" groups that had taken to the streets to protest the Walker-Bennett budget.

The theme of Bennett's "budget" legislation could be found in the Fraser Institute book *Discrimination, Affirmative Action and Equal Opportunity*, discussed on page 127. Bennett's attacks on public sector workers were previewed in another institute book, *Unions and the Public Interest*, which recommended that

> public employment can be cut directly when public employees become too expensive, either by automating their functions or contracting them out to companies in the private sector. When advantageous, the public employer should be free to accomplish this cut in public employment by layoffs, rather than having to rely on attrition alone.[51]

The Bennett government's abolition of rent controls—allowing rents and landlord profits to rise—also had its roots in Fraser Institute publications. Walker "rejoiced" when the Socred government announced the abolition of rent controls as part of its cutback program. He congratulated the government for having the "foresight and political courage to abandon this form of intervention."[52] Since he had invested so many of the institute's resources in anti–rent control, anti–housing regulation propaganda, this was a high-profile win. His success in British Columbia sparked landlords from Quebec and other provinces to meet with him seeking advice on how to end rent controls in their jurisdictions.[53] It was also a high-profile victory for corporate power and propaganda and a significant setback in the movement for social and economic rights that had commenced in the post–Second World War era.

Grant Devine's Conservative government in Saskatchewan was next to promote a pro-business agenda, especially during its second term of office. Like the Bennett government, it downsized government programs and services, but its main claim to fame was its privatization program, which transferred many public assets to private hands, often the hands of government friends. Michael Walker didn't directly advise the Devine cabinet the way he did in British Columbia. But the Fraser Institute held a major conference on privatization which was attended by a throng of Saskatchewan government ministers and policy advisers. And the Saskatchewan Conservatives received advice on privatization from two Margaret Thatcher advisers invited to Canada by the Fraser Institute and the National Citizens Coalition. At the same time, Saskatchewan business leaders set up their own think-tank in the mould of the Fraser to direct and justify Devine's privatization initiatives.

Grant Devine rode into power in 1982 using a formula that would be refined by Preston Manning: combine a populist theme—"we need a government that cares about people"—with a corporate, conservative theme—"government is too big"—and roll these into one message in which the populist theme predominates—"there is so much more we can be," University of Regina historian James Pitsula and political scientist Kenneth Rasmussen wrote in their history of the Devine years.[54] But the action was on the business side of the ledger— cut government, deregulate business and let the people look out for themselves. Using Decima Research, the same pollsters employed by Bill Bennett, Devine won a sweeping victory in 1982.[55] Like Thatcher and Bennett, he did little in his first mandate to implement the business agenda. By the time of the next election, however, Devine was slipping badly in public opinion polls mainly because of a declining farm economy.

Devine was able to cajole massive farm aid from his friend Brian Mulroney to help squeeze back into office in 1986. The New Democrats lost the election on the day—halfway through the campaign—Mulroney announced his government would provide $1 billion in assistance to western farmers. Almost overnight the point spread between the Tories and New Democrats in rural ridings jumped from 3 to 13 percent. On election day, the NDP won more votes, but the Tories won the majority of seats, sweeping Saskatchewan's rural ridings, thanks to Mulroney's favour.[56]

Privatizing Saskatchewan's vast array of Crown corporations was not raised as an issue during the campaign, which was about building the province and diversifying the economy, standard fare in Saskatchewan elections. If Devine was planning a massive sell-off of Saskatchewan's Crown corporations, he would have to move cautiously because they remained popular in a province where social democrats had reigned almost uninterrupted since the 1940s. Another non-issue was the state of the province's finances. But once the election was over, Devine was able to use a newly discovered dismal state of the budget to win support for privatization. Before the election, the projected budget deficit was said to be under $400 million. During the election, Devine admitted it might be as high as $500 million. But after the election, the projected deficit ballooned to nearly $1.3 billion, the largest ever recorded in the province.

Drastic measures would be needed, Devine warned the people, to prevent the province's finances from spiralling out of control.[57] Was this a plot, as NDP leader Allan Blakeney charged, to run up a huge debt in the first term and use it as an excuse to cut services and sell assets in the second? Support for this view could have been found a year before the election, when a group of prominent Saskatchewan Tories visited Britain to study how the Thatcher government privatized the telephone company.[58] Whether contrived or not, Devine used the deficit to slash spending, fire thousands of government workers and privatize Crown corporations.

The government moved quickly on its downsizing program, in the blitz-krieg fashion recommended by Milton Friedman and implemented by Bill Bennett and also by the Labour government of New Zealand. It lopped $800 million from expenditures and mounted a comprehensive attack on the welfare state by going after the so-called "special interests" that preoccupy conservatives. These cuts were unpopular, notes then NDP adviser Mark Stobbe, so Devine was receptive to a message from his business backers that privatizing government assets could be sold as good news for the province, diverting public attention from his cuts to spending, programs and jobs.[59]

In July 1987, the Fraser Institute held a major conference on privatization at the Bayshore Inn in Vancouver. Two top Thatcher advisers were big drawing cards: Madsen Pirie was head of the libertarian Adam Smith Institute, and Oliver Letwin, a defeated Tory candidate for the British House of Commons, and later, director of the international privatization unit for N.M. Rothschild Bank. Saskatchewan sent the largest delegation of any government to the conference, larger even than B.C. The roll call of attendees should have been instructive: the minister in charge of Saskatchewan Government Insurance, plus a company vice-president and a political aide; the president of Saskatchewan Housing Corporation; both the chair and president of the Crown Management Board; the chairman of the Potash Corporation of Saskatchewan, a Crown corporation soon to be put on the privatization block; the premier's principal secretary; a cabinet policy analyst and a government policy analyst who would later become research director for the Institute for Saskatchewan Enterprise— all crowded into the conference rooms to pick up tips on how to privatize without provoking a public backlash.[60] Pirie was brought to Regina several months later by the National Citizens Coalition, where he extolled the virtues of privatization to a crowd of 1,200 government and business executives. Dozens of copies of Pirie's paper "The Buying out of Socialism" made the rounds of Saskatchewan's public servants, and tapes of Pirie speeches circulated among members of the Conservative caucus.[61] Pirie and Letwin were soon added to the Devine government payroll.[62]

Later, Philip Fixler, of the libertarian Reason Foundation in Santa Monica, California, spoke to the Regina Chamber of Commerce and the Saskatchewan Urban Municipalities Association. A Reason Foundation specialty was providing arguments for privatizing municipal services. Fixler told his audience that everything should be privatized, including the police force and the fire department. The campaign to hype privatization reached its climax at the Conservative convention in November 1987 when Devine told the delegates that all Crown corporations, except the utilities, were candidates for transfer to the private sector.[63]

While Conservative Party members were onside with the plan, the government had to convince the grassroots that privatization was good for everyone. The government set up a Department of Public Participation to supervise and coordinate all privatization activities. Oliver Letwin was hired as a public-participation consultant at $22,000 a month, to help formulate the government's program and sell it in the province, speaking to groups like the chamber of commerce. Privatization's business and academic supporters met at Regina's exclusive Assiniboia Club in the summer of 1988 to create an "independent" group to study privatization. The meeting led to the creation of the Institute for Saskatchewan Enterprise (ISE), which was loosely modelled on the Fraser Institute. It was given the job of marshalling the evidence to back up the government's privatization claims.[64] ISE's board consisted of a handful of university administrators and a larger contingent of Saskatchewan corporate executives. Like most pro-business groups, the institute billed itself as non-partisan and non-ideological. "It [privatization] is not ideology," ISE chair Roger Phillips, head of the Inter-Provincial Steel Co. (Ipsco), asserted. "It's plain common sense," he said, anticipating the propaganda approach taken by the Mike Harris government in Ontario several years later.[65] Phillips was a long-standing Fraser Institute trustee and espoused the libertarian creed of Milton Friedman. In a speech to the Regina Chamber of Commerce a few days after the election, Phillips proposed the idea that business had no responsibility to society except to create wealth.

One Crown corporation after another was put up for sale. At a Conservative fundraising dinner, Letwin praised the Saskatchewan program as one of the best-planned schemes he had ever seen. Everything was running smoothly with little public opposition.[66] That opposition appeared, explosively, when the government put SaskEnergy, the natural gas division of SaskPower, on the auction block. Since Devine had promised not to privatize any utilities, he evoked widespread hostility with this move. When the vote on the privatization bill was called, the NDP walked out of the legislature for seventeen days and returned only when Devine promised not to proceed. His government was wounded, but Devine still pushed ahead with the sale of the Potash Corporation. This action was accomplished only after Devine moved for closure on the debate and rammed it through. Devine had turned this Crown jewel into a desirable property for investors by assuming $622 million in long-term debt, which taxpayers would have to support.

Saskatchewan voters never flocked to support the privatization of public assets the way its evangelizers envisioned. ISE sputtered to a close when its privatization conference attracted only a quarter of the expected delegates, who heard fifty-four privatization zealots speak about their positive experiences.[67] Devine's support continued to crumble and he suffered a crushing defeat in the 1991 election, which brought the New Democrats under Roy Romanow to power. Just before the election, Devine told *Financial Post* columnist John Schreiner, "We've moved [people] so far that you've forever changed Saskatchewan . . ."[68] To some extent, this was certainly true. But Devine's legacy consisted of something different: the largest accumulated debt in the province's history, a handful of Crown corporations privatized, and a record of corruption. Nearly half the Tory caucus was found to have participated in illegal diversions of taxpayer dollars into Conservative Party coffers to fund party activities or line the pockets of individual MLAs. Privatization propaganda in that province would take years to recover.

Ten years before Lewis Powell's famous memo to the U.S. Chamber of Commerce launched the corporate reaction to progressive advances, Alberta premier Ernest Manning and his son Preston committed themselves to creating a national "pure" Conservative party that could roll back the onslaught of "socialism." Ernest had been approached by several wealthy and influential business leaders to set up such a party. To devise policies for this party, which they saw as either an expanded Alberta Social Credit or a realigned federal Conservative party, these corporate executives, some of whom later became involved with Reform, set up an organization called the National Public Affairs

Research Foundation (NPARF) in 1965, more than half a decade before the neoconservative and libertarian think-tanks appeared on the scene. They were led by Alberta oil executive Bob Brown, who headed Home Oil, an early Fraser Institute backer. The NPARF's purpose was to introduce conservative ideas into public debate to consolidate the forces on the right. It was not created in the mould of the think-tanks established later; it did work for governments and industry (particularly in the oil and gas sector). It held public meetings and circulated its papers to political leaders, academics and business people. Preston was hired as "policy researcher." His first assignment was to produce a white paper on human resources development for his father's government. In it, Manning promoted individual enterprise and small government and opposed universal social programs and government enterprise, themes that would infuse the Reform Party platform twenty years later.[69]

Another Manning assignment was to assist his father in writing a slim paperback titled *Political Realignment: A Challenge to Thoughtful Canadians*, which argued that social conservatism must be wedded to free enterprise to create a viable alternative right-wing political force. The vehicle could be the federal Progressive Conservative Party, they wrote, but if the cause of conservatism continued to decline, then a new party, one committed to social conservatism, would emerge. Ernest used the book as a political stratagem in the 1967 PC leadership convention. He didn't formally enter the race, but let it be known he was open to a draft by convention delegates. The book told the delegates what they could expect from him as leader. But it was too early for the Mannings' conservative ideas. As Trevor Harrison notes, neither a draft nor realignment occurred. The convention chose Red Tory Robert Stanfield, a former Nova Scotia premier and heir to a wool fortune.[70] Colin Brown quit the party in disgust, bought his first full-page ad in the *Globe and Mail* and would soon found the National Citizens Coalition. Ernest Manning retired the following year and scooped up a handful of prestigious corporate directorships, including one at the Canadian Imperial Bank of Commerce, plus a Liberal-bestowed seat in the Senate. These latter two appointments raised eyebrows, but did not inflict lasting damage on his reputation as a social conservative. The NPARF carried on until it was superseded by the Canada West Foundation and the Fraser Institute. Preston Manning stayed on at the foundation for another year and then, in partnership with his father, launched a successful business-consulting career, with clients like Nova Corp., Syncrude and Trans Alta Pipelines.[71] One noteworthy project was a paper he prepared for the Business

Council on National Issues. In this report Manning argued that "basic economic rights," or property rights, should be entrenched in the Constitution. Murray Dobbin explains that "big business pressed hard for the entrenchment of these rights in the constitution leading up to the negotiations over the [1982] Charter of Rights." In a rare defeat of the BCNI, property rights were not included in the Charter, but remained "a major plank in the Reform Party's constitutional platform."[72]

Manning would have to wait it out through the reigns of Trudeau and Mulroney until the time was ripe for his pure conservative party. As long as the Conservatives were in opposition, he knew there would be little chance. People on the right who were angry with the Liberal government—and there were many—would gravitate to the Conservatives regardless of who was leader. The Conservatives would have to gain power and there would have to be enough dissatisfaction with the Conservative government for his new party to have an opening. As Murray Dobbin saw it, "Preston Manning has always been clear about both his political agenda and his preferred political vehicle for achieving it: it is a radical free-market agenda and it would be brought to fruition on a wave of popular anger."[73]

Manning knew his time was near when, shortly after the 1984 election, some conservative businessmen concluded that Mulroney was "not a real Tory," in the sense that he and his father used the term. The election was barely over when a group of fifty "wealthy high rollers" began meeting at the Ranchmen's Club in Calgary. They were looking for a new party of the right to form or join. The *Alberta Report* informed its readers that the dissident business elite enlisted the support of the National Citizens Coalition and the Fraser Institute to advance their goal of pushing Canada's political economy further to the right. The Fraser Institute had just advised the B.C. government to move quickly and sharply to the right, and the National Citizens Coalition rose to national prominence through its lavish spending in the 1984 election to attack the National Energy Program, the NDP and the Canada Health Act. The Calgary business sector's problem was to determine which political party could (or would) bring about the changes they desired. There seemed no immediate alternative to the Tories, except for a gaggle of right-wing splinter groups with little credibility. The business elite was willing to give the Tories a chance. R. Campbell Todd, president of Prairie Pacific Energy Corporation and a spokesperson for the Ranchmen's group, said that Mulroney had "just six months to set the course or his mandate will begin to drift."[74]

The Mulroney government did many things to annoy westerners, but the worst was its decision in the fall of 1986 to give the CF-18 fighter maintenance contract to Canadair-CAE of Montreal over Bristol Aerospace of Winnipeg, despite federal evaluations that recommended acceptance of Winnipeg's lower bid. The politically motivated decision caused an immediate furor. Anger spread from Manitoba to all parts of the West because the decision provided a clearly understood symbol of alienation. Support for the federal Tories eroded.[75] Ted Byfield was already arguing for a new political party in the pages of the *Alberta Report.* "The system doesn't work . . . What we need is a credible western party," he wrote just before the CF-18 debacle.[76]

The Canada West Foundation (CWF) was supposed to be non-partisan, but it became a rallying point for those angry enough with the Liberals and Conservatives to entertain the notion of a new, western-oriented party. This think-tank was created after a conference to study the feasibility of creating one large prairie province to give the region more political clout was held in Lethbridge in 1970. The conference concluded this was not possible, but research on the West should be expanded by a new organization. Financial backing for the foundation came from some of western Canada's wealthiest tycoons: Fred Mannix (Calgary billionaire construction, coal and energy magnate); James Richardson (Winnipeg stockbrokerage business, seed and fertilizer, grain elevators, oil and gas); Max Bell (newspapers, oil and gas); and Arthur Child (chair of Burns Food, left a million dollars to the Reform Party on his death).[77] The foundation researched the economic and social character-istics of the West (including B.C. and the North) and made proposals for how the region should develop. The Canada West Foundation differs from the Fraser Institute in that it accepts government grants for its work—about a third of its budget—and it developed connections to western political parties, which the Fraser did only behind closed doors. The CWF is not a neoconserva-tive or libertarian propaganda organization, because its proposals often suggest a role for government in economic development. But, like the Fraser Institute, it cultivated important business connections.

Stan Roberts, CWF president, was an early promoter of a new western party. He had been a marketing consultant, former president of the Canadian Chamber of Commerce, active Liberal and vice-president at Vancouver's Simon Fraser University. The big money came from eighty-four-year-old Francis Winspear, a Victoria accountant and millionaire who had lived in Edmonton. In 1980, Roberts and Winspear organized a Canada West

Foundation conference in Calgary to discuss western grievances and consider the creation of a new party. That conference went nowhere. They teamed up again in 1987, when Winspear gave Roberts $100,000 to get the new party going. Through their CWF contacts they linked up with other groups wanting political realignment. Manning was already being seen as the right leader for the party. Roberts became a candidate for leader, but dropped out when he saw how conservative it was becoming under Manning's influence.

The oil industry was dubious about the new party. Calgary had recently emerged as a third financial centre in Canada. Oil and gas were its heart and soul, but real estate, construction, petrochemical, ranching and agribusiness interests were influential. As Manning critic Murray Dobbin notes, Alberta was Texas North and wanted its own party. The Prairies had just experienced a proliferation of marginal protest parties that flared up and disappeared almost overnight. These parties failed in part, Dobbin suggests, because "their political style and imagery repulsed . . . the powerful oil industry whose interests were almost exclusively tied up in free market economic policies."[78] Manning, as a frequent oil-industry consultant, took great pains to ensure his political grouping would not alienate the oil companies.

Business chronicler Peter C. Newman reports that Manning called his closest advisers "the Posse." They were mostly from Calgary and mostly connected to the oil patch. The most influential, perhaps, was Jim Gray, co-founder and president of Canadian Hunter, a major gas producer. Gray was connected to the national corporate elite through his directorships in CNR, Edper Investments, Brascan Corp. and Nova Scotia Power. He was a leader in the fight against the National Energy Program. Known as the "ayatollah" of conservatism, he was the person who aspiring right-wing politicians had to see before launching their careers.[79] Gray encouraged Manning's political career while keeping his membership in the federal Conservative Party. He was later a backer of Ralph Klein's 1992 Alberta Conservative leadership bid. But as a Mormon, Gray opposed the Klein government's legalization of video lottery terminals and was kicked out of Klein's inner circle.

Other advisers, Newman notes, included Ed McNally (independent brewer, founding member of the Posse; staked Manning's nascent political movement); Jack Pirie (independent oil executive, loaned Manning space at Sabre Petroleums for his first political storefront, long-time Fraser Institute trustee); R. Campbell Todd (Ranchmen's Club group, Prairie Pacific Energy Corp.); Ellen Todd (Manning's event organizer, son became Stockwell Day's chief of staff); Gordon Shaw (Imperial Oil, Manning fundraiser); Robert Muir (long-time Calgary lawyer for Dome Petroleum); Doug Hilland (one of city's largest private investors); David Elton (executive director, Canada West Foundation, replacing Roberts); Cliff Fryers (Calgary tax lawyer, member of the Ranchmen's Club, would become Reform's chief fundraiser); Ron Wood (news director, CKXL Radio); Jack and Sheila Mackenzie (made fortune in oil and used it to endow the Marigold Foundation, which did research and groundwork before the party was formally created).[80]

Only a handful of Manning's advisers were from outside Calgary. These included Winspear and Manning family friend Dr. Charles Allard, who was assembling a major media empire in the West. Wealthy Edmonton developer Jack Poole organized a series of informal lunches to introduce Manning to the upper echelons of business and law in that city. Ted Byfield brought to the enterprise the means to disseminate the ideology of the new party. He attended some of the formative meetings of the Reform Association. His articles heralded the need for the new party and chronicled its birth and growing pains. He gave the keynote address at the conference called to decide whether to form the new party.[81]

At Reform's founding convention, Manning told delegates the party should be "ideologically balanced" so it could draw support from Liberals, New Democrats and Conservatives.[82] But this was a smokescreen. Manning's strategy was to promote a free-market, small-government agenda by disguising it as a western populist movement. Western Canada's problems would be solved, not with western Canadian solutions, but with pro-business, anti-government ones, which weren't necessarily the same. From its birth in 1987, the Reform Party was positioned on the far right of the political spectrum.[83] Manning claimed otherwise. He needed to attract a broader range of voters if he was to be successful.

Harnessing two forces together—the mass power of broad-based discontent and the financial power of those supporting an unfettered free-market philosophy—was Manning's party-building task. He had worked for the oil industry for twenty years and saw himself as the person who could exploit people's grievances for corporate purposes. The business agenda had to remain hidden from public view because of its unpopularity with most Canadians, who still believed that government has a productive role to play in people's lives. The agenda was buried beneath the more popular issue of western alienation, which was based on a sense that Ottawa had not dealt fairly with the West in its policies and funding priorities. With his party's fortunes soaring after the 1988 election, Manning was invited by Conrad Black to address the Toronto Club. He received a "rousing ovation" from the cigar-chomping blue-blooded audience, which included three Big Five–bank chairmen. They evidently liked his message 'that government must reduce spending and be "fiscally responsible."[84]

Reform claimed to be a populist party in which the grassroots control the leadership and determine the policies. Simon Fraser University political scientist David Laycock explains that at "the centre of all populist ideology is an essential social antagonism between groups, identified as 'the elites' and 'the people.'"[85] In earlier times the elites—the enemy—were variously bankers, big business or the Canadian Pacific Railway. They were special interests opposed to the interests of the people, who had collected in parties like the Progressives, United Farmers, Canadian Co-operative Federation and even the Social Credit League of Alberta in the early days under William Aberhart (Preston Manning's godfather). Manning claimed that Reform was merely an updated expression of these populist movements. Many Reform activists believed they were part of a genuine populist party controlled by the grassroots.

But the truth, Laycock argues, is that Reform was a neo-populist party in which populism, based on political and regional alienation, is yoked to capitalism and social conservatism. It was Manning's genius that a party strongly supportive of inegalitarian social and economic policy was able to present itself as the party of the people. In the Reform cosmos, the business elite mysteriously disappears as the people's enemy and is replaced, oddly, by the people themselves, or at least specific groupings of people which are called "special interests." Radical-conservative populists like Manning define special interest groups as those that support the welfare state, oppose tax cuts and propose that social resources be allocated on the basis of non-market principles. They ask for and benefit from government efforts to offset the market's unequal distribution of benefits and opportunities—a guiding principle of the welfare state. Laycock provides one list of these special interests: "feminist lobby groups, Native organizations, ethnic and cultural minority groups, state-aided arts and cultural organizations, providers of state-subsidized legal assistance to the poor or traditionally disadvantaged, the management and employees of virtually all Crown corporations and state agencies, and all public-sector unions." They are the groups business wants removed from political influence.[86]

Manning and his advisers were forging Reform into an agent of reaction, one that would give political life to the emerging counterthrust to the social and economic gains since the Second World War. Reform was poised to contribute a new definition of equality to Canadian political discourse. In this new view, social justice didn't require the state to redistribute resources through taxation and social programs as it had in the previous four decades. In the new reality, these special interests were transformed into undeserving beneficiaries of such state action. Reform argued that the disadvantages faced by minorities were deepened by such state action—the law of unintended consequences (see page 80). Welfare for poor people creates more poor people. Ordinary people—potential Reform supporters—are victims of the machinations of special interests and the bureaucrats who support them.[87]

Reform ran candidates in seventy-two western ridings in the 1988 election, which was mainly about free trade. It did not win any seats but took 8.5 percent of the votes in those ridings and more than 25 percent in some Alberta and British Columbia ridings. Reform's strategy was to capitalize on discontent with the Tories, but since both parties favoured free trade, this wasn't easy to achieve. Many conservative voters disliked Mulroney, but worried that a vote for Reform would split the free trade vote and open the door to a Liberal, or worse, NDP, victory.

The National Citizens Coalition's web site says it is independent of all political parties, but the organization maintained close links to one party: Reform.[88] At Reform's founding convention in 1987, David Somerville told reporters, "If NCC supporters notice a remarkable similarity between the political agendas of the Reform Party of Canada and the NCC, it may be because an estimated one-third of the delegates are NCC supporters."[89] Yet despite the close fit between the two organizations, they remained separate. Somerville met with Winspear and Roberts in Vancouver several years before Reform's birth, to discuss the possibility of a new party. And after Reform was created, Winspear and Roberts travelled to Toronto in an unsuccessful attempt to interest the NCC in joining. Founder Colin Brown was ill with cancer—he died several months later—so the meeting took place with Somerville, who had been appointed president. The two groups couldn't agree on methods for influencing the political system. The NCC wanted Reform to remain non-political while Reform wanted the NCC to join them.[90]

The groups are different but complementary. The NCC is a classic grass-roots propaganda organization. Its goal is to influence public opinion by spending millions of dollars from unnamed corporate backers for ads in mainstream media—mainly during election campaigns when voters are paying closer attention to the issues. The ads promote a corporate agenda to cut government's ability to provide programs and services and attack workers' right to organize in unions. Its secondary activity is to mount legal challenges to government laws limiting third-party advertising during elections. If these laws are effective, the NCC would have to revamp its operational model.

Because of the secrecy surrounding the NCC's backers, "Canadians have no way of knowing if private insurance companies are paying for NCC campaigns against health care or if Cargill is behind their attack on the 'Soviet Empire' Wheat Board," comments Council of Canadians chair Maude Barlow.[91] Big business has always been wary of supporting the organization publicly, but a 1980s investigation of the NCC's advisory board by *This Magazine* revealed members with ties to thirty-nine major Canadian corporations. These included Canadian Pacific, Brascan, Canadian Imperial Bank of Commerce, Bank of Montreal, MacMillan Bloedel, Canada Trust, Power Corp., Bell Canada, Stelco, Abitibi Paper and eight major insurance companies. Almost all were Fraser Institute members.[92]

The NCC's success in defeating a federal law limiting third-party spending during elections overnight turned the organization into a propaganda powerhouse. In July 1984, the Alberta Court of Queen's Bench upheld an application from the NCC to overturn the federal government's Bill C-169, which would amend the Canada Elections Act to ban newspaper and broadcast ads by third parties—such as the NCC—for or against particular candidates or parties during an election period. All parties in the House of Commons supported the legislation, which was designed to ensure that elections remained as level a playing field as possible. But Brown and the NCC fought the law on the grounds it violated free speech provisions of the Canadian Charter of Rights and Freedoms. The NCC was portrayed in the mainstream press as a champion of free speech and Colin Brown was featured in newspapers across the country. In reality, the removal of the legislation reinforced the right of the wealthy to spend their money to influence public opinion in their favour. The NCC's backers spent $300,000 fighting the legislation. Ottawa decided not to appeal the ruling because the appeal would have to be filed during an election period and the optics would be disastrous for the government.[93]

The NCC used the Alberta court decision to intervene in the 1984 election, spending $700,000 fighting the National Health Act (despised by the private health insurance industry) and the National Energy Program (despised by the oil patch). It also put up $100,000 to denounce the NDP (despised by business in general). The NEP campaign was so successful that a Calgary millionaire reportedly offered to bankroll a western branch office for the NCC in that city. Making full use of the 1984 judicial ruling that allowed third-party involvement in elections, proponents and opponents of the Free Trade Agreement (FTA) entered the fray in full force during the 1988 election. In addition to the spending by the two sides, the NCC spent $840,000 exposing the "frightening agenda" of the NDP, which opposed the deal. New Democratic Party leader Ed Broadbent, they screamed, was "very, very scary." The NCC was on the rise. By 1991 it would claim a membership of 39,000 and an annual budget reported to be $2.4 million.

By the end of the 1980s, the fledgling business-sponsored propaganda infrastructure had achieved some successes. The Fraser Institute and its libertarian allies guided two provincial governments in downsizing their operations and making them more business friendly, and diminishing the social and economic rights of their citizens. The Canada West Foundation helped organize the Reform Party. The C.D. Howe Institute and the Business Council on National Issues fought and won the battle for a free trade agreement, which would go far in tying the hands of democratically elected governments. The National Citizens Coalition worked on that campaign too, and also fought successfully for the right of business to intervene in election campaigns. But Canadian corporate propaganda lagged behind American efforts. In the U.S., dozens of foundations and corporations were financing scores of libertarian and neo-conservative think-tanks, creating a climate of ideas that supported the election of Ronald Reagan. He slashed taxes on corporations and the wealthy and deregulated the economy, undermining government's ability to protect the environment and public health and safety. Brian Mulroney had won re-election and the Free Trade Agreement, but he was no Reagan. He disappointed business because of his lack of progress on the corporate agenda.

No Canadian foundation had stepped up to adequately fund conservative think-tank activity. There were too few think-tanks to create an echo chamber, which amplifies conservative messages and forces mainstream media to pay attention. The media were losing their suspicions about the think-tanks, but beyond the regional *Alberta Report* and limited-circulation magazine *The Idler*, Canada had no dedicated right-wing press. Nor had Canadians established any flak organizations (see page 70) to attack corporate media for being too liberal. The Fraser Institute had recently set up a quasi flak organization called On Balance, but its target was mainly the CBC. All this would soon change. The 1,200 conservatives and libertarians who gathered in the Calgary Hyatt Regency's Imperial Ballroom for the Fraser Institute's thirtieth-anniversary festivities indeed had real reason to celebrate success.

CHAPTER 5

The Propaganda Machine in Action: the 1990s and Beyond

During the 1990s, a smoothly functioning conservative ideas-generating machine emerged in the West, echoing the rise of the American foundations and think-tanks that were successfully pushing the American political agenda to the right. Sitting in the driver's seat is the Calgary School, a grouping—cabal?—of neoconservative and libertarian academics and political activists in the political science, economics and history departments at the University of Calgary. Like all groupings of the right, they comprise economic and social conservatives, who often have conflicting views on the role of the state in enforcing moral values. But they coalesced around arguments to attack special interest groups, slash social programs, downsize government, deregulate the economy and cut taxes. Over this decade, the Calgary School was able to disseminate its ideas to a wider audience and attract other conservative organizations to the city thanks to increased business and foundation funding and a supportive reception from the corporate media. The National Citizens Coalition moved its headquarters to Calgary to be closer to the action, while the Canadian Taxpayers Federation opened its office in nearby Edmonton. Calgary is home to the Canada West Foundation and the National Foundation for Family Research and it's where the short-lived Canadian Property Rights

Research Institute was based. Alberta's conservatives were supported by the business-friendly *Calgary Herald* and by Ted Byfield's *Alberta Report.*

As the tale is told, the Calgary School was inevitable because of western alienation in a country dominated by the concerns of Ontario and Quebec. It was supposed to be the voice of the excluded. Yet, a 1998 study by the Center for Strategic and International Studies, a neoconservative think-tank based in Washington, D.C., concluded differently. This study claimed that the West, acting through these professional intellectuals, exercises an overpowering influence on federal politics. Study author David Rovinsky reported that in the nineties the West became the "motor of Canadian political thought."[1] Gone were the days when Canada's conservative think-tanks had to look outside the country for the intellectual heft of a Milton Friedman or a Friedrich Hayek, as the Fraser Institute did in its early years. In 2004, the year of the Fraser Institute's thirtieth anniversary, a third of the Fraser's senior academic fellows worked at the University of Calgary, while another Calgary Schooler directed the institute's Alberta office.[2]

The Calgary School impelled federal and provincial governments to focus on reducing deficits and cutting taxes and programs. It stirred up a backlash against liberal immigration and multiculturalism policies and disparaged First Nations. Calgary School members fabricated a crisis of alleged judicial activism since the enactment of the Canadian Charter of Rights and Freedoms, following a script written by the American Federalist Society. And it incited English Canada to take a hardline stand against Quebec.[3] The climate the Calgary School helped create in Alberta was a factor in Ralph Klein's four election victories in the face of deep cuts to social programs. Taking his inspiration from Klein, Mike Harris implemented his own brand of government-cutting and program-slashing in Ontario several years later. And several years after that, Gordon Campbell followed the same route in B.C. But the Calgary School's greatest influence was federal. It helped shape the political direction of the Reform Party and Canadian Alliance and dominated the thinking of Prime Minister Stephen Harper, who studied under Calgary School professors, selected one as a close adviser, and the student of another as his chief of staff.

Shadia Drury warns that the Calgary School "is a Canadian appropriation of American neo-conservatism."[4] She was a member of Calgary's political science department for twenty-seven years, frequently locking horns with her conservative colleagues before leaving for the University of Regina. Drury is an expert on Leo Strauss, the intellectual fount of the neoconservative movement, who spawned Straussians like former World Bank head and former U.S. deputy defense secretary Paul Wolfowitz and leading neocon polemicist Irving Kristol, whose impact on the corporate propaganda system was described in Chapter 3. Strauss and two other émigrés, German political philosopher Eric Voegelin and Austrian Friedrich Hayek, are the Calgary School's philosophical inspiration. As Chapter 3 explains, Strauss believed in the inequality of humanity. An elite must rule on behalf of the ignorant public and must hide the truth by writing in code. "Using metaphors and cryptic language," philosophers communicated one message for the elite, and another message for "the unsophisticated general population," explains philosopher Jeet Heer. "For Strauss, the art of concealment and secrecy was among the greatest legacies of antiquity."[5] That legacy is continued by today's elite, which, Drury argues, includes the Calgary School. It's not surprising Strauss's ideas attracted legions of young university students who could imagine themselves as the intellectual elite, sending coded messages to each other, undecipherable by the ignorant crowd. But a serious problem arises when such youthful fantasies are carried into adult life, especially by senior government officials and prominent university professors.

Strauss recommended harnessing the simplistic platitudes of populism to galvanize mass support for measures that would, in fact, restrict rights. Does the Calgary School resort to such deceitful tactics? Drury believes so. Such thinking represents "a huge contempt for democracy," she told the *Globe and Mail*'s John Ibbotson. The 2004 federal Conservative election campaign run by the Calgary School's Tom Flanagan was "the greatest stealth campaign we have ever seen," she said, "run by radical populists hiding behind the cloak of rhetorical moderation."[6] The Calgary School has successfully hidden its program beneath the complaint of western alienation. "If we've done anything, we've provided legitimacy for what was the Western view of the country," Calgary political scientist Barry Cooper told journalist Marci McDonald. "We've given intelligibility and coherence to a way of looking at it that's outside the St. Lawrence Valley mentality."[7] This statement may be Straussian code. On the surface, it's easy to understand Cooper's complaint and the Calgary School's mission. But the message could mean something very different to those in the know. For "St. Lawrence Valley mentality," they might read "the Ottawa-based modern liberal state." And for "Western view," they might read "the radical conservative attack on democracy." "We've legitimized the radical-right attack on the Canadian democratic state," Cooper may be saying.

To decipher the Calgary School's code, we need to look at the professors who taught its members. Tom Flanagan is said to be the School's informal leader. He was born in Illinois and attended Notre Dame University in Indiana. There he came under the influence of Eric Voegelin, whose work provided a framework that, McDonald reports, "reconciled his Roman Catholic faith with his family's conservative politics."[8] A central Voegelin thesis is that our souls have lost the capacity to experience the divine. As a result, we have been seduced into trying to make the world a better place—through Marxism, secularism, progressivism or liberalism. The "isms" must inevitably make things worse. We will solve our political problems, Voegelin claims, only when we recover our religious experience.[9] Voegelin's work is a plea to return to the authoritarian Middle Ages. Voegelin taught at Louisiana State University during the forties and fifties and at the University of Munich during the turbulent sixties. He spent his last fifteen years as the Henry Salvatori Distinguished Scholar at the neoconservative Hoover Institution on the campus of Stanford University. Salvatori, whose fortune came from oil exploration, was the benefactor of another foundation that funded the conservative counterthrust for three decades.

Flanagan pursued his Ph.D. at Duke University in Durham, North Carolina, where Voegelin disciple John Hallowell headed the political science department and edited Voegelin manuscripts. Hallowell challenged the modern political philosophy of positivism and worked to revive the works of Aristotle and reaffirm the relevance of Christian perspectives in politics. At Duke, Flanagan met Barry Cooper, a Canadian also doing his Ph.D. in Voegelin studies. They shared a carrel in the library and became lifelong friends.

Marci McDonald recounts the early years of Calgary's political science department and the offer to teach there Flanagan received from E. Burke Inlow, the department's first head. Inlow had been recruited from an assignment with the Pentagon, where, as an expert on Iran and the Far East, he provided intelligence to people the U.S. government was sending to the Middle East. Inlow sought out Flanagan because his mandate was to counter the "prevailing leftist currents" on most Canadian campuses. Inlow also hired Antony Parel, a Jesuit-trained expert on Machiavelli, from Radio-Vatican in Rome.[10] Machiavelli was a figure of abiding concern to Strauss and Voegelin. Strauss wrote about Machiavelli as the first thinker of the modern age who rebelled against the classics and the Christian tradition. Machiavelli was an important antecedent to the Enlightenment's relativism, a development that Strauss, Voegelin and

the Roman Catholic Church despised. By 1975, Parel was head of the department and recruited Voegelin scholar Barry Cooper and two recent Ph.D.
graduates who studied under a student of Leo Strauss.

Los Angeles–born Ted Morton went to Colorado College and then the
University of Toronto, where Straussians Walter Berns and Allan Bloom were
teaching. The two scholars left Cornell University in 1969 after becoming disgusted by the campus's student radicalism. They settled in for nearly a decade
of relative peace at the Canadian university. Rainer Knopff also did his graduate
work at the University of Toronto. Former Straussian Anne Norton claims that
Bloom, far more than Strauss, shaped the Straussians who governed in the
United States under George W. Bush. Paul Wolfowitz, the most famous
Straussian, studied more intensively with Bloom than with Strauss. "Bloom
taught both the most powerful and most vociferously ideological of the
Straussians," she writes.[11] The year Morton finished his doctoral studies at
Toronto and followed Knopff to Calgary, Bloom left for Chicago and Berns for
the American Enterprise Institute.

Bloom became a highly visible figure several years later with the publication of his book, *The Closing of the American Mind*, which critiques the modern
liberal university and how it fails its students. The great books of Western
thought and the eternal verities contained in them, Bloom complained, have
been devalued and replaced by relativism and self-interest. The result was a
void in the souls of students, which cynical student leaders filled with the
aimless social movements of the 1960s.[12] The book was wildly popular, selling
over a million copies and making Bloom a rich man.

Voegelin shared many traits with Strauss. Both turned to ancient philosophers for answers to contemporary political problems. Both fled the Nazi regime
to assume teaching posts in the U.S. Both heaped scorn on the liberal West
because it lacked the moral fibre to stand up to totalitarianism. (And both
would likely add terrorism to the challenges facing the West if they were alive
after 9/11.) They went further and, like Friedrich Hayek, accused liberal democracy itself for being responsible for the rise of Nazi and communist regimes. Both men were lionized by the conservative right. One difference is that
Strauss's influence is widespread in government and academia, while Voegelin
has been largely ignored, except in a few centres like Calgary. Barry Cooper has
written or edited four books on Voegelin, including a translation of his volu-
minous correspondence with Strauss, titled appropriately *Faith and Political
Philosophy*.

Tom Flanagan combines academic and political interests: building a conservative movement (through his publications) and a conservative party (through his activism). Once in Canada, Flanagan became interested in Louis Riel, whose Metis rebellions for land and self-government he saw as an attempt to found a messianic movement. Voegelin had a phrase for this: "immanentization of the eschaton." In Jewish and Christian thinking, the eschaton is the end time, when God will transform earth into heaven. Immanentization of the eschaton thus means "utopianism," which Voegelin regarded as the central error of modern society.[13] Man can never create heaven on earth and all attempts to do so are doomed to failure with disastrous consequences. Flanagan turned this obscure thought into a cottage industry.[14]

Flanagan's incendiary 2000 book, *First Nations? Second Thoughts*, argues that the First Nations were merely the "first immigrants" in North America, preceding the French and British by a few thousand years. Consequently there could be no indigenous entitlements, he concludes. Aboriginals were simply a people conquered by "Europeans with a higher degree of civilization."[15] Reserves should be turned into private property and opened up to free-market exploitation and Aboriginals should be assimilated. The book won the $25,000 Donner Book Prize as the best public policy book of the year. This may not be surprising given that Donner subsidized Flanagan for the book's research to the tune of $20,000. The foundation also gave him $5,000 to publicize his revisionist book, *Riel and the Rebellion: 1885 Reconsidered*.[16]

Ted Morton describes himself as "every liberal's nightmare: a right winger with a Ph.D.," but many right wingers have Ph.D.s, especially in the era after Strauss, Voegelin and Hayek. Morton joined Calgary's political science department in 1981 and remained there for twenty-three years. Like Flanagan, Morton combines incendiary scholarship with conservative politics. He supported the American-style Triple-E Senate (equal, elected and effective) and was elected as a Reform Party senator-in-waiting in the election called by Alberta premier Ralph Klein, but not recognized by Prime Minister Jean Chrétien. In 2001 Morton served as parliamentary director of policy and research for the Canadian Alliance. In 2004, having abandoned his hopes for the Senate, Morton was elected as an MLA in the provincial election, and in 2006 came in third in the race to succeed Klein.

In 1996, Morton and Barry Cooper obtained Olin Foundation support for a lecture series that promoted a strict constitutional view of the democratic state and attacked so-called judicial activism. Featured speakers in the lecture series included the head of the Voegelin Institute at Louisiana State University.[17] But Morton's most stinging attacks were co-written with Rainer Knopff. The former Walter Berns students collaborated on three books in which they apply American neoconservative views to the Canadian legal system, particularly to the Charter of Rights and Freedoms. They launched their most provocative work, *The Charter Revolution and the Court Party*, with a Donner-hosted banquet at Toronto's Intercontinental Hotel.[18] Morton and Knopff dedicate the book to Berns.

When Berns left Toronto, he took a more prominent role in the neoconservative movement. He was appointed a resident scholar at the American Enterprise Institute, where he remained for twenty-five years. He was a consultant to the Reagan government and a member of the board of directors of the Institute for Educational Affairs, the organization set up by Irving Kristol and William Simon to identify and support promising conservative scholars. Berns taught at Georgetown University in suburban Virginia where he was a John M. Olin professor.[19] Over the next ten years, he received $1.3 million from conservative foundations for his work at Georgetown.[20] His corporate and foundation backers must have been enthused by his strictly limited view of government as an historical institution, an approach followed by Morton and Knopff. Berns's book, *Taking the Constitution Seriously*, "could well have been the subtitle for nearly all the courses he taught at Cornell," writes Jeremy Rabkin, who carries on the Berns tradition at the university.[21] To "take seriously" meant for Berns to respect the legal, philosophical and rhetorical traditions that underlie the constitutional plan bequeathed to Americans by the constitutional framers. We should be guided today by what a handful of aristocratic men thought two hundred years ago is the book's message.

Following Berns, Morton and Knopff oppose the Charter of Rights and Freedoms because, they contend, all the rights necessary for representative democracy are contained in Canada's founding documents. In the U.S., Alexander Hamilton insisted in *Federalist Paper No. 84* that the proposed Constitution was "itself, in every rational sense, and to every useful purpose, a bill of rights."[22] For Canadians, who follow the Westminster parliamentary tradition, Morton and Knopff also find our rights are protected by the practice of parliamentary sovereignty. Partisan debate and public deliberation will inevitably produce sound public policy that respects rights. If rights are protected and respected, they ask, why do we need special legal instruments like the Charter?

Their answer is that the Charter's existence is the result of a plot by the right's perennial bogeyman—special interest groups. Unable to achieve what they wanted by pressing legislators, Morton and Knopff argue, these groups ferociously lobbied the Trudeau government for an expansive charter and, once it was enacted, "turned to the courts to advance their policy objectives."[23] These special interests—feminists, anti-poverty organizations, gay rights groups, prisoners' and refugees' rights groups—use the courts to constitutionalize the preferences they could not achieve through the legislative process.[24] Feminists and their ilk stand accused of using the courts, not to protect the fundamental core of existing rights, but to change public policy through the judicial creation of new rights.

Astonishingly, the Morton-Knopff analysis ignores two overarching influences on modern democracy: corporate power and corporate propaganda. As they see it, representative democracy works because coalitions of minorities form majority governments. In the real world, however, corporate power dominates other interests and, through the techniques of propaganda, can manipulate public opinion sufficiently to achieve the results it desires. Morton and Knopff use the phrase "government by discussion" approvingly,[25] but that is naive or perhaps deceptive, as Leo Strauss might advise. Minorities could coalesce and discuss all they want, but still have little impact on most legislative outcomes without business support.

The Calgary scholars also seem not to have noticed that business uses the courts to advance its interests to greater effect than all other interest groups combined. Strauss would alert us to this glaring omission. Morton and Knopff are sophisticated scholars, he might advise his students. They must know that business consistently uses the courts to create and expand its rights, rights that were not foreseen by the American founding fathers or the lords of Westminster. That they have chosen not to discuss corporate power may be a Straussian signal that it must remain hidden from the masses. If corporate power became a public issue, the consequence could be great turmoil within the capitalist order. This cannot be allowed to happen. So the Calgary School developed the dual strategy of obscuring corporate power and the possibility that it can be democracy's enemy and focusing instead on easily attacked targets like special interests. The strategy was adopted in whole cloth by Preston Manning, Stephen Harper and the Reform Party founders, perhaps during their discussions with the Calgary School the year the party was created. Early populist parties railed against various business elites—bankers, eastern businessmen or the Canadian Pacific Railway. Reform was backed by the western business elite, so it couldn't target business. Special interests and government bureaucracies that support them had to be turned into the enemy. Flanagan's attacks on First Nations, Cooper's work undermining the CBC, and Morton and Knopff's knocks against the courts and special interests, merge into one philosophy with one hidden mission.

The Calgary School's influence was expanded when Tom Flanagan and Stephen Harper joined forces as a result of their mutual interest in the ideas of a third European émigré. Friedrich Hayek's ideas on minimal government inspired the wealthy libertarian think-tank backers several decades earlier; Margaret Thatcher was an outspoken devotee. [See discussion on p. 101] Flanagan found Hayek in the late seventies, around the same time as Thatcher. Harper arrived at the University of Calgary several years later to study economics and was introduced to Hayek's work, which became the foundation of his graduate studies. He studied under conservative economist Robert Mansell who, according to the *Globe and Mail*'s John Ibbotson, was "more of an associate of the Calgary School than a charter member."[26] At Mansell's urging, Preston Manning hired Harper to do policy research for the soon-to-be-born Reform Party. Manning asked political science department head Roger Gibbins, the Calgary School's chronicler who had replaced Antony Parel, to recruit some faculty members to help fashion a platform. Marci McDonald reports that Manning and Harper met Flanagan and his colleagues during these brainstorming sessions.[27] Thanks to the Calgary School's influence, the party's rallying cry "The West Wants In" and its policy Blue Book were infused with Straussian duplicity. As we've seen, "the West" was code for the neoconservative virtues of limited government and equal opportunity for all, independent of government programs. The phrase "the West Wants In" thus means that Canada needs smaller government and fewer social programs. There is no room for special interests, except for business, in this rendition of Canada.

Flanagan soon became disgusted with Brian Mulroney's ongoing deficits and joined the Reform Party. The same year, he took a job as Manning's director of research, while Harper was Manning's policy chief. Flanagan soon became discouraged by Manning's constant consultations with the party's grassroots and quit before his contract ran out. Harper was ready to quit too, but Flanagan and his other advisers urged him to soldier on. Harper was elected in the 1993 election that saw the Reform wave sweep the West and win fifty-two seats. But he left the party before the 1997 election and joined the National Citizens Coalition, first as vice-president and later, president.

That same year, Flanagan and Harper launched a four-year writing partnership while they were repositioning Harper for his return to party politics. Their first effort was an article titled "Our benign dictatorship," which was published in the Donner Foundation–financed magazine the *Next City*. They argue that a coalition between Reform and the Bloc Québécois was one way for conservatives to seize power.[28] In one of their last writing collaborations, recalling the states' rights movement in the U.S., Flanagan and Harper were two of six signatories to an open letter to Alberta premier Ralph Klein. Dubbed the "Alberta Agenda," this was a manifesto calling on Alberta to use all of its constitutional powers to reduce federal government influence: withdraw from the Canada Health Act, collect its own income tax, set up a provincial pension plan, replace the Royal Canadian Mounted Police (RCMP) with a provincial police force and push senate reform back onto the national agenda. A third signatory was Ken Boessenkool, a policy adviser to Stockwell Day when he was Alberta finance minister, and then a researcher at the C.D. Howe Institute, and later a lobbyist for Hill and Knowlton. The group included Andrew Crooks, chairman of the Canadian Taxpayers Federation and Calgary School professors Knopff and Morton.[29]

Stephen Harper's program is the conservative agenda advocated by his Calgary School advisers, but his task, like that of Straussians, is to hide his true intent and pretend to be in the mainstream, which is all the "bewildered herd" (journalist Walter Lippmann's view of the public) can comprehend. When Harper won the Canadian Alliance leadership in March 2002, Flanagan came back. This time there would be no more wasted effort talking to the "little people." Flanagan brought in Alberta Agenda signatory Ken Boessenkool, who became the Conservatives' director of policy. Ian Brodie, a former student of Ted Morton, who taught at the University of Western Ontario, became executive director of the Conservatives, and later, Harper's chief of staff. And, of course, Flanagan had Harper.

The corporate propaganda system requires prodigious amounts of cash to establish think-tanks, support conservative scholars, publish their works and disseminate the results widely in the media. Like all academics, conservatives are supported by taxpayers who pay their salaries (although an increasing fraction is contributed through student tuition fees) and provide their offices, computers, lecture halls and labs. Taxpayers also supply a substantial portion of academic-research funds. Ted Morton and Rainer Knopff's attacks on special interests were supported by grants from the federal government's Social Sciences and Humanities Research Council (SSHRC). Morton was also supported by the Calgary Institute for the Humanities and the Bora Laskin National Fellowship in Human Rights Research. Moreover, he received a research grant from the Earhart Foundation, a prominent contributor to corporate propaganda efforts and especially to students of Strauss. As for Rainer Knopff, he received multi-year support from the Donner Canadian Foundation.[30] Donner provided nearly $1 million for Calgary School research, for Barry Cooper's attacks on the CBC, Flanagan's attacks on Louis Riel and for the Fraser Institute to open a Calgary office under Cooper's supervision.

During this decade, the Donner Canadian Foundation was the lifeblood of conservative and corporate propaganda in Canada. It's safe to say that the corporate counterthrust would have made little headway in Canada without Donner's support. Certainly the Calgary School would not have been as effective. A little background: steel magnate William Donner came to Canada after a dispute over income taxes in the United States. He set up the foundation in 1950 and when he died three years later, most of his money went to the foundation. Through four decades, the primary funding targets were medical research and other good works. The family established an American granting operation in New York City called the William H. Donner Foundation. The American foundation was administered from Canada and followed the same "good-works" policy. During the Reagan years, the West Coast, more right-wing, branch of the family gained ascendancy in the American foundation and adopted the agenda-driven activism of the major conservative foundations. In the early nineties, the family decided to move the Canadian foundation to the right. By then Donner's Canadian endowment was about $135 million, making it one of the country's largest, Krishna Rau reported in *Canadian Forum*.[31]

The foundation hired Pittsburgh-born Devon Cross as president. Cross had been program director of the Smith Richardson Foundation in New York—financed by the Vicks VapoRub fortune—supervising a granting program of $12 million a year, directed largely to libertarian and neoconservative propaganda efforts. Cross's mission at Donner, apparently, was to create a national network of libertarians and neoconservatives, paralleling the highly structured ones in the United States.[32] Allan Gotlieb was appointed chair of Donner's board of directors. Gotlieb had been Brian Mulroney's ambassador to Washington and helped push the Free Trade Agreement through. After retiring from public service, Gotlieb was appointed chair of Burson-Marsteller Canada, the leading public relations firm, giving him a finger in treetops and grassroots propaganda efforts.

Cross organized a meeting of about a dozen conservative journalists and academics at the Intercontinental Hotel in downtown Toronto. The guest list included columnists Andrew Coyne and Terence Corcoran, then at the *Globe and Mail*; Fraser Institute economist John Robson and his brother William, a C.D. Howe policy analyst. Also present was University of Montreal political scientist Stéphane Dion, who became Jean Chrétien's intergovernmental affairs minister, and later, leader of the Liberal Party. Cross asked them how their ideas could have greater influence on public discourse. Coyne suggested a conservative magazine. Two years later, with a Donner grant of $1.4 million, the *Next City* commenced publication under the auspices of Toronto-based Energy Probe Research Foundation. Coyne and then *Globe* columnist Robert Fulford were contributing editors.[33] *Next City* published articles calling for parent-run charter schools (publicly funded schools that can set their own goals and hire their own personnel), the privatization of medicare, an end to government subsidies to the arts and the Harper-Flanagan piece on how conservatives could seize power. Margaret Thatcher was the magazine's patron saint. *Next City* lasted four years until its Donner funding ran out, but its spirit lived on in the *Financial Post* through regular columns by *Next City* editor Lawrence Solomon.

With its new grant-making program in place, Donner poured two to three million dollars a year into conservative efforts. Some of the more significant grants were:[34]

- $450,000 over three years to start the Atlantic Institute for Market Studies (AIMS), a libertarian think-tank in Halifax, plus another $620,000 for AIMS programs
- $450,000 to the Fraser Institute, to transform government debt into a crisis and move it to the top of the public agenda, plus another $2.3 million for ongoing support
- $400,000 to launch *Gravitas*, another right-wing magazine
- an additional $225,000 to Energy Probe, to set up a Consumer

Policy Institute, which proposed replacing public medicare with individual medical savings accounts and private insurance, and privatizing public transit

- $325,000 to the anti-union, Christian organization Work Research Foundation, to promote freedom of association, which would hobble unions
- $700,000 to the Society for the Advancement of Excellence in Education, to promote charter schools and undermine public education
- $450,000 to the University of Victoria, to establish a Centre for Municipal Studies, to promote privatization and contracting out of municipal services
- $435,000 to the Frontier Centre for Public Policy in Winnipeg, and $500,000 to the Montreal Economic Institute (MEI), for start-up funding, plus additional ongoing support for these two regional libertarian think-tanks
- $300,000 to start up and support the Dominion Institute, to push the study of history away from Canada's cultural mosaic and back to the lives of the great men and women and the events of which they were part
- $200,000 to the Fraser Institute for the Donner Awards in the Delivery of Social Services, to undermine government by ostensibly demonstrating that the voluntary sector does better than the public sector in delivering social services (so who needs government?)
- $100,000 to the Fraser Institute to start CanStats, to criticize and harass mainstream media and push them to the right, as if they needed much pushing
- $190,000 to the National Foundation for Family Research and Education, to attack public daycare

In 1999, Donner cut back its funding for conservative efforts when some family members decided they wanted more input into the granting process. Before then, about two-thirds of the annual funding went to conservative causes. The foundation started supporting projects like migratory-bird conservation, mountain bongo antelope repatriation and integrated whole-person care at McGill University. It continued funding conservative projects at a level of about $1 million a year, or 25 percent of total granting.[35] The same year, Donner added Ken Whyte to its board. Whyte had started his job as editor of Conrad Black's long-awaited radical-conservative paper the *National Post*. This dual appointment permitted effective dissemination of Donner-funded propaganda even at the lower level of support.

Meanwhile, other foundations were recruited to support the corporate counterthrust. Albertan Max Bell made a fortune investing in oil and gas and using his profits to buy newspapers. Together with several other tycoons he formed FP Publications, which became one of the largest chains in Canada in the 1960s. He set up the Max Bell Foundation shortly before his death at the Montreal Neurological Centre at McGill University. Thirty percent of the amount awarded each year—about $1 million—went to McGill. Bell was a founder of the Canada West Foundation, which directed a sizable grant to that think-tank too. The remaining money went to health care projects like cancer pain management, acute-care nursing and infectious veterinary diseases.

Four years after Donner began funding the right, Bell remade itself. David Elkin left his post as long-time head of Canada West to become Bell's president; Michael Walker joined the board; and the foundation changed its mandate from funding in the areas of health, Canada and the Asian Pacific and veterinary sciences to "support [for] projects which educate Canadians about public policy alternatives."[36] "Public policy alternatives" is code for the corporate agenda—smaller government, privatization, deregulation. The propaganda function was clear. Bell began funding Fraser and C.D. Howe and the new general-purpose think-tanks, apparently coordinating its efforts with Donner and other conservative funders. The Society for the Advancement of Excellence in Education (SAEE), which in its early years propagandized for charter schools, was a major beneficiary of both foundations. It would likely never have existed without their support. Bell also supported a Fraser Institute program to promote private sector school chains.

Max Bell's board of directors was dominated by corporate executives. Two of Canada West co-founders, Ronald Mannix and James Richardson, who were among western Canada's wealthiest tycoons and early backers of the Reform Party, chaired the foundation for most of its life. Walker left the board in 2003, his mission presumably accomplished. One board addition the following year—Jim Gray, Reform Party and Ralph Klein backer and long-time Canada West Foundation chair—tied the foundation even closer to the business elite. A second appointment was Tom d'Aquino, president of the Canadian Council of Chief Executives, a move that may indicate closer ties to the eastern business establishment.

Walker reined in two more foundations to support Fraser programs such as school choice, the Lotte and John Hecht Memorial Foundation, whose money came from selling arms, and the W. Garfield Weston Foundation, whose money comes from a less colourful source—selling biscuits. John Hecht was a Vancouver-based weapons merchant who sold arms to the Middle East—playing both sides of the 1960s Arab-Israeli conflict—and in most other regions of the world. Hecht was a personal friend of George H.W. Bush and raised money for Bush's presidential bid. Hecht may have been involved in the illegal Iran-Contra affair, selling arms to Iran to provide funds to arm the Contra rebels in Nicaragua. He pumped his profits into a Vancouver real estate empire and also owned properties in Europe, Israel, Argentina and the United States. Hecht died in 1988 on his European honeymoon with his second wife. He left the bulk of his fortune, estimated at between thirty-two and one hundred million dollars, to his charitable foundation,[37] which provides funds in two areas: alternative medicine in the treatment of cancer; and economic education promoting the free market. This second program was custom-made for Walker. The Hecht Foundation provides hundreds of thousands of dollars to the Fraser Institute's student-recruitment programs, which are described later in the chapter.

Galen Weston is head of Canada's third wealthiest family (after the Thomsons and the Irvings). He and his family are becoming a more important funding source for conservative think-tanks. Most of the W. Garfield Weston Foundation's funding is for "good works." It is lead funder for Canadian Merit Scholarships, which enables high school students to attend university. It also leads in donations to the Nature Conservancy of Canada to purchase ecologically significant properties, and the Royal Ontario Museum. But, beginning in 2003, Weston financed the Fraser Institute's school vouchers program, which sends poor children to private and religious schools. Weston also contributes to the institute's school report card program which ranks all schools in a province. Each year the rankings find that private schools, which can control entry, and schools in wealthier neighbourhoods always top the lists. Weston provides awards for schools that topped the lists and those that showed the greatest improvement from the previous year. Vouchers and school rankings work together to undermine confidence in the public school system. By 2007, the last year for which figures were available, Weston had donated $12 million to the Fraser Institute's education programs.[38]

Money is also supplied directly by corporate Canada. Few Canadian think-tanks reveal their sources of corporate backing. This is not required under the Income Tax Act. The Fraser hasn't released a list of corporate members since the 1980s and has never revealed the amount of member contributions. A partial understanding of corporate backing can be gained by examining think-tank boards since members are most likely invited to join because of their financial contributions. The Fraser's board of trustees includes a representative from Pfizer, the world's largest drug company. Just coincidentally, since Walker claims no trustee can tell the staff what to do, the Fraser has a pharmaceutical policy division, which attacks Internet pharmacies that provide cheaper drugs for Americans, disparages critics of drug company policies regarding distribution of HIV/AIDS drugs in Africa, attacks generic drugs and opposes the ban on direct-to-consumer advertising of prescription drugs. All of these programs benefit Pfizer. The board also includes financial investors from Vancouver and Toronto. Coincidentally, cutting corporate and income taxes is a Fraser mainstay. There's big and small oil and gas money from Calgary represented on the board as well. Also coincidentally, the Fraser has supported so-called climate change deniers for a decade.

The same links between the interests of board members and institute activities are found at most think-tanks. The Halifax-based Atlantic Institute for Market Studies proposed privatizing New Brunswick Power and allowing electricity rates to rise; the president of Emera Inc., the largest private utility in the region, which would be a prime beneficiary of the policy, chaired the AIMS board. AIMS proposed "modernizing" the Newfoundland fishery by allowing industry to shut down "inefficient" plants; the president of Fishery Products International, which owns dozens of these inefficient plants, is on the board. And AIMS proposed doing away with zoning and planning regulations on land development; the CEO of Empire Co., an owner of shopping malls and office buildings and a residential land developer, is on the advisory council.[39]

Do business executives join think-tank boards because they support ongoing activities—as the think-tanks claim—or does their money help create new directions and programs? A rare glimpse of the role of corporate funding in shaping Fraser Institute programs was obtained as a result of the 1998 Master Settlement Agreement between forty-six U.S. state Attorneys General and the major tobacco companies. A condition of the agreement was that the tobacco companies had to make public, and post on dedicated web sites, all of the documents used in the discovery phase of legal actions brought by the states against the tobacco industry for Medicaid costs associated with smoking-related diseases. More than forty million pages of documents were made public. They include a series of letters written in 2000 by Sherry Stein, the Fraser Institute's chief fundraiser, and Michael Walker to the British American Tobacco Co., the world's second-largest tobacco company and owner of Imperial Tobacco, which controlled 70 percent of the Canadian market. The letters reveal that the Fraser Institute had set up a social affairs centre to promote free market solutions to social policy problems like poverty, drug use, smoking and gun control. Tobacco company Rothman's International was providing $50,000 a year for this work and Philip Morris, "generous support."

With this and other funding, in 1999 the Fraser published a book by two tobacco industry consultants, *Passive Smoke: The EPA's Betrayal of Science and Policy*, and held two day-long conferences in Ottawa. This package of initiatives was timed to coincide with the looming prospect of a spate of bylaws being enacted by municipalities across the country, and by the federal government, to regulate smoking in public places. A bylaw had just come into effect in Victoria, British Columbia, to ban smoking in all indoor public places. The book, by Gio Gori and John Luik, argues that these bylaws are ill considered because the link between second-hand smoke and lung cancer had not been proven. The book attacks the 1993 decision of the U.S. Environmental Protection Agency that declared second-hand smoke to be a carcinogen. It was followed by the two conferences, which worked in sequence, the first attacking the need for regulation and the second attacking regulation of smoking. Neither the book nor the conferences mentioned the tobacco industry funding.

At the end of 1999, Rothman's was bought by British American Tobacco (BAT), and the Fraser Institute lost this funding source. It commenced a year-long campaign to replace, and add to, the money. Writing to BAT's chairman Martin Broughton, Sherry Stein asked him to take over Rothman's funding commitment and consider a new initiative for a risk and regulation centre. She asked for $50,000 a year for each centre. BAT funding for this new centre would help the Fraser "provide the factual information that will seriously counter the risk activists and their misleading and misguided propaganda," Stein wrote.[40] Later in the year, Fraser Institute director Michael Walker reiterated these requests in his pitch to BAT's international scientific affairs manager, Adrian Payne. Walker focused on the new Centre for Studies in Risk and Regulation. He railed against the "agitators for a 'zero-risk' society [who] have become increasingly successful in advancing their cause, often basing their case on exaggerated junk science scares."[41] The targets of these nasty agitators were environmental quality, second-hand smoke, pesticides and genetically modified foods. With BAT financial assistance, the Fraser Institute would set the record straight. BAT would not be alone in supporting the new centre, Walker reassured Payne. The institute had already

> met with a number of your colleagues in the industry to discuss this proposal and all are on side and have implied that they will support the Centre with comparable contributions. The companies they represent are Imperial Tobacco Company Ltd., JTI Macdonald Corp., and Rothman's Benson & Hedges Inc. We have begun discussions as well with Philip Morris International Inc., and Brown and Williamson Tobacco in the U.S. Others we will approach for support are in the food, biotechnology, and chemical industries.[42]

Later in the year, Stein presented three proposals for BAT's support. It could contribute: $30,000 for the launch of the centre, featuring guest speaker John Stossel, a well-known television personality and anti-regulation zealot; $42,000 to distribute an anti-regulation book called *Safe Enough?*; and/or $48,000 for a project that would show regulation was too costly to be effective. The letters from Stein and Walker don't indicate which, if any, of these projects BAT did support, but they all took place. The letters also don't indicate that Brian Levitt, the CEO of Imasco, BAT's Canadian subsidiary, was a Fraser Institute trustee during this period.

The Fraser and Howe institutes carved out a national presence, one on the right and the other further to the right, while the Canada West Foundation established its domain as a conservative think-tank focused on western concerns. With Donner support, business set up three new regional think-tanks during the nineties. First was the Atlantic Institute for Market Studies (AIMS) in Halifax in 1994. It was followed in 1999 by the Montreal Economic Institute (MEI) and the Frontier Centre for Public Policy in Winnipeg. The Fraser Institute set up a branch office in Calgary to tap into the Calgary School; later established a Toronto satellite office to support the work of the Harris government; and in 2007 opened a branch office in Montreal. The regionalization of corporate-sponsored propaganda followed the American model, where state-based think-tanks were established in most states to provide a conservative business-oriented perspective on policy issues at state and municipal levels.

These think-tanks followed the same formula. The first, and most crucial, step is to locate a policy entrepreneur who can run the institute and bring together the other elements. All three think-tank leaders had solid libertarian credentials as members of Friedrich Hayek's Mont Pèlerin Society. They were also members of the Civitas Society, the secretive association of libertarians and social conservatives discussed later in the chapter. AIMS president Brian Crowley has the most experience of the three and is the only one with an economics background. He earned his doctorate in political economy from the London School of Economics and, like Eric Voegelin, became a Salvatori fellow, at the Heritage Foundation in Washington, D.C. Before becoming president of AIMS, he was president of the Atlantic Provinces Economic Council and before that, taught economics, politics and philosophy at Dalhousie University in Halifax. Crowley was an adviser to Nova Scotia and Manitoba governments on the Charlottetown and Meech Lake accords. He's a director of the Society for the Advancement of Excellence in Education. Crowley is a member of the Frontier Centre for Public Policy's research advisory board. He maintains a connection to the Heritage Foundation as an adjunct faculty member of the Heritage's Center for Media and Public Policy. He was on Ralph Klein's Advisory Council on Health where he helped move the council's recommendations towards a two-tier system. Crowley is a frequent commentator on political and economic issues for the CBC and Radio-Canada. The Harper government appointed Crowley to a two-year term as a visiting scholar in the finance department. Harper called AIMS "dollar for dollar the best think tank in the country."[43]

Leading the Frontier Centre is Peter Holle, who describes himself as an authority on cost-saving strategies in government and public sector "reform." He was an adviser to the corrupt administration of Saskatchewan premier Grant Devine when he privatized Crown corporations and sold off public assets, often to friends of the government. After Devine's defeat in 1991, Holle started the Manitoba Taxpayers Association and then went to the Canadian Taxpayers Federation before moving to the Frontier Centre.[44]

The Montreal Economic Institute's first policy entrepreneur is Michel Kelly-Gagnon, the youngest of the group, being only twenty-eight when appointed MEI president in 1999. His education and work background provide little indication of his abilities in the field of corporate propaganda. He was educated as a lawyer and then became chairman of a company that specializes in in-house employee training. But he had solid libertarian credentials as an alumnus of the Institute for Humane Studies, which provides scholarships for promising conservative students, and membership in the Mont Pèlerin Society.[45]

Once a leader is recruited, the organization needs to obtain charitable tax status from the Canada Revenue Agency (CRA) so that it can receive grants from foundations (which can donate only to tax-exempt organizations). In this way, taxpayers subsidize the propaganda work, which is often designed to undermine their interests and diminish their rights. Next, the organization must raise sufficient funds. A small think-tank needs $300,000 a year to operate. All three think-tanks received seed funding from Donner. In the case of AIMS, Donner provided $150,000 a year for three years as start-up funding, and then continued to support major projects. Donner funding to AIMS is supplemented by contributions from the Big Five banks, regional brokerage houses and corporate law firms, Atlantic Canada's largest corporations, major national corporations such as Imperial Oil, Inco and Southam (now CanWest Global) and the foundations of the McCain, Pirie, Sobey and Weston families.[46]

The other think-tanks tapped similar sources. The Montreal Economic Institute opened its doors in 1999 with its Donner grant. The rest of the money was raised from other foundations and the local business elite. André Desmarais, president of Power Corp. and then prime minister Jean Chrétien's son-in-law, hosted a discreet fundraising dinner in the early days. The Montreal corporate elite turned out in force: SNC-Lavalin, Bell Canada, National Bank, Groupe Transcontinental, Imasco, Merrill Lynch and Standard Life. Desmarais's sister-in-law, Helene Desmarais, was a co-founder and chairs the board of directors.[47]

Next, the think-tank needs to recruit advisers to frame its research. They are almost always from the conservative-libertarian end of the political spectrum. The Frontier Centre's board of research advisers contained one person of a mildly liberal, pro-environment persuasion. This person had coordinated Manitoba's sustainable development initiative and was a member of the Canadian delegation to the Earth Summit in Rio de Janeiro in 1992. He lasted less than a year before departing. Most of the others were staunchly libertarian and have remained on the board for a decade: an American expert on private sector provision of public services; an American economist affiliated with three conservative think-tanks; a Swede who advises the Greater Stockholm Council on bringing the private sector into the public health system; the president of the Michigan-based libertarian Mackinac Center for Public Policy; an American libertarian public policy consultant; an American specialist in public–private partnerships; Brian Crowley from AIMS; and two members of New Zealand's Labour government during the 1980s, when it led the world in downsizing, deregulation and privatization.[48]

The funding is used to pay for studies by academics, whose work is compatible with the think-tank's conservative goals. It must also build a staff of reliable researchers and analysts who do much of the day-to-day research, writing and promotion of the institute. With a budget of $12.7 million in 2007, the Fraser supports a staff of sixty-six, plus twenty-two senior fellows, making it by far the largest think-tank in Canada.[49] Donner's $200,000 grant to the C.D. Howe Institute for its Border Papers series was paid largely to Howe staff analysts and to academics from the University of Toronto, Carleton University, the University of British Columbia, the University of Western Ontario and York University to produce papers that justified deeper economic and social integration with the United States.

The studies produced by a think-tank all seem to head in the same direction. AIMS's mandate is to determine "whether and to what extent market-based solutions" can be successfully applied to Atlantic Canada's problems. Not surprisingly, perhaps, AIMS discovered that the market could solve virtually all of Atlantic Canada's problems. In short order, AIMS recommended privatizing the Atlantic fishery, airports, local government and public education; reforming taxes; cutting government spending and unemployment insurance; and deregulating the economy. Applying "market-based solutions" to the purported problems of public education was a recurring theme in early AIMS studies. Promoting charter schools was a priority, perhaps because charter schools was a priority with Donner and Max Bell, the think-tank's funders for this work. One publication argued that universities should "operate like private businesses," organizing curriculum to meet the needs of "clients" rather than leaving it to the "whims" of faculty.[50]

The mission of the Frontier Centre for Public Policy is to apply market principles to the economic and social life of Manitoba and Saskatchewan. It covers issues like agriculture (privatize the wheat board), poverty (reduce by cutting taxes and regulations), housing (reduce zoning bylaws), environment (protect by entrenching property rights), health care (promote health care industry), education (increase school options such as vouchers) and Aboriginal governance (move from band to individual ownership).

Another element in the process of establishing a successful think-tank is to launch the institute with a study that is controversial and obtains lots of media coverage. The audience is twofold: policy-makers who sit up and take notice of the new player, and local business people who, hopefully, begin contributing to the think-tank's efforts. The Montreal Economic Institute's first publication was titled *Statism and the Decline of Quebec*, and attacked Quebec's Quiet Revolution. The conventional wisdom is that the Quiet Revolution represented a period of enormous provincial progress and economic expansion. During the 1960s, the Quebec government became the agent of provincial development, nationalizing power companies, imposing greater regulation on an out-of-control private sector and establishing Crown corporations to produce goods and services the private sector wouldn't. Author Jean-Luc Migue, an economist with the École nationale d'administration in Quebec City, took a contrary position. He alleged that government intervention represented "a sort of slow-motion catastrophe" that discouraged private investment, slowed growth and resulted in significantly higher unemployment. Economic growth under Union Nationale premier Maurice Duplessis was quite strong in the years before the Quiet Revolution, he claimed. But instead of carefully analyzing Quebec's economic performance, Migue follows the script written by Hayek. (Migue had won the Sir Antony Fisher Silver Medal and was a member of the Mont Pèlerin Society.) In his interpretation, governments are always more concerned with expanding their fiefdoms than complying with the need of citizens for lower tax and regulatory burdens, if that's what most citizens want or need. It was standard libertarian fare. Nonetheless, Migue's book received favourable treatment in Quebec's anglophone and francophone press.[51]

The final ingredient in the formula is to obtain media coverage for the think-tank's products. All think-tanks are preoccupied with their media impact. In an early annual report AIMS said the institute strives to take "the AIMS message to new readers," and to reinforce the message with old ones. "Calls from the regional and national media seeking comments on current issues continue to come in at a rate of approximately one a day, giving aims a substantial presence [in] printed and broadcast reports," AIMS president Don Cayo reported.[52] Cayo and senior policy analyst Fred McMahon (who later moved to the Fraser Institute) were "published regularly in five influential Atlantic dailies," the annual report noted, "one Western paper and the *Globe and Mail.*" Cayo was substituting for Brian Crowley, who had taken a two-year leave to join the editorial board of the *Globe and Mail*, where he could promote the libertarian agenda on a national stage. Cayo, in turn, was managing editor and editorial page editor of the *Telegraph Journal*, New Brunswick's leading provincial paper. He took his own two-year leave of absence to head AIMS while Crowley was in Toronto. After Crowley returned to AIMS, Cayo went back into the newspaper business and followed libertarian news editor Neil Reynolds to Vancouver, where Cayo first became the *Vancouver Sun's* editorial page editor under Neil Reynolds, and then a business columnist, when Reynolds brought in libertarian economist Fazil Mihlar from the Fraser Institute to run the newspaper's opinion pages.

As the nation's largest think-tank, the Fraser Institute has the greatest media presence. A draft media plan leaked in 1997 revealed a rare glimpse of the organization's ambitious plans for media penetration, tailoring the institute's activities to attract the most coverage. In 2007, the Fraser Institute issued 225 news releases and media advisories and placed 282 op-eds, more than doubling the 2006 success rate. The number of news stories referencing the institute in media around the world climbed to 6,243, an increase of 24 percent over 2006. "Reaching decision makers, policy makers, and the public through the main-stream media remains one of our primary tactics," the institute's 2007 annual report states.[53] The Fraser's Communication Department slices and dices its media successes: nearly four hundred mentions across more than fifty countries of the economic freedom report; more than six hundred mentions in Canadian media for the hospital waiting list survey; more than one thousand hits for the school report cards. The Weston Awards for winning schools allows the Communication Department to "customize and personalize our message for specific communities," the annual report notes.[54]

Along with its undeniable media success has come occasional scrutiny, when institute studies were found to have serious flaws even though they re-ceived generous media coverage. In 2000, Alberta health researcher Kevin Taft checked the sources in a Fraser study that backed the Ralph Klein government's plan to allow private hospitals to operate in the province. The study claimed that a survey of reports comparing public and private hospital performance revealed "the advantages to private provision of hospital services. Those advan-tages are lower costs and higher quality," the study concluded, "enabling more and better health care to be purveyed to Canadians, enhancing health out-comes."[55] But the evidence in the study, Taft found, didn't support this conclu-sion. He compared the claims for the superiority of for-profit hospitals the institute made in its study against the original research papers it cited. He found many discrepancies, including papers in which the institute ignored findings that countered its desired conclusion and those in which the institute misreported their conclusions. Nonetheless, the report received favourable coverage in the *Globe and Mail* and *Calgary Herald*, which ran a positive opinion piece by Calgary School professors Barry Cooper and David Bercuson.

Another example of outside scrutiny of Fraser Institute research occurred in the mid-1990s when the institute held two conferences on the right to work, a perennial favourite of institute researchers. The conferences—in Toronto and Calgary—came out, predictably, in favour of right-to-work legislation and lower minimum employment standards. After the conferences, Ontario Conservative MPPs defended a bill in the legislature "that would make weak employment standards laws even weaker," wrote Lynn Spink, an adjunct professor at York University's Centre for Research on Work and Society. The MPPs "used figures from one of the conference papers" to make their case. "The numbers turned up again in *The Globe and Mail Report on Business*," she commented, "as if they were the gospel truth." Spink decided to take a closer look at the Fraser Institute's research and organized a review of papers from the Toronto conference. The reviews were written by progressive labour lawyers, economists and social scientists at universities in Canada, New Zealand and the United Kingdom.[56] One paper by Fazil Mihlar, then a Fraser Institute staff economist, was examined by Martha MacDonald, a professor of economics at Halifax's St. Mary's University. She claimed that Mihlar "misrepresents many points and makes unsupported assertions that employment and business growth in some U.S. states is caused by 'right to work' laws." Mihlar's work, she concluded, was "fuelled by simplistic market analysis and virulent anti-union ideology."[57] A paper by Charles Hanson, an economist at the University of Newcastle Business School describes "the British Disease"—the high number of strikes, low productivity and poor quality of goods and services that characterized the United Kingdom before the election of Margaret Thatcher in 1979. Hanson suggests the economy turned around as a result of Thatcher's "radical reform" of trade union law. David Coates, a professor of labour studies at the University of Manchester, says, however, in contrast to what Hanson claims, trade unions were not the prime cause of pre-1979 U.K. economic underperformance and the Thatcher years were not a period of unbridled U.K. economic success. Says Coates: "Hanson's assertions are half-true and misleading at best and simply wrong in a number of key respects."[58]

The Fraser Institute's Tax Freedom Day campaign has also been challenged. This is supposedly the day when the average Canadian family has earned enough income to pay its total tax bill for the year and can start working for itself. The Canadian Centre for Policy Alternatives (CCPA) claims the Fraser employs a problematic method to calculate the tax burden of the average Canadian family.[59] The institute uses the statistical average income—total income earned in Canada divided by the total number of families. But since some families earn a great deal of income, this approach raises the average income significantly, as well as average tax paid. Median income should be used, the CCPA argues. This is the income level at which 50 percent of Canadian families earn more and 50 percent earn less. It is lower and will push Tax Freedom Day weeks earlier. In 2006, the latest year for which statistics are available, Statistics Canada calculated the median after-tax income of Canadian families at $58,3000 and the average after-tax income at $67,000, which is 16 percent higher.[60] Also distorting the results, says the CCPA, is the fact that the Fraser bases its calculation on households with two or more individuals. This increases the amount of taxes paid because two-or-more-person households earn, on average, greater incomes ($67,600 after taxes) than single-person households ($28,500). And to the extent Canada's tax system is progressive, Canadians with lower incomes pay a smaller share of their income in taxes, so the Fraser's approach overestimates the taxes paid by typical Canadians. Despite these defects, Tax Freedom Day is one of the institute's most successful media events. The 2008 edition was covered by most major Canadian newspapers.

In 2006, an exhaustive critique of a Fraser Institute environmental publication was undertaken by University of British Columbia environmental scholars Hilda McKenzie and Bill Rees. They examined the six editions of the institute's "Environmental Indicators" report published between 1997 and 2004. The institute argues that in contrast to the "alarming claims about environmental degradation and related health impacts" that fill newspapers, the institute's own research found that "things are, in fact, improving dramatically in the developed world as improvements in technology, higher incomes, and democratic systems have created an ever-increasing ability to protect the environment."[61] Rees and McKenzie were curious as to how the institute's researchers could reach these conclusions given the "scientific consensus on the seriousness of problems such as climate change and biodiversity loss."[62] Their analysis recites a litany of problems with the report.

First, the report filters out global problems such as global warming and biodiversity—arguably the most significant indicators of the state of the ecosphere—because its goal, it says, is to provide a picture of national environmental quality. The report abstracts Canada from the rest of the world and ignores the overwhelming role played by industrialized nations in contributing to escalating carbon dioxide emissions. It does refer to these issues, but as secondary indicators only, which are not used to compile a country's record.

Nor does the report compare improvements in Canada and the U.S. with those in other high-income countries. According to evaluations of environmental performance by the Organisation for Economic Co-operation and Development (OECD), Canada and the United States ranked 28th and 29th, respectively, out of twenty-nine countries. True, Canada has made improvements in domestic air quality, Rees and McKenzie note, but most other OECD countries have made greater improvements and increased the gap with the two North American countries. A third omission they cite is the role of government regulation in bringing about improvements. The report argues against government regulation at every turn and attempts to attribute improvements to the market, when they are obviously caused by toughened regulation.

Other problems Rees and McKenzie document include:

ignoring the reasons for the improvements it does document, reasons (government regulation and the movement of polluting industrial activity to other parts of the world) that would undermine its own premises and ideological objectives; including only 4 of its 10 indicators in its summary index showing improving environmental quality; minimizing human-induced effects in comparison to the alleged effects of natural processes, exaggerating uncertainty and misrepresenting the degree of scientific consensus on key issues; misframing the scale of problems; dismissing major concerns; and providing no critical assessment of the adequacy of current regulatory standards.

The 2002 edition of the Fraser Institute's "Environmental Indicators" reports that overall environmental problems in the United States were 19 percent less severe in 1995 than in 1980, and in Canada 17 percent less severe. "Given the methodological distortions behind the construction of the index," Rees and McKenzie conclude, the precision is an example of "crackpot rigour." "Environmental Indicators" is a brownlash report, they argue, "which works to minimize the seriousness of ecological problems and to fuel a backlash against environmental regulation." Despite its many flaws, "the report's 'good news' conclusions are reported on in the mainstream media as if based on sound analysis."

While the libertarian propaganda machine was bulking up during the nineties, the Canada West Foundation was nourishing and embellishing an enduring narrative of western alienation, based on Calgary School scripts. The foundation was created in 1970, financed by western Canada's wealthiest corporate executives as an alternative to a single prairie province that could match the clout of Ontario and Quebec. It never received the media attention the Fraser Institute was able to attract because it had little interest in grassroots propaganda. Its purpose was treetops—to reach business, political and bureaucratic leaders. In 2003, the CWF was reporting a "deep-seated belief" among western-ers that "the government of Canada doesn't listen [to them], doesn't under-stand, and doesn't care." A 2004 CWF poll found that 65 percent of westerners felt their provincial interests were "poorly" or "very poorly" represented in Ottawa.[63] But under cover of this concern for regional grievances, the CWF promoted the same corporate and conservative ideas as the Fraser and the Calgary School.

Ten years earlier, during the federal budget consultations that led to the deep spending cuts in Paul Martin's 1995 budget, the foundation organized a meeting in Calgary of 108 western Canadians to meet with Martin. "We have here women, the disabled, immigrants, racial minorities," Canada West presi-dent David Elton said in introducing the meeting. "But we hope everybody sees themselves not as spokespersons for special interest groups but as Canadians." However, one special interest group did prevail, one that wasn't even identified by Elton: business, which was unanimously opposed to any kind of tax increase to cut the federal deficit. Business voices were the only ones quoted in media reports of the consultation. Don't raise taxes, cut program spending instead, was the message sent to Ottawa from the West, or at least Canada West's version of the West.[64] It's not known if women, the disabled, immigrants and racial minorities signed on to the business agenda, which would mean deep cuts to social programs that largely benefited them.

Three years later, the CWF supported the Klein government's drastic cuts to social services by promoting the idea of a "welfare society." A report entitled "Issues and options for change: social services for the 21st century," distinguished between a "welfare state," where the government plays the central role, and a "welfare society," where the community is predominant. "We've made it too easy for people to say 'let the government look after it,' especially when there is no real financial need," Elton explained. "We're trying to find a way that will make the system work even better than solely under government."[65] But Elton was wrong to claim welfare was provided "solely under government." Many not-for-profit and for-profit organizations participate in the welfare state. And there's a precedent for community-provided welfare: the nineteenth century.

Under the cover of regional alienation, the CWF also pushed for a two-tier health system. Canadians are tired of federal-provincial jurisdictional wars, claimed Professor Roger Gibbins, the Calgary School chronicler who replaced Elton as president when Elton moved to the Max Bell Foundation. They are more concerned about "a slippage of responsible government." And to make matters worse, he said, politicians "have an irresistible attachment to public funding as an aspect of our national identity." We need an "alternative view," one that doesn't see the solution as simply providing more money. While surgical waiting lists lengthen, "the debate over healthcare is increasingly sterile," Gibbins claimed.[66] To make the debate more fecund, one supposes, simply allow a greater role for for-profit health care.

Canada West Foundation's pro-business slant was evident even in a major initiative it called the Natural Capital Project. This project was supposed to help close the "counterproductive gap that exists between environmental interests on the one hand and business interests on the other," the foundation wrote in its 2004 annual report.[67] How would the foundation achieve this laudable goal? By ignoring environmental interests and focusing solely on what business wanted. The external advisers Canada West selected for this project proved the point. They were stacked with representatives from forestry and oil and gas companies. There wasn't one representative from a genuine environmental organization, aside from Ducks Unlimited, which restores marshlands so that oil and gas executives and Calgary School professors can shoot ducks. Close the gap between two groups by eliminating one of the groups. Gap closed!

As well as general-purpose libertarian think-tanks, Donner's deep pockets supported the creation of a variety of single-issue organizations. Typical are the Society for the Advancement of Excellence in Education, whose goal is to undermine the public school system and promote charter schools; the Consumer Policy Institute, to promote private transportation alternatives and medical savings accounts, which are designed to privatize medicare; and the Canadian Constitution Foundation, to attack medicare and human rights commissions.

Perhaps the most successful—*National Post* columnist John Fraser called it "wildly successful"—is the Dominion Institute, which says its mission is to create "active and informed citizens through greater knowledge and appreciation of the Canadian story."[68] But what is "the Canadian story"? The Dominion Institute's version is great men and important events. The organization was funded by the Donner Canadian Foundation, evidently, to challenge the prevailing social-history approach taught in most schools, which emphasizes race, ethnicity, gender and class. These are precisely the so-called special interests that the Calgary School has ferociously attacked and demonized. The Dominion Institute's mission is to ensure special interests have little role in Canadian history. Like many Donner-backed projects, the propaganda function is central. "Everything we do at the Institute," executive director Rudyard Griffiths explained to John Fraser, "is done with an idea to how it will play in the media. We measure success in hundreds of media hits for each project."[69]

Griffiths and a group of young conservatives obtained seed funding of $150,000 from Donner to start the institute. The founders included *Ottawa Citizen* columnist Dan Gardner, Mike Chong, a rural Ontario Conservative MP whose web site tells us he is "a conservative who believes in fiscal prudence, limited government, free enterprise . . ." Another founder is Duncan Jackman, son of long-time Tory fundraiser Hal Jackman. Duncan chairs the family's holding company, E-L Financial Corp., with assets of about $6 billion.

The Dominion Institute attracted conservative historians like Jack Granatstein and Margaret MacMillan. The federal government also jumped on board because institute programs are designed to fit with various departmental mandates: war veteran visits to schools are sponsored by Veterans Affairs and Canadian Heritage; Passages to Canada—stories told and written by prominent immigrants to Canada (UNESCO ambassador Kim Phuc, author Shyam Selvadurai, Ken Wiwa, and MPs Ujhal Doshanjh, Mario Silva and Hedy Fry)—is sponsored by Citizenship and Immigration Canada. The corporate elite, too, was enamoured of the project because it so gracefully dovetailed with the corporate agenda: cut support for minority groups and increase support for the military. Within a few years, the institute's budget rose to $1.5 million. About half comes from government and the rest from corporations (Bell Canada, Magna International, Random House) and corporate-backed foundations such as Historica (the banks, ManuLife Financial, CN, CanWest Global, Imperial Oil, PetroCan) and Operation Dialogue (AGF Management, Scotia Capital Markets).

The Dominion is also supported financially and editorially by CanWest Global and the *Globe and Mail*. The *Globe* complained in one editorial that "[s]choolchildren learn all about the story of women, the story of natives, the story of the labour movement, but little about the story of the country as a whole."[70] Could this story of "the country as a whole" perhaps be the story promoted by the Dominion and its corporate backers: the lives of the prime ministers, the wars, the great events and the great men who shaped them? Every year on the day before Canada Day—the Dominion people wish it was still called Dominion Day[71]—the institute releases a survey measuring how little Canadians know about important dates and events. And every Canada Day, the *Globe* runs a front-page story decrying the abysmal state of Canadians' historical knowledge. The *Globe* sponsors Passages to Canada, which the Dominion frames as a "personal search for identity and belonging." Absent is any mention of immigrant groups or the dynamics of immigrant communities. The critical-thinking section of the teachers' resource booklet asks:

> In Canada, immigrants are encouraged to retain their native customs and traditions. This policy, known as multiculturalism, is central to the contemporary Canadian identity. However, some argue multiculturalism makes unifying this country more difficult. What is your view? Why?[72]

The people who argue against multiculturalism are not identified. Might they be Calgary School professors or the Dominion Institute itself?

The National Citizens Coalition celebrated its thirtieth anniversary in 1997, claiming with pride to be "Canada's largest independent organization for the defence of our economic and political freedoms." Several years before that important event, Reform MP Stephen Harper told an NCC meeting that the breakdown of the consensus that once governed the country was a significant advance. "Universality has been severely reduced: it is virtually dead as a concept in most areas of public policy." These achievement are "due in part to the Reform Party of Canada and . . . the National Citizens Coalition."[73]

One way the NCC works to break down the national consensus is to fight for the right of business and the wealthy to run their own political ads during election campaigns. After its triumph in defeating the law limiting third-party advertising in 1984, the NCC succeeded in overturning similar laws passed by the Mulroney government, and by the NDP government in British Columbia. In 2000, Parliament passed yet another law designed to limit the voices of the wealthy during elections. This time the government strategy was not to forbid third-party advertising, but to set limits by stipulating that a third-party group or individual could not spend more than $150,000 nationally on advocacy ads during an election campaign and no more than $3,000 in any one riding. This law was overturned once again by the Alberta Court of Queen's Bench and upheld by the Alberta Court of Appeal. It went to the Supreme Court of Canada, which ruled against the NCC in a six-to-three decision. The court action was called the "Harper case" because it was launched by the NCC while Stephen Harper was president. By then, he was leader of the Conservative Party and was disappointed by the decision. "I don't think there should be any limits that would unduly restrict third parties from getting their message out," he said, adding that if elected prime minister, "we'll ensure there aren't any undue restrictions on the exercise of free political speech."[74]

Harper knew the third parties, but he wasn't talking. The NCC opened an office in Calgary, just after the Klein government brought in its dramatic cuts to government programs and services. Alberta's budget-cutting initiatives made it, "for someone interested in public policy, the most exciting place to be in Canada," the NCC's David Somerville effused.[75] Reform and the NCC drew even closer through Harper's efforts. Harper sat for one term as the Reform MP for Calgary West. He didn't run in 1997, sparking speculation that he had major problems with the direction Preston Manning was taking the party, such as too much consulting with the party's grassroots. The same year he joined the NCC as a vice-president under Somerville and, when Somerville retired in 1998, took his place as president. Meanwhile, Rob Anders, who was running the NCC's Canadians Against Forced Unionism project, took over Harper's Calgary West seat as the Reform MP. (Harper resigned as NCC president in August 2001 to run for the leadership of the Canadian Alliance.)

Although freedom of speech is the organization's avowed aim, lack of free speech is taken to extremes within the NCC. The organization doesn't list its officers, board members, donors or finances. Nor does it have annual general-membership meetings. The organization's constitution distinguishes between voting and public members. The vast majority of members are in the public category. They pay dues but have no say in the NCC's operations. They are not entitled to receive notice about any meeting, nor are they permitted to attend or vote at these meetings. Voting members, on the other hand, have all the power. A quorum of two voting members can choose leaders and determine policies. In effect, a small cadre of directors and corporate and foundation backers run the organization like a private lobbying club. University of Western Ontario business professor Donald Thain, one of the few directors of the NCC ever to speak publicly about the workings of the organization, and one of the even fewer not from the corporate sector, told *This Magazine* in the mid-eighties that "the coalition is really Colin Brown and a few close friends and colleagues."[76] The NCC is not shy about its secret ways. "No one, absolutely no one," Somerville once said, "is forced to donate one cent to the National Citizens Coalition. It's a strictly voluntary organization and if they don't like the campaigns we're doing, if they don't think we're running them very well, they don't give money."[77]

The NCC set up a group called Ontarians for Responsible Government to oppose the "ruinous" economic policies of Bob Rae's NDP government. Its goals were to pressure the Rae government to moderate its "radical" agenda, to defeat the New Democratic Party, elected to office in 1990, in the next provincial election and to ensure the next government embraced free enterprise and smaller government.[78] The organization spent $600,000 during the 1995 election to defeat Rae. It waged "all-out electoral war" against the "People's Republic of Ontario." Snarled Colin T. Brown, son of the NCC founder, "We want to wipe them off the electoral map."[79] And he did, with the assistance of the corporate media.

The Fraser Institute launched a program in 1988 that would have far-reaching impact on advancing the corporate agenda. This program, aimed at students, is actually a half-dozen initiatives through which the institute "is cultivating a network of thousands of young people who are informed and passionate about free-market ideas and who are actively engaging in the country's policy debate," as the organization's publication *Frontline* puts it.[80] The initiatives are separately funded but work together as a comprehensive package of recruitment and intellectual grooming. These programs outgun in magnitude, scope and longevity anything that the progressive left has mounted through unions and social justice organizations.

Over 17,000 students have come in contact with at least one of the student programs, the institute claims. "Developing talented students sympathetic to competitive markets and limited government" through these programs "is one important way that the Fraser Institute is working towards changing the climate of opinion in Canada."[81] Graduates have spread into politics, academia, other think-tanks and the media.

They're especially proud of Ezra Levant, who was a student of the Calgary School's Tom Flanagan and attended his first student seminar in 1992. He was asked to join the student leaders' colloquium in Vancouver and became an intern, where he wrote the book *Youthquake*, which was distributed and publicized by the institute. Levant tapped into the American conservative movement as a Koch Foundation Summer Fellow in Washington, D.C., and attended various Institute for Humane Studies and Liberty Fund events. After graduating from law school and articling, he worked for several years as a parliamentary assistant to Preston Manning and Stockwell Day. From there he did a two-year stint on the editorial board of Conrad Black's *National Post*, which was dominated by conservative ideologues. Next, he entered electoral politics and was nominated for the Canadian Alliance in the riding of Calgary Southwest. He attracted national attention when he initially refused to resign his nomination so that party leader Stephen Harper could run. After some high-profile deliberation, Levant resigned. He practiced law briefly at a libertarian firm in Calgary and wrote a weekly column for the *Calgary Sun* and *Winnipeg Sun*. In January 2004, along with other Fraser Institute alumni, he started the socially and economically conservative magazine *Western Standard*, which took over the mantle from the defunct *Alberta Report*.

Another star graduate of the Fraser's student program is Danielle Smith, who started her career at a Calgary student seminar. She went on to a year-long internship at the institute, publishing some of her attacks on environmentalism in the institute's *Canadian Student Review*. She then worked for the short-lived Canadian Property Rights Research Institute and was hired as an editorial writer for Conrad Black's *Calgary Herald*, arriving in the editorial office just as the workers went on strike for a collective agreement. She later became host of CanWest Global's Sunday talk show for several years. Smith was subsequently appointed the Alberta director of the Canadian Federation of Independent Business. (The Fraser Institute's former environmental director is the B.C. director.)

Other student program graduates include Rob Anders, Conservative MP for Calgary West, who ran the National Citizens Coalition's Canadians Against Forced Unionism project and was considered to be among the most right-wing members of the Conservative caucus. Sonia Arrison was a program officer at the Donner Canadian Foundation and then worked at the Fraser Institute where she specialized in deregulation and privatization. She then became director of technology studies at the California-based Pacific Research Institute, where former Fraser Institute staffer Sally Pipes runs the organization. Marc Law attended the student leaders' colloquium and went on to work for the Fraser as an economics researcher until he started Ph.D. studies in the United States. He became an assistant professor of economics at the University of Vermont, where he specializes in historical studies of regulation. Craig Yirush is a professor of history at UCLA, where he studies early American history. Yirush worked his way through the ranks at the Fraser Institute, attending student seminars and the student leaders' colloquium. He volunteered at the 1992 Mont Pèlerin Society general meeting, was a Fraser intern and attended workshops and sessions at the Institute for Humane Studies.[82]

The student seminar has become the Fraser's initial recruitment tool. The net is cast wide for promising candidates, with up to a dozen day-long seminars held each year in cities across Canada on the full range of libertarian topics: how the market protects the environment; how smaller government leads to greater prosperity; and why we need to privatize health care to save it. A big draw is that the seminars, including coffee and lunch, are free and held in prominent downtown hotels. Seminars are free because they are sponsored by corporate and foundation backers: Lotte and John Hecht Memorial Foundation (B.C. seminars), W. Garfield Weston Foundation (Toronto), EnCana Corp. (Calgary and Edmonton), CanWest Global (Winnipeg). Individuals and companies can sponsor specific components: one student costs $120, lunch is $1,875, coffee break, $500, speakers' travel and accommodation, $4,000. An entire seminar costs a tax-deductible $17,000.

The seminars mix lectures and small-group discussions, presented from a narrow ideological perspective. Discussion groups are led by staffers from the Fraser or its sister libertarian think-tanks like the Montreal Economic Institute. Lecturers are senior fellows at the institutes or executives from the National Citizens Coalition or the Canadian Taxpayers Federation. Featured guest speakers run the gamut from Tony Clement, then minister of health in the Mike Harris government, to *National Post* columnist Colby Cosh, to Brian Day, president of the private Cambie Surgery Clinic in Vancouver. In short, the range of expertise presented at the seminars runs from right to far right.

Students, in contrast, cover the political spectrum; there is no way the institute can weed out college and high school students with progressive views who come, often out of curiosity. But that doesn't matter. The skeptical ones can participate and enjoy a free lunch. At the end of the day they are offered a warm "thanks for coming and participating," and are never contacted again. Those whose views are approved by the institute, in contrast, are identified for further orientation, writes journalist Patti Edgar, who attended a seminar as a University of Victoria student in 2000.[83] They might be asked to enter the student-essay competition, which is sponsored by the Manning Centre for Building Democracy. Recent topics have ranged from "How can property rights protect the environment?" to "Eliminating world poverty: what is the best approach?" and to the 2008 topic, "The Canadian healthcare system: Why is it broken and how can it be fixed?"

The best essay receives $1,000, second prize is $500 and there's a separate $250 prize for the best high school essay. The winners of the 2008 contest argued that health care is in crisis, not because of inefficiencies in the system or underfunding, but because it is run by a government monopoly that insulates economic activity from the efficiencies and innovations of competition. The winning essay argued that by adding more private sector services and private insurance to health care incrementally, political opposition to demonopolization by "statists" and "chauvinists" can be overcome. The winning high school essay was titled "The case for capitalist healthcare." That all winning entries are similar should not be surprising, given that to ensure that students come up with the right answer, the institute provides lists of sources, which are restricted primarily to libertarian publications and web sites.[84] Students, apparently, receive no credit for critiquing the topic.

The 2009 topic is the positive relationship between economic freedom and global prosperity. Students are asked if economic freedom is the most effective way to pull a nation out of extreme poverty. To make sure students are on the right track, they are urged to start by exploring the Fraser's Economic Freedom of the World project, which ranks governments around the world in terms of how friendly they are to business and investment.

Winning essays are published in the institute's *Canadian Student Review*. This twelve- to twenty-four-page quarterly publication showcases short articles by conservative students, Fraser Institute staffers and some academics. In 2007, 68,000 copies were distributed free of charge—thanks to the Hecht Foundation—to campuses across Canada through a network of sympathetic professors and student organizations.

The long-standing student colloquium re-emerged in 2007 in a new format sponsored by the Liberty Fund of Indianapolis. Over two days of intensive discussion, students examined the topic "Liberty and Free Markets." A basic reading for the 2008 colloquium, entitled "Liberty and Public Choice," was the Fraser Institute's annual "Government Failure in Canada" report.[85]

The linchpin program is the internship. About four hundred university and college students apply each year for ten intern positions in the Fraser's Vancouver, Calgary and Toronto offices. Successful applicants are paid $2,000 a month for four months to train as junior policy analysts. They work on specific projects with institute analysts that will lead to publishable reports. The program, which costs about $100,000 a year, is financed partly by the Donner and Bell foundations. Interns participate in policy briefings and a weekly discussion club, develop their presentation skills and plug into networks of conservative experts in their field of research. Interns work on projects such as the school report card, the annual mining survey and new products, like the Regulatory Process Transparency Index for states and provinces, which will measure the "burden of regulation" and undoubtedly find that Canadian provinces rank dead last in North America, with Alberta being the best of a bad lot. One intern worked on an economic sustainability index, while another worked on a project to prove private schools are better for the poor than public schools. In 2007, a new product, funded by the Max Bell Foundation, was open to internship applications; this will profile successful private sector school chains.[86]

A recent addition to the student programs is teacher-training workshops on economic principles. This program is designed "to enlighten high school teachers on the principles of economics."[87] But only principles of economics that support a property-rights, market-based approach to economic activity are presented. Each year, more than fifty teachers participate in the one-day program in Toronto and Vancouver. The Fraser Institute estimates that ninety students are influenced by the participation of each teacher who uses the material in his or her lesson plans. The program is financed by three foundations: London Drug (chairman Brandt Louie is a Fraser Institute trustee), Weston and Donner.

The Fraser Institute's student recruitment programs, the intellectual output of the Calgary School and the millions of dollars supplied by the Donner Canadian Foundation would be for nought if these achievements could not eventually be translated into political success. The Mulroney Conservatives splintered into

Reform in the West, Bloc Québécois in Quebec and a Progressive Conservative rump in Ontario and Atlantic Canada. The meltdown was seen, in part, to be a result of Mulroney's betrayal of conservative principles. Ever since, conservatives have sought to "unite the right." What they seemed to mean, though, was to move further to the right.

Conservative stalwarts David Frum and Ezra Levant organized a conference in 1996 to assess the potential for strategic voting between Reform and PC candidates in the next election. Called "The Winds of Change," the conference was closed to the press. This was odd because some members of the press were present. Lorne Gunter, a columnist with the *Edmonton Journal* and an *Alberta Report* alumnus, even helped organize it. Gunter eventually withdrew, "feeling his continued participation might compromise his role as political commentator," another political commentator, Michael Valpy, commented.[88] The conference went nowhere, but the attendees did agree to establish a discussion group called the Civitas Society, after the Roman word "civitas," a body of people constituting a politically organized community. The founding directors include some of Canada's most prominent conservatives, such as *Alberta Report*'s Ted Byfield, the Calgary School's Tom Flanagan, David Frum and Ezra Levant, Gwen Landolt of the conservative REAL Women of Canada, the National Citizens Coalition's David Somerville, C.D. Howe president William Robson, Tom Long of the Mike Harris Tories, and Michael Walker. The ties to Stephen Harper were close and became even closer by the election to the Civitas board of Ian Brodie, who would become Harper's chief of staff.[89] This secretive, politically organized community of 250 libertarians and social conservatives, which allows no public access to its web site, became influential in shaping conservative strategy in the years leading up to Harper's 2006 election victory. Gunter served as Civitas president the year Harper was elected prime minister. He was succeeded by AIMS president Brian Lee Crowley.

Reform became the official opposition after the 1997 election, but failed to win seats east of Manitoba. Reform and the Progressive Conservatives each won about 19 percent of the vote. The combined vote would have been enough to win the election or, at least, reduce the Liberals to a minority. But to create a genuine right-wing party, the Red Tories, those who were conservatives but still saw a role for state intervention, would have to be jettisoned. Manning, to further his decades-long quest for the "pure" conservative party, promoted a united alternative as a political movement to unite Reformers and Blue Tories, who favoured small government and lower taxes.

Harper resigned his seat in the House of Commons to become vice-president of the National Citizens Coalition. A week after the 1997 election, he gave a speech to the American organization the Council for National Policy, which was meeting behind closed doors in Montreal. The *New York Times* called this group "a club of a few hundred of the most powerful conservatives" in the United States.[90] *Rolling Stone* reported it had "funnelled billions of dollars to right-wing Christian activists." It was at this Montreal meeting that the plot to impeach President Bill Clinton was reportedly hatched.[91]

The meeting was secret, but the text of Harper's speech was published on the Internet by CTV eight years later.[92] Was Harper hatching his own plot to form a genuine right-wing party? After calling Canada a "Northern European welfare state in the worst sense of the term," Harper complained that the Progressive Conservative Party is "very definitely liberal Republican. . . . In fact," he continued, "the leadership of the Conservative [P]arty was running the largest deficits in Canadian history. They were in favour of gay rights officially, officially for abortion on demand. Officially—what else can I say about them? Officially for the entrenchment of our universal, collectivized, health care system and multicultural policies in the constitution of the country." Reform was nothing like that, he told the conservative power brokers, being "much closer to what you would call conservative Republican." And that's where he would take the new party.

The unite-the-right movement was given a boost by Conrad Black's vanity paper, the *National Post*. From the first day of publication, the paper made it clear it would be a political player as well as a newsgathering operation. The lead story on that first day was not news in the sense of reporting on something important that had happened. Instead, the paper revealed that Alberta premier Ralph Klein agreed to be a speaker at a unite-the-right conference to be held in Ottawa four months later. Klein would make the case for a united-conservative alternative, the story informed readers.[93] It was agenda-setting, not news. The *National Post*, under the editorship of soon-to-be Donner Foundation trustee Ken Whyte, would beat the unite-the-right drum on every possible occasion. And eventually the *National Post*'s efforts paid off.

In 2000, Reform members voted to disband their party and create the Canadian Alliance. But Reform leader Preston Manning was defeated in the leadership race by Christian fundamentalist Stockwell Day, Klein's treasury minister. Civitas Society founder Tom Long came in third. The Canadian Alliance fared poorly in the election that year, even with significant corporate backing. Four of the five Big Banks donated about $100,000 each, while a big Calgary oil and gas law firm, Fraser, Milner, Casgrain, kicked in $130,000. The largest contribution, $250,000, came from a Toronto-based land development group.[94] This was no longer a populist party, if it ever was. Day was replaced by Stephen Harper in 2002, and Harper was able to repair much of the damage Day had caused. Red Tory Joe Clark retired as Progressive Conservative leader, eliminating a major obstacle to a shift to the right. PC leadership winner Peter MacKay of Nova Scotia promised he would not negotiate with Harper and the Canadian Alliance, but that's what he soon did. The prospect of a dismal result by both CA and PC parties in the next election led to protracted negotiations and an agreement to create a new party. As well, corporate backers were unhappy because they had to donate to so many parties. In the non-election year of 2002, for instance, Scotiabank contributed $40,000 to the Tories, $45,000 to the Alliance and $69,000 to the reigning Liberals. There were just too many bets to be hedged. The negotiations between the two parties were chaired by billionaire heiress Belinda Stronach of Magna International, providing an appropriate corporate backdrop to the proceedings. In short order, the party was formed, Stephen Harper elected leader, Paul Martin reduced to minority-government status and Harper elected prime minister in another minority government.

In less than two decades, Harper moved from graduate student working with Calgary School professors, to head of the National Citizens Coalition, to prime minister. He achieved this amazing transformation by blurring and reversing long-held positions. To become their prime minister, Harper had to commit himself to the values and priorities of most Canadians, at least until he won a majority government. And even then, his radical plan for a Canada governed by economic and social conservatism would have to be implemented patiently and incrementally.[95] He said as much in his speech to the seventh annual Civitas conference in Toronto in 2003. Like all Civitas gatherings, this one was supposed to be off the record, but was reprinted by Ted Byfield in his "Citizens Centre Report."[96] Harper claimed that the ideas of the economic conservatives—the libertarians—have already been adopted by government. As a result of the Reagan and Thatcher revolutions, Harper argued, "socialists and liberals began to stand for balanced budgeting, the superiority of markets, welfare reversal, free trade and some privatization." Of course, much more needs to be done, he reassured them: deeper and broader tax cuts, further reductions in debt, further deregulation and privatization and the elimination of corporate subsidies. But the arguments for this program have already been won, he declared, perhaps paying silent tribute to the Fraser Institute, the Calgary School and the rest of the corporate propaganda machine. The task was to move forward on values questions.

The corporate elite doesn't care much about values questions like abortion rights, gay marriage, gun control and child pornography. These do not help the bottom line and may even hurt it if a company came out in opposition to or in support of abortion rights, for instance. But there aren't enough economic conservatives in the country to win a majority Harper government. The task for Harper is to bring social conservatives of various stripes into the Conservative tent. Harper urged a return to social conservatism and social values, to change gears from "neocon" to "theocon," in Ted Byfield's apt, but worrisome, phrase, echoing visions of a future not unlike that painted in Margaret Atwood's dystopian work *A Handmaid's Tale*.

The state should take a more activist role in policing social norms and values, Harper told the Civitas audience. To achieve this goal, social and economic conservatives must reunite as they did in the United States, where evangelical Christians and business ruled in an uneasy coalition during the George W. Bush years. Red Tories must be jettisoned from the party, he said, and alliances forged with ethnic and immigrant communities, who vote Liberal, but espouse traditional family values. Harper reminded his audience that this was the successful strategy counselled by the radical conservatives under Ronald Reagan to pull conservative Democrats into the Republican tent. Movement towards the goal must be "incremental," he insisted, so the public won't be spooked. And this goal would need the support of the corporate media every step of the way.

CHAPTER 6

Gateway to the Public Mind

A debate has raged in newspapers around the world for over a decade about the ban on DDT. This pesticide, whose scientific name is dichlorodiphenyltrichloroethane, was widely used with great success during and after the Second World War to control insects that spread typhus and malaria. After the war, manufacturers made it available for use by farmers to protect crops like cotton. Production and profits soared. In just one year, 1959, 80 million pounds of the chemical were applied worldwide.

But even as DDT was coming into common use, scientists were expressing concern about possible environmental hazards. Rachel Carson's 1962 book, *Silent Spring*, raised the alarm that DDT and other pesticides were poisoning wildlife and endangering human health. She reported that thinning bird shells and declining bird populations were linked to DDT and cautioned that bald eagles eating fish laden with DDT were threatened with extinction. The chemical was subsequently banned in the United States and Canada in the early seventies and in most developed countries by the eighties. Later research found that DDT is a persistent organic pollutant that migrates from warm to cold climates after its release into the environment, eventually poisoning the traditional foods of Arctic peoples. It is a recognized carcinogen linked to breast and liver cancer and is suspected of disturbing embryonic development and reproduction in humans. In 2001, ninety-two countries and the European Community (EC) signed the United Nations Stockholm Convention banning the production and use of eleven persistent organic pollutants, but allowing exemptions for DDT. The ban, which came into force in 2004, continues to be controversial.

The reason for the controversy is the resurgence of malaria. DDT was dramatically effective in reducing malaria in many Third World countries. When the flow of the pesticide to these countries was reduced to a trickle in the seventies, the incidence of malaria soared. The World Health Organization (WHO) estimates that in 2006, 247 million people had the disease, causing nearly a million deaths, mostly of African children under five years of age.[1]

Should DDT be completely banned, as environmental groups like Greenpeace wish to see as its ultimate fate? Or should it be brought back into common use, at least in the Third World, as the Congress of Racial Equality (CORE) and Africa Fighting Malaria (AFM) argue? Isn't it ridiculous, those two groups ask, to worry about declining bird populations when millions of children are dying? And when framed as a choice between birds and children, the answer should be obvious. But is this the right question for the public to be asking? Might there be more to the debate? And how could someone get the facts on the controversy? Most people rely on the news media to keep them informed. To make responsible decisions about the ultimate fate of DDT, Canadians need accurate information and balanced viewpoints on the subject, but the story Canadians received about DDT was neither accurate nor balanced.

In the years since the Stockholm Treaty was signed, readers of Canadian newspapers have not had an opportunity for Greenpeace's position on DDT to be explained to them by Greenpeace itself. The only information they received about this environmental organization's position on DDT was conveyed by the organization's foes. *National Post* readers learned, for instance, courtesy of then columnist Elizabeth Nickson, that "groups like Greenpeace . . . serve their own ideological agenda, and want to keep the Third World permanently mired in poverty, disease and death. So far it has succeeded," she commented.[2] Greenpeace, with 100,000 members in Canada, actually supports limited DDT use to combat malaria, but readers of Canadian newspapers may have missed this information. CORE and Africa Fighting Malaria, on the other hand, have no members in Canada, yet were given space in the Canadian press to speak for themselves and to be represented in a positive light by their allies.

Early in 2004, the year the Stockholm Convention was to come into force, a *National Post* column introduced Paul Driessen, author of the book *Eco-Imperialism: Green Power, Black Death*, who railed at "wealthy, powerful First World environmental pressure groups" who "reveal an unbelievably callous, paternalistic, eco-centric attitude." Among their crimes, Driessen charged, these eco-imperialists pressured African governments to abandon DDT because it jeopardizes birds. Birds over blacks: is that what environmentalists want?[3] The *Post* repeated the eco-imperialism charge later in the year, when Driessen visited Winnipeg on a book tour. "Environmental activists who've never known starvation, never had to live without electricity, never had to watch their children die of malaria or dysentery, must no longer be allowed to put their anxieties, priorities and agendas ahead of the desperate pleas, the most basic needs, of destitute people who wish only to improve their lives and save their children's lives."[4] It was powerful rhetoric, with no reply from environmental activists in the *Post*.

The charges were repeated by the *Globe and Mail*'s Margaret Wente in a column titled "Bring back DDT: Eco-imperialism is killing African children." Wente featured Niger Innis, head of CORE, whose message was that wealthy Western countries had an "irrational aversion" to the use of DDT and successfully banned its use worldwide. As a result, African nations couldn't use this chemical to wipe out malaria and millions of African children were dying every year. Quoting Innis, she concluded that "First World environmentalists have saddled the Third World with debt and death."[5]

Writing in the *Ottawa Citizen*, Richard Tren, director of AFM, claimed that new European Union (EU) regulations that may effectively ban pesticides such as DDT was "a victory for the environmental lobby and a defeat of sound science," putting "the lives of millions in poor countries in danger."[6]

The problem with the coverage of the DDT issue and with the eco-imperialism charge is that they are based on falsehoods that the media did not investigate. Former CBC-TV *National News* anchor Knowlton Nash once said that ". . . our job in the media . . . is to . . . provide a searchlight probing for truth through the confusing, complicated, cascading avalanche of fact and fiction."[7] In this case, the media let their audiences down; fiction prevailed over fact.

Despite what the pro-DDT organizations alleged, DDT was not banned for use in mosquito control and could continue to be used in twenty-five countries in malarial regions. In these countries, limited amounts of DDT can be sprayed on the inside walls of houses to combat malaria-carrying mosquitoes. "The environmental community is collaborating with the World Health Organization to ensure that the phase-out of the remaining uses of DDT does not undermine the battle against malaria and the well-being of people living in malarial zones," the United Nations Environmental Programme reported when the treaty came into force. Even Canada's northern indigenous people, who were being poisoned by DDT, supported its continued use. According to Sheila Watt-Cloutier, president of the Inuit Circumpolar Conference Canada, "Canada's indigenous people would refuse to be a party to an agreement that threatened the health of others," she wrote in a letter to the *Globe and Mail* during treaty negotiations, "notwithstanding the threat of POPS [persistent organic pollutants] to their own health."[8] Spraying DDT onto the inside walls of houses is just one part of the battle. Other elements include hanging insecticide-treated bed nets to protect sleeping children, tracking outbreaks and treating people infected with the disease. As well, researchers are developing safe, affordable and locally effective alternatives to DDT.[9] This information was largely omitted in media coverage of the issue, which was framed starkly as DDT or death.

Both CORE and Africa Fighting Malaria claim the incidence of malaria skyrocketed after DDT was banned in the United States and the developed world. This is not true either. Key to the resurgence of malaria was that mosquitoes developed resistance to DDT because of its widespread use in agriculture. Ironically, rather than improving life, using DDT actually resulted in the resurgence of malaria. As early as the mid-fifties, researchers noted that DDT was losing its effectiveness. The rapid evolution of DDT-resistant mosquitoes was widely reported by such establishment media as *The Economist*, the *Washington Post*, and the *Globe and Mail*. Immunity to DDT was said to be the main cause of malaria's comeback, yet this information seems to have fallen into a rabbit hole as far as current media coverage of the issue is concerned.

How did the media get it so wrong? The answer lies, perhaps, in a document that came to light as a result of the 1998 Master Settlement Agreement between U.S. state Attorneys General and the tobacco industry. Among the forty million pages of industry documents posted on the Internet were two letters from AFM's Roger Bate to Philip Morris executives requesting funding for an anti-malaria campaign and a six-page document outlining AFM's strategy of falsehood and misrepresentation.[10]

Africa Fighting Malaria was formed during the negotiations that led to the Stockholm Convention. The name is misleading. The organization is based in Washington, D.C., not Africa. And the board of directors comprises, not Africans, but Americans. Its staff and directors have links, not to African social movement organizations, but to Western libertarian and neoconservative think-tanks like the American Enterprise Institute, the Institute of Economic Affairs, Tech Central Station, the Liberty Institute and the Atlas Economic Research Foundation. The anti-malaria campaign was intended to beat back environmental regulation. Using the plight of poor people was the vehicle to achieve this goal.

Titled "International public health strategy," the document outlined the steps necessary to defeat the environmental lobby. Roger Bate introduced himself by explaining that "my work . . . has focused on highlighting the dangers for governments of concentrating on minuscule risks to health, primarily because of pressure from loud interest groups." But eliminating these minuscule risks, Bate argued, "reduce[s] wealth and freedom . . ." The environmental movement "has been successful in most of its campaigns," Bate offered, "as it has been 'politically correct.'" Environmentalists are winning because they can claim to speak for the fish, birds, bears and whales, and in the case of Africa, the elephants. Bate recommended picking "issues on which we can divide our opponents and win. Make our case on our terms, not on the terms of our opponents—malaria prevention is a good example." Was a malaria-prevention campaign being offered to the funders because malaria was such a scourge it should be eliminated? Or was it, perhaps, being proposed for strategic reasons, such as defeating the "loud interest groups"? Bate recommended a recipe for success: fashion "the correct blend of political correctness" (having "oppressed blacks" as your membership) and arguments (being able to claim that "eco-imperialism was undermining their future and their right to self-determination").

According to Bate, to help disseminate the AFM message, sympathetic journalists should be recruited. "Target messages to show . . . journalists how to make political capital out of supporting our ideas," Bate recommended. "How do we recruit . . . journalists . . . to advocate the position?" he asked. One approach is the "contrast of western indifference to death in LDCs [less-developed countries] . . . and preoccupation with virtual risks in [the] west." The message Bate proposes to sell is that environmentalists fret about minimal risks at home while they ignore the deaths of millions overseas.

Bate denied that AFM received money from Philip Morris in response to his funding request. He also denied receiving any money from pharmaceutical or chemical companies.[11] Nonetheless, Aaron Swartz of the national watch group Fairness and Accuracy in Reporting (FAIR) notes, "AFM has very much followed the plan Bate laid out in his original funding pitch to corporations." And CORE followed a similar route.

In her *Globe* column on eco-imperialism, Margaret Wente assured readers that Roger Innis was "neither a shill for industry nor a raging neo-con," but the spokesman for the Congress of Racial Equality, which, she explained, was "a leading African-American advocacy group." In fact, Innis was a shill for industry and a raging neocon. And the Congress of Racial Equality had not been a leading African-American advocacy group since the 1960s. At that time CORE had been at the forefront of the struggle for equal rights, as a pioneer in the use of non-violent direct action to challenge segregation. CORE collapsed in the seventies and the remnant was taken over by Roy Innis (Niger Innis's father), who moved the organization to the Republican right.[12] In recent years CORE used its African-American facade to work with conservative groups to attack organizations like Greenpeace and undermine environmental regulation. It's fair to say that CORE was for sale to anyone with a need for visible black cheerleaders in its campaign. CORE also engaged in campaigns supporting genetically engineered foods. Innis could be seen leading a pro–free market, anti–Kyoto Accord counter-demonstration outside the ExxonMobil annual shareholders' meeting in Dallas, Texas, after CORE received $40,000 from the oil giant.

In 2003, Innis formed a partnership with one of the most aggressive anti-environmental organizations to launch a campaign to popularize the term "eco-imperialism." The Center for the Defense of Free Enterprise (CDFE) had earlier claimed credit for coining the term "eco-terrorism" and creating the so-called wise-use movement. Its funding comes from conservative foundations, forest-products companies, ExxonMobil and DuPont, a leading producer of DDT.[13] Leaning heavily on the use of symbolic days for their propaganda value, the two groups formed the Economic Human Rights Project on Martin Luther King Day, 2004, and kicked off their campaign on Earth Day with the publication of *Eco-Imperialism: Green Power, Black Death* by Paul Driessen, who is a fellow at the CDFE.[14] Driessen is also a senior fellow at the Committee for a Constructive Tomorrow, a libertarian think-tank whose researchers and advisers are prominent industry-backed global warming deniers.[15] (Roger Bate is on this organization's board of advisers.) The committee received $540,000 from ExxonMobil between 1998 and 2003.[16]

The strategy for the eco-imperialism campaign is to exploit the plight of poverty-stricken peoples in order to undermine environmental regulation and further the interests of its sponsors in the energy, chemical and forestry industries. These anti-environmental, pro–free market organizations have successfully used the media to persuade the public and decision makers that DDT should not be completely banned so it can be used to conquer malaria. They set up one special-purpose organization—Africa Fighting Malaria— and utilized an existing one—Congress of Racial Equality—to put a poor black face on their efforts. But behind the facade was a network of free market, libertarian think-tanks and their corporate sponsors pulling the strings. The strategy was effective. "Groups are latching onto the emotional impact of the malaria story, which is truly a human tragedy, to discredit environmentalists," admits John Balbus, chief health scientist with the American-based organization Environmental Defense.[17] Malaria was just the opening salvo. Already on the agenda are oil drilling in sensitive areas (the poor need as much cheap oil as possible), genetically modified foods (they will feed the hungry) and damming rivers for electricity production (the poor should not have to live without electricity). But parading the plight of the poor in front of the world media was not accompanied by any plans to improve the poor's social and economic conditions.

News is not propaganda, but the success of propaganda depends on reaching target audiences through the news media. Writing about the first Gulf War, British investigative reporter Philip Knightley asked, "So how today can the ordinary newspaper reader and television viewer distinguish the news from the propaganda? The answer is that he cannot. Good propaganda is too subtle to be instantly identifiable."[18] True, Knightley was commenting on propaganda in wartime, but the DDT-malaria campaign was all-out war on the Greens. The public would hear little about eco-imperialism if it wasn't mentioned in the press. It is discussed on some blogs and web sites, but how many people read them and how many believe them? Almost everyone reads newspapers, listens to radio talk shows or watches news on television, at least some of the time. There can be no propaganda without the participation of the news media. Propaganda is effective because the news media are perceived by their audiences to be generally free of propaganda and not beholden to corporate or other special interests. "Letters to the editor do indicate that some people consider the news media to be biased in specific instances," writes media scholar James Winter.

"But generally, people tend to regard the media as reasonably objective entities which, in most instances, present a fairly diverse spectrum of views."[19]

Underlying the public's trust in the media is the notion of the free press. In the United States, the idea of a free press is as old as the nation itself. The First Amendment to the U.S. Constitution says that ". . . Congress shall make no law . . . abridging the freedom of speech, or of the press . . ." In Canada, the idea of a free press predates Confederation, but official recognition came only with the 1982 Charter of Rights and Freedoms, which proclaims that "[e]very-one has the following fundamental freedoms: . . . freedom of thought, belief, opinion and expression, including freedom of the press and other media of communication . . ." The rationale is that the press must be free and independent so it can inform the public without fear or favour. As U.S. Supreme Court Justice Lewis Powell (author of the Powell Manifesto, see page 95) wrote in words quoted by Anthony Lewis of the *New York Times*: "No individual can obtain for himself the information needed for the intelligent discharge of his political responsibilities . . . By enabling the public to assert meaningful control over the political process, the press performs a crucial function in effecting the societal purpose of the First Amendment."[20] Powell's words would apply equally to the Charter's communication clause. The press has a responsibility to society and in return society protects the press. The statement of principles of the Canadian Newspaper Association, representing daily newspapers across Canada, states that ". . . the operation of a newspaper is a public trust, and its overriding responsibility is to the society it serves . . ."[21]

Our faith in the free press is based on the notion of the "marketplace of ideas." As U.S. Supreme Court Justice Oliver Wendell Holmes wrote in a classic dissent, "The best test of truth is the power of the thought to get itself accepted in the competition of the market" through "free trade in ideas."[22] True, Holmes was in the minority in that decision, but his words have outlived it. The market-place of ideas was most salient in the nineteenth century, when hundreds of newspapers reflected every interest and point of view, and flooded the nation's fledgling newsstands. The papers that provided the most truthful accounts would be sought out by the careful, rational reader, so the theory went. These papers would thrive, while those that presented false or less truthful ideas would fall by the wayside. Society would be better off because it was well served by a free press, which presented the truth about its affairs. The marketplace of ideas has faded in significance, particularly in the United States, where most metropolitan areas are served by only one paper. But perhaps it still operates in locations like Toronto, where six papers (*Toronto Star, Globe and Mail, Toronto Sun, National Post, Metro, 24 Hours*) with different ideological slants vie for readers' attention. Toronto has such a free and unfettered press, democracy should thrive there, one might conclude.

The marketplace of ideas is an excellent concept, but doesn't reflect several news media realities. It has been long noted by critical media scholars like Dallas Smythe that the media do not operate in a market for ideas but in one for audiences. Their market is advertisers, and their product is not truthful ideas but desirable audiences, which they sell to advertisers. Ad dollars account for 75 to 80 percent of newspaper revenues and 100 percent of revenues for television and radio. Thus, in Toronto, each paper tries to lure advertisers away from the competition. They do this by presenting the advertisers with a more desirable readership demographic than the other papers. And they attract readers with an appealing package of news, information and entertainment, which may or may not contain truthful ideas. The bias in deciding what's news is towards attracting wealthier audiences that can be sold at higher rates, not fearlessly exposing the truth regardless of who is implicated. But not every paper can attract wealthier audiences. In two- and three-newspaper cities they compete for demographic segments. In Vancouver, for instance, the *Vancouver Sun* targets higher-income, better-educated readers, while *The Province* courts those with lower income and education.

Media owners push the press further from the free press ideal. How independent can the news be when seven conservative billionaires and multi-millionaires have a hammerlock on mainstream Canadian news media.[23] They all took big hits as a result of the 2008 financial meltdown, losing an average 25 percent of their net worth, but are still ranked among the wealthiest Canadians. They are the Thomson family, which controls CTV and the *Globe and Mail* (net worth $18.5 billion), the Ted Rogers family, which owns *Maclean's*, *Chatelaine*, Rogers Wireless, Cable and Radio ($5.1 billion), Paul Desmarais, who owns seven Quebec papers including *La Presse*, among others ($4.1 billion), Allan Slaight, who sold Standard Broadcasting ($2.0 billion), the Shaw family, which owns Shaw Cable, Corus Entertainment and Corus Radio ($1.2 billion), Randall Moffat of Moffat Communications ($600 million), the Peladeau family, which owns Quebecor and Sun Media ($415 million) and the Asper family of CanWest Global (at $341 million, down 60 percent). Sure they're in it for the money. Return to shareholders is the fundamental value of all commercial news media and the ultimate objective of all media managers. There are several ways to increase profits: increase revenues by raising prices charged for subscriptions and rates charged to advertisers, if they can attract more affluent readers; or cut costs and divert more revenue to the shareholders. Cutting costs means primarily cutting the number of journalists working for them, making the search for truthful ideas more difficult.

As the roll call of billionaires and multi-millionaires demonstrates, the media barons have been successful in the news business, even given the dramatic downturn of 2008. They're also in the game for the power and influence that media ownership can buy. This fact has been evident since the nineteenth century, when aspiring politicians like William Lyon Mackenzie and Amor de Cosmos raised their profiles and promoted their political programs by starting newspapers. The *Globe and Mail* was established in the 1930s when mining magnate Bill Wright purchased the *Globe* and its chief competitor, the *Mail and Empire*. He wanted the newly merged entity to reflect the view that "anything that is of advantage to mining is of advantage to the country as a whole,"[24] an early version of "what's good for General Motors is good for the country." George McCullagh, Wright's publisher, was a Bay Street broker who became wealthy buying and selling gold-mining stocks. He was a devout practitioner of the religion of free enterprise and made sure the *Globe*'s pages reflected the advantages of free markets and less government interference. Along with praising capitalism, the *Globe* condemned unions and social reform. Conrad Black was merely following long-established tradition when he launched the *National Post* as a vehicle to spread his ideology and agenda over the political landscape. Losses of $200 million in the first few years of operation didn't seem to deter him from his mission.

University of Windsor's Jim Winter notes that in the 1940s, George Orwell identified the tendency of the British press towards a consensus as to which stories were newsworthy. This was laid out in his preface to *Animal Farm*, which was removed from the original publication—perhaps because it focused on thought control in Western democracies and not the Soviet Union—and reappeared only later with the original manuscript:

> [T]here is an orthodoxy, a body of ideas which it is assumed that all right-thinking people will accept without question. It is not exactly forbidden to say this, that or the other, but it is 'not done' to say it, just as in mid-Victorian times it was 'not done' to mention trousers in the presence of a lady. Anyone who challenges the prevailing orthodoxy finds himself silenced with surprising effectiveness. A genuinely

unfashionable opinion is almost never given a fair hearing . . . in the popular press . . .[25]

Orwell was clear as to why this was so: "The British press is extremely centralized, and most of it is owned by wealthy men who have every motive to be dishonest on certain important topics." Journalist Linda McQuaig made the same point when she wrote that "we must always remember that virtually all media outlets are owned by rich, powerful members of the elite. To assume that this fact has no influence on the ideas they present would be the equivalent to assuming that, should the entire media be owned by, say, labour unions, women's groups or social workers, this would have no impact on the editorial content."[26] Given that big business finances the production and distribution of news, it would be naive to expect the media to question seriously the structure of society or to entertain far-reaching proposals for change.

Media barons are members in good standing of Canada's corporate elite and many are active members of the Canadian Council of Chief Executives, the most powerful and influential corporate lobby in the country, as was discussed in Chapter 1.[27] At a high-level chief executives conference in 2000, then CanWest CEO and tax lawyer Izzy Asper called the tax system "anti-business, anti-private sector, and anti-entrepreneurial." Canadians were anti-business, he charged, because the education system was "tilted against the ideas of business, enterprise, entrepreneurship and profit." Canada should be more like the U.S., he railed, where "these ideas are revered."[28] They also seem to have been revered by CanWest newspapers and television stations.

For one hundred years the press has been a profit-making enterprise operating in a capitalist system and has thoroughly assimilated the values of business. The owners' ideological convictions and interests in influencing the political agenda, and their reliance on advertising dollars for their revenues, create an ideal context for disseminating corporate propaganda messages. They became rich under the current system of inequality and are unlikely to favour any change except perhaps a return to the greater inequality of the early twentieth century, which is one goal of corporate propaganda. They are unlikely to want a fairer tax system or to encourage their news organizations to advocate for such a system. The influence of advertising revenue and the ideological solidarity of a governing elite, ensure the narrow consensus of the agenda for discussion. Free press always means free from government interference; corporate interference is never considered.

The Asper family's pro-business, anti-government tilt is not hard to find. Along with its twelve daily metro newspapers across Canada, the *National Post*, thirty-odd community papers and television news broadcasts on the Global network, for several years CanWest offered *Global Sunday*, which it billed as "Canada's number one current affairs talk show." A February 2005 show featured a panel discussion on federal government equalization policy. The purpose of equalization is to ensure that provincial governments have sufficient revenues to provide "reasonably comparable levels of public services at reasonably comparable levels of taxation." The left-wing perspective on equalization is that it helps fund programs that define who we are as Canadians, such as education, health care and social services. Canadians in every province should have roughly equal access to these programs, the left says.

This perspective was not raised by the three-member panel. Instead, two of the panellists offered right-wing viewpoints.[29] Ken Boessenkool, a former adviser to Stephen Harper and a Fraser Institute contributor, argued that non-renewable resource revenues should not be included in equalization, meaning that some provinces, Alberta in particular, would have permanently lower taxes and richer services. Boessenkool, who had become an Ottawa lobbyist for non-renewable resource companies, was one of six authors of the Alberta Agenda, a proposal to build a fiscal firewall around the province. The second panellist was prominent Queen's University economist Thomas Courchene, an early member of the Fraser Institute editorial advisory board, but since 1980, a senior fellow of the C.D. Howe Institute. Courchene offered that in the post-NAFTA world, provinces trade north-south and "too much equalization east, west will impair" regional economies. Economics apparently trumps equalization. The third panellist, *National Post* columnist John Ivison, didn't have any answers to the equalization question, but his right-leaning credentials were on display in recent columns in which he wrote that public health care was a monopoly controlled by health care workers and hospitals, the CBC was the "Corpse" without any viewers, and child care sucked up "vast gobs of money."

The program's rightward tilt was likely not accidental. The model for this format could be found on the Fox News channel's falsely balanced *Hannity & Colmes* debate show. This show pitted the aggressive conservative Sean Hannity against the mildly liberal, often conciliatory Alan Colmes, in a format "where conservatives outnumber, out-talk and out-interrupt their liberal opponents," as Fairness and Accuracy in Reporting explains the strategy.[30] *Global Sunday* followed a similar formula, tilting sharply to the right. Progressive and left-wing perspectives on public policy issues were blanked out—they didn't seem to exist in *Global Sunday*'s world.

Host Danielle Smith had a long history of advocating for the libertarian right. She started her career as an intern at the Fraser Institute, then, after stints as a Reform Party worker and Edmonton school trustee, she launched the Canadian Property Rights Research Institute. This short-lived organization was sponsored largely by Alberta ranchers. Its goal was to promote the principle that private property rights take priority over human rights and environmental protection. Smith opposed endangered species legislation and bans on smoking in indoor publicly accessible places. She left the property rights organization in 1999 to join the *Calgary Herald* as an editorial writer, where she crossed the picket line to write her first column two weeks after her newsroom colleagues went on strike for a first contract. In this piece she applauded the Fraser Institute's environment director—without revealing her own institute connection—for claiming there is no crisis regarding endangered species, therefore no government legislation is required.[31] Typical of her editorials was one she wrote lauding the work of researcher Fred McMahon from the libertarian Atlantic Institute for Market Studies (and later at the Fraser Institute), who argued that jobs flourish when businesses earn big profits, and businesses earn big profits when governments cut taxes and unions give up their outlandish demands.[32]

Smith oversaw a parade of *Global Sunday* panels slanted to the right. In one discussion with the title "The Nanny State: Should Government Be in the Business of Babysitting?," public-daycare advocate Martha Friendly of the University of Toronto had to fend off the other three panellists, two of whom were ideologically opposed to any form of daycare. The fourth panellist favoured daycare but, as spokesperson for the Quebec-based Coalition for Private Daycare, required the participation of for-profit providers.[33] When the topic was "State of the Union—Gay OK?," two constitutional lawyers faced off on the two sides of the issue, University of Toronto law professor Lorraine Weinrib arguing in favour of same-sex marriage and constitutional lawyer David Brown, who was counsel for the Association for Marriage and the Family in Ontario, arguing against. But the balance was upended by the presence of Joan Crockatt, a senior editor from the *Herald*. Instead of providing context for the issue, which would be the expected role, Crockatt claimed, somewhat bizarrely, that "judges don't make laws . . . laws are made by Charter attorneys, not by judges . . . judicial activists would like Canadians to believe" that judges make laws.[34] Another political panel featured Barbara Yaffe and Lorne Gunter, two conservative CanWest pundits along with Robert Fife, the CanWest News Ottawa bureau chief, as if he was supposed to provide left-wing balance.[35]

In October 2004, the program added a new segment called "The Final Round." This was supposedly a hard-hitting boxing match between two combatants: in the right corner, Ezra "Hammer" Levant, and in the left, Stephen "Leftie" LeDrew. The viewer could vote each week on which pugilist delivered the knockout punch. But was LeDrew really on the left? The *Fontana Dictionary of Modern Thought* defines the left as the "label applied to a range of radical political views and to those holding them." And it says that radicalism "has always been associated with dissatisfaction with the status quo and an appeal for basic political and social change."[36] As former president of the Liberal Party of Canada and long-time Paul Martin supporter, LeDrew does not fit that characterization. Middle of the road is closer to the mark.

His opponent, Ezra Levant, on the other hand, was a genuine radical right winger, a rightist being someone who vigorously defends capitalism and attacks government intervention in economic affairs. Levant was an adviser to Reform/ Canadian Alliance leaders Preston Manning and Stockwell Day and spent two years on the *National Post*'s editorial board. He was publisher of the *Western Standard*, an Alberta-based conservative magazine with an agenda that spanned topics from anti-gun control, to anti-Kyoto, to anti–same sex marriage, to pro–private enterprise.

Some of their debates revealed the rightward torque to *Global Sunday*. In one program Smith asked LeDrew and Levant this question: George W. Bush has assured Paul Martin that "the U.S. missile defence plan does not involve the weaponization of space . . . Should Canada sign on?" Levant replied first: "Of course we should . . . Who do we trust more—the crazy ayatollahs of Iran . . . or George Bush? . . . We should sign on if we mean to be good allies." Then it was LeDrew's turn: "Bush is an honourable fellow . . . but no one knows what the deal is . . . Let's get the facts and then we'll deal with it."[37] This was hardly a counter to Levant. The argument that we should not join under any circumstances was not raised. As far as *Global Sunday* was concerned, this viewpoint, possibly held by a majority of Canadians, was not worth discussing.

In another program, the question for debate was: "What role, if any, does the state have in the cribs of the nation?" LeDrew replied that "young couples with both parents working need a financial break . . . daycare or a tax credit and the state should provide it." Levant offered that we should "lower taxes . . . so one parent [can afford] to stay home." The argument for the benefits of non-profit, publicly supported daycare was not raised. In fact, LeDrew said that "no one's talking about Moscow Central," blurring the performance of excellent non-profit daycares, such as those at universities and colleges, with some mythic totalitarian Soviet system.[38]

It was a tight little world out there in CanWest's Calgary studio. When Smith introduced Levant each week she didn't mention their close ties. It wasn't just that they were both conservative University of Calgary students and had been Fraser Institute interns during the nineties. Nor was it just that when Smith headed the Canadian Property Rights Research Institute, Levant was on the organization's board of advisers. There was an even closer link. Smith was married to Levant's business partner in the *Western Standard*. Smith's husband at the time, Sean McKinsley, was former executive assistant to two Canadian Alliance MPs and former executive director of the Alberta Taxpayers Association. McKinsley runs a polling and PR firm called JMCK Inc., which had some interesting clients, such as the Canadian Taxpayers Federation, the Canadian Alliance, the *Calgary Herald* and CanWest Global Television, which offered his wife's program.[39]

Many of us have strong opinions about what's important in the world, even though we may have little direct involvement with events and issues beyond our daily lives. Our knowledge of the world beyond our immediate experience comes largely from the news media. How the press treats events and issues has an impact on what we know and believe. Current understanding of media influence is summed up by the famous statement of American political scientist Bernard Cohen. He wrote in his 1963 book, *The Press and Foreign Policy*, that the press may not be successful much of the time in telling people what to think, but it is stunningly successful in telling its readers what to think about.[40] Newspapers convey to us the relative importance of the topics they report each day. Is the story on the front page or an inside page? Is it the lead story on the front page? How big is the headline? How long is the story? Is there an accompanying picture or graphic? Does the story appear in the news for more than one day? Television news presents fewer items, so even a mention on the evening news conveys the message this item is important. Additional cues are provided by a story's placement in the lineup and the amount of time spent on it. News on the Internet largely follows the lead of the traditional media since it is derivative of those sources.

For current affairs shows like *Global Sunday*, simply putting a topic up for debate among experts (even if they skew right) signals that the topic is important. "For all the news media"—newspapers, television, radio and even the Internet—"the repetition of a topic day after day is the most powerful message of all about its importance," writes Maxwell McCombs, the University of North Carolina professor who has studied agenda setting for three decades.[41]

The first agenda-setting research was undertaken by McCombs during the 1968 U.S. presidential election. He found a close match between the issues reported in news coverage of the campaign and those reported as key in the campaign by undecided voters.[42] More than four hundred studies confirm that the media agenda (the items receiving the most frequent and most prominent coverage) sets the public agenda (the issues members of the public think are worthwhile to hold opinions about). Of course, what people think is important is influenced by factors other than what the media report. People talk to each other about items they see or read on the news and these conversations can lead them to accept or reject a particular agenda item. Someone who is unemployed will know that unemployment is an important issue to be addressed, even if the media do not report it. Or the media might report that unemployment is not a problem, which will contradict the unemployed worker's experience. But most items reported in the news are beyond the individual's direct knowledge and experience.

Chapter 1 discussed the outpouring of studies and conferences sponsored by the Canadian Council of Chief Executives, the C.D. Howe Institute and others in the aftermath of 9/11. These mostly urged deeper integration with the United States and were faithfully reported by the mainstream news media. According to agenda-setting theory, the avalanche of supportive media coverage wouldn't convince Canadians that deeper integration was essential for Canada's survival, but it would persuade them that integration was an important issue that needed to be addressed.

If, on the other hand, a topic is rarely or never discussed in the media, it has almost no chance of being deemed important by the public. Leonard Pitts, a columnist with the *Miami Herald*, observed that "in a world where media set the public agenda and drive the dialogue, those things media ignore may as well not exist."[43] NewsWatch Canada is a media-monitoring project in the

206 Not A Conspiracy Theory

School of Communication at Simon Fraser University in Burnaby, British Columbia. NewsWatch calls items left off the media agenda "the missing news," whose absence creates blind spots in public perception. These are stories or trends that Canadians should be aware of because of their significance, but have been underreported or omitted entirely from coverage. Frequently some stories receive adequate coverage, but significant dimensions or angles to the story may be omitted. One blind spot studied by NewsWatch researchers is the media's apparent unwillingness or inability to cover the power and biases of media corporations themselves.[44]

Further evidence that important news is missing from the media lineup is provided by the findings of the American research group Project Censored. Each year professors and students at Sonoma State University in southern California comb the commercial and alternate press seeking stories of significance that have been underreported in the commercial press. They assemble a list of the top twenty-five most significant but underreported stories of the year.[45] For 2008, some of these stories—with consequences for Canada—were:

- The U.S. and European Union are vigorously pursuing increasingly destructive regional and bilateral trade and investment agreements that require enormous and irreversible concessions from developing countries, while offering little in return (#4)
- At least twenty states have passed laws allowing public–private partnerships to build and run highways, with investment firms picking up infrastructure cheaply to maximize profits (#9)
- Pure water is growing more scarce because corporations, municipalities and the military are polluting U.S. waters—often with little or no accountability (#17)
- The U.S. free-trade model is meeting increasing resistance as peoples' movements around the world are building powerful alternatives to neoliberal exploitation (#19)

These are all stories that Americans and Canadians should know about because they have important public policy dimensions, but they have been largely shut out of the mainstream American (and Canadian) news media. Instead, they were reported in alternative print and online publications such as consortiumnews, Common Dreams, moonofalabama.org, CorpWatch,

Democracy Now, Global Research, SciDev.Net, Mother Jones and Tomdispatch. com, none of which reach mass audiences.

Media emphasis on certain issues, such as crime or political corruption and not on others, such as media concentration or corporate propaganda, determines which issues members of the public think are important. A new publisher arrives at a newspaper and, to make his mark, increases the paper's coverage of crime and accidents. Soon people become concerned about the safety of the streets. But there is no increase in robberies or car crashes, only in the frequency with which they are reported on the front page. Some issues are brought into the foreground of people's minds while others are pushed into the background. By simply keeping an issue "alive" by reporting on it for some duration, the media may transmit to the public more than just information, but also a subtle message concerning the legitimacy of the issue. This is not to say that most news media have an agenda they try to push onto their readers and viewers. That may be the case with CanWest's *Global Sunday*, the *National Post* and, increasingly, *Maclean's* magazine, but the agenda exists for most media because they must select and highlight a few stories as the most important of the day.

Why do the media select and emphasize certain stories and not others? Almost everything the American president does, from visiting Iraq, to stopping for a BeaverTail during his state visit to Canada, is newsworthy. So are the activities of most national leaders, such as the Canadian prime minister and provincial premiers. Another influence on the media agenda is the news reported by elite newspapers such as the *New York Times, Washington Post* and *Globe and Mail*. Many newspapers and television news broadcasts turn first to the *Times* or the *Globe* to determine what's important that day, what they should be covering. Third are the norms and ground rules that govern newsroom operations. From assigning stories, to suggesting sources, to editing and placing stories, newsroom practices are carefully organized so that the news operation runs smoothly. But the interest in efficiency inevitably influences the media agenda.

Journalists can cover only a fraction of what occurs each day. Their lives are made easier by communications officers and public relations practitioners who represent government agencies, corporations and other important news sources. They provide the newsroom with substantial amounts of information organized in a way to make it immediately usable.[46] A study of the *New York Times* and the *Washington Post* over twenty years revealed that nearly half of all news stories that had appeared in their pages were based on news releases, news conferences and background briefings paid for by source organizations.[47] These two papers are among the largest, wealthiest, best-staffed and most important in the American media system. As we've just seen, they set the agenda for many American and Canadian news organizations. That they rely so heavily on subsidized news from source organizations is a little-known fact that has implications for our understanding of propaganda dissemination.

Think-tanks also subsidize news. Their corporate and foundation backers pay them to undertake studies and package them for free distribution to the media. If the Fraser Institute can influence the issues the media report and comment on, it will influence the issues people consider important. And if it can influence the public agenda, it can push governments in desired directions. The institute's school rankings are not only controversial, but expensive to prepare. They have provided CanWest and Sun Media papers with hundreds of pages of free copy. Along with dozens of pages given over to detailed school rankings, the think-tank supplies ready-made stories that newspaper education reporters can easily rewrite under their own bylines. Again, this is not the media telling us what to think—only carefully controlled brainwashing experiments can do that—but telling us what to think about. Even strong supporters of public education will likely conclude, reading year after year about the disparities between private and public schools, that there must be problems in education that need to be addressed. And it's been effective. In at least five Canadian court decisions in recent years, the institute's rankings have been cited in child custody cases. Perhaps the public system needs to be supplemented with taxpayer-financed vouchers that allow students to attend private schools. And the propaganda purpose is achieved.

The Fraser Institute understands the critical importance of the media in shaping public opinion. The institute's leaked—Michael Walker said "purloined"—1997 draft five-year plan, "Towards the new millennium," revealed an ambitious program of continued media "penetration." The five-year period is long past and the Fraser has, no doubt, fashioned other media penetration plans. But this document provides a rare glimpse of think-tank thinking. In it, Walker bragged that the Fraser had "outpaced not only each and every one of our competitors, but the sum total of their efforts in [the creation of a media presence]." He pointed proudly to a fax-broadcasting system, which facilitated mass mailings of institute releases and increased the institute's presence on talk radio across the country. He noted that the institute was the focus of 105 hours' worth of coverage on the Cable Public Affairs Channel (CPAC), which is watched by a surprising number of people. CPAC coverage flows from the institute's round-table luncheons and the conferences it hosts. The key, Walker reported, was "the controversial or novel topics which have been covered by these conferences."[48]

As for the future, Walker vowed that the focus during the next five years would be "the expansion of our penetration of the national media." He proposed to double the institute's $2.5 million budget—a target he easily met— with a sizable portion going to media outreach and influence. He described ambitious plans to develop a database of journalists who respond to the institute's material and catalogue the extent to which particular journalists cover its news releases. He would create a regular column for Canadian newspapers on health care issues, publish two studies a year dealing with educational-choice issues and publish one book a year demonstrating a private property market-based solution to an environmental problem. Finally, the institute would become the central point of reference for economic information about social policy issues. Each new project area the institute undertook "will have a component focusing on the approach to the media and to other second hand dealers in ideas," a characterization which points to the fact that news media create no ideas themselves and must get them from somewhere, preferably from Walker and his staff at the Fraser.

Some initiatives never came to fruition because new opportunities arose. In 1997, the Internet was still marginal, but by 2002 was pushing its way to centre stage, and the institute moved to Internet distribution. At the 2002 annual general meeting, chairman Ray Addington was able to boast that "the Institute's web site . . . regularly attracts more visitors than the web site of any other public policy organization in the country."[49] As well, Walker claimed in the annual report, the institute had dramatically increased its penetration of mainstream media. Mentions of the Fraser Institute in Canada's major newspapers doubled over the five-year span. One reason for the large increase, though, was the appearance of Conrad Black's National Post, which, in 2002, published articles by Fraser staffers or mentioned the think-tank nearly every other day. The institute's communications department recorded over four thousand media stories in 2002. It estimated this coverage was worth more than $9 million in advertising equivalency, a measure the think-tank uses to gauge public impact. Projects that "provided a tangible empirical focus for the policy concern" were key in the media penetration efforts, as the five-year plan predicted. These are projects like Tax Freedom Day, the Hospital Waiting List Survey, the Economic Freedom of the World Index, and the School Report Card.[50] They are misleading but attract media attention because they can grab headlines and are easy to report. They are also effective as propaganda because most people tend to accept statistics as being authoritative. They are also effective agenda-setting devices because many indexes are published annually and soon become part of the landscape of ideas.

While Michael Walker, Brian Crowley of AIMS and other think-tank entrepreneurs were devising strategies to move their ideas into the commercial media, the media were moving in their direction and becoming more receptive to their messages. Newspapers have been pro-business since they became businesses themselves in the late nineteenth century. As businesses, they exist to earn a profit for their shareholders. They thus generally favour policies that boost business and oppose policies that detract from business success. Within that general framework, however, there was room for a variety of perspectives. Independent-newspaper owners in small and medium-sized cities want to boost business, but also promote the general welfare of the community. They had to reflect, or at least respect, the political leanings of their readers. Even when papers were gathered together in the Southam chain, there was a hands-off attitude from head office. Local editors determined their papers' positions on local issues. As one example, the *Vancouver Sun* endorsed the Mike Harcourt New Democrats in the 1991 provincial election.[51]

But the days of local independence are over, as the media barons followed American trends and pushed their properties further to the right, ending up closer to the propagandists. The *Vancouver Sun*, for instance, went overboard during the 2005 provincial election in its praise of the business-friendly Gordon Campbell Liberals and its vilification of the New Democrats who, if anything, were more moderate than Harcourt had been in 1991.[52]

Early in 2005, Ted Rogers shook up his flagship *Maclean's* magazine by hiring one of the top media figures in the country to be the magazine's new editor. Ken Whyte was editor-in-chief of the *National Post* under Conrad Black and the person most responsible for making that paper amenable to propaganda efforts. Whyte worked under the Aspers for two more years after Black sold the paper to them, before leaving. After several years in the wilderness, he ended up as publisher and editor at *Maclean's*, a previously inconceivable coupling of positions in one person because it combines business and editorial functions, which traditionally were assiduously separated. What will take priority: editorial integrity or corporate profit? Or perhaps they are merging.

Whyte's hand appeared about two months after he took over in the form of an interview with Allan Gotlieb, who was critical of the Liberal government's international-policy statement because it didn't "reflect a vision of a single North American market,"[53] repeating the message of the deep-integration campaign. Whyte and Gotlieb were both on the Donner Canadian Foundation board, which was still promoting deeper integration. This connection was not revealed to *Maclean's* readers. The following week *Maclean's* featured a fawning cover story about Conservative leader Stephen Harper, who was, the magazine informed readers, known to be "icy and inflexible," but "up close he's anything but."[54] And the week after that, the magazine offered a report about the need to "fix" the health care system by contracting out medical procedures to private clinics.[55] This was written by a former colleague of Whyte's at the *Alberta Report*. Whyte took little time before raiding the *National Post* for writers and managers. *Maclean's* was becoming indistinguishable from the *Post*.

The *Post* itself was created by Conrad Black who ramped up the remaking of newspapers when he became their largest owner in Canada. He went on a buying spree during the 1990s and ended up owning 60 of Canada's 105 dailies under his company, Hollinger Inc., including many major ones. He immediately began diverting money paid to reporters into shareholders' pockets, where, in his view, the company's cash belonged. The day after Hollinger completed its purchase of the *Regina Leader-Post* and *Saskatoon StarPhoenix*—giving Black ownership of all five papers in the province—employees of the papers were summoned to meetings in hotels in Regina and Saskatoon. Once there, they were herded into different rooms. The occupants in one room in each hotel—dubbed the "Death Room"—were told they were losing their jobs and would not be returning to the papers, ever. A total of 182 employees were fired, about 25 percent of the two papers' staff.[56] The goal of these and other cuts was to reduce newsroom staff to one person for every thousand papers sold, a ratio which seems to have been concocted by management to justify such severe cuts. In his first three years controlling Southam, Black eliminated nearly a third of the workforce.

Besides enriching shareholders, deep staff cuts facilitate the job of propagandists. With fewer reporters to dig into stories and obtain information and viewpoints from alternative sources, newsrooms are more likely to go with the handouts from official and known sources. And with the threat of further staff cuts looming over the newsroom if profit margins were still not high enough, few reporters would want to be noticed by management for seeking out critical and progressive sources when it was patently clear what the proprietor wanted. News releases and opinion pieces from conservative think-tanks became more likely to receive favourable attention. Nor did it hurt that Black's long-time partners, David Radler and Peter Whyte, and Black's wife, Barbara Amiel, all joined the board of trustees of the Fraser Institute, while Hollinger contributed $99,000 to the think-tank's building fund.[57]

Black's next priority was to remake the *Ottawa Citizen*. Located in the nation's capital, this paper had the greatest potential to influence the national agenda, since Black did not own a national paper or one based in Toronto. He planned to increase *Citizen* circulation by targeting upscale, conservative *Globe* readers and by moving the paper to the right. Editor James Travers and editorial page editor Peter Calamai were too leftist for Black and were forced to resign. As Travers admitted, "On social policy issues, I think we are quite far to the left of Mr. Black's point of view."[58] Black replaced Travers with Neil Reynolds, a former president of the fringe Libertarian Party of Canada. Asked several years later, when he was editor of the *Vancouver Sun*, what his paper believed in, Reynolds replied to his baffled audience at the UBC School of Journalism, "Low taxes, lower taxes, very low taxes . . . limited government and the innate moral right to globally trade," a viewpoint that may reflect libertarian doctrine but hardly does justice to the viewpoints of many readers.[59] Under cover of creating "a paper for readers," Black and Reynolds transformed the *Citizen* from a moderate voice into a strident champion of conservatism. They replaced Calamai with William Watson, a conservative economist from McGill University, who published with the C.D. Howe and Fraser institutes. They reached into the Fraser Institute itself for the deputy editorial page editor, John Robson, who had been a policy adviser for both the institute and the Reform Party. They also added: Adrienne DeLong Snow, the managing director of the Donner Canadian Foundation, David Warren, the founder and editor of the *Idler*, a socially conservative literary magazine that went under in the early nineties; and Dan Gardner, who came to the *Citizen* from the offices of Ontario education minister John Snobelen and Premier Mike Harris.[60] (In Black's view the *Citizen* had been too critical of the Mike Harris government. These appointments could right that perceived wrong.) To maintain balance, Black retained some long-time liberal *Citizen* columnists and promoted several reporters to the editorial board.

Black was also concerned about the *Montreal Gazette*, which he felt was soft on Quebec separation. Editor Joan Fraser resigned abruptly because Black's views were so incompatible with hers. She did this after one of Black's associates on the Southam board said she had to go.[61] Black later brought in Peter Stockland, editorial page editor of the *Calgary Herald*, to head the paper. Stockland was a notorious Quebec nationalist basher for the Sun newspaper chain. He was so hated by francophone Québécois that his family had to move temporarily from its Quebec City home. Stockland was a conservative and a devout Catholic. He called the National Action Committee on the Status of Women "a clique of rad-fem nutbars."[62]

To move the rest of the papers expeditiously to the right, Black hired a half-dozen conservative columnists from outside the Southam chain: his wife, Barbara Amiel, to write about foreign affairs, Andrew Coyne from the *Globe* to write about national politics, and Giles Gherson, also from the *Globe*, to write about economics. He hired Mordecai Richler, a strident anti–Quebec nationalist, and George Jonas, Amiel's ex-husband, to disseminate his crusty, socially conservative views on society. Their columns went out to all Southam papers and helped shift the chain to the right. On occasion Black wrote his own editorials and ordered his papers to run them in prominent positions. Who can forget October 1996, when he instructed all his daily newspapers to run a column he wrote, even telling them to run it on the op-ed page and title it "Conrad Black's response to the CBC." The CBC documentary *The Paper King* was judged to be even-handed by outside observers, but Black considered it "a smear job" and a "televised kangaroo court," which featured a "dreary procession of tired and authoritarian leftists trotted through [the] program." Like a herd of barking seals most papers did exactly as he ordered.[63] Some even ran news stories about Black's editorial and the irresponsibility of the CBC, probably hoping the boss would appreciate their enthusiasm for his cause.

Black's great project was launching a new national daily, the first in North America since *USA Today* was established in the early eighties. It would be his personal vehicle for promoting his agenda. He chose his editor carefully. Ken Whyte was already working for him at *Saturday Night* and was successfully pushing it to the right. The two chose their editors as much for their ideology as for their journalistic skills. Neil Seeman was a recent graduate of the

University of Toronto law school who wrote a letter to Black railing about the left-wing faculty at the institution. Seeman then attended graduate school at Harvard and moved directly onto the *National Post* editorial board. He had no journalistic experience, but he did oppose affirmative action, pay equity and Liberal corruption.[64] He left after several years to work as a senior researcher for the National Citizens Coalition. He then moved briefly to the Fraser Institute, to start its new flak organization, CanStats, which is described later in this chapter.

Other media organizations also opened their pages to think-tank propagandists. Many were already members of the Fraser Institute. The *Globe* hired AIMS president Brian Crowley for a two-year secondment, and Owen Lippert, a senior adviser at the Fraser, for a four-month stint writing editorials. In the spring of 1996, columnist Gordon Gibson started appearing regularly in the *Globe* writing on western issues. "Gibson was initially identified as 'a senior fellow in Canadian studies at the Fraser Institute,'" writes James Winter. "It made him sound like an academic teaching at a university rather than a representative of a corporate lobby group which is dedicated to free enterprise capitalism."[65]

To understand the media's agenda-setting prowess, consider the case of the Canadian Alliance—Conrad Black helped create it. On its very first day of publication, October 27, 1998, the *National Post*'s lead story speculated that Alberta premier Ralph Klein might be a speaker at a conference scheduled to be held the following February titled the "United Alternative." This was not news in the conventional sense because nothing had actually happened. Instead, it was the launch of an agenda-setting campaign by the paper. The front-page story was accompanied by two more inside: one, a column in which Preston Manning urged Joe Clark to join the United Alternative (UA); and a second which explained that the PCs were toast unless they joined the UA. The *Post* offered an editorial as well, criticizing Clark for opposing "the neo-conservative ideas that have revitalized the Right in every other advanced country."[66]

On the second day of publication, the *Post* continued with another barrage. It led with a front-page story describing how the PCs were rejecting the call to unite with the UA and how Klein was urging Clark to join the alliance. A second story inside the paper described a meeting in Calgary of UA organizers. There was no editorial, but there was a long opinion piece by Stephen Harper, who was then "out of politics" as president of the NCC. Harper urged Clark to "respond positively to Reform's proposal for a United Alternative."[67]

The fate of the UA, which morphed into the Canadian Alliance, was intertwined with Hollinger. One link was Ezra Levant, who worked as an assistant to Preston Manning, then wrote editorials for the *Post*, and then ran as a candidate for the Alliance, before withdrawing to allow party leader Stephen Harper to run in a by-election. Another link was long-time Black partner and Hollinger executive Peter White, who worked quietly behind the scenes to create a Canada-wide party that could win the 2000 federal election. White was principal secretary to Brian Mulroney and then president of the PC Canada Fund, where he wrote a letter on Hollinger stationery asking for money to support PC leader Jean Charest. When Red Tory Joe Clark won the Tory leadership, White and other right-wing Tories left the party and began the quest for the United Alternative. White recruited Tom Long as part of the strategy to break out of the western Canadian ghetto and attract Bay Street funding. Long had worked as an aide to White when White was Mulroney's special assistant for appointments. And when White moved back to the private sector to head one of Black's companies, he brought in Long to be his executive assistant. Somehow the paper's subscription list fell into Long's hands. Conrad Black denied he was supporting Long, but when the story broke, Long hastily returned the list.[68] One *National Post* reporter anonymously complained to the satirical magazine *Frank* that *Post* journalists "look like 'whores' selling out to Long and the Alliance. It hurts the credibility of the newspaper and as a journalist that works for it, I'm profoundly upset. But nothing surprises me, they've got all these people on the editorial board and management side that are Alliance members."[69]

The result of the 2000 election must have been a great disappointment to Black. Long had lost the CA leadership race to western Christian fundamentalist Stockwell Day, who made almost no inroads in Ontario, electing only two candidates in that seat-rich province. Despite two years of aggressive agenda-setting and framing of conservative issues, Black's propaganda efforts had not paid off. He put his Canadian newspapers up for sale. The consensus was that he had been blocked by his archrival Jean Chrétien in his quest to acquire a peerage in the British House of Lords, which seemed only fitting to Black as an enormously successful Canadian media baron. Chrétien invoked a rarely used parliamentary resolution to deny Black the appointment. Black would not be able to achieve his ambition if he remained a Canadian citizen. But if he gave up his citizenship he would have to give up his newspapers, since only Canadians could be owners. Besides, the *Post* was losing fistfuls of money, about $100 million so far.

A year after the Canadian Alliance defeat, Black had a buyer in Izzy Asper, owner of CanWest Global Communications, who had just achieved his dream of creating a second private Canadian television network, Global TV. Asper paid an astronomical $3.5 billion for twelve major dailies, 50 percent of the *National Post* and buckets of debt from which he and his family never recovered. Hollinger ended up with a 15 percent share of CanWest. Black and chief lieutenant David Radler were elected to the CanWest board. Black retained the other 50 percent of the *Post* and continued to control the paper's editorial direction. But eight months later, Black threw in the towel and sold the other half to Asper.

In response to the Aspers' moves, Bell Canada Enterprises, Canada's dominant telecommunications firm, acquired the CTV Television Network and the *Globe and Mail*, to create a second Canadian media empire. Canada entered an era of unprecedented media concentration six months later when the Canadian Radio-television and Telecommunications Commission (CRTC) approved the CanWest and Bell Canada takeovers. A third media conglomerate was assembled by the Peladeau family, which acquired the Sun Media newspaper chain, the Vidéotron cable TV network and the TVA broadcasting network. Such a degree of cross-ownership was unrivalled. Ownership of print and broadcast news outlets in the same market had been made illegal by the Trudeau government in the early 1980s, but the policy was reversed by Brian Mulroney a year after he took office.

The Aspers carried on with Black's conservative political agenda and added a few wrinkles of their own. Criticism of Prime Minister Jean Chrétien and the Liberals was not tolerated, at least until family patriarch Izzy Asper died. Asper was leader of the Manitoba Liberal Party in the 1970s and a long-time supporter of the federal Liberals. But the Asper offspring moved further right. After CanWest took over the papers, son David joined the Fraser Institute board as well as that of the Frontier Centre for Public Policy, the libertarian think-tank in the Aspers' hometown of Winnipeg, while son Leonard joined the boards of the C.D. Howe Institute and the Canada West Foundation. The record of the Aspers' contributions to political parties casts further doubt on the staunchness of their Liberalness. During the election year of 2000, CanWest and its subsidiaries gave $81,506 to the Liberal Party and individual Liberal candidates. But it also gave $37,466 to the Canadian Alliance and some of its high-profile candidates, like Stockwell Day and Preston Manning. The Aspers actually gave more to Day ($3,000) than they did to Chrétien ($2,000). They gave nothing to the Progressive Conservatives, New Democrats or Bloc Québécois.[70] The pattern continued in the following elections. In 2003, the last year in which corporations could donate large sums to political parties, the Aspers gave $59,000 to the Liberals and $26,000 to the Canadian Alliance.

After Neil Reynolds transformed the *Ottawa Citizen* into a more conservative publication, Black sent him to the West Coast to perform the same operation on the *Vancouver Sun*. Reynolds brought in Don Cayo to be his editorial page editor. Cayo had worked under Reynolds at the *St. John Telegraph-Journal* in New Brunswick and had taken a two-year leave to head the libertarian Atlantic Institute for Market Studies while AIMS president Brian Crowley worked at the *Globe and Mail*.[71] After two years as editorial page editor, Cayo became a *Sun* business columnist, where he often wrote columns supporting Fraser Institute positions: private auto insurance is cheaper than public insurance; privatizing the fishery is better for conservation; pegging the Canadian dollar to the U.S. greenback will enrich all Canadians; only the market can save medicare; taxes take too much out of the family budget; Canada's laws are too union friendly; Fraser Institute figures on poverty are more credible than Statistics Canada's; investing in sweatshops is good because it lifts people out of poverty; we need a regulatory-freedom day just like Tax Freedom Day; and British Columbia can be as wealthy as Alberta, we just need to cut taxes for business and the rich.[72]

Cayo's place as editorial page editor was taken by Fazil Mihlar who had been hired by Reynolds as an editorial writer. Mihlar had been the director of regulatory studies (i.e., deregulation) at the Fraser Institute. Besides filtering letters to the editor and opinion pieces on the op-ed page, Mihlar often wrote a weekly column on the marvels of capitalism. His format was to focus on economic studies that apparently had just come across his desk. He didn't disclose that some of these studies came from corporate-backed libertarian think-tanks.

In an October 2004 column, Mihlar promoted individual unemployment accounts (IUA) as the solution to the problems in Canada's employment insurance program.[73] This is odd because the major problem with employment insurance is that the period of qualification had been greatly extended and the benefits reduced, meaning that fewer Canadians could benefit from this key social safety net program. In the IUA scheme, employer and employee contribute equally, but, unlike the current system where contributions are pooled in a large insurance fund, the IUA would be owned individually by the employee, who can invest the funds as she sees fit. If she loses her job, she can access the funds until they are used up. Let's hope she didn't invest in Enron or Nortel.

Mihlar's source for this scheme was a paper by two professors at Central Michigan University in Mount Pleasant, Michigan. It might seem difficult to track down such an obscure study from such an obscure place. But Mihlar neglected to inform his readers of a more important affiliation of the professors: one was an adjunct scholar with the Mackinac Center for Public Policy, a libertarian think-tank in nearby Midland, Michigan, while the other was on the Mackinac's board of scholars. Individual unemployment accounts were a creation of the Mackinac Center, not Central Michigan University. Mackinac is one of dozens of libertarian think-tanks spread across North America. Privatizing unemployment insurance, as Mihlar proposed, would be a victory for this think-tank network and one more nail in the coffin of a collective society.

Like the other think-tanks, Mackinac's success is rooted in the deep pockets of conservative foundations. It is funded by the Walton Family Foundation (money from anti-union Wal-Mart), the Ruth and Lovett Peters Foundation (Procter & Gamble, supports National Right to Work Legal Defense Fund) and Dow Chemical Co.[74] In addition, the authors of the IUA study received a grant from the Earhart Foundation (oil money, supports free-market scholars). Their study was published by the Independent Institute in Oakland, California.[75] This organization is funded by Earhart, and the David H. Koch (oil billionaire), John M. Olin (chemicals and munitions) and William E. Simon (financier, key mover of modern conservative movement) foundations, among many others.[76] The study was also posted on the web site of the Heartland Institute in Chicago. Heartland is supported by the Charles G. Koch (oil billionaire's billionaire brother) and Barre Seid (Chicago industrialist) foundations as well as by some of the oil giants.[77] The study's brief appearance in Canada was on the *Vancouver Sun*'s editorial page, with a reprint in the *Windsor Star* the following Saturday.

Over a fifteen-month period Mihlar discussed six reports by the National Bureau of Economic Research (NBER), but never mentioned the conservative slant of its output. The NBER is headed by Martin Feldstein, who was Ronald Reagan's chief economic adviser and a guru for "Bush-enomics." The NBER received over $10 million from conservative foundations, including Smith Richardson.[78] This foundation, whose money comes from Vicks VapoRub, started funding the NBER's work on the privatization of social security in the mid-nineties, a project which had moved to the top of the Bush agenda.[79] The progress of this idea illustrates the system's agenda-setting prowess: conservative foundations support think-tanks that support sympathetic scholars to write reports that are disseminated by the think-tanks and commercial media. After constant repetition over a prolonged period, the proposals end up on the political agenda.

Mihlar devoted a column to the work of Tyler Cowen, identified simply as a professor at George Mason University in Fairfax, Virginia.[80] Cowen's contribution is to apply market principles to arts and culture. Mihlar does not mention that Cowen also heads the James Buchanan Center for Political Economy, and the Mercatus Center, and is vice-chairman of the Institute for Humane Studies, all located at the university. George Mason is a hotbed of libertarian and conservative activity. Over the years it has received more than $45 million from conservative foundations.[81] In a column highlighting the work of another George Mason University scholar, Mihlar agreed with Bryan Caplan's assertion that people are too irrational to understand how individual greed can be in the interests of society and how economic, environmental and social conditions are getting better. If people were more rational, Caplan claimed, they would better appreciate the market economy. Mihlar neglected to mention that Caplan is an adjunct scholar at the libertarian Cato Institute, information that would help Mihlar's readers better assess Caplan's biases.[82]

To be fair, Mihlar did discuss articles by business and management experts without a covert ideological agenda except, perhaps, for an emphasis on the centrality of capitalism. He discussed a number of studies by global consulting firm McKinsey & Co., and suggested variously that

- Canada should outsource medical care to India;
- bus drivers should work split shifts to increase efficiency;
- high-tech firms need to improve efficiency; and
- companies need to wring more profits from their servicing activities.

Mihlar cut his ties to the Fraser Institute years before he wrote his *Vancouver Sun* op-ed pieces. Nevertheless it is fair to say that the placement of former Fraser Institute researchers Mihlar at the *Sun*, Danielle Smith at the *Calgary Herald* and John Robson at the *Ottawa Citizen* represented a significant success for the institute. When Michael Walker announced he was stepping down after thirty years at the think-tank's helm, Ezra Levant effused that "newspaper editorial boards from coast to coast are sprinkled with his alumni."[83]

It was a brilliant strategy. Having people in editorial positions brings libertarian ideas into the acceptable range of opinion in commercial media.

Corporate-backed think-tanks operate a dual strategy to get their messages in the media. As the Fraser Institute's five-year plan indicates, they court the press to obtain favourable coverage. But they also club the press when necessary. The weapon of choice is the charge that the media are too liberal and do not give conservatives a fair shake. Monitoring the media was one of the strategies recommended by Lewis Powell in his 1971 memo to the U.S. Chamber of Commerce that launched the third counterthrust. (See discussion on p. 58.) The right began accusing the press of liberal bias in the early 1970s. They're still at it more than thirty years later. Even though the corporate media are not liberal, conservatives continue to make the accusation because it is useful to do so. If the press can be accused of being too liberal and leftist, the right's extreme positions will seem moderate in comparison.

Edward Herman and Noam Chomsky called this activity flak, which they defined as "negative responses to a media statement or program."[84] (See p. 70.) Flak occurs every day when individuals write letters to the editor commenting on something that appeared in yesterday's paper. On occasion, organized groups complain about the treatment afforded them by a particular newspaper. But the greatest impact of flak was achieved by organizations set up specifically to criticize and harass the media. These organizations are financed by the same corporations and foundations that back the think-tanks. Four media-monitoring organizations in the United States have the task of rooting out supposed liberal bias and ensuring that the media reflect business-friendly, conservative positions. "They are quoted frequently and forcefully on a variety of topics," writes Trudy Lieberman, a health care activist and journalist, in her book *Slanting the Story*.[85] Lieberman explains the peculiar definition of "liberal bias" espoused by conservatives. Bias doesn't necessarily mean prejudice, but simply a point of view or the dissemination of information that right-wing organizations would rather the media ignore. This could be information about government help for the poor, the homeless or the weak, or even a discussion of the poor, homeless and weak, information that conflicts with the objectives of the right. Stories on victims of spending cuts are biased, they say, because there aren't equivalent stories on victims of tax hikes (even though tax hikes are rare). Bias could also mean giving short shrift to conservative solutions to a problem, discussing a flaw in the conservative approach, or simply omitting information presented by the right.[86]

The first flak group in the United States was Accuracy In Media (see page 70), which was set up in 1969 and predates Powell's memorandum by several years. Conservative economist Reed Irvine, who worked at the U.S. Federal Reserve, was upset over media coverage of the Vietnam War. He believed that favourable reporting on the Viet Cong by American media helped the North Vietnamese win the war. Irvine was a strident anti-communist; through AIM he led several high-profile campaigns to detail the media's liberal bias. In his view, these news stories and documentaries highlighted the evils of capitalism while glorifying the Soviet Union and various socialist movements.[87] The organization grew spectacularly during the 1970s, with funding from major oil companies and Richard Mellon Scaife's foundations. AIM says its mission is to "critique botched and bungled news stories and set the record straight on important issues that have received slanted coverage."[88] But Herman and Chomsky see a darker purpose. The function of AIM, they say, is "to harass the media and put pressure on them to follow the corporate agenda and a hard-line, right-wing foreign policy.... It conditions the media to expect trouble (and cost increases) for violating right-wing standards of bias."[89] Irvine was a frequent participant in television talk shows, and his letters to the editor and commentary were published regularly in the media. The media felt obligated to provide careful responses to his detailed attacks on their news and commentary.[90] With the demise of the Soviet Union, AIM turned its guns on the "hysteria" perpetrated by "radical environmentalism" and debunked "myths" such as global warming. AIM regularly targeted the United Nations, Hillary Clinton and Dan Rather, while it ferociously protected the Bush administration from any criticism.

The Center for Media and Public Affairs was established in 1986 by Linda and Robert Lichter in Washington, D.C. It calls itself non-partisan and oddly this label has stuck, even though its first fundraising letters were signed by Ronald Reagan, Patrick Buchanan and Reverend Pat Robertson, who helped mobilize fundamentalist Christians to take over the Republican Party. The Lichters' research was first published by the American Enterprise Institute and they received money from the Bradley, Olin, Smith Richardson and Scaife foundations.[91]

The Lichters' claim to fame was a study which purported to prove that reporters at the nation's top newspapers, newsmagazines and television networks voted Democratic more frequently than the country as a whole. The study also claimed to demonstrate that on questions measuring economic and social views, the "media elite" was to the left of the "business elite." The catch is that the Lichters didn't compare reporters' views with those of the general public, but with CEOs and other top executives at six Fortune 500 companies. Of course, the views of reporters will be more liberal than those of very conservative business executives. Nearly everybody's will be. In fact, the majority of reporters and editors were conservative on five of six economic questions. On one question, 63 percent of media respondents supported less regulation of the economy, making them more conservative than the general public, but more liberal than the 86 percent of CEOs who favoured less regulation. This latter comparison was the one publicized.[92]

On social issues, the reporters and editors were liberal. They supported environmental protection, affirmative action, women's rights, gay and lesbian rights and sexual freedom. But these are views shared by most Americans, with the exception of the religious right. The finding that the media were conservative on economic issues was lost in the stampede to attack the newly discovered "liberal media." We should note that the Lichters never canvassed media owners who, by a wide margin, vote Republican.[93]

Robert and Linda Lichter and their corporate and foundation backers achieved tremendous success in their campaign to tar the media with the liberal brush. But a study by sociologist David Croteau of Virginia Commonwealth University found that "on select issues from corporate power and trade to social security and medicare, to health care and taxes, journalists are actually more conservative than the general public." The study also found that "journalists are mostly centrist in their political orientation."[94] This study, unfortunately, was not reported as well as the ones claiming liberal bias. As a result, the liberal media claim has been disseminated so widely that it achieved the status of urban legend, both in the United States and Canada.

In Canada, the *Ottawa Citizen*'s David Warren has been on a crusade to "out" the liberal media. In Warren's world, the liberal media accuse the Israelis of perpetrating massacres while pretending that the Palestinians want something other than to drive Israel into the sea. The liberal media, Warren charges: like the United Nations the way it is; become outraged when Islamic terrorists are successfully prosecuted; hate the Stephen Harper Conservatives; love Pierre Berton (Warren hated him because he epitomized the liberal media); use repulsive images from Iraq to undermine U.S. foreign policy; and generally provide disinformation on the war in Iraq. He's mentioned the liberal media phantom in three dozen columns, but never once—Berton aside—identified a single news organization or journalist who might be a member of this nasty group. As with most charges made by flak organizations and their supporters, the liberal media charge is vague, but, ironically, continues to be recycled through the "liberal" press itself.

In 1997, Lichter established a new organization called STATS, for Statistical Assessment Service. It sounds official, but is engaged in the same mission as its parent organization, harassing the media. Funding for STATS comes from the Olin, Scaife and Donner foundations. STATS addresses a real problem: the difficulty the press has in reporting complex science stories. Science reporters don't always get the facts right. A study by the First Amendment Center found that 89 percent of scientists surveyed expressed "only some" or "hardly any" confidence in the press. News organizations often go for sensational rather than important stories that may be less interesting to readers. And each paper has its own editorial slant, determining which stories to cover and which to ignore.[95] STATS seems to exploit this problem to discredit scientific findings critical of corporate practices. It uses reports from industry front groups, such as the Greening Earth Society (Western Fuels Association), and Harvard Center for Risk Analysis (Amoco, Dow Chemical, General Motors, Monsanto, Procter & Gamble) to debunk legitimate science stories.[96]

STATS' modus operandi is important for Canadians to know about because it served as a model for a new division of the Fraser Institute which opened in 2002 called CanStats—the Canadian Statistical Assessment Service—with funding from the Donner Canadian Foundation. Most of us don't have the time or resources to sift through complex policy papers, the CanStats web site explained before it was shut down in 2006. So we rely on the media to tell us. But what if the media don't get it right because they slant the coverage? CanStats is there to "point out the inaccurate use of scientific, technical and social scientific information in public policy debate."[97] The main problem is that in its four years of existence, CanStats pointed out alleged inaccuracies in the science of environmentalists, health activists and others who criticize industry, but never found any inaccuracies in the science of industry-backed studies. It presented its mission as a public service, but CanStats seemed to be in the employ of industry, particularly industry that pollutes the environment or exposes people to health-and-safety risks.

In 2004, CanStats published more bulletins on aquaculture than on any other subject, except for its output debunking the science of global warming. Why might the Fraser Institute be so interested in defending the interests of fish farmers? Michael Walker says his organization's research program is insulated from its sources of funding. So it must have been just coincidence that the institute's largest benefactor was the Weston family, which, at the time, owned a major B.C. salmon-farming operation. This subsidiary was performing poorly and losing millions of dollars every year. It needed all the help it could get could be one interpretation of CanStats efforts.

An April 2004 CanStats bulletin attacked the CBC, a common Fraser Institute target over the years, for distorting scientific findings about sea lice on wild salmon. CanStats accused the CBC of misreporting a press release from the National Research Council of Canada (NRC). The CBC distortion, the bulletin alleged, began in the headline to its story. The NRC press release was titled "Aquatic scientists divided on role of sea lice from salmon farms in decline of native salmon in B.C." The CBC headline read "Sea lice threatens salmon run, says researchers," according to the CanStats bulletin.[98] On the face of it, this certainly looks like a distortion by the public broadcaster. The problem is that the CBC was not reporting on the National Research Council press release, which was issued on March 2. The CBC news item appeared on April 28, nearly two months later. The NRC was not mentioned in the CBC story, which was a report on the work of salmon researcher Alexandra Morton. CanStats' claim of CBC distortion was a deception. CanStats took the liberty of adding an "s" to the word "researcher" in the CBC headline. To make a fallacious point, CanStats misrepresented the headline of the CBC item, which referred to a single researcher, Morton, and not multiple scientists, as in the NRC study.[99]

That this was not simple sloppiness but a strategy of disinformation became clear in the next CanStats bulletin, in October, on fish farming. Here, CanStats repeated the bogus CBC headline with the word "researchers" instead of "researcher." CanStats went on to amplify the NRC news release, which explained that scientists were divided on the role of sea lice in declining wild salmon populations. The release contained the views of Morton, the bulletin noted, as well as those of Scott McKinley, a University of British Columbia professor who heads an organization called AquaNET. McKinley disagreed with Morton's conclusions, saying there could be other explanations for declining wild salmon populations, aside from the threat from sea lice from farmed-salmon operations. The CanStats charge was that the CBC was guilty of bias because it did not include the views of McKinley, once again glossing over the fact that the CBC was not covering the news release.[100] That McKinley would be defensive of the fish-farming industry may not be surprising given that AquaNET is a consortium of fish farmers, university researchers and government agencies working to promote the industry.[101]

The October CanStats bulletin also complained about the unequal coverage given by the media to critical and supportive farmed-salmon studies. One study that found much higher levels of cancer-causing polychlorinated biphenyls (PCBS) in farmed salmon than in wild salmon received extensive coverage, CanStats reported, while a just-released study that found no difference in PCB levels in farmed and wild populations received no coverage in the mainstream Canadian press, aside from one *Vancouver Sun* story. CanStats' conclusion? By giving unequal coverage to the studies, the media were "playing politics" and "support[ing] the cause of alarmists."

There's another explanation for the disparity in coverage, one that CanStats ignored. The first study that received wide coverage was undertaken by credible, independent researchers from a number of universities using very large samples and published in the reputable peer-reviewed journal *Science*.[102] The study that received coverage only in the *Sun*—and which led the *Sun* to erroneously frame the issue as duelling science—was bogus.[103] It was underwritten by Salmon of the Americas, an industry front group, was not published in a peer-reviewed journal, let alone in any journal, and its details were not made public.[104] CanStats overlooked these flaws in the study. In its analysis of fish-farming coverage, CanStats relied on the work of Dr. Charles Santerre, a professor of food and nutrition at Indiana's Purdue University. Santerre's oft-repeated claim, almost a mantra, is that salmon, farmed or wild, is safe to eat since contaminants are well below standards established by some regulatory agencies (except for the U.S. Environmental Protection Agency). In the interests of accuracy, CanStats should have acknowledged that Santerre consults for Salmon of the Americas.

In the last of its series defending fish farming, CanStats went directly after researcher Alexandra Morton. In November, online daily newspaper *The Tyee* published an excerpt from Morton's essay, which appeared in the book *A Stain Upon the Sea: West Coast Salmon Farming*. In the excerpt, Morton describes her heroic efforts to find out if escaped farmed Atlantic salmon can survive in B.C. waters. She examined the stomach contents of dozens of these fish that had been caught by B.C. fishermen, looking for evidence of wild food. She did find some evidence to this effect, as well as other indications that the fish might be able to spawn, which would set the stage for species invasion.[105] Morton's work was suggestive and certainly not conclusive, but that did not stop CanStats from mounting a stinging attack in its next bulletin, titled "A Stain Upon the Science." The article quibbled with Morton's numbers and concluded her work was "junk science" and "scare literature."[106] Meanwhile, Weston put its fish-farm operations up for sale and the science of aquaculture no longer seemed an important line of inquiry for CanStats.

CanStats was retired from service after only four years as a media attack dog. Perhaps the Fraser could not come up with additional funding for it after the Westons pulled out. Along with its dubious ruminations on fish farming, CanStats provided similar critiques of global warming coverage. It pumped out a series of bulletins purporting to demonstrate the many ways media got climate change wrong, claiming variously that: the earth was cooling, not warming; there were more polar bears than ever before; and there was no scientific consensus about climate change. This last claim echoed an anti–Kyoto Protocol column by the *Globe*'s Margaret Wente in August 2005. Wente featured retired meteorologist Madhav Khandekar, without revealing his connection to Friends of Science, an industry-financed group of climate change deniers.[107] In this piece, Wente asserted that "hundreds of peer-reviewed papers in scientific journals have questioned the link between human activity and global warming." Like CanStats' denials about scientific consensus, this was a falsehood. University of California history of science professor Naomi Oreskes looked at 928 climate sciences papers published in refereed scientific journals between 1993 and 2003. She found that "none of the papers disagreed with the consensus position" that climate change was occurring and was very likely caused by human activity.[108] Oreskes's paper had been published and was posted on the Internet when Wente wrote her column and CanStats issued its bulletins, so it was available. By not mentioning this study, CanStats and Wente wittingly or unwittingly became participants in the massive, twenty-year-long campaign financed by the fossil fuel industry to confuse the public about the threat climate change poses to the planet.

CHAPTER 7

Delaying Action on Climate Change

"Support for Kyoto plunges," a front-page *Globe and Mail* story screamed at the beginning of November 2002.[1] The story reported a survey by polling firm Ipsos-Reid, which suggested that 44 percent of Canadians wanted the federal government to ratify Kyoto, while an equal number—45 percent— wanted Ottawa to withdraw from the accord and develop a made-in-Canada plan. A poll done a month earlier by the same firm found that 74 percent of Canadians supported implementing the accord, with only 21 percent opposed. Bizarrely, the federal government's own polling firm had just released numbers that suggested massive support for Kyoto, with 78 percent approving ratification. This dramatic collapse in support for Kyoto was disastrous news for environmentalists, who had fought for cuts to carbon dioxide emissions since the alarm about climate change was first raised in 1988. It would also be bad news for Prime Minister Jean Chrétien, who pledged his government would ratify the accord by the end of 2002, just two months away. How could he proceed when Canadians were turning against it? But the poll contained good news for the fossil fuel and automobile industries, which had fought emission controls from the beginning.

It was also wonderful news for the anti-Kyoto government of oil-rich

Alberta. Yet what did it expect, given that it had commissioned the poll in the first place? As became quickly evident, the reason for the different results is that the second Ipsos-Reid survey included the option to withdraw from Kyoto and develop a made-in-Canada solution. The pollster was criticized for including this option because it was not provided in its earlier survey. The results of the two surveys were not comparable and the *Globe* article was "fraudulent," federal environment minister David Anderson charged.[2] Ipsos-Reid president Darrell Bricker defended his firm's use of the phrase, which, he said, is legitimate and indicates there is an "emergent view . . . that Canadians are open to a 'made in Canada solution' that may be different from the Kyoto Protocol."[3] Bricker's problem, though, was that a made-in-Canada solution to climate change didn't exist. He admitted as much in his defence of the poll question "To suggest that the phrase is irrelevant to the current debate on the accord is to deny the importance of rhetoric in shaping public opinion. As social scientists, it is our job to test the impact of rhetoric."

The *Globe*'s own Hugh Winsor described the rhetoric succinctly: "Why should we subject ourselves to some foreign deal struck an ocean away when the alternative is a good old homegrown alternative, This is a no-brainer . . ."[4] Perhaps, but as we'll soon see, the made-in-Canada plan was created in the U.S. and would not slow global warming, which is what most Canadians said they wanted. It was a conscious attempt to mislead Canadians into believing a credible alternative existed. Remember Alex Carey's definition of propaganda: "communication where the form and content are selected with the purpose of bringing a target audience to adopt attitudes and beliefs chosen in advance by the sponsors of the communication."[5] In this case the target audience was Ontario, where Chrétien's parliamentary majority resided. Liberal MPs and the voting public were being manipulated into turning their backs on the international treaty. The sponsors of the communication were big oil and the government of Alberta. Were Ralph Klein and the oil patch in cahoots? According to Greenpeace campaigner Josh Matlow, their relationship was "kind of like that of an organized crime boss and his 'legitimate business activities.' They'll all deny any connection to each other, one operating above-ground while the other does its work in the shadows."[6] But who is the boss of bosses, the premier of Alberta or the president of Imperial Oil?

The first media mention of a made-in-Canada solution to climate change occurred in March 2002, in the business section of Canada's two national dailies, the *Globe and Mail* and the *National Post*. The story was about the change in leadership at Imperial Oil, Canada's largest integrated oil company. The author of the phrase was Robert Peterson, Imperial's outgoing president. "I am of the view they are going to rethink this and come to a conclusion that there's got to be a made-in-Canada solution," Peterson told business reporters in Calgary.[7] Peterson, who had been called a dinosaur for his implacable opposition to emission-reduction proposals—"not all the fossils are in the fuel," Maurice Strong, who chaired the 1992 United Nations Conference on Environment and Development in Rio de Janeiro, once said about him—made this comment a month after George W. Bush unveiled an industry-friendly plan that would barely slow emissions of carbon dioxide and other greenhouse gases, let alone cut them. Peterson told an Imperial Oil annual meeting that the Kyoto agreement was "bad science and flawed public policy." There were "too many theories chasing not enough facts to support the theory of global climate change," he said,[8] parroting the line of the industry front group, the Global Climate Coalition.

Peterson's promotion of a made-in-Canada solution found a receptive audience with the oil revenue–dependent Alberta government. It was as if Peterson gave the marching orders and Alberta saluted. Yes, Peterson was the boss of bosses. Two weeks later, the phrase popped up again, seemingly emanating from the mouth of Alberta environment minister Lorne Taylor. The *National Post* headline writer wrote, "Alberta offers Kyoto alternative: 'Made-in-Canada' solution to greenhouse gas emissions to be unveiled at energy summit." But what Taylor said was that the province was working on a "U.S.-style plan to reduce greenhouse gases . . ."[9] Alberta's plan, Taylor said, would be based on the same principles as Bush's recent climate-change policy. It emphasized financial incentives for developing technologies that reduce carbon emissions. So the made-in-Canada plan would be based on the made-in-the-U.S. plan, which would:

- Not cut emissions, just slow down the rate of increase;
- Allow voluntary, not mandatory, reporting of emissions; and
- Provide tax credits for renewable energy and fuel-efficient cars that look good, but are too small to have much impact.

In the following weeks, Taylor's call for Canada to follow the lead of the U.S. received a flood of support from western Canadian newspapers. Typical were these headlines:

- Canada will have to join with the U.S. in developing a strictly North American plan to reduce emissions (*Vancouver Sun*, 16 April 2002)
- Canada should follow the lead of the U.S. and get out of the pact now (*Calgary Sun*, 15 April 2002)
- [Environment Minister David] Anderson should allow the Kyoto Protocol to rest in peace, and start preparing Plan B (*Calgary Herald*, 4 April 2002)
- They would do better to pull the plug on Kyoto and start over (*Winnipeg Free Press*, 16 April 2002)

Three weeks after Taylor's announcement, Alberta premier Ralph Klein addressed the Canadian Association of Petroleum Producers' (CAPP) annual dinner in Calgary. He said he would work with the oil industry and the United States to find a "North American solution" or a "made-in-Canada solution" to climate change, using the phrases interchangeably.[10]

Then two things happened. "U.S.-style plan" and "North American solution" disappeared from the rhetoric—would Darrell Bricker's respondents say yes to a "U.S.-style plan"?—leaving only the "made-in-Canada solution." And National Public Relations (NPR), the Canadian affiliate of giant PR firm Burson-Marsteller, took over the campaign to defeat Kyoto ratification. The oil patch had panicked when Jean Chrétien said that he hoped to ratify Kyoto by the end of the year. On September 26, NPR launched the Canadian Coalition for Responsible Environmental Solutions (CCRES), whose mission was to instill the phantom made-in-Canada solution in the public mind.[11]

The CCRES was a textbook example of an "Astroturf" organization and Burson-Marsteller wrote the book. Astroturf organizations are grassroots coalitions that are actually backed by the industry they seem to be opposing. If the oil and auto industries oppose controls on global warming, they will be dismissed as special interests and ignored. But if they can bring in other business and community interests and create the impression of a grassroots campaign, they have a better chance of winning. As Rick Hyndman, the Canadian Association of Petroleum Producers' senior policy adviser on climate change later acknowledged, Canadians were unlikely to view CAPP, the voice of the oil patch, as a credible source.[12] Time for an Astroturf coalition.

The introduction of the coalition took great pains to point out that the organization represented "a broad cross-section of Canadian industry," that it was made up of "representatives of more than twenty-five business organiza-tions, industry associations and consumer advocacy groups" and that the members of the coalition "account for the vast majority of Canada's private sector jobs, investments, exports, training and research and development."[13] This wasn't just the fossil-fuel guys protecting their turf, they were saying. The oil industry was in the background at the news conference that introduced the coalition to the public. Lead speakers came from the three broadest business associations: the Canadian Chamber of Commerce, the Canadian Council of Chief Executives and the Canadian Manufacturers and Exporters. Pierre Alvarez, president of CAPP, spoke last, noting the diversity of interests repre-sented in the coalition. Imperial Oil's outgoing president, Robert Peterson, and Tim Hearn, his successor, were nowhere to be seen. But behind the seemingly wide representation was the fact that virtually all the money that went into organizational activities, such as expensive saturation TV ads in Ontario, esti-mated to cost $225,000 a week, came from the deep pockets of the petroleum producers.[14] Nor were there any consumer-advocacy groups in the coalition, which did include the Used Car Dealers of Ontario, hardly the consumer's fiercest advocate.

Burson-Marsteller has a record of unparalleled success in resisting environmen-tal initiatives and in supplying corporate greenwash by framing environmentally destructive corporations as friends of the environment. Nuclear power-plant maker Babcock and Wilcox used the firm to restore its reputation after the Three Mile Island disaster in 1979. Burson-Marsteller assisted Union Carbide after Bhopal in 1984 and Exxon after the *Exxon Valdez* oil spill of 1989. It worked for the B.C. Forest Alliance to attack environmental campaigns to save old-growth forest. In 1992 it was hired to greenwash the image of big business and ensure the corporate viewpoint was well stated and received at the Earth Summit in Rio de Janeiro. It set up the Business Council on Sustainable Development (BCSD), with fifty-eight top executives from polluters such as Chevron, Shell, Volkswagen, Mitsubishi, Dow Chemical and DuPont. The Burson-BCSD triumph was to prevent the summit from dealing meaningfully with climate change.[15]

In 1993, in a campaign similar to the one it would run in Canada, Burson-Marsteller helped organize a front group called the American Energy Alliance to defeat Bill Clinton's proposed BTU tax on fossil fuels. This tax was the centrepiece of Clinton's plan to combat global warming, which would reduce U.S. emissions of greenhouse gases to their 1990 levels by the year 2000. When the National Association of Manufacturers and the American Petroleum Institute (API) were the only "visible BTU critics, they got nowhere," *Fortune* magazine reported in 1993. But then Burson brought hundreds of small- and medium-sized companies, farm organizations and consumer groups into the alliance. "[W]hat had once appeared a typical big-business lobby was transformed into a grassroots movement."[16]

The goal of the campaign, according to *Time* magazine, was to undermine support for the Democratic president by sowing dissent in the Democrat-controlled Senate. The coalition paid Burson more than a million dollars to deploy forty-five staff members to drum up as much grassroots outrage as possible and direct it at swing Democrats on the Senate Finance Committee. These included David Boren of Oklahoma and Max Baucus of Montana, states with powerful oil and coal constituencies. Winning just one Democratic vote would be enough to stop the tax in the committee where the Democrats held an eleven-to-nine majority. (All Republicans would vote against it.) They used the most effective argument against the legislation they could muster, that it would cost jobs. The National Association of Manufacturers estimated the potential loss at 600,000 nationally. Alliance members provided separate estimates for Oklahoma and Montana, to drive the message home.

Burson's operatives "drafted anti-BTU editorials and sent them to copy-hungry weekly newspapers . . . They commissioned local economists to produce studies about potential job losses and then organized rallies and press conferences to publicize the results," *Time* reported. They used phone banks, fax machines, TV and print ads, and appearances on radio and talk shows to generate an avalanche of calls and letters to the senators. One new technique was to call a client's potential supporters, see if they're mad as hell—and if so, patch them right through to their senator's office, even if the constituent didn't know the representative's name.

In Billings, Montana, *Time* reported, Citizens for a Sound Economy, an oil industry–funded anti-tax group, placed full-page ads in the *Billings Gazette*, inviting residents to a noon lunch and rally to hear about the evils of the president's proposal. More than 150 local residents heard a Washington economist explain that the BTU tax would cost every Montana family $500 a year and deprive the state of 1,500 jobs. In Oklahoma, Citizens for a Sound Economy inundated the state with radio and TV ads criticizing the tax and urging constituents to call their representative. The University of Oklahoma's College of Business Administration released a study estimating that the BTU tax would cost the state 11,000 jobs. On the eve of major rallies in Tulsa and Oklahoma City, Boren came out against the tax and it was dead.[17]

Fast-forward nine years: same goal, different political system. The objective here was to undermine support for the Liberal prime minister by drumming up as much grassroots outrage as possible about Kyoto and directing it at Ontario MPs, who formed the bulk of Chrétien's majority in the House of Commons. A primary target was the seventy-member Liberal auto caucus, consisting mainly of Ontario MPs with auto-parts or vehicle-assembly factories in their ridings. These operations could be affected by measures to meet the Kyoto goals.[18] National Public Relations also targeted the provincial govern-ment of Ernie Eves, which was wavering in its support for Kyoto. The PR firm swung into high gear towards the end of October. A key operative was Guy Giorno, the former chief of staff to Ontario premier Mike Harris and the ulti-mate Tory insider, who would become Stephen Harper's chief of staff six years later. Giorno organized a shrimp-and-wine reception for Tory cabinet minis-ters and executives from coalition affiliates to help bring the government into the anti-Kyoto camp. Greenpeace campaigner Josh Matlow crashed this party and reported on it in *Now Toronto*. Two days later NPR sent an e-mail to every member of the provincial parliament (MPP) at Queen's Park. It was sup-posed to go only to Tory MPPs. Liberal and NDP members released the e-mail to the public. It revealed NPR's bait-and-switch strategy: claim Kyoto was useless because it didn't deal with smog and pollution, issues of concern to southern Ontario residents. Sample questions, answers and talking points were included: "Will the Kyoto Protocol reduce smog? Acid rain? Air pollution? No. No. And no."[19] In this part of the campaign NPR was successful. A week after the reception, Ralph Klein came to Toronto to personally convince Eves to join him and B.C. premier Gordon Campbell in opposition to Kyoto. Klein and Eves emerged from a seventy-five-minute meeting united in their efforts to undo Kyoto. "Every province should come up with their own solution to their own problems in their own sectors of the economy and their own industry," Eves said, in an eye-glazing distortion of any conceivable plan to attack climate change on a global basis.[20]

Less than a week later the coalition launched its prime-time ads, which ran on regional networks across Ontario. In the thirty-second spots, a sincere-looking woman or man walks across the screen criticizing the federal government's rush to ratify. "We deserve a Canadian approach," the woman purrs, "that produces immediate results and invests in our environmental future—a Canadian plan that reduces emissions without costing jobs, damaging our economy or our standard of living."[21] The ad urged Canadians not to sign a contract without knowing the cost and called on viewers to "ask your member of parliament to stop the rush to ratify Kyoto."

It was during NPR's saturation ads that the Ipsos-Reid poll claiming a collapse of Kyoto support hit the front page of the *Globe*. The timing seemed coordinated. The poll was commissioned by the Alberta government, but there was little separation between Klein and the coalition. When the coalition opened its web site—called madeincanadasolution.com—several weeks earlier, it was featured on the Government of Alberta web site.

Also during the saturation TV campaign, propaganda work continued to cast doubt on the benefits of Kyoto. In an action reminiscent of the work of Citizens for a Sound Economy in defeating the Clinton BTU tax, the Canadian Taxpayers Federation commissioned a study to show how implementing Kyoto would hit the average Canadian's paycheque. The report was prepared by Fraser Institute fellow Ross McKitrick of the University of Guelph. This brief study was long on rhetoric and short on analysis. It told us, for instance, that CO_2 is not a contaminant. "It puts the fizz in your pop and the bubbles in your beer," so how could it be bad? The study claimed that Kyoto-related costs would reduce average net income by $2,700 a year by 2010. "In light of the fact that Kyoto yields no economic or environmental benefits this is obviously a bad deal and should be rejected," McKitrick wrote, but provided little evidence to support this conclusion.[22]

A few days after NPR's saturation ads wrapped up and McKitrick's study received wide publicity, a second PR firm was brought in to do battle with the accord. Imperial Oil and Talisman Energy were dissatisfied with the effectiveness of the made-in-Canada campaign and hired APCO Canada to organize a gathering of scientists "skeptical" of the treaty, as part of a last-ditch effort to derail ratification. APCO runs a small operation in Ottawa but is part of a global PR firm headquartered in Washington, D.C., with high-level contacts to both parties. An APCO specialty is supporting rogue scientists who are financed by industry and purport to challenge established scientific thinking. APCO organized the Advancement of Sound Science Coalition (TASSC), which was originally funded by Philip Morris USA, to attack epidemiological studies that implicated second-hand smoke in increased rates of lung cancer and heart disease in non-smokers. Such studies could not be allowed to stand, given the tobacco industry's position that harm from smoking was regrettable, but due to individual choice. This work was essential in Philip Morris's efforts to limit the impact of regulations designed to curb second-hand smoke. APCO then widened the catchment to include other industries with poisoning or polluting problems. TASSC was so successful that for a few years it was tasked with a lead role in opposing Kyoto.[23]

APCO's assignment for Imperial Oil and Talisman was to bring together a roster of climate-change "skeptics" to reveal Kyoto's "science and technology fatal flaws." All scientists are skeptics because the scientific process requires continuing questioning of established theory. Thousands of climate scientists have moved from skepticism to a difficult consensus that climate change is occurring, is caused by human activity and will have serious consequences for humanity. A handful of scientists, most of whom APCO invited to Ottawa, claim it is not occurring.[24] They are called "skeptics" by the media but are usually funded by the fossil-fuel industry. "Paid deniers" may be more accurate. Several months after the Kyoto meetings in 1997, for instance, the National Environmental Trust, a U.S.-based consumer and environmental watchdog group, unearthed a $5-million plan spearheaded by the American Petroleum Institute, along with Exxon, Chevron and the Southern Co. Within the plan was a campaign "to maximize the impact of scientific views consistent with ours on Congress, the media and other key audiences." They would do this by "[recruiting] a cadre of scientists who share the industry's view of climate science and [training] them in public relations so they can help convince journalists, politicians and the public that the risk of global warming is too uncertain to justify [action]."[25] This cynical approach helped create a sense that widespread disagreement existed among scientists, and led the public and politicians to conclude that since the global-warming debate was not over, action was not yet warranted.[26] And every year action was delayed was one more year the fossil-fuel industry could reap its record profits.

Heading the APCO roster was Patrick Michaels, a researcher at the libertarian Cato Institute and a research professor at the University of Virginia. Michaels had written two books and many opinion pieces for the *National Post* and other newspapers that deny global warming. He edits two publications that criticize research by the Intergovernmental Panel on Climate Change (a group representing the consensus of 2,000 international climate scientists) and claim that global warming, if it is occurring, will actually be beneficial. These publications are sent free to hundreds of journalists and generate extensive publicity for his views.[27] Michaels rarely mentions that his publications are funded by Western Fuels, a coal-industry front group, the German Coal Mining Association, the Edison Electric Institute, an association of electric-utility companies and Cyprus Minerals, a backer of the anti-environmental Wise Use movement.[28]

In 2006, Michaels received $100,000 from the Intermountain Rural Electric Association (IREA). This organization wrote a letter to other energy cooperatives asking for additional contributions for Michaels. IREA's general manager wrote that "[M]ost of the electric power furnished by rural electric cooperatives is produced by coal-fired power plants. That will also be true for the foreseeable future. This then raises a concern about all the publicity on global warming and the costly measures being advocated to control CO_2 emissions."[29] Was industry buying science to back its anti–global warming propaganda, as some environmentalists claimed? Michaels enhanced his credibility by donning the mantle of state climatologist of Virginia. But in 2006, the Virginia government disowned him, saying it no longer had authority to appoint a state climatologist and hadn't had this authority since 1980, the year he was appointed.[30]

Fred Singer was another participant on the APCO panel. Like Michaels, Singer is a denier who receives extensive media attention and funding from energy-industry stalwarts such as ExxonMobil, Shell, Arco, Unocal, Sun Energy and the American Gas Association. He is former chief scientist for the U.S. Department of Transportation and executive director of the Science and Environmental Policy Project (SEPP). This organization was set up in 1990 with funding from Reverend Sun Myung Moon's Unification Church. SEPP is no longer affiliated with Moon, but Singer continues to write for the Moon-owned *Washington Times*. Singer hadn't published his work in any peer-reviewed scientific journal for two decades, except for one technical comment. He became an "independent" consultant, writing letters to the editor and testifying before Congress that ozone depletion and global warming aren't real problems. He has consulted for the Global Climate Coalition, the fossil fuel–backed lobby that dominated global-warming propaganda.[31]

Canadian deniers at the conference included Tim Ball, who billed himself as "the first Canadian climatology Ph.D." and said he'd worked as a professor of climatology at the University of Winnipeg for twenty-eight years. These claims are not true. Many prominent Canadian climatologists, including Kenneth Hare (University of Montreal, 1950) and Timothy Oke (McMaster, 1967), received their Ph.D.s before Ball received his in the U.K. in 1982. He's not even a climatologist. His thesis was about climate change in central Canada between 1714 and 1850, and it was earned in historical geography, not climatology. Nor did Ball work as a professor of climatology at the University of Winnipeg for twenty-eight years. He was an instructor and lecturer in geography for twelve of those years before receiving his Ph.D., and then taught for twelve years as an associate and full professor, in geography, not climatology. Ball doesn't have any significant research publications on climate change. He hadn't published a peer-reviewed paper since the early nineties, when he wrote one on the migration of geese. Several were published in the 1980s based on Ball's thesis, which was about weather during the Hudson's Bay Company exploration years.[32] Ball sued University of Lethbridge environmental scientist Dan Johnson and the *Calgary Herald* because of a letter Johnson wrote to the *Herald* questioning Ball's academic credentials. In its statement of defence, the paper had this to say about Ball: "The plaintiff is viewed as a paid promoter of the agenda of the oil and gas industry rather than as a practicing scientist."[33] It was an interesting comment, given that the *Herald* provided Ball eight columns in the paper and identified him as a Ph.D. in climatology and professor for twenty-eight years.

Despite his questionable qualifications, for a few years Ball was in high demand by the front groups sponsored by the fossil-fuel industry. Ball's particular niche was his argument that since 1940 the world's climate has actually been cooling. The conclusion of the Intergovernmental Panel on Climate Change that the world is heating up, is wrong, he argues, because it used "distorted records." With so-called undistorted records in hand, Ball has called the scientific theories connecting human sources of CO_2 and global warming: "ludicrous," "the greatest deception in the history of science," "junk science," a "hoax," "dogma" and mythology, among other epithets.[34] Ball is promoted by the National Center for Public Policy Research, which received $225,000 from ExxonMobil, Tech Central Station (which also receives support from General Motors) and EnviroTruth.org. He's given policy briefings to the Fraser Institute and the Frontier Centre for Public Policy in Winnipeg. And he's on the Scientific Advisory Board of the Calgary-based Friends of Science, whose funding is "not exclusively from the oil and gas industry," according to the University of Calgary's Barry Cooper, who funnelled money to this organization through a university account, which is described below.[35]

The APCO-assembled deniers had minimal impact on federal MPs and bureaucrats. They were too late. The campaign faltered. Chrétien issued a directive that the vote to ratify Kyoto would be regarded as a confidence motion and the government could fall if Liberal backbenchers, perhaps swayed by Guy Giorno and APCO, voted against it. Sarnia Liberal MP Roger Gallaway, whose riding contains a major greenhouse gas–emitting Imperial Oil refinery, was against the accord and said he would stay away from the House the day the vote was taken. Toronto area MP Roy Cullen had a number of concerns and was torn about what to do. He declared that he would speak against the accord but vote for it.[36]

Despite Burson-Marsteller's track record in convincing people to support measures that actually go against their own interests, this time the manipulators could not create enough fear and confusion to twist people's deep feelings about the need to protect the environment for their children and grandchildren. Ipsos-Reid's fallacious poll aside, ongoing public opinion surveys that asked the same questions found strong support for Kyoto. ". . . [F]rom late May until [November 7], the overall national level of support has been remarkably stable," Frank Graves, president of Ekos Research Associates, which had polled for Environment Canada over that period, wrote in a rebuttal to Ipsos-Reid. National Public Relations' expensive propaganda campaign did not shift public opinion enough to create the change desired by industry.[37] The campaign failed everywhere except Alberta, where the Klein government ran its own radio, television and newspaper ads and disseminated industry-friendly messages through industry-friendly newspapers, such as the *Calgary Herald*.

For the fossil-fuel industry, however, the game wasn't over. All it needed was the election of an industry-friendly prime minister. When Jean Chrétien announced he wasn't running again and wanted to leave Kyoto Accord ratification as a legacy, he rendered himself impermeable to everything the PR flaks could throw at him. Paul Martin would be more compliant with industry wishes if he won a majority in 2004. He had the right credentials: a solid business background, support from the business Liberals and even some backing from the Alberta oil patch in the person of Murray Edwards, a securities lawyer, oil-industry financier and Liberal fixer. And Martin's track record spoke of an affinity for business. He could point to his deep social-spending cuts and his tax cuts for the wealthy, initiatives that must have been appreciated by the highest echelons of the business elite. But when he won only a minority of seats, Martin couldn't operate as the usual majority-government dictatorship, doing business's bidding regardless of public opinion. So he waffled, placating voters by supporting Kyoto in his public utterances, but also pleasing business by doing little to move the file forward.

As for Stephen Harper, scrapping Canada's participation in Kyoto was adopted as official Conservative Party policy before the 2006 election. He introduced the policy into the election campaign cautiously, given that most Canadians were still supporting Canada's adoption of the Kyoto targets. Usually, when a government or political party announces a new policy, it chooses a location that resonates with the policy. To announce the launch of a new day-care program, it goes to a centre with lots of cute little tykes milling about. For a new environmental initiative, it selects a pristine wilderness location and flies the media in by helicopter. The optics reinforce the message. But Harper made his Kyoto announcement in Halifax, a location which does not spring to top of mind when thinking about carbon dioxide emissions. (Auto manufacturing factories? Petrochemical plants? Coal-fired electricity plants?) And it was folded in with two other major policy reversals: reopening discussion of a missile defence agreement with the Bush administration and reversing the Liberal government's groundbreaking deal with Canada's Aboriginal peoples.

Each policy shift was important enough to warrant a full day's media attention, but by collapsing them together, and by announcing them in Halifax late in the campaign, Harper's advisers ensured none of the policies would be adequately examined by the media. The leader's position was on the record, but with little salience, just as planned.

Nor did the press rise to the challenge of decoupling the issues. The Liberal-supporting *Toronto Star* placed the Hydra-headed story on its front page, but led with the missile defence debate issue. Harper's intention to pull out of Kyoto wasn't mentioned until the tenth paragraph.[38] Other papers, most supporting Harper, carried the story, but not on the front page. The *Globe and Mail* made its lead story that day the latest seat projections by its in-house pollster, but admitted, not far into the story, that the numbers were dubious. The *Globe* also ran on its front page the non-story of the very distant family relationship between Harper and actor Robb Wells, who plays Ricki in the TV show *Trailer*

Park Boys. In a page-six story titled "Harper not bound by Liberal initiatives"—as if the Kyoto Accord was some cockamamie idea hatched by Liberal spin doctors—*Globe* reporter Brian Laghi didn't get around to Kyoto until paragraph eleven. The story, when finally told, was that Harper judged Canada's Kyoto commitment a failure. "It's necessary for Canada to develop our own plan," he said, reviving the oil industry's 2002 made-in-Canada canard.[39]

For successfully stating his party's policy without attracting media or public scrutiny, Harper could thank his election war-room operatives. A key strategist during the election was Ken Boessenkool, a long-time Harper ally. After Harper lost the 2004 election, Boessenkool joined lobbying and PR firm Hill and Knowlton where he picked up some powerful fossil-fuel clients, such as ConocoPhillips.[40] Conoco's merger with Phillips Petroleum created North America's third-largest integrated oil and gas company. Like other oil giants, ConocoPhillips would benefit if Canada pulled out of Kyoto. The company admitted that implementing Kyoto would create significant expenditures, but had made no plans to prepare for these charges against earnings.[41] Much cheaper to make Kyoto go away.

Boessenkool resigned his lobbying jobs and went into the war room when the election was called. Other lobbyists helping the campaign, such as long-time communications aides Yaroslav Baran and Sandra Buckler, also ceased representing their clients. But during the campaign and after the victory, their colleagues were still representing big-oil interests. Baran's firm, Tactix Government Consulting, and Buckler's, GPC Public Affairs, represent dozens of the largest CO_2 emitters, such as Syncrude Canada, Shell Canada, the Canadian Petroleum Products Institute, the Canadian Trucking Alliance, Fording Coal, BP, Canadian Oilsands Investments, the Canadian Vehicle Manufacturers Association, as well as ConocoPhillips. Meanwhile, groups that support Kyoto, such as Greenpeace and the Sierra Club, had no representatives in the war room.

Climate change became news in 1988 when top U.S. National Aeronautics and Space Administration scientist James Hansen testified before Congress that he was 99 percent confident that global warming was here. The story made the front pages, perhaps because the country was experiencing a scorching summer. It was one of the hottest on record to that point and culminated in a prolonged drought.[42] The intersection of science and weather led to the creation of the Intergovernmental Panel on Climate Change, a United Nations–mandated body of two thousand climate science experts to study global warming. With such a huge selection of expertise involved, unanimity was never possible, Sir Robert May, former chief scientific adviser to the British government, explained. All opinions were considered as the IPCC "produce[d] narrowing bands of distribution of opinion," he wrote, "not two sides, but more often a distribution of opinion with a sort of consensus round the middle, and sometimes outlying spikes." May argued that "the way the IPCC has gone about its business, embracing dissent, putting out the facts and letting opinion contend in the market place, is a sound example of how science can inform policy making."[43]

But this didn't happen for nearly twenty years because the fossil-fuel industry went to great lengths to prevent climate science from informing policy-making. Its return to shareholders could be placed in jeopardy. Just 122 corporations are responsible for 80 percent of all CO_2 emissions. Four global oil and gas companies—ExxonMobil, BP/Amoco/ARCO, Royal Dutch/Shell, and Chevron/Texaco—produce the oil that contributes 10 percent of the world's carbon dioxide emissions. Six coal companies account for nearly 5 percent of CO_2 emissions. Auto companies like General Motors, Ford and DaimlerChrysler that promote gas-guzzling sport-utility vehicles, are major contributors. The three largest electric-power companies—American Electric Power, The Southern Company, Tennessee Valley Authority—produce CO_2 emissions at the same level as oil companies.[44] Any mandated reductions in emissions would affect corporate profits. It was essential that business continue as usual. The corporations, the front groups they set up, the advertisers and public relations experts they hired, and the deniers and think-tanks they funded, worked for twenty years to counter the conclusions of the IPCC and convince politicians and the public that global warming was not a real threat. According to a landmark study of the oil industry at the turn of the century, big polluters used five strategies to frustrate action on climate change: deny (claim climate change is not proven); delay (argue we don't know enough to justify drastic action); divide (use threats of job and income loss to divide critics); dump (move operations to countries with few regulations); and dupe (use all available techniques of environmental greenwash).[45]

The fossil-fuel industry was so successful in sowing doubt and confusion about the true extent of global warming that when the evidence became incontrovertible—disappearing glaciers, open water at the North Pole—it was too late to do much about it, except to start a debate on how to adapt to a rapidly warming planet. If governments had accepted the scientific consensus early enough, there was a "chance of altering the early trajectory of development in India and particularly China, which are now starting to rival American contributions to the earth's carbon overload," environmentalist Bill McKibben wrote in 2006.[46] Thanks to the fossil fuel–funded attacks on the IPCC, though, the challenge to slow down and then reverse global warming was made that much more daunting.

The IPCC was no sooner formed when about fifty companies in the mining, oil and gas, electricity, automobile, and chemical industries created a front group called the Global Climate Coalition (GCC). Exxon and the American Petroleum Institute were key backers. Its mission was to convince Congress and the media that the idea of human-caused global warming was not true and if the IPCC's scientific evidence became persuasive, it would argue that a warming planet was beneficial.[47] The coalition kept the discussion focused on whether or not there was a problem, thus preventing discussion about what should be done.

The GCC hired E. Bruce Harrison, a leading public relations strategist on environmental issues. Harrison got his start in anti-environmental PR in the 1960s by helping agricultural-pesticide manufacturers attack Rachel Carson and her book *Silent Spring*. In their campaign to discredit Carson, Harrison and his colleagues used the emerging practice of "crisis management," which has been described as a mélange of "emotional appeals, scientific misinformation, front groups, extensive mailings to the media and opinion leaders, and the recruitment of doctors and scientists as 'objective' third-party defenders of agrichemicals."[48] Harrison used many of these tactics to discredit the IPCC and environmental groups who argued that greenhouse-gas emissions had to be controlled. Their strategy was to spread the notion that global warming was a dangerous myth and to emphasize the lack of absolute proof.[49]

The coalition, along with other business lobbies such as the Business Council for Sustainable Development, ensured that the United Nations Framework Convention on Climate Change at the 1992 Earth Summit in Rio, which would reduce greenhouse emissions globally, was fatally weakened. The GCC was responsible, the same year, for gutting a House of Representatives energy bill that would require industry cutbacks of CO_2 emissions and place a ten-year moratorium on offshore oil and gas drilling. In 1993, the coalition distributed a $250,000 video documentary, *The Greening of Planet Earth*, to a thousand environmental reporters across the country, arguing that increased atmospheric CO_2 would boost crop production and feed the world's hungry.[50]

The IPCC's 1995 consensus document concluded that global warming was indeed occurring, so industry switched messages, continuing to complain about the lack of proof, but also warning of "serious adverse consequences for economic development and growth around the world" if fossil-fuel use was curtailed.[51] In preparation for the Kyoto meeting in December 1997, the GCC ran a $13-million advertising campaign aimed at undermining support for the climate treaty.[52] In a series of ads on the op-ed pages of the *New York Times* just before and after Kyoto, Mobil emphasized the high degree of uncertainty over the impact of human carbon emissions. We "don't know enough about global warming," the ads said, and then scared readers with predictions of job losses and "difficult choices" for Americans. "How much prosperity are Americans willing to forego?" the ads asked. "How much more tax will they have to pay?" The Kyoto Protocol could put "the U.S. at a disadvantage," Mobil warned, and claimed that actions to prevent climate change could "wreak havoc" on our nation. Americans should not take any "quick-fix" measures and were advised to "stop, look and listen before we leap."[53] These messages anticipated those of the Coalition for Responsible Environmental Solutions half a decade later.

The threat of job loss was an effective weapon to divide critics, as we saw earlier in the defeat of the Clinton BTU tax in 1993. A 1997 study by Wharton Econometric Forecasting Associates (WEFA) (not connected to the well-known business school) predicted that 2.4 million jobs, $300 billion in GDP and $2,700 per household—a figure curiously identical to Ross McKitrick's for the Canadian context five years later—would be lost by signing the Kyoto Accord.[54] This study was then cited by the oil industry as evidence that fighting climate change would bring unnecessary hardship. But a critical examination by the progressive Economic Policy Institute found that the authors had included parts of the Kyoto document that had not been agreed to by the parties. WEFA also relied on worst-case assumptions to produce the scariest results. Still more disconcerting, the National Environmental Trust discovered that the study was funded by the American Petroleum Institute, and noted other suspicious connections between the study and the GCC, Shell and Texaco. Despite these revelations, the GCC propaganda was astonishingly successful. The Senate voted 95 to 0 to condemn Kyoto.

ExxonMobil and its allies pressed into service the full weight of the tree-tops propaganda machine. In the United States, the company pumped millions of dollars into a maze of organizations to spread doubt and confusion in the public mind. *Mother Jones* magazine tallied forty organizations funded by

ExxonMobil to undermine scientific findings on climate change and to support the science skeptics. Between 2000 and 2003 (the limits of the study), Exxon provided $8.6 million to these groups.[55] These included:

- $960,000 to the American Enterprise Institute. ExxonMobil CEO Lee Raymond was a vice-chair of AEI's board of trustees and Dick Cheney a former senior fellow. Three weeks after Cheney assumed the U.S. vice-presidency, he met with Raymond for a half-hour. The subject of their discussion was never disclosed.

- $1.4 million to the pro-market Washington, D.C.–based Competitive Enterprise Institute (CEI), which worked for more than a decade to derail efforts to combat climate change. Its contribution is the claim that global warming is a European plot to damage American competitiveness. One CEI initiative was a 2005 campaign in Europe to persuade business, politicians and the media that the European Union should abandon its commitments under Kyoto. CEI's global-warming policy director attacked the United Kingdom's chief scientist for his pro-Kyoto stance and was consequently censured by the British House of Commons. CEI set up a front group called the European Sound Science Policy Coalition modelled on the Global Climate Coalition. The immediate target was to get German utility company RWE to join the fledgling coalition.[56]

- $252,000 to the Committee for a Constructive Tomorrow, where Paul Driessen, who wrote *Eco-Imperialism: Green Power, Black Death*, is a senior fellow. Many prominent global-warming deniers are academic and scientific advisers to this organization, which denied climate change for more than a decade.

- $40,000 to the Congress of Racial Equality. CORE was a leading civil rights organization in the 1960s, but was taken over and moved to the far Republican right. (See Chapter 6.) Its unique niche is to accuse environmentalists of "eco-imperialism" because they want bans on toxic pesticides and controls on carbon emissions, which, CORE claims, hurt African-Americans. CORE mounted a counterdemonstration to shout down environmentalists picketing ExxonMobil's shareholders meeting in Irving, Texas.

- $60,000 a year to the Fraser Institute. The money may have been used for policy briefings by Tim Ball, whose unique, but bizarre, contribution is that the earth is cooling, not warming.
- $140,000 to the Hoover Institution, a prolific generator of anti–global warming propaganda. Hoover publications deny that global warming is occurring, ("Who says the globe is warming?," by Thomas Sowell) or claim it is a hoax ("New age fanatics and the upper muddle class," by Fred Singer), while another line of output accepts that global warming is occurring but says it's a good thing ("Happiness is a warm planet," by Thomas Gale Moore). Hoover senior fellow Michael Boskin is a member of ExxonMobil's board of directors and the board's important Public Issues Committee. Boskin is a star conservative academic. He chaired George H.W. Bush's Council of Economic Advisers and received the National Association of Business Economists' Adam Smith Award in 1998.[57] Condoleezza Rice was a Hoover senior fellow and a Chevron Corp. director before entering the Bush administration.
- $305,250 to Citizens for a Sound Economy. This is the group that worked with Burson-Marsteller's Astroturf group to defeat Bill Clinton's BTU tax in 1993.

Here's how it fits together. Sallie Baliunas is a Harvard–Smithsonian Institution astrophysicist who has been providing scientific cover for global-warming deniers since the mid-nineties. She is a senior scientist at the George C. Marshall Institute (received $310,000 from ExxonMobil), where Marshall CEO William O'Keefe was a former ExxonMobil lobbyist, senior official of the American Petroleum Institute and chairman of the Global Climate Coalition.[58] Baliunas co-wrote (with colleague Willie Soon) the Fraser Institute pamphlet *Global Warming: a guide to the science* (receives $60,000 a year from ExxonMobil). Baliunas is "enviro-sci host" of TechCentralStation.com (received $95,000 from ExxonMobil) and is on science advisory boards for the Committee for a Constructive Tomorrow ($252,000) and the Annapolis Center for Science-Based Public Policy ($427,500). She has given speeches before the American Enterprise Institute ($960,000) and the Heritage Foundation ($340,000). The Heartland Institute ($312,000) publishes her op-ed pieces. She is not lying when she says she receives no direct funding from ExxonMobil, but the money surrounds her.

Why might the oil giant be so taken with Baliunas? With colleague Willie Soon, she first claimed that solar effects could account for the earth's warming. When that theory was discredited, they then wrote a paper that claims the twentieth century hasn't been all that warm. This paper was published in an obscure journal, *Climate Research*, and partially funded by the American Petroleum Institute.[59] It became a mini-bible for deniers. But the editor-in-chief and two other editors of *Climate Research* resigned, saying the paper should not have been published because of methodological errors in the research and a deficient peer-review process at the journal.[60]

In 1999 the Global Climate Coalition lost some of its clout because of ongoing pressure from climate-change activists. Concern about their environmental reputation with consumers led the two European-based oil giants, British Petroleum and Shell, to drop out of the coalition. They were followed by Ford, Daimler-Chrysler, Texaco, the Southern Company and General Motors. The GCC soldiered on, transforming itself into a lobby group for trade associations instead of individual companies. And since trade associations like the American Petroleum Institute, Automobile Manufacturers Association and Western Fuels Association were still participating in the GCC, the companies that withdrew from the coalition were still involved, but in a less obvious way. The American Petroleum Institute, which represents both Shell and BP, continued to deny the problem of climate change and delay solutions. Shell and BP could sound environmentalist for their European customers, but didn't need to change very much in the way they operated.

After George W. Bush assumed the U.S. presidency, ExxonMobil obtained more direct access to American climate-change policy-making than it did as a leader of the GCC.

- Just weeks after Bush took office, an ExxonMobil official sent a memo to the White House asking it to replace, "at the Request of the United States," the chairman of the IPCC. Dr. Robert Watson was chief scientist at the World Bank. His crime was that he was too "aggressive" in calling for urgent action on climate change. The Bush administration then successfully lobbied other countries for a more acceptable candidate, one who was not as adamant as Watson. They thought they had their man in Dr. Rajendra Pachauri, an Indian economist who had worked closely with the electric-utility industry. Unfortunately for Exxon, the new chairman came to embrace the science and called for deep cuts in CO_2 emissions if humanity was to survive.[61]

- The same year, in a more successful move, ExxonMobil proposed that the White House make scientist Harlan Watson (no relation to Robert), then working as a Republican aide for the House Science Committee, "available to work with the team" of Americans attending international climate-change meetings. Bush went further and appointed Harlan Watson as the nation's chief climate negotiator, and Watson faithfully touted the Bush administration's record on climate change.[62]

- Larisa Dobriansky was appointed deputy assistant secretary for national energy policy at the Department of Energy, where she managed the Office of Climate Change Policy. Dobriansky promoted Bush's voluntary programs, public–private partnerships and incentives to industry. She was previously a lobbyist with the law firm Akin Gump, where she worked on climate change for ExxonMobil.[63]

- Lawyer Philip Cooney headed the American Petroleum Institute's "climate team" which led industry opposition to Kyoto. He was appointed chief of staff at the Council on Environmental Quality under Bush. In 2005, Cooney watered down global-warming reports by government scientists. When his actions were revealed, he resigned and took a job at ExxonMobil.[64]

In Canada the Fraser Institute and *National Post* were the primary channels for global-warming denial. Their role was to repackage for Canadian consumption material written mostly by industry-sponsored American deniers. They also extracted maximum mileage out of Canada's own hearty band of naysayers. Behind the Fraser Institute's anti–global warming work lies the fact that every major oil, gas, petrochemical and coal company in Canada are, or have been, members of the institute. These include Imperial Oil, Shell, Texaco, British Petroleum, Chevron, Gulf, Westcoast Energy, Alberta Natural Gas (later EnCana Corp.), Dow Chemical, DuPont, Alcan and the Canadian Petroleum Association.

The month after the Kyoto Protocol was adopted in 1997, the Fraser published a book, edited by the institute's environmental economist, Laura Jones, titled *Global Warming: The Science and the Politics*. The book is a compilation of articles by American global-warming deniers. Familiar names include Sallie Baliunas, Willie Soon, Robert Balling, Sherwood Idso and Patrick Michaels. Jones's introduction frames the discussion: ". . . global warming is not a settled issue. The scientists [in this volume] raise important questions about the validity of the hysteria over global warming. It is time to revisit these questions."[65]

Jones promoted the denial thesis at every opportunity. In one *Fraser Forum* piece, she claims that extreme weather events are not related to global warming, which isn't occurring, but if it is, it's too small to be harmful and is probably beneficial.[66] This article utilizes four sources, three of whom are American deniers who contributed chapters to her book. The fourth is a survey of climatologists by Citizens for a Sound Economy, the ExxonMobil-funded advocacy group. This group's message is that Kyoto could cost Americans $400 billion a year, give governments sweeping new regulatory authority and export jobs and industries overseas—all without providing any environmental benefit.[67]

In another *Fraser Forum* piece, Jones defines the precautionary principle thusly: "attempting to prevent future catastrophic but highly unlikely events is justified whatever the cost of prevention." This definition, however, is at odds with the common understanding of precaution. The most widely used description of the precautionary principle is found in Article 15 of the Rio Declaration on Environment and Development: "In order to protect the environment, the precautionary approach shall be widely applied by States according to their capabilities. Where there are threats of serious or irreversible damage, lack of full scientific certainty shall not be used as a reason for postponing cost-effective measures to prevent environmental degradation."[68] Although the principle, as defined here, seems cautious and measured, Jones calls it "reckless" because "assuming no huge technological breakthroughs in the near future, achieving the reduction targets set out at Kyoto will be incredibly costly." One cost will be twenty-five thousand additional deaths per year in the U.S. alone.[69] Her source for this startling claim is the Washington, D.C.–based Competitive Enterprise Institute (CEI). This is yet another ExxonMobil-backed libertarian think-tank at the leading edge of the corporate campaign against global warming. In a study provocatively entitled *Could Kyoto Kill?*, CEI author Frank Cross estimates that each additional regulatory cost of $10 million will "induce" one premature death and a loss of one thousand dollars per person per year, as a result of global-warming policies.[70]

After Kyoto's ratification by Parliament in 2002, Jones became an "adjunct scholar" at the Fraser Institute and then chief lobbyist for the Canadian Federation of Independent Business in British Columbia, where she carried on her anti-regulation work. Her position at the institute was filled by Kenneth Green, director of the environmental health and safety program at the Reason Institute, a Los Angeles–based libertarian think-tank that specializes in fighting environmental regulation, claiming it is an affront to liberty.

Reason's anti–global warming propaganda is based on the claim that "climate change has been a natural phenomenon [sic] throughout the course of time." Do man's activities affect climate? "That is still open to debate," Reason's web site informs us in a reasonably sounding way. "Some would say none at all while others will say that it is dramatic."[71] Reason is funded by a number of conservative foundations, the American Petroleum Institute, ARCO, BP Amoco, Chevron, Koch Industries, Shell Oil, Western States Petroleum, the Big Three auto companies, and carbon dioxide–spewing airlines. ExxonMobil provided $381,000 between 1998 and 2005.[72]

Green promoted the same fossil-fuel interests during his three years at the Fraser. The month after Canada ratified Kyoto, Green coordinated an issue of *Fraser Forum*, featuring six articles about climate change.[73] Green's contribution is an article titled "Kyoto Krazy." He claimed, amazingly, that the science of global warming was still unsettled (in 2003!). There are two sides to the debate, he wrote. On one side are "environmental pressure groups" like the David Suzuki Foundation, which believes "the law is on their side, that they've been terribly conscientious about consultation and cooperation, that there really is a free lunch and Canadians can achieve draconian reductions in energy use at low cost." On the other side, he says, are "more pragmatic researchers in the private sector and academia" who have shown that "Kyoto Protocol ratification will provide little benefit and will likely lead to real and wrenching economic impacts that will negatively affect the well being of Canadians." Green, however, cites only one such pragmatic researcher in the private sector and academia, his Fraser Institute colleague, Ross McKitrick.[74]

Green continues his bizarre comparisons. On one side is a group "such as the United Nation's [sic] Intergovernmental Panel on Climate Change, which has published reports suggesting that a warmer climate would cause major ecological disruption necessitating urgent action." But other scientists, he goes on, "have shown that the threat of global warming is overstated by the United Nations." Here too, Green cites only one source, McKitrick, who is an economist, not a scientist. In Green's world, one economist with an agenda negates two thousand climatologists who have fashioned a difficult consensus. Green also refers to the work of Sallie Baliunas and Willie Soon, who "explain" that global warming is a "natural and largely beneficent phenomenon," due primarily to sunspot activity. His reference is from Soon and Baliunas's 2001 Fraser Institute pamphlet, which was based on their 1995 book, which had been discredited by then.

In their own contribution to Green's *Fraser Forum* issue, Soon and Baliunas provide an excerpt from their 1995 book, which argues that sunspot activity could be responsible for global warming. The Calgary School's Barry Cooper, who runs the Fraser's Calgary office, weighed in with an article that claims ratification was all about politics and nothing else. He offers variously that Chrétien forced ratification (a) to put Paul Martin in a tight spot; (b) to exploit another opportunity to take a crack at the Americans; and (c) to promote further centralization of power in Ottawa at the expense of Alberta. Take your pick.[75] These reasons "have been advanced," Cooper claimed, to explain Chrétien's decisive action, but provides no sources or references for who advanced them. As to the possibility that Chrétien acted because he was convinced global warming was a threat, Cooper is silent.

Green left in 2005 to become executive director of the Washington, D.C.–based Environmental Literacy Council, which provides industry-friendly learning materials for American schoolchildren. This organization receives funding from many of the same sources as Reason: the American Petroleum Institute, ExxonMobil, the Sarah Scaife Foundation and the Charles G. Koch Foundation.[76] Green also became a "visiting fellow" at the American Enterprise Institute, which had launched its National Research Initiative to "support, publish and disseminate" research by academics and other intellectuals on pressing public policy issues.[77] Yet Green went beyond the activities of supporting, publishing and disseminating research while at the AEI. Just before the IPCC's Fourth Summary Report was due to be released in February 2007, Green authored a letter on AEI letterhead offering $10,000 each to scientists and economists to write articles disputing the IPCC findings.[78] Perhaps the AEI used some of the $960,000 it received from ExxonMobil, and perhaps ExxonMobil's CEO, who was vice-chairman of the AEI's board of trustees, played a role in this gambit. It's not known how many scientists took the money.

After Green left the Fraser Institute, global-warming propaganda tailed off, but not before the institute scored its biggest coup, the prolonged attack on the

IPCC's "hockey stick" by Ross McKitrick and Stephen McIntyre. McKitrick, who wrote the anti-Kyoto study for the Canadian Taxpayers Federation, was an environmental economist at the University of Guelph with no background in climatology. He first appeared as a Canadian denier at a briefing sponsored by the Cooler Heads Coalition at the libertarian, industry-backed Competitive Enterprise Institute in Washington, D.C. Here he attacked the "climate alarmists," the two thousand climatologists of the IPCC, and first applied his "regulation-costs-more-than-the-good-it-would-do" mantra.[79] McKitrick wrote his first *National Post* opinion piece in 2001, making the point that Kyoto was a "disastrously expensive policy commitment" based on "pervasive ignorance."[80] The *National Post* must have liked this approach since it gave him a podium five times the following year.

Steve McIntyre was a semi-retired Toronto mining and oil-exploration consultant without a Ph.D. or even a master's degree; in other words, he had no pedigree in the climate-science world. McKitrick met McIntyre through an anti–global warming online discussion group and they began working together while the denial lobby was organizing to prevent Canada's ratification of Kyoto. In 2003 they published a paper, with Fraser Institute support, alleging that serious errors had been made in one climate-change study known as the hockey stick. This study had been published in *Nature* by Michael Mann and his colleagues for the IPCC in 1998. It claimed that temperatures in the northern hemisphere have been rising since 1900 after remaining relatively constant for the previous nine centuries, describing the basic shape of a hockey stick. The paper synthesized "12 data sets—such as the width of tree rings and the isotopic composition of ice cores—to generate a chart of temperature variation in the Northern Hemisphere."[81] Many studies by other researchers have used other methodologies to replicate the hockey stick results, but McIntyre and McKitrick and other climate-change deniers relentlessly attacked this one paper. The hockey stick became their straw man. They built it up to the point where it came to stand for the entire IPCC effort, and then attempted to tear it down. For three years, until the basic shape of the hockey stick was largely confirmed in 2006 by a National Academy of Sciences panel, the climate-change world was ripped apart as the anti-Kyoto propaganda machine waged all-out war on scientific consensus.

The battle was ludicrous in some ways. Jim Hansen of NASA, who is recognized as the father of global-warming research, wrote to Environmental Science and Technology Online: "Although I have been carrying out research in the atmospheric science and climate field for more than four decades, I have never heard of either of them. That perhaps tells you something."[82] The essence of McIntyre and McKitrick's criticism was whether certain North American tree rings, called the "bristlecone pine data," should have been included in Mann's analysis. Mann and others argued that it didn't matter if these data were not included. "Particular concerns with [these] data were addressed in the follow-up paper," Mann's associates Gavin Schmidt and Caspar Ammann wrote on the climate scientists' web site, "[B]ut the fact remains that including these data improves the statistical validation over the 19th Century period and they therefore should be included."[83] McKitrick and McIntyre also charged Mann with withholding adverse statistical results, but Schmidt and Ammann noted that studies using other types of data "agree that the late 20th century is anomalous in the context of the last millennium, and possibly the last two millennia."

The faint call emitted by the duo was picked up and amplified by the right-wing echo chamber until it became a huge roar, impossible to ignore. In Canada, McIntyre and McKitrick's work was hyped by the *National Post* and other CanWest papers; in the United States, the business-friendly *Wall Street Journal* was the heavy hitter. The journal in which McIntyre and McKitrick published their study, *Energy & Environment*, was controversial in scientific circles, in particular because the journal does not follow standard academic procedures for peer review. It was found in just twenty-six libraries around the world, only fifteen of which were at universities.[84] Many scientists have never heard of it. But *Energy & Environment* published manuscripts by climate-change deniers that were rejected by peer-reviewed journals. The journal's editorial board contains several well-known deniers and editor Sonja Boehmer-Christiansen is a denier herself. Her mission, she says, is to give the deniers a voice. Once the articles are in print, the denial lobby can leverage the publication into the political realm.

That's what happened with McIntyre and McKitrick. They were flown to Washington, D.C., to brief lobbyists from the National Association of Manufacturers and the staff of Republican senator James Inhofe of Oklahoma, as a vote neared on a bill to cap fossil-fuel emissions.[85] Inhofe chaired the Environment and Public Works Committee, which is in charge of Senate legislation on the environment. Not surprisingly, given his oil-industry constituency, Inhofe is one of the most strident anti-Kyoto members of Congress. He asked if the threat of global warming was "the greatest hoax ever perpetrated on the American people." His answer? "It sure sounds like it." Inhofe used McIntyre and McKitrick's work to bully senators who might be wavering in their opposition to the bill and it was defeated. The oil industry contributed $320,000 to Inhofe between 2001 and 2006, while electric utilities added $195,000.[86]

Within two weeks of the publication of the McIntyre and McKitrick article in *Energy & Environment,* Canadian deniers fanned out across the country to spread the good news. They were given an accommodating platform from CanWest papers. Kenneth Green, then still at the Fraser Institute, published an op-ed piece in the *Calgary Herald* claiming that 2003 had been "a very bad year for advocates of the Kyoto Protocol." Thanks to the work of McIntyre and McKitrick, he wrote, the hockey stick was no more. In the *Vancouver Sun,* columnist Michael Campbell, who was not known to have any expertise in climate science, called the M&M paper "arguably the most damaging attack to date on the science behind Kyoto," and alleged that Kyoto was "perhaps the most potent weapon in the arsenal of those who oppose western capitalism." Libertarian columnist Lorne Gunter claimed in the *Edmonton Journal* (reprinted in the *Windsor Star*) that M&M had "destroyed the hockey stick theory," which was, he pontificated, the "holiest of holies in the greenhouse priests' liturgy." Also in the *Windsor Star,* long-time denier Tim Patterson of Carleton University, called *Energy & Environment* a "prestigious" journal and claimed that M&M's work "completely demolishes" the hockey stick curve.[87]

In early 2005, McIntyre and McKitrick hit pay dirt with the publication of an article criticizing the hockey stick in a peer-reviewed journal, *Geophysical Research Letters* (GRL). Within two weeks of the article's publication, McIntyre was featured in a long, front-page piece in the *Wall Street Journal.*[88] McIntyre's astonishing rise to fame was documented in a study by *Environmental Science and Technology* (ES&T), an online publication of the American Chemical Society.[89] Thousands of studies on global warming are published every year. Very few are ever reported by the mainstream media.[90] ES&T found that the *Wall Street Journal* had published only three news stories reporting new climate-change research in peer-reviewed science journals over a one-year period: a 169-word Associated Press story, a 576-word report on a news conference announcing the results of a study, and the 2,209-word McIntyre article. Michael Oppenheimer, a professor of geoscience and international affairs at Princeton University, told ES&T that "the story gave an undeserved amount of attention to a controversy that most scientists regard as ludicrous." Caspar Ammann worked at the National Center for Atmospheric Research in Boulder, Colorado. Like M&M, he reanalyzed Mann's data, but unlike them, found Mann's method to be "robust even when numerous modifications are employed." Yet Ammann's work received no media coverage.[91] Some news organizations, it seemed, were lining up on the side of the deniers.

The GRL article led to a blizzard of stories in CanWest papers. The day the article was published, the *National Post* featured it as front-page news. Titled "Canadians find flaw in Kyoto 'hockey stick,'" the story exemplifies how the *Post*'s editorial position influences its news judgment. Like the *Wall Street Journal*, M&M's study is the only one of hundreds published each year that obtained front-page coverage in the *Post*. The *Post* also ran a Terence Corcoran editorial entitled "Let science debate begin" (as if the deniers hadn't been debating the science since Exxon funded the Global Climate Coalition fifteen years earlier). The same day, the *Post* published the first of a lengthy two-part series by Dutch science writer Marcel Crok lauding M&M's work. Crok was not known as a denier, yet he claimed that "even GRL . . . now acknowledges a serious problem with the prevailing climate reconstruction by Mann and his colleagues."[92] This claim received a sharp retort from the public information officer of the American Geophysical Union, the scientific body that publishes GRL. The journal "acknowledges no such thing," he wrote. GRL "takes no position on the validity of the research it publishes, only that a paper is worthy of being put before the scientific community for its consideration."[93] In the following days, the *Post* published pages of letters, which, curiously, all seemed to come from deniers and their supporters. It also published two anti–United Nations rants from Peter Foster, a piece by McIntyre, one by denier Tim Patterson, plus another editorial from Corcoran.

Other CanWest papers also put the cudgels to the hockey stick. Not surprisingly, the *Calgary Herald* was a hotbed of anti-Kyoto rhetoric. It published pieces by Mark Milke, former head of the Canadian Taxpayers Federation, and Barry Cooper, the Calgary School political scientist who directs the Fraser Institute's Calgary office. In a flight of non-academic fancy, Cooper compared the science behind the hockey stick with science in the Soviet Union under Stalin. Then the *Herald*'s Danielle Smith entered the fray. Smith, a former Fraser Institute intern, was then an editorial writer and host of CanWest's *Global Sunday* television talk show. The day before her Sunday show, Smith profiled Ross McKitrick as a hero who stood up to Environment Canada's "One-Tonne Challenge," which, presumably, was worthless because it relied on the science behind the hockey stick. McKitrick was the "garden party skunk" who discovered the fatal problems in the methodology. On Sunday she interviewed McKitrick, showering him with puffball questions. The next day, the interview was transformed into news and reported in the pages of the *Ottawa Citizen* and *Windsor Star*.[94]

Back in the United States, Republican representative Joe Barton of Texas took up the attack for big oil. Barton chaired the powerful House Committee on Energy and Commerce, which controls House legislation affecting oil companies. (Barton received $189,000 from the oil and gas industry and $250,000 from electric utilities for the 2006 election.[95]) In June 2005, he wrote to Mann, his colleagues and several science groups, demanding a detailed accounting of their government and private funding, data and methods. Barton asked for nothing from McIntyre and McKitrick. The fossil fuel–backed conservative political machine was flexing its muscles and intruding into the world of science. Scientists worried this was a tactic to intimidate climate scientists from further linking global warming to human activity. Barton wrote: "Provide the location of all data archives relating to each published study for which you were an author or co-author." Barton also asked for the scientists' curriculum vitae, lists of all sources of support for research and the computer code used to generate the hockey stick analysis.[96]

To bring sanity back to the House of Representatives, four months later, Sherwood Boehlert, the New York Republican who chaired the House Science Committee, called for an independent review of the 1999 Mann paper and related research. (Boehlert received virtually no funding from oil and gas companies or electric utilities.) The task was given to the National Academy of Sciences, which advises Congress and the government. A twelve-member panel was convened and six months later the panel's report exonerated the hockey stick graph. The 155-page report found it "plausible that the Northern Hemisphere was warmer during the last few decades of the 20th century than during any comparable period over the preceding millennium." But because there were "substantial uncertainties" regarding surface temperature changes prior to AD 1600 due to the relative scarcity of precisely dated evidence, the panel had "lower confidence" in the record for this period.[97]

That assessment didn't stop the denial lobby for an instant. Without missing a beat, the *Post*'s Terence Corcoran distorted the panel's findings by claiming it "essentially upheld McIntyre and McKitrick and threw out the 1,000-year claim."[98] The newspaper provided no news coverage about this study, so *Post* readers had only Corcoran's unique interpretation to go by. Two weeks later, McIntyre and McKitrick were given yet another podium in the *Post*. They repeated their attack on the hockey stick and this time trained their guns on the National Academy of Sciences panel, along with Michael Mann.[99]

For many citizens, their understanding of global warming derives from what they read or watch in the media, not from an extensive knowledge of science.[100] So whoever has access to the media will have more opportunity to persuade public opinion. Consider the case of a researcher with science council funding who works at a Canadian university and discovers a new piece of evidence that global warming is occurring. The evidence and the argument of the research are likely abstract and difficult for him to explain to a general-assignment reporter writing the story, so the research receives little, if any, coverage. Consider next the case of an economist who does little original research herself, but is funded in part by the fossil-fuel industry to spread the word that global warming is not occurring, and if it is, we don't need to do anything about it, especially cut back on our use of fossil fuels. She is associated with a right-wing think-tank with a staff of media specialists and government lobbyists, whose primary function is to get pro-industry messages into the media.

Add to that the predisposition of corporate-controlled media to filter out news or views critical of business. The result is a news system largely devoid of stories describing the links between business activity and environmental degradation. Very few stories were published in Canadian or American papers about ExxonMobil's funding of the deniers. Add the further predisposition of reporters to present news in a balanced fashion, looking for two sides to a story. If the two thousand climatologists of the IPCC release a study stating that the evidence for human causes of global warming just became stronger, a conscientious reporter will seek out a statement from a denier such as Tim Ball or Ross McKitrick for the sake of balance.

In contrast with most news organizations, the *National Post* makes little pretense of being balanced, in its opinions or even in its news. In April 2006, the *Post* published a letter addressed to Stephen Harper and signed by sixty "accredited experts in climate and related scientific disciplines," as they described themselves. They wanted Harper to begin a debate on the Kyoto Protocol. This was an odd request given that the theory of climate change had been debated since 1988, when NASA scientist James Hansen declared global warming was here. That statement has been subjected to extensive, prolonged and worldwide scrutiny, especially after the fossil-fuel industry set up the Global Climate Coalition. The sixty experts denied "alarmist forecasts" of global warming and attacked "the confident pronouncements of scientifically unqualified environmental groups," whose goal was to capture "sensational headlines."[101]

Only nineteen of the "accredited experts in climate and related disciplines" were Canadian. Some were experts in paleoclimatology, which looks at climate changes over millions of years, so an increase of one or two degrees in the past hundred years would not be worthy of their consideration. Some still seemed to believe that sunspots could account for warming, even though that theory had been discredited. Signatories of the published letter included Patrick Michaels, Fred Singer, Tim Ball and Sallie Baliunas. They included non-climatologists like economist Ross McKitrick. Geographer Sonja Boehmer-Christiansen, editor of *Energy & Environment*, signed on too.

The deniers' letter was followed two weeks later by one from ninety supporters of Kyoto. This group called itself "climate-science leaders from the academic, public and private sectors across Canada." Unlike the deniers, they were all Canadian and they were all climate scientists; no weasel phrases like "related scientific disciplines" were included. Their point was simple. The evidence was conclusive that warming has occurred and most of it was attributable to human activity. These conclusions, they wrote, were supported by the vast majority of the world's climate scientists. Harper's assignment was to get on with developing an "effective national strategy" to deal with climate change.[102]

Financial Post editor Terence Corcoran seemed to think debate rather than action was required. He ran the letter from the Kyoto supporters, but accompanied it with an editorial attacking their credibility. Their crime was that some were federal government scientists and some had received peer-reviewed government grants. Therefore, what they had to say must be socialist-inspired rubbish.[103] The pro-Kyoto scientists were subjected to another blistering attack the following week, this time by Reuven Brenner, a McGill University economist and adjunct fellow at the libertarian Cato Institute, who had done studies for the Howe and Fraser institutes and Shell Oil. Brenner's point was that the ninety scientists were actually taxpayer-funded "activists and lobbyists who masquerade as scientists."[104]

The sixty-expert letter was organized by a group called the Friends of Science, a Calgary-based coalition of oil-patch geologists, Conservatives, prominent climate-change deniers and public relations practitioners. The president is an oil and gas consultant. The vice-president worked as a geologist for major petroleum producers in Canada and the North Sea. The society was organized in 2002, as the Chrétien government was preparing to ratify Kyoto. Its first action was to bring prominent deniers to Ottawa in a last-ditch effort to sideline Kyoto ratification. That exercise was paid for by Imperial Oil and Talisman Energy and choreographed by the APCO public relations firm, as reported earlier in this chapter.

With Harper's victory, APCO and the Friends of Science believed they had a second chance to get rid of Kyoto and adopt the phantom made-in-Canada solution. But they had to ensure their oil-industry funding would remain hidden. Otherwise, they would not be credible with the public. How they did this was the subject of a 4,200-word story in the Globe and Mail in 2006 by Charles Montgomery.[105]

According to Montgomery, Barry Cooper set up a fund at the university called the Science Education Fund. Donors could give to the fund through the Calgary Foundation, which administers much charitable giving in Calgary. Its policy is to guard the identities of donors. The Science Education Fund then provides money for the Friends of Science. Thanks to this clever scheme, oil-industry backing was rendered invisible.

In 2004, the society pumped $400,000 into a twenty-five-minute video entitled Climate Catastrophe Cancelled, which promoted the relatively minor uncertainties around global warming while ignoring the widely accepted certainties. Between 2004 and 2006, the Science Education Fund received an additional $200,000. In the run-up to the 2006 election, Friends aired thirty-second radio spots that attacked Kyoto, targeting 200,000 Ontario residents in ridings where the Liberals were thought to be vulnerable. Were they effective? After the ads were aired, the Friends' web site reported receiving 300,000 visitors and the Tories did win several of the seats.[106] After Harper's victory, Friends distributed thousands of copies of Climate Catastrophe Cancelled to politicians and news organizations across the country. In April they wrote the letter to Harper urging him to pull out of Kyoto. In May he did.

Meanwhile, Charles Montgomery's lengthy Globe and Mail feature about the Friends of Science was picked up by SourceWatch, a directory of propagandists created by public relations industry critics John Stauber and Sheldon Rampton. The spotlight beamed on Friends' dubious funding arrangements led the University of Calgary to conduct an internal audit, which concluded that its trust account had been used to "support a partisan viewpoint on climate change." The university shut down the account and contacted Elections Canada about an apparent violation of the Elections Act.[107] Elections Canada ruled that the ads didn't violate the law. They were not "election advertising" because they attacked the Kyoto Protocol and the science of climate change, and not specific candidates or parties.[108]

The spotlight also revealed that Morten Paulsen, Preston Manning's former communications director, had received a one-year contract to promote Friends' anti-Kyoto message. Paulsen was also working for oil giant ConocoPhillips at the time and had worked on the 2006 Conservative election campaign.[109] The *National Post* did not report these developments, but had gone on an attack-dog rampage when Montgomery's exposé first appeared in the *Globe*. Montgomery wrote his article, *Post* resident enforcer Terence Corcoran charged, because "Mr. Montgomery comes from the same ideological school" as Noam Chomsky.[110] There, that'll teach ya, don't mess with us global-warming deniers. It was a rare insight into the intersection of interests by the oil industry, industry-funded front groups, radical conservative academics, corporate media and Conservative Party apparatchiks.

And while the *National Post*, the Friends of Science, Calgary Schooler Barry Cooper and their allies continued to muddy the waters, action on global warming was delayed for nearly two decades. ExxonMobil CEO Lee Raymond retired at the end of 2005. His shareholders showered him with a $400-million retirement package, the use of an Exxon jet, car and driver and a million-dollar consulting deal. They had a lot to be thankful for. After taking over Mobil for $82 billion, Raymond guided the combined oil giant to the largest profit in human history, US$36 billion. (And profits kept going up after his retirement, reaching $45.2 billion in 2008.) Shareholders were happy with shares that had risen 500 percent in value during the years he was doing everything he could to prevent action on global warming.[111] Retired *Boston Globe* reporter Ross Gelbspan, author of the best-seller *Boiling Point*, however, sees things differently than ExxonMobil shareholders. For him, the deniers and their corporate sponsors were "criminals against humanity."[112]

CHAPTER 8

Killing medicare ... To Save It?

There's a growing chorus across the land which argues that it's really
pretentious to define ourselves as a nation by the way we pay for a prostate exam
and ridiculous to claim cultural integrity by the way we pay for a pap smear.

So begins *Medicare Schmedicare*, a point-of-view documentary about
Canada's health care system, which was broadcast on CBC-TV twice during
the 2005 federal election campaign. The video then cuts to Vancouver orthopaedic surgeon Brian Day in the operating room of his privately owned Cambie
Surgery Centre.[1]

"Brian Day is a leader in the middle-class revolution tired of the contradictions built into the system," long-time filmmaker Robert Duncan begins his
documentary, which is an attack on public health care. Its thesis is that one-tier
medicare is a myth and the villain is medicare's founder, Tommy Douglas, former
Saskatchewan premier (1944–61). Duncan claims "We've been swallowing the
medicare myth, saluting an emperor who has no clothes (over a picture of Tommy
Douglas) . . . Big surprise, Tommy, a parallel private system already exists."

The attack on Douglas is ironic because just before this program was
broadcast, the CBC postponed a miniseries on Douglas's life, set to air a week
before the federal election. The combination of the two decisions provoked a
storm of protest. Complainants had a right to be upset. The Duncan video was
financed largely by Canadian taxpayers.[2] People who want and benefit from
medicare unwittingly financed this attack on it. Should the CBC, as Canada's

public broadcaster, be supplying programs that celebrate the handful who can afford to buy private care? they asked.

Eva Czigler, acting head of CBC network programming, wrote a boiler-plate response to the complaints. The Douglas program was pushed back because of the "appearance of partisanship" if it was aired during the election campaign, she wrote. Fair enough. The Douglas program, Czigler explained, emphasized Tommy Douglas's "profound commitment to socialism" and would surely be lambasted by the right. *Medicare Schmedicare* is different, she argued, because "the views of those who advocate 'two-tier' medicine are not the only views heard . . . throughout, the documentary returns to a staunch critic of the 'for fee' system . . ."[3]

That would be Mike McBane, a researcher with the Canadian Health Coalition, an organization of unions and social justice organizations working to protect medicare. Duncan pulls every trick in the book to make McBane look bad. Duncan allows five private-medicine practitioners, filmed in their professional contexts, to speak and set the frame for the documentary before he turns to McBane. Looking down on McBane is a large picture of Tommy Douglas, the guy Duncan has just slagged. McBane is earnest in his criticism of private medicine, but is made to have a weak television presence. He's confined to a seat in a cramped office, with bad lighting and a solitary camera angle for the entire production, looking artificial and stilted in his owl glasses and crum-pled shirt. In contrast, his thirteen adversaries are out in the real world walking around, talking, joking, looking professional and in charge, and viewed from many camera angles.

It's not that Duncan couldn't find anyone else to defend medicare. In fact, he spent a day interviewing Dr. Michael Rachlis, one of public health care's most effective advocates. But Rachlis doesn't appear in the documentary. Apparently his presence was left on Duncan's cutting-room floor, leaving McBane to hold up the side. Duncan uses other tried-and-true propaganda tricks to disparage medicare. The Institute for Propaganda Analysis (IPA) can help us here. This organization was created to educate Americans about the widespread use of political propaganda in the pre–Second World War period. It is known for identifying basic devices, words and phrases that indicate a deceptive purpose to communication.[4] *Medicare Schmedicare* is evidence the IPA's work is still relevant today.

"Glittering generalities" are virtue words like "democracy" or "civilization" about which we have deep-seated ideas. The IPA calls them glitter words because "they mean different things to different people." Duncan's best glitter word is "choice." One private-clinic operator says that "choice is a good thing, having choice in the delivery of health care." But if the choice is to pay $25,000 for a new hip in a Bellingham, Washington, hospital, how relevant is that word to most of us? Choice does not serve our best interests, but expensive, privatized medicine is sold to us by giving it a name we usually like.

Another glitter word is "revolution." Duncan uses this word at the beginning and end of the documentary. "Brian Day is a leader in the middle-class revolution tired of the contradictions built into the system," Duncan begins. According to the *Fontana Dictionary of Modern Thought*, a revolution is sudden radical change in ruling classes and social institutions. Think French Revolution, Russian Revolution.[5] But private medicine is what we used to have. The correct word is "reaction," as Chapter 2 notes: a return to an earlier order of society when the wealthy and privileged possessed the rights and entitlements they believe society owed them, such as the right to obtain their own medical treatment. Day is leading the *reaction* against public health care and blocking progress towards a more just, equal and enlightened society.

Day himself combined both glitter words in a talk he gave to the Fraser Institute several months later. The title of the talk was "Canada's common sense revolution in medicare reform," and the topic was "The introduction of choice for Canadians seeking healthcare."[6]

Euphemism is another propaganda device whose purpose is to "pacify the audience in order to make an unpleasant reality more palatable." One classic example is that during the Second World War, the United States changed the name of the War Department to the Department of Defense. Duncan's best euphemism is calling private medicine a "parallel system." This cunning phrase was invented by Canada's doctors in the mid-nineties. It is cunning because, as we all remember from grade 6 geometry, parallel lines never meet. The private system does not intersect with the public system and consequently will have no impact on it. The reality is, of course, that if the private system is allowed to grow unchecked, the public system will be destabilized.

The Bandwagon is a propaganda technique used to convince us that "everyone else is doing it and so should [we]." Says Duncan, "There are now too many medical options and too many people using them to still believe there's only a one-tier system in Canadian health care." But, as the IPA points out, there's never quite as much of a rush to climb on the bandwagon as the propagandist tries to make us think there is. Duncan's documentary accounts for the health treatment of perhaps thirty thousand Canadians, or 0.1 percent of the population. Some bandwagon!

Medicare Schmedicare demonstrates how far Canadian thinking has changed in a decade. It seems that Canadians are more amenable to the messages of this documentary, that medicare is finished and private care can fix things up. If this is the case, though, it may not be a result of fundamental problems with medicare. The cause, more likely, is the steady stream of propaganda emanating from those with a vested interest in its demise. And those interests, like the people portrayed in *Medicare Schmedicare* who laud private care as the solution to our health care ills, neglect to mention that private care is what we used to have. The situation was so desperate that there was an outpouring of support for publicly financed care. Granted, even if private health care becomes entrenched, there will still be a public system. But how long would it be until, instead of a parallel system, we are faced with a two- or three-tiered system such as exists in the United States, where those on the bottom tier have no medical insurance and those in the middle, with partial coverage, can see their lives ruined by one calamitous illness?

Duncan admitted his film was propaganda, although he didn't define what he meant by this. CBC's ombudsman Vince Carlin reviewed the documentary in light of the numerous complaints the CBC received. In response to Carlin's questions, Duncan wrote that his film took a "personal point of view approach," based on the philosophy of Canadian filmmaker John Grierson, who argued "that propaganda should come FROM the People TO the Government."[7] The problem in *Medicare Schmedicare* is that the propaganda comes, not from the people, but from the narrow interests who benefit from private care.

In his report, Carlin identifies many inaccuracies and falsehoods in Duncan's work. Duncan claims that Tommy Douglas's dream of one-tier medicine was dead. Carlin notes that "neither Douglas nor the Health Act called for 'one-tier' medicine, but for universal coverage, a different concept." Carlin then says that "in the program, it states that the system no longer covers some of these things [dentistry, optometry or drugs] when it never did." Duncan lets his "proponents of private health care give what sound like authoritative numbers of wait-times and even about people dying on waiting lists." Carlin found many problems with Duncan's numbers. One glaring misrepresentation was Duncan's use of "mean waiting time" for the average instead of "median waiting time." The mean is the statistical average—all waiting times are added up and divided by the number of people waiting. The median waiting time is the

264 Not A Conspiracy Theory

waiting time experienced by the middle patient; half the waiting times are longer and half shorter. Mean waiting times are longer because a few patients endured very long waits. These are real and devastating for the handful, but they distort the average person's experience. And, Carlin notes, some provinces have made innovative changes to cope with waiting times, countering Duncan's claim that the system is "brain dead."

Why does the private system continue to expand when, in most cases, it contravenes the Canada Health Act? Duncan responds that Health Canada and provincial health authorities appear to be suffering from "temporary blindness or permanent amnesia." This answer is unsatisfactory because it ignores how power is exercised. A better answer is that the clinics survived and expanded, not because of government blindness or amnesia, but because of the private health care industry's economic and political clout.

Just before the Christmas recess in 2003, the B.C. legislature passed a bill that would give the province the power to audit doctors and clinics and levy penalties on those that accept payments for medical treatments that should be covered by B.C.'s Medical Services Plan. The legislation was required, Health Minister Colin Hansen explained, because "B.C. has an obligation under the Canada Health Act to ensure patients get the medically required care they need without any unnecessary cost to themselves." If patients pay extra, Health Canada could withhold transfer payments.[8] The legislation could put the clinics, including Brian Day's Cambie Surgery Centre, out of business. For a few days following the bill's passage, readers of Vancouver's two daily newspapers were blitzed with stories about how some individuals were saved from lives of misery and pain because of the availability of private medical clinics. The headlines tell the story:

- "I'm a firm believer in the public system . . . but . . . I'm not willing to wait a year," knee patient says (*The Province*, Friday 5 December)
- Clinics stop surgeries, fear for survival: New BC legislation already leading patients to seek treatment in the U.S. (*Vancouver Sun*, Friday 5 December)
- Medical system "failed" board of trade official (*Vancouver Sun*, Saturday 6 December)

- Private surgery ban will kill Olympic careers: Athlete (*The Province*, Sunday 7 December)
- Stock up on pain killers, the wait just got longer (*The Province*, Monday 8 December)
- Medical broker reopens cross-border health care (*Vancouver Sun*, Monday 8 December)

Then the stories stopped. Curiously, the two Vancouver papers saw no need for stories about the good job that publicly funded hospitals were doing, which is odd given that they must account for the vast majority of surgeries performed in the province. Ten days later, Premier Gordon Campbell announced that Bill 92, the Medicare Protection Amendment Act, "has not been proclaimed and it is not our intention to proclaim it."[9]

What happened between the flurry of stories and Campbell's back-tracking? Did the newspaper stories change Campbell's mind? Or was some other script being played out? Was it a case of temporary blindness or permanent amnesia as Duncan claimed? We don't know what went on behind closed doors, but the government admitted that anger from private clinics played a factor in its decision. "We were very taken aback by the loud and vociferous concern that came from the doctors," Health Minister Hansen explained.[10] But groups often express loud and vociferous concern—and may even take to the streets—and yet the government doesn't back off. Something else was at work, as the newspaper stories would reveal.

Front and centre were personal stories of people who *might be* affected by the legislation. Darcy Rezac, managing director of the Vancouver Board of Trade, said he would be in a wheelchair if he had been forced to wait—maybe two to three years—for knee surgery in British Columbia. He went to a private clinic in Washington State and had both knees operated on within two weeks. (He didn't disclose how much the operations cost.) And now Bill 92 would force B.C. clinics to close. British Columbians who couldn't afford the Cadillac treatment Rezac received would be sentenced to years of pain and diminished mobility. Please keep the clinics open![11]

The next day it was Amber Allen's turn. The twenty-eight-year-old athlete wanted to play soccer for Canada in the 2004 Athens Olympics, but might not be able to go. She tore a knee ligament and had to choose between waiting eight months for surgery in a public hospital or three weeks for a private-clinic operation. She opted for the private clinic and paid for the procedure out of her own pocket. Allen was angered that the province was planning to close the clinics when, at the same time, it was lobbying hard for the 2010 Olympics. "It's like saying that Canada is promoting disposable athletes," she complained, noting that athletes are prone to injuries and need to get prompt treatment. Please keep the clinics open![12]

On Monday, Rick Baker was featured. He is a medical broker who refers Canadian patients to U.S. clinics and hospitals for a fee. He has a deal with some of them and gets a discount for the patients he refers. Part of the discount he passes on to the patient and the rest he keeps. Baker expects Bill 92 will help his business substantially. But do we want people like Baker to flourish? If we don't keep the clinics open, he'll get rich. Is that what we want?[13]

A second trend in the stories is that the sources quoted were heavily weighted in favour of private clinics. Over the five days, nineteen sources spoke for the clinics, while only six spoke for public care. Doctors Brian Day and Mark Godley, proprietors of private clinics who would benefit the most from the deep-sixing of the legislation, were featured prominently. They did not discuss how much they would benefit personally, but instead focused on the claim that what they were doing would save medicare. Other pro–private clinic sources quoted in the stories were the president of the B.C. Medical Association, athletes and their representatives who wanted the clinics, including the Vancouver Canucks' general manager. Also featured were other doctors who operate private clinics and patients who had benefited from privately financed procedures. The handful of opposing voices included Debra McPherson, the president of the B.C. Nurses' Union, and Chris Allnut, the business manager of the Hospital Employees Union, who both clearly held vested interests in favour of protecting medicare. Terrie Hendrickson, the coordinator for the BC Health Coalition, a pro-medicare group, was quoted in two stories but placed last, as if an editor suddenly remembered, "Oh yes, we need to look balanced."

The stories were too neat, especially when there were no compensating stories about the achievements of the public system. It looked like—and it was—a well-executed public relations campaign. Hill and Knowlton, one of Canada's largest and most politically connected PR firms, was retained to do media and lobbying work for the Coalition for Health Care Options. (The Institute for Propaganda Analysis would call "options" a glitter word, having relevance only for the wealthy.) This organization had no office, phone, or web site. Twelve private clinics, including those run by Day and Godley, had come together to oppose the legislation.

Constructing front groups that obtain excellent media coverage and achieve the results desired by its clients is a Hill and Knowlton specialty. The firm worked for Big Tobacco for many years, blurring the link between smoking and lung cancer. In 1991, the PR firm masterminded the Kuwaiti government's efforts to convince the Americans to go to war against Iraq. Hill and Knowlton set up a front group called Citizens for a Free Iraq, without saying it was financed by the Kuwaiti government, which pumped about US$12 million into Hill and Knowlton's coffers for this assignment. At one point, 148 Hill and Knowlton functionaries were working on the file. The firm was responsible for a great media-manipulation coup, the emotionally moving testimony of a fifteen-year-old Kuwaiti girl named Nayirah. She told a U.S. congressional committee a story about Iraqi soldiers barging into a hospital with guns, pulling hundreds of premature babies from incubators and leaving them to die on cold hospital floors. Three months later the United States invaded Kuwait, thanks in large part to Nayirah's story. It was a lie. Nayirah was not a peasant girl as she claimed, but a member of the Kuwaiti royal family and the daughter of the Kuwaiti ambassador to the United States. She was nowhere near the hospital in question at the time of the alleged incident and had been coached in her false testimony by a vice-president in Hill and Knowlton's Washington office.[14]

In Canada, the firm specializes in cleaning up the image of industries and companies with poor reputations. These include:

- Task Force on Food Biotechnology in Canada, a coalition of food-industry groups, to promote genetically modified foods as environmentally benign solutions to world hunger[15]
- Mining Association of Canada, to clean up the mining industry's image as environmental rogue[16]
- Talisman Energy, to repair the company's tattered image as a supporter of human rights abuses in war-torn Sudan[17]
- Ethyl Corp., to block legislation banning a gasoline additive alleged to be harmful to the environment and human health.[18]

Promoting the interests of the health care industry is another Hill and Knowlton specialty. It works for Big Pharma firms like GlaxoSmithKline, Merck Frosst Canada, Bristol Myers Squibb and the industry's chief lobbyist, Canada's Research-Based Pharmaceutical Companies (known as Rx&D).[19] To be successful in convincing a government to change a policy, a PR firm must have functionaries who are well connected and know how the system works. Hill and Knowlton executive Bruce Young was registered in Victoria, British Columbia, to lobby for the Coalition for Health Care Options. Young is a long-time federal Liberal insider and was an adviser to Liberal MP David Dingwall when he was minister of health, so he knows the system from the Ottawa end. Young was hired by Hill and Knowlton in 2000 to head up its Vancouver office. He left in 2004 to become senior special adviser in B.C. to Prime Minister Paul Martin, readying the Liberals for the election that year. After Martin's narrow minority victory, Young moved back into lobbying, this time to open a B.C. office for Earnscliffe Strategy, another influential lobbying firm. Young picked up some prestigious clients, including Rx&D.[20] Given that drug costs are the fastest-rising component of health care, large doses of misleading messaging are required to prevent British Columbians from venting their wrath on Big Pharma and focus instead on the alleged ills of medicare.

A second Hill and Knowlton lobbyist working on the private-clinic file was Sandra Stoddart-Hansen, a vice-president of public affairs and later, general manager of B.C. operations. Stoddart-Hansen has an insider's understanding of British Columbia's health care system, having been vice-president of human resources for B.C.'s children's and women's hospitals in Vancouver in the early nineties.[21]

The Coalition for Health Care Options was mentioned only once in the stories, when a woman named Astrid Levelt was identified as a spokesperson. She told the *Vancouver Sun* that her group of private-treatment centres feared that the legislation would drive them out of business.[22] Levelt was more than a spokesperson, though. She was former general manager of Mark Godley's False Creek Surgical Centre. Levelt had left Godley's organization to become director of business development for another organization, Ambulatory Surgical Centres Canada, which helps physicians and surgeons set up their own private-surgery facilities.[23] They must have been confident that the provincial legislation would not hold them back from their private practices. Hill and Knowlton's job for the private clinics was to defeat the legislation and open minds to the alleged potential of private clinics. Mission accomplished.

Robert Duncan was as wrong as one can be. The success of the private clinics had nothing to do with government "temporary blindness or permanent amnesia" and everything to do with backroom lobbying and media manipulation.

Near the end of his documentary, Duncan applauds Montreal as the private-medicine capital of Canada, but does not tell us how this happened. He neglects to mention the work of the Montreal Economic Institute. Since 1999, this business-sponsored organization has spread anti-government, anti-medicare messaging across the province. The MEI was one of three regional libertarian think-tanks established in the nineties, along with the Frontier Centre for Public Policy in Winnipeg and the Atlantic Institute for Market Studies in Halifax, as described in Chapter 5.

Michel Kelly-Gagnon, MEI executive director, explained to the *National Post* that "we are trying to change the climate of opinion in Quebec." The Fraser Institute and C.D. Howe Institute "do good work but they fail to penetrate Quebec. The message needs to come from within the tribe," he said.[24] What Kelly-Gagnon didn't say, though, was that the message to the tribe would be created, not by the tribe, but by the chiefs—Quebec's corporate elite. MEI's president was a senior vice-president of the National Bank, Quebec's leading financial institution. Prominent backers include corporate heavyweights SNC-Lavalin, Bell Canada, Groupe Transcontinental, Imasco, Merrill Lynch, Standard Life and the foundations of several wealthy businessmen.

A key message to the tribe, repeated frequently, as is necessary if propaganda is to be effective, is that Quebec's public health care system has failed and needs to be replaced with a parallel system of private and public care. The institute publishes "economic notes" on health care, with titles like "Health care financing: squandering billions is not the answer," "Turning to the private sector in health care: The Swedish example," "Health care reforms: How far can we go?" and "Using private insurance to finance health care." The MEI also sponsors a public opinion survey by Leger Marketing that purports to show increasing acceptance of private health care. The June 2004 survey found 51 percent of Canadians supported private care; the April 2005 survey found a marginal increase to 52 percent. The December 2005 survey, taken during the federal election, found support had jumped to 58 percent, while a survey nine months later found support edging up to 60 percent. These results received prominent coverage in many of Canada's major papers and especially in the *National Post*, where most of them ended up as front-page stories.[25]

The catch is the phrasing of the question: "Would you find it acceptable or not if the government were to allow those who wish to pay for health care in the private sector to have speedier access to this type of care while still maintaining the current free and universal health-care system?" The assumption that the "current" system will be maintained is doubtful. Critics have attacked this assumption. If private health care flourishes, they argue, there is only one source for the human resources needed to staff it—the public system. Doctors and nurses who practice in publicly funded hospitals will move over to the private clinics, diminishing the resources available for medicare. Brian Day, who makes the parallel system argument in *Medicare Schmedicare*, reduced his billings to the B.C. Medical Services Plan from $180,000 to $55,000, when his clinic doubled in size.[26] He has substantially decreased his participation in the public system. Who will take his place? The Canadian Health Services Research Foundation reports that "countries with parallel public and private health-care systems . . . appear to have larger waiting lists and longer waiting times in the public system than countries with a single payer system such as Canada." Doctors who practice in both systems naturally devote more of their practice to their higher-paying private patients.[27]

To increase the credibility of their anti-medicare message, the MEI's corporate backers forged close links with Quebec's medical establishment, re-creating the business–physician alliance that existed earlier in the century. This alliance resisted, but could not stop, the introduction of medicare, first in Saskatchewan and then nationally. Now they have another chance. One MEI physician board member was secretary-general of the Canadian Medical Association (CMA). Edwin Coffey, a gynecologist and professor in McGill University's Faculty of Medicine, is an MEI senior fellow. Coffey is a past-president of the Quebec Medical Association and served on the board of the CMA. He was Quebec's representative on the CMA's Working Group on Health Care Financing in Canada. This group was set up at Coffey's urging to study how to "permit the emergence and development of both alternative and complementary private health care insurance and health care arrangements."[28]

Coffey was a prolific pamphleteer for the private-medicine cause, receiving an accommodating welcome from the corporate chiefs' anglophone scribe the *Montreal Gazette*. Every six months Coffey wrote the same anti-medicare opinion piece and every six months the *Gazette* published it. That the *Gazette* would provide so much space for so little content should remind us that the corporate media were members in good standing of the anti-medicare coalition forty years earlier, along with doctors and business. Evidently they still are.

In one piece, Coffey lumped Canada with Cuba as the "only countries where outdated Marxist-inspired health legislation bans private medical and hospital services and private insurance alternatives to the governments' monopolistic plans." (He forgot North Korea.)[29] Actually, Coffey's ideology got in the way of the facts. A Cuban orthopaedic hospital has a for-profit division that earns US$20 million a year providing surgery to patients from elsewhere in Latin America. The money is channelled back into Cuba's public system.[30]

A year later, in a column ironically titled "Too much rhetoric in health-care debate," Coffey slathered on the rhetoric himself when he complained about supporters of public health care who "prefer the Marxist notions of class struggle, distributive or social justice and the envy-based prescription of egalitarianism."[31] In 2004 he was still complaining about the "radical Marxist and egalitarian factions," who lobbied for universal, publicly-funded medical and hospital insurance.[32] Coffey's Gazette columns tailed off after 2004, but he continued arguing for increased privatization of health care in other venues.[33]

The MEI expends considerable ink pushing for greater participation in health care by the private insurance industry. Typical is its November 2005 economic note urging the use of private insurance to finance health care because public financing has reached a "dead end," echoing Robert Duncan's complaint.[34] The MEI promotes what it calls "duplicate insurance," which provides for care in private establishments with coverage by the public system. Individuals could pay additional amounts to be treated in the private system. "As long as no public funds are pledged to cover the care, this form of insurance for treatment in a fully parallel private sector would comply with the Canada Health Act," the MEI's research director, Valentin Petkantchin, wrote in the National Post.[35]

It may not be surprising that the MEI promotes the private insurance industry, given that a prominent backer is the Desmarais family. Through its ownership of Power Corp., this family is Canada's eighth wealthiest, with a net worth of $4.1 billion, slipping four places from 2007. Andre Desmarais, Power Corp. co–chief executive officer—and, as mentioned earlier, Jean Chrétien's son-in-law—organized a dinner party in 1999 to get the think-tank off the ground.[36] And his sister-in-law, Helene Desmarais, wife of Paul Desmarais Jr., Power's other CEO, chairs the MEI board. A few years earlier she wrote a report for the city of Montreal suggesting that downtown Montreal should become an international centre for the health care industry. That's health care as profitable industry, not public service. Business and profits, she recommended, not treatment and care.[37]

Power Corp. owns three Canadian life insurance companies, including Great West Life, the largest provider of supplementary health insurance in Canada. The company earns revenues by selling insurance for services not covered by medicare and for critical illness, extended health, disability and long-term-care benefits insurance. Extending private health care coverage to Canadians who might already be purchasing Great West Life insurance for non-medicare services would be a natural for the company.

The Desmaraises' support for the Montreal Economic Institute may soon pay off. The family can thank the work of another MEI researcher, Dr. Jacques Chaoulli, for this. Chaoulli is well known as the appellant in the 2005 Supreme Court of Canada decision which ruled that prohibitions against private health insurance in the Quebec Health Act are inconsistent with the Quebec Charter of Human Rights and Freedoms. Robert Duncan did mention this decision in his documentary, but his bias was evident: "Those who support a parallel private system announced the court had recognized there was no sense giving a heart transplant to a system that was brain dead," while "those who cling to one tier saw it as a victory for the establishment, a conspiracy of social and business elites had ganged up to destroy Medicare." He then cut to critic Mike McBane, who must be one of those who "cling" to one tier. Duncan was correct that the Chaoulli decision was a victory for the elites who had conspired to destroy medicare. The Chaoulli decision could create private inroads into basic health care coverage, at least in Quebec. And if Great West Life and other private insurers can make it work for them in that province, other provinces will follow.

Jacques Chaoulli is an odd poster boy for privatized health care. Trained in France, he started practicing medicine in Quebec in 1986. Eight years later he launched a crusade for twenty-four-hour emergency house calls. These calls contravened Quebec law, which requires physicians with less than ten years of practice to work a certain number of hours in a health care facility, a requirement he had not met.[38] Chaoulli lobbied everyone he could, including the premier and the medical association, to no avail. After meeting with rejection, Chaoulli went on a hunger strike. In its fourth week, his supporters, patients and the media convinced him to stop the strike but continue the fight. He left the public system only to discover that his patients were prohibited from obtaining private insurance to cover his services. He then spent a year and a half researching health care systems in other countries and so-called freedom of choice, which is a right that can be exercised only by the better off.[39] The year before the MEI was established, Chaoulli wrote a book touting a parallel private system. Soon-to-be-MEI researcher Edwin Coffey wrote the forward to the French-language book *Pour une Question de Vies ou de Morts* (*A Question of Life or Death*).

The same year, 1998, Chaoulli and a patient who had waited months for a hip replacement, decided to take their case to Quebec Superior Court. The case took six years to wend its way to the Supreme Court, which rendered its decision supporting private health insurance in June 2005. Chaoulli wants Quebecers to have the right to buy private insurance, which they can then use to buy medical services from non-participating doctors, but still receive treatment in publicly funded hospitals. No wonder the doctors, who seek more money, and the Desmarais family, which would benefit from the private insurance business, backed him.

It wasn't long before Chaoulli set up a private, for-profit medical-brokering service which would provide patients speedy access to doctors for a fee. The Chaoulli Group was planning to include doctors who practiced in the public and private systems. Individuals who registered for the service would pay Chaoulli a $150 annual fee, $20 for every medical referral after the first one, and then pay the doctor a fee for the service. But the Quebec government filed a formal complaint with the Quebec medical services board, and Chaoulli withdrew the fees for services by doctors who were in the public system.[40]

With the participation of the private insurance industry in the Montreal Economic Institute, the historic anti-medicare alliance was re-established: the medical associations, big business, the private insurance industry and the media are all working to destabilize medicare, just as they tried to prevent it from coming into existence forty years ago. And with the election of the Conservatives in January 2006, this coalition at first had more clout than ever in the federal cabinet. MEI vice-president Maxime Bernier was elected as the MP for the Beauce region of Quebec, winning the seat held formerly by his father. Harper appointed Bernier minister of industry. Like all industry ministers, Bernier's job was to represent business interests in cabinet. And, like the Desmarais family, Bernier was preoccupied with health care as an industry, not as a public service. He was the MEI's spokesperson when the Chaoulli decision was handed down. He applauded the ruling, which, he claimed, supported the MEI's arguments for greater freedom for patients, insurers and health care providers.[41] Greater freedom for insurers could benefit MEI backer Desmarais, but Bernier had an even closer connection to private health care insurers. Before taking on the job as spokesperson for the institute, he was vice-president of corporate affairs at Standard Life of Canada, another of the country's largest private insurers and another possible beneficiary of Chaoulli.

Two months after the 2005 Supreme Court ruled in the Chaoulli case, two-thirds of the delegates to the Canadian Medical Association's annual convention in Edmonton endorsed the right of all Canadians to buy private health insurance if they couldn't get timely access to public care.[42] In an editorial the next day, the *Globe and Mail* justified the vote as "mainly a sign of how frustrated doctors and most Canadians are with a single-payer public system . . ."[43] The *Globe*'s editorial writer must have been ignorant of medicare's history. Many doctors are strong advocates for medicare, but their organizations have fiercely opposed public health care from its earliest days. This vote was nothing new. Over the years, doctors formed alliances with the private insurance industry and with other business organizations to fight public health plans proposed by provincial and federal governments, just as they came together once again in the Montreal Economic Institute.

The same media amnesia was evident in 2006, when delegates to the CMA convention in Charlottetown elected Brian Day to lead their organization. B.C. doctors had the right to elect their nominee to the position of CMA president in 2007–08, the post being rotated among the provincial medical associations. Day's B.C. victory was hailed as "stunning"; Day was the "dark-horse candidate" and "a pioneer."[44] But how stunning and how dark-horse really? The last time British Columbia had a turn, ten years earlier, the province's doctors voted for Victor Dirnfeld, who was an originator of the expression "parallel system" and an advocate for it. The *National Post*'s headline ran "Doctors signal dismay, pick private-care chief."[45] The story claimed doctors were "frustrated" with the health care system. Doctors have always been frustrated by medicare, but not for the reasons the *Post* suggests. They seem to want the security of government payments, plus the ability to boost their earnings through private fees. They may be frustrated because they are having difficulty with the private-fees side of the equation.

Doctors and business first joined together in British Columbia during the ravages of the Depression to defeat public health insurance in that province, despite substantial public support, writes Antonia Maioni in her history of health insurance in the United States and Canada. The government of Liberal B.C. premier Thomas "Duff" Pattullo, facing a rapidly growing radical opposition, proposed a compulsory health-insurance plan for lower-income workers and voluntary participation for everyone else. Business unanimously opposed the scheme, which would require contributions by employers. Boards of trade, chambers of commerce and the B.C. Loggers Association ganged up on the plan.[46] Doctors initially supported the scheme because it meant they would be paid for treating the indigent and working poor. But when no money was forthcoming from Ottawa, Pattullo eliminated coverage for the poor, meaning doctors would have to continue to treat them as charity cases. Doctors also resisted the proposal to give the provincial government influence over setting fees. The bill was passed by the B.C. legislature, but was not implemented because of doctor opposition. At the CMA convention, the B.C. health plan was a topic of heated discussion about the dangers of "socialized medicine."[47]

Business and doctors came together again in 1957 when the federal government introduced the Hospital Insurance and Diagnostic Services Act (HIDSA). This was the first of two programs that would define medicare, in which federal funds were allocated to provinces with a universal hospital-insurance program. By the mid-fifties, more than 40 percent of Canadians had some form of non-profit or commercial hospital insurance. The insurance was not cheap, nor was it based on ability to pay. Canadians were paying half the costs of hospitalization and two-thirds of the costs of medical care out of their own pockets.[48]

The CMA opposed HIDSA, charging that universal, compulsory hospital insurance was the first step towards socialized medicine. It proposed voluntary, private health insurance or physician-sponsored plans that would retain fee-for-service practice and physician autonomy. For its part, the Canadian Chamber of Commerce decried "state medicine" and the abuses it claimed were inevitable by "persons demanding treatment as a right for imaginary ills or illnesses," Colleen Fuller writes in her history of medicare.[49] Private insurers, Fuller reports, called public hospital insurance a "Trojan Horse" that would "destroy . . . freedom of choice." Healthy, high-income earners, who were the industry's target market, would no longer be able to choose one of the many policies designed with them in mind, and instead would be forced onto public health plans. "Compulsory health insurance cannot be separated from state medicine and socialism," the industry asserted. The groups coalesced around the proposal that the government provide subsidies to the poor—so-called "hopeless risks"—to enable them to subscribe to private health plans. On the other side, organized labour strongly championed universal health insurance for all Canadians. The Trades and Labour Congress and the Canadian Congress of Labour had merged into the Canadian Labour Congress (CLC) in 1956, which put great pressure on government to bring in the hospital-insurance legislation. Pressure also came from the Co-operative Commonwealth Federation (CCF) opposition in Parliament and from most provinces, which wanted federal financial support for their hospital plans. But the legislation was not passed until the Liberal government of Louis St. Laurent was defeated and replaced by John Diefenbaker's Progressive Conservatives in 1957.[50]

When Saskatchewan premier Tommy Douglas announced in early 1959 the Saskatchewan government's plan for a "complete transfer of medicare expenditures from the private to the public sector," the coalition of interests opposed to public health care panicked. Physicians, business, insurance companies, drug companies and the Sifton family, owner of the *Regina Leader-Post* and the *Saskatoon StarPhoenix*, united to fight what they saw as socialism and the destruction of the economy. The CMA had come out in favour of privately financed, privately provided health care. In contrast, the public strongly favoured medicare.[51] The 1960 provincial election was framed as a referendum on the government's medicare plan. When Douglas won the election, he believed he had a mandate to proceed. But he soon went to Ottawa to become the first leader of the newly formed New Democratic Party. His successor, Woodrow Lloyd, introduced the legislation, which came into effect in July 1962.

The opposition peaked with a doctors' strike that began the day the plan started on July 1, 1962, and lasted twenty-three days. The Sifton newspapers called July 1 "the day when Freedom died," and relentlessly attacked medicare and the CCF government.[52] In the end, both sides made concessions. The doctors agreed that medicare in Saskatchewan would be universal and compulsory and the government would be the sole collector of revenues and disburser of payments. The government backed off from its plan to make doctors salaried, full-time practitioners. It also agreed that the government health agency would not oversee the quality of care provided under the plan. Doctors would keep their right to set standards of care and working conditions. They could choose not to join the plan and were allowed to extra-bill their patients at higher rates.[53]

Doctors and the insurance industry worked together to blunt attempts by other provinces to introduce health care programs in the mould of Saskatchewan. They succeeded in Alberta, Ontario and British Columbia. In Alberta, Social Credit premier Ernest Manning launched a campaign against "socialistic" health insurance that represented "the flagrant violation . . . of freedom of choice in a free society." The "Manningcare" plan reflected two principles shared by doctors and private insurers: voluntary health insurance for the majority and means-tested government subsidies to enable lower-income residents to purchase private insurance.[54] This was the model adopted by British Columbia and Ontario.

The battlefield shifted once again to Ottawa, where the Pearson government was readying medicare legislation. The adoption of medicare would mean the end of private health insurance and extra billing by doctors, Colleen Fuller notes. Instead of universality, the doctor–insurance industry lobby called it "compulsion."[55] Canadians would no longer have the freedom to choose if they would be insured and by whom. In their view, this was some kind of violation of a fundamental principle in a free enterprise, democratic society. Instead of having more than 120 insurers to choose from, Canadians would be forced to insure under a single government monopoly.[56] But the tide of public opinion was flowing against them. In the end, the Medical Care Insurance Act passed by a vote of 177 to 2 in the House and medicare came into effect on July 1, 1968. The private insurance industry had to reorganize its revenue sources. Many companies, like Great West Life, turned to the extended benefits market to expand. Doctors resigned themselves to lower, but still respectable, incomes. They continued the fight for a larger share of health care dollars.

Federal fifty-fifty cost-sharing with the provinces, which had persuaded the provinces to sign on, came quickly under fire because of rapidly escalating costs. In 1977, governments shifted to federal block grants of tax points plus cash-equalization payments under the Established Programs Financing Act. These transfers were supposed to grow each year, but almost immediately the cash portion of the transfer was cut back because of Trudeau's "Six and Five" anti-inflation program.

In the early eighties, some doctors became unhappy with contract settlements in an era of high inflation. They complained their fee schedules were too low compared with American doctors' earnings. Nothing prevented them from opting out of medicare and charging whatever they could. But doctors also liked the deal they got under medicare, where they were treated as independent entrepreneurs and guaranteed a high level of income. They wanted to continue to reap the benefits of medicare and also extra-bill patients. They threatened to move south en masse if they couldn't continue to do this. In response, the Trudeau government (with the agreement of the Conservatives) brought in the Canada Health Act (CHA) in 1984, which banned extra billing and strengthened

Ottawa's role in the medicare system. The law raised the five principles of medi-care—universality, comprehensiveness, portability, public administration and accessibility—to the level of national standards, which the provinces had to meet before Ottawa would transfer cash to them. "No compliance, no cash," was the mantra from Ottawa.[57] Few doctors pulled out of medicare. They lost the extra-billing fight, but looked for other ways to boost their incomes. By the mid-nineties that approach became evident. Canada needed a "parallel sys-tem," they discovered, so that they could operate private health clinics and still remain within the public system. Now they just needed to convince Canadians that a parallel system was necessary and, in fact, inevitable.

They were helped enormously in their quest for higher incomes by gov-ernment cuts to medicare, throwing the system into a state of near crisis. No sooner had the Trudeau government enacted the Canada Health Act than the Liberals were out and Brian Mulroney in. His Progressive Conservative gov-ernment immediately began to undo the federal government's newly acquired clout in defining and protecting medicare. First, he reduced the rate of growth of cash payments and in 1990 froze the level of cash transfers for five years, in the name of cutting the deficit. In total, the Mulroney government cut health care payments to the provinces by $30 billion. Then, in 1993, Mulroney was out and Chrétien in. Paul Martin's 1995 budget wreaked further havoc on health care funding. It fused social welfare programs into a new block fund called the Canada Health and Social Transfer. The cash transfer to the provinces was cut by a third, or $6 billion, out of a total of $18 billion.

With reduced funding, the federal government was hardly in a strong position to police the Canadian Health Act. It looked the other way when provinces allowed—and even encouraged—doctors to open surgical clinics. Ottawa's mantra of "no compliance, no cash" was transformed into the pro-vincial governments' response "no cash, no compliance," Fuller observes sar-donically. Faced with severe federal cuts and the desire to exercise their own claims to jurisdiction over health care, the provinces closed hospitals and delisted services. In public, though, everyone pledged allegiance to the principles of the CHA.[58]

If history is any guide, the Stephen Harper government is likely to con-tinue the trend to private care. Like all premiers and prime ministers, Harper must profess support for medicare because of its popularity. But this support is not credible, given Harper's opposition to the plan his entire political life. As Preston Manning's chief policy adviser, Harper developed Reform's policy of "provincializing" health care, a move that would undermine the CHA's national standards. According to Murray Dobbin, Harper and Manning blocked Reform constituency resolutions supporting universal medicare and promoted user fees, extra billing and private insurance. Harper took credit for assisting Mulroney and Martin in eroding medicare. In a speech to the National Citizens Coalition before he was appointed president, he bragged that "universality has been severely reduced. It is virtually dead as a concept in most areas of public policy."[59]

Harper was president of the National Citizens Coalition for five years before returning to active politics in 2001. The NCC had been set up by private-insurance broker Colin Brown specifically to fight medicare. The organization poured hundreds of thousands of dollars into the 1984 election to defeat the Canada Health Act. Its full-page ads asked Canadians if they would like to have "their open-heart surgery done by a civil servant," and warned them that "more Canadians will die" if the CHA was implemented. Then, as leader of the Canadian Alliance, Harper urged Ottawa to allow the provinces to establish more privately owned hospitals and other undefined privately delivered services. But he stopped short of private-payment schemes. "The payer is the health-insurance plan," he said.[60] Which is what Ralph Klein said too.

In Alberta, spending on health care remained "remarkably stable" during the seven-year reign of Progressive Conservative premier Don Getty (1985–92), report journalist Gillian Steward and Kevin Taft, a health policy analyst who subsequently became leader of the Alberta Liberal Party.[61] Spending kept up with inflation, but did not increase beyond that. Yet from the moment he became premier in 1993, Ralph Klein went into "communications overdrive" to hammer home the point that spending during the Getty years had been "out of control." As late as 1999, when Klein spoke at a Fraser Institute lunch honouring him for the third year in a row for "fiscal performance," Klein distorted the truth again and said that public program spending had been "uncontrolled" before he came to power.[62] The Klein government's campaign to impress on the public mind that health funding was out of control had succeeded, even though the claim was not based on facts. And because spending on health care had skyrocketed, it had to be cut.

And cut deeply, write Steward and Taft. In his first three years as premier, Klein slashed per capita spending on health care by 18 percent, adjusted for inflation, single-handedly creating a health care crisis.[63] Nearly 15,000 health care workers in Alberta lost their jobs or had their positions downgraded, and thousands of hospitals beds were closed. Waiting lists for services grew longer and became a frequent subject of debate in the media. "Public confidence in the health-care system eroded . . .," Steward and Taft conclude. The cuts soon ended and funding began to climb again, but "the sense of crisis did not lift," they observe. In Calgary, to balance its books, the Calgary Regional Health Authority shut down one hospital, sold another and demolished a third, while retaining four newer facilities.[64]

Shortly after the Grace Hospital was closed, private investors leased the third floor of the facility from the Salvation Army, the hospital's owners. The investors, called the Health Resources Group (HRG), extensively renovated the ward, adding top-of-the-line surgical suites and post-operative recovery rooms.[65] The HRG opened shop as a thirty-seven-bed medical clinic providing surgical procedures that did not require an overnight stay, a stipulation that would turn the centre from a clinic into a hospital. Klein was not ready for that yet. The HRG tried to keep its beds filled with clients referred by Alberta's Workers' Compensation Board, the RCMP, Aboriginal Affairs and the armed forces, organizations that are legally allowed under the CHA to bypass medicare waiting lists. The HRG kept up its efforts to obtain provincial approval for procedures requiring an overnight stay, but was rebuffed. Finally, in 1999, Klein announced plans to introduce Bill 11, which would allow private companies to contract with regional health authorities for overnight surgical procedures, such as hip replacements. This was good news for the HRG investors, but another three years would pass before the Klein government finally approved the HRG as a facility to provide surgeries that require overnight stays, in 2002.[66]

Around the same time the HRG opened its clinic, in Vancouver orthopaedic surgeon Brian Day secured twenty-two investors, including fourteen doctors, to put up $100,000 each, obtained a $2.6-million bank loan, put up the rest of the money himself, built the Cambie Surgery Centre, and offered the same mix of CHA-acceptable services as the HRG. Day was responding to similar cuts to health care spending by the B.C. government, which, surprisingly, was run by the Mike Harcourt New Democrats. The clinic was a money-maker and its expansion financed, several years later, not by doctors, but by foreign investors who were attracted to the profits they could see in private health care.[67]

Private clinics and the health-insurance industry need to persuade Canadians that medicare is in crisis and the only way to save it is to expand private enterprise within the medical system. And they need to claim that what they are doing is for the public good and, only secondarily, if at all, for themselves. To accomplish this goal, they first had to crush what they regarded as the Canadian "entitlement mentality," Colleen Fuller suggests. Most Canadians consider access to health care a fundamental right and not a matter of money.[68] Remember Robert Duncan's opening words in his film *Medicare Schmedicare*, which ridicule our pride in medicare: "There's a growing chorus across the land which argues that it's really pretentious to define ourselves as a nation by the way we pay for a prostate exam and ridiculous to claim cultural integrity by the way we pay for a pap smear."

Private medicine should be a hard sell, but with a roster of public relations companies, corporate-sponsored libertarian think-tanks and supportive corporate media backing the venture, the task of wringing more profit out of medicare was rendered easier. Organizations like the PR company Hill and Knowlton and think-tank the Montreal Economic Institute do not engage the public in debate and discussion but deceit and manipulation, as was discussed in Chapter 1. The PR firm used front groups and carefully placed news stories to create false impressions, while the think-tank produced objective-looking studies in which conclusions are likely determined before the studies are done. Rarely do they reveal who finances their work. They are out to convince Canadians that private medicine and private insurance have a vital role to play in the Canadian health care system when, in fact, they serve only a few. Their success will drain resources away from the public system. If their goals are achieved, the public system will be destabilized.

Most corporate media supported a parallel system. In 2005 and 2006, *Globe and Mail* editorials welcomed the B.C. government's intention to pay private clinics for medically necessary procedures;[69] claimed that private care is coming down the pike and we'd better start talking about it;[70] and reiterated this point while claiming that the doomsday clock for medicare-as-we-know-it is roughly three minutes away from midnight.[71] In 2007 the paper reversed gears and toned down its unabashed boosterism. It argued that private clinics are not a panacea for a stretched system but may help shore it up;[72] claimed that medicare needs practical new answers such as private clinics for its chronic and urgent problems;[73] cautioned governments not to allow private payment for publicly provided services;[74] and warned that the unrestricted use of private insurance would damage the public system.[75]

The *National Post* was not as nuanced. The paper's editorial writers fumed at Canada's "antiquated, socialistic health system . . . Nowhere else in the free world—indeed nowhere else in the entire world outside of Cuba and North Korea—are citizens prohibited from buying private health insurance to pay for their essential health needs," it bellowed.[76] The paper claimed variously that: Canada needs a mix of private and public care if we are to get the care we deserve;[77] we should examine the feasibility of allowing private insurance companies to deliver funding to health care;[78] allowing doctors to work in private and public systems and patients to pay to have some procedures done will save medicare.[79] Through constant repetition, the media agenda becomes the public agenda: health care is indeed in crisis and government must allow more private sector participation. Dozens of polls seem to suggest that Canadians believe there is a crisis requiring private enterprise solutions. And the public agenda morphs into the government agenda.

"Parallel system" is less threatening than "two-tier," the term formerly used to describe private financing and provision of health services. "Parallel system" has great propaganda merit. "Two-tier" suggests a hierarchy of availability: if you're on the second tier, then you must be a second-class citizen. If you're on a parallel track, in contrast, you're separate but equal. The first use of the term "parallel system" in Canadian newspapers in relation to health care appeared in the *Montreal Gazette* in 1986. This article described legislation introduced by the Quebec government to guarantee access to health and social services in English. The government promised the new law would not lead to a "parallel system" of services.[80] The term was first used to refer to private health care by an opponent of the free trade agreement during the 1988 election. "We're going to see a private health-care system operated by American corporations. This will create a competitive and parallel system for the more affluent," predicted Graham Stewart, director of reform programs for the John Howard Society of Ontario.[81]

But it was the Canadian Medical Association that brought the term into the public realm. In an editorial opposing a private system, the *Windsor Star* wrote in 1995: "Last week [the general council of the Canadian Medical Association] defeated a motion that would have surely set the stage for a vigorous physician-supported lobby to introduce the parallel system. But the vote was very close—88-68 . . ."[82] The phrase next appeared in a letter to the editor in the *Vancouver Sun* from B.C. Medical Association president Victor Dirnfeld, who was on his way to becoming CMA head: "The BCMA ... does suggest that a private parallel system will go a long way to free up clogged waiting lists without sacrificing the public system."[83] And several months later the phrase appeared again, this time in a report from the CMA convention in Sydney, Nova Scotia: Doctors who support "a private parallel system say it would mean the injection of more money into a public health-care system ..."[84] In 1998 the Montreal Economic Institute's Jacques Chaoulli wrote his book arguing for a parallel system and started his court challenge to government-funded medicare. The parallel system had arrived.

Like the Montreal Economic Institute, the Fraser Institute isn't mentioned in Robert Duncan's documentary, but it too can take credit for raising the alarm about medicare's viability. The institute has attacked public health care almost since the day it was founded by high-powered corporate executives in the mid-seventies. In 1979, just five years after it opened, the institute published a book entitled *The Health Care Business: International Evidence on Private Versus Public Health Care Systems*. This book urged an end to publicly subsidized health insurance and services and a new system of compulsory private insurance and market-based hospital services.[85] In the twenty-five years since that publication, the institute has churned out an impressive array of books, studies and reports, all of which, astonishingly, reach the same conclusion, that the private sector does a better job of financing and providing health care services than the public sector.

To investigate this surprising concurrence of findings, Kevin Taft set out to check the sources in one important study the Fraser Institute produced in 2000 to support the Klein government's plan to allow the HRG and other private hospitals to operate in the province. Titled "How private hospital competition can improve Canadian health care," the study was prepared by Martin Zelder, a graduate of Milton Friedman's Chicago School of economics, who was director of health policy research at the institute. Zelder surveyed the literature comparing public and private hospital performance. He concluded that the evidence revealed "the advantages to private provision of hospital services. Those advantages are lower costs and higher quality, enabling more and better health care to be purveyed to Canadians, enhancing health outcomes."[86] But did the evidence he surveyed actually come to these conclusions? Not according to Taft, who compared the claims for the superiority of for-profit hospitals

284 Not A Conspiracy Theory

Zelder made in his paper against the original research papers Zelder cited. Taft found many discrepancies.[87]

Papers in which Martin Zelder ignored findings that countered his desired conclusion:

- "[A]s hospital market structure becomes more competitive . . . the hospitals in the market will become less efficient"
- "The findings support the hypothesis that . . . greater competition is associated with higher rather than lower costs"
- "For-profit hospitals may choose to operate only in areas where returns on investment are likely to accrue," but public hospitals need to operate where medical services are necessary
- "Have for-profit hospitals . . . achieved savings by reducing the quality of care, the amount of charity care and community benefits, or the provision of services?"

Papers in which Martin Zelder altered their conclusions:

- Says Zelder: "They discovered that for-profits had significantly lower cost per admission and per day than non-profits." Says the study: "Hospitals in more competitive environments exhibited significantly higher costs of production than did those in less competitive environments."
- Says Zelder: This study is a "subtle test of non-profit inefficiency" which "implicitly [confirms] . . . that non-profits maintain more slack." But the study does not conclude that non-profit hospitals are inefficient. Says the study: "Government and private not-for-profit hospitals behave differently than for-profit hospitals."
- Says Zelder: The study "found no significant difference in cost between for-profits and non-profits." Says the study: "Investor-owned chain hospitals earned their higher profits by charging more rather than by costing less."
- Says Zelder: "They discovered that adjusted costs per admission and per day were not significantly different between for-profit and non-profit hospitals." Says the study: "Investor-owned chain hospitals generated higher profits through more aggressive pricing practices rather than operating efficiencies."

To hear Lawrence Solomon tell it, David Gratzer is a hero of medicare because he brought medical savings accounts (MSAS) to the public's attention. Solomon heads the Toronto-based Urban Renaissance Institute. He wrote in the *National Post* that "MSAS were once obscure notions, discussed avidly by policy wonks . . . Then David Gratzer, at the time a mere medical student, described MSAS and their potential in a book called *Code Blue*. The description struck a chord in a country concerned about the direction of medicare, the book won a coveted award and MSAS were no longer obscure."[88]

In a medical savings account plan, government or an employer deposits a certain amount of money in every individual's account each year. Individuals are responsible for spending the money as they see fit, for health services such as doctor's appointments, medications or physiotherapy, any of which may be provided in the public or private sectors. If they don't spend all the money in their account by the end of the year, they can keep it for themselves or allow it to accumulate. As well, people must purchase insurance to cover their health care costs above the amount contributed into their MSA to cover catastrophic health care expenses. There is a gap between the amount contributed to the MSA and the level at which catastrophic insurance kicks in. The gap amount must be paid by the individual.

Solomon says that MSAS promise to contain health care costs, boost the quality of health care and empower the poor by giving them more say in health care decisions that affect their lives. These are all laudable goals, no doubt, but beneath Solomon's rhetoric, MSAS look more like a device to transform medicare from a predominantly public system into a private one.

Solomon makes it seem as though Gratzer single-handedly put MSAS on the public agenda. This claim is false. Gratzer was a promising young conservative medical student at the University of Manitoba who was recruited by the Fraser Institute in the mid-nineties. How conservative? He would compare the Canadian health system to the "old Soviet Union. They lined up for toilet paper," he once told *Vancouver Sun* columnist Don Cayo. "We line up for heart operations or cancer care."[89] In 1997, he co-wrote, with Fraser Institute health economist Cynthia Ramsay, an article entitled "Crucial debate clouded by political expediency," which appeared in the *Fraser Forum*, touting the American private-financing-and-delivery model of health care.[90] (Later, when the dysfunctionality of the American system became apparent, Gratzer became a fan of the Singapore model, discussed below.) A condensed version of the Gratzer-Ramsay article was published in the *Edmonton Journal* and reprinted in the *Montreal Gazette*, which always seemed to be looking for new material attacking medicare. Gratzer also won a prize for his essays from the Virginia-based Institute for Humane Studies, which identifies promising conservative students and supports their careers.

Then the Donner Canadian Foundation entered the picture. Donner was described in Chapter 5 as the lifeblood of conservative propaganda during the 1990s. Donner soon began promoting Gratzer's career. His book, *Code Blue*, which attacks medicare and argues for medical savings accounts, won the $25,000 Donner book prize in 1999. Gratzer didn't invent MSAs, but got the idea from a Toronto-based organization called the Consumer Policy Institute (CPI).[91] This organization was started with a $225,000 grant from Donner to disseminate propaganda about the advantages of MSAs and private insurance. (Over 90 percent of CPI's ongoing funding comes from corporate sources.) Interestingly, Lawrence Solomon was the Consumer Policy Institute's executive director, but he neglected to mention this fact in his article praising Gratzer.

Gratzer next received a podium from which to trumpet his views, courtesy of *National Post* editor Ken Whyte—a Donner Foundation trustee—for a monthly column attacking medicare. Typical is a column praising a study done by his former colleague Cynthia Ramsay, neglecting to mention his collaboration with her. Ramsay studied health care systems in eight countries and found, perhaps predictably, that Singapore came out on top. Why? Because of its medical savings accounts–based system.[92]

Gratzer's work was picked up by the burgeoning network of libertarian thinks-tanks across Canada. While still a medical student at the University of Manitoba, he was appointed a policy analyst at the Frontier Centre for Public Policy in Winnipeg. The Atlantic Institute for Market Studies, the Montreal Economic Institute and the Frontier Centre, which each received about a half-million dollars in seed funding from Donner, reprinted Gratzer's *National Post* columns, commissioned him to write articles for their publications and showered him with fawning interviews. The result was an anti-medicare echo chamber in which a few articles based on little substance were bounced back and forth and amplified from a distant din into a roar. Gratzer then moved into the American market, becoming a senior fellow at the libertarian Manhattan Institute, debating health care policy at the American Enterprise Institute and National Center for Policy Analysis (where the Consumer Policy

Institute first picked up the MSA idea) and writing articles for conservative publications like the *Weekly Standard* and the *National Review*.

Gratzer frequently promoted MSAS, but was vague on the justification for their use. He claims they would save money, but a study published in the *Canadian Medical Association Journal* concluded that the MSA approach would cost a lot more.[93] A research team at the University of Manitoba found that an average of $730 per person per year was spent on doctors and hospitals in Manitoba between 1997 and 1999. But 40 percent of the Manitoba population spent less than $100 a year and 80 percent spent less than $600. The highest-using 1 percent of the population accounted for 26 percent of all spending. In contrast, the lowest-using 50 percent accounted for just 4 percent of expenditures. The researchers concluded that most Manitobans were already making responsible health care decisions. MSAS wouldn't help here.

But if each Manitoban received $730 a year and 40 percent are only spending $100, that's a lot of extra cash the government has to dole out. The study estimates a huge $505-million reward. As for the 1 percent of Manitobans who incur 26 percent of health care costs, how would they pay? The study concludes that "no feasible model can significantly reduce costs unless the entitlement is set so low and the catastrophic level so high that there is no longer reasonable insurance against health care costs."[94] Lawrence Solomon called this study "so stupid in design that it would be guaranteed to fail," but provided little evidence to back this assertion beyond the name-calling.[95]

MSAS have been tried on a nationwide scale in Singapore, and Gratzer uses the experience in this small city-state to justify its adoption by Canada. However, several studies indicate that health care costs continued to rise in Singapore for a decade after MSAS were introduced. The main factor in cost escalation was competition between hospitals. They didn't compete by lowering prices, but by recruiting the best-known physicians with higher pay and by using the most sophisticated, expensive technology, explains health policy expert William Hsiao, of the Harvard School of Public Health.[96] In 1993, with costs still rising, the government introduced a raft of cost-containment measures, such as placing price caps on services delivered in public hospitals, imposing predetermined subsidy rates and bed numbers on all hospitals and restricting eligible benefits, says Samuel Shortt, director of the Centre for Health Sciences and Policy Research at Queen's University.[97] Lower costs were achieved through government-imposed rules, not by the free enterprise magic of MSAS.

Gratzer claims that Singapore spends less that Canada on health care.

"Singapore, incidentally, spends less than 4 percent of its gross domestic product (GDP) on health care; we spend three times that," he wrote in the *Canadian Medical Association Journal*.[98] This is a bit of an exaggeration. In fact, Singapore spent 4.3 percent of GDP on health care the year Gratzer wrote his article, while Canada spent 9.6 percent, which is 2.2, not three times, as much. And Gratzer doesn't explain that one reason Singapore spends less is that it has a younger population, which requires fewer health services. In Canada in 2005, 18 percent of the population was over sixty years old; in Singapore, only 12.2 percent was over sixty. Canada has 50 percent more older people. Consequently, Singapore doesn't have the same pressure on its system that Canada's older population exerts. Another factor is the ethos among Singapore immigrants to rely for health care on oneself and one's family, rather than on the state. Finally, many patients in Singapore turn to Traditional Chinese Medicine, whose costs are not included in official health cost tallies.[99]

In the end, notes William Hsiao, only a small portion of total health care expenditures—8.5 percent in 1995—came from government-funded medical savings accounts. Patients themselves paid 57.7 percent of health care expenditures directly out of their own pockets.[100] Singapore is primarily a privatized system, but Gratzer and Solomon obscure this fact for their readers. In Canada, governments pay about 70 percent of all health care bills, while private insurance and individuals pay the other 30 percent. In Singapore, the ratio is reversed: government pays only 36 percent while private payers pick up the rest. Are MSAS a veiled effort to undermine the Canadian tradition of universality? They would force poor and lower-middle-class Canadians, critics charge, to decide how they should spend their MSA money. Should they take their child to a clinic for an earache, which, if untreated, could lead to infection and possible hearing loss?[101] Or should they spend the money on medication for a parent's stomach ulcer?

Is medicare brain dead, as Robert Duncan claims? Has the public system outlived its ability to provide good-quality care to all Canadians? Not according to Dr. Michael Rachlis, who is an effective champion for public health care. In a study for the Canadian Centre for Policy Alternatives, Rachlis suggests several intriguing ways to reduce wait lists using public sector solutions. Might this explain why Duncan neglected to include his interview with Rachlis in the documentary *Medicare Schmedicare*? Rachlis proposes establishing specialized public, short-stay, surgical centres.[102] For-profit clinics have been successful because they specialize in a few procedures and can introduce innovative practices into their work, he notes. Public clinics could do the same and more. They would be cheaper because administrative costs would be reduced and return to shareholders eliminated. Such clinics already exist. Rachlis points to Toronto's Queensway Surgicentre, which is a division of the Trillium Health Centre, a public hospital, and the largest free-standing surgical centre in North America. It does surgeries at a 10 percent lower cost than the hospital and with fewer delays.[103] In 2001, the Manitoba government bought the Pan-Am Clinic from its private sector owners. It operates as a unit of the Winnipeg Regional Health Authority. Consequently, the cost of cataract surgery at the now-public clinic fell from $1000 to $700.[104] "The public system should shift as many minor procedures and low-risk elective surgeries as possible, [such as] hip and knee replacements, to short-stay public, specialized clinics," Rachlis recommends.[105]

Rachlis also proposes applying queue-management theory to wait lists. He argues that analyzing flow in air-traffic control and manufacturing demonstrates how better coordination and flow of queues can dramatically reduce wait times. Instead of every surgeon maintaining a separate wait list, patients could be served more quickly if each jurisdiction maintained a single list.[106] There is no shortage of such solutions if the political will is present, Rachlis concludes. But the twenty-year propaganda campaign to undermine medicare and legitimize the parallel private system, has sapped political will to an alarming extent.

By 2000, Canadians were worried about medicare's future. Angus Reid surveys conducted in 1991 and 2000 indicate a substantial decrease in the percentage of Canadians who thought highly of the quality of health care. In 1991, 26 percent of Canadians rated the system as "excellent" and 35 percent, "very good." In 2000, these figures plummeted, with 7 percent saying "excellent" and 19 percent, "very good." The 2000 survey also revealed that 80 percent of Canadians felt that health care in their province was in crisis.[107] In 2008, an Ipsos-Reid poll found that seven out of ten Canadians thought the overall quality of health care would be the same (39 percent) or worse (32 percent) in ten years.[108]

But these opinions about health care do not mirror people's actual experiences with the system, according to an analysis of Statistics Canada data by geographers Kathleen Wilson and Mark Rosenberg. They conclude there is no crisis, at least according to the Canada Health Act criterion of accessibility to medically necessary health care services regardless of ability to pay. In 1994, Statistics Canada began measuring people's actual health status and their utilization of health services across Canada. Respondents were asked the question "During the past twelve months was there ever a time when you felt you needed health care but you didn't receive it?" The researchers found that in 1999 only 5.9 percent of Canadians aged twenty-five and older reported not receiving care when needed. The four most commonly cited reasons were "waiting time," "health care not available," "cost as a barrier to care" and "care not available in the area."[109] A series of follow-up questions were posed for those who answered yes. While the percentage of the population reporting not receiving care when needed was small, it had increased since the statistical agency began collecting data in 1994. Wilson and Rosenberg speculate that accessibility may become an issue in the future. They conclude that "the results of the analysis suggest that most Canadians continue to enjoy reasonable access to health care services . . ." Their paper, they write, "remind[s] us that there are differences between perceptions and behaviour."[110]

Propaganda scholars should be impressed by the success of the campaign to convince Canadians that their health care system is in crisis, when objectively it may not be. True, it took nearly two decades of negative communication by public health care's enemies. And true, people still haven't given up on their dream of a system in which all citizens can receive high-quality medical care regardless of their ability to pay. Of course, chronic underfunding has placed the system under great stress. Even so, medicare advocates like Michael Rachlis have shown how medicare can be made more efficient and effective. But medicare's enemies don't want the public to hear these things and worked overtime to ensure they don't. Joseph Goebbels, who first pointed out the necessity for endless repetition if propaganda is to work, would have marvelled at the prolific outpouring of attacks on medicare as the medical establishment and elites banded together to beat down this challenge to their power-and-wealth, with the assistance of public relations firms and libertarian think-tanks. Why should the largely healthy rich pay for the health care of the less-healthy poor? And why should doctors, the ultimate entrepreneurs, not be able to earn as much money as they can?

Medicare is a cherished social program. The threat of an incapacitating illness without the ability to pay for its treatment led Canadians to demand a public health-insurance scheme decades ago, despite the concerted opposition of the medical profession, the private insurance industry, the corporate media and conservative governments. Under medicare, the risk of an individual's ill health is shared by all. Despite attempts by Robert Duncan, Brian Day and the Fraser Institute to reframe privatization as a "common sense revolution," it doesn't make much sense to most Canadians.

CHAPTER 9

Targeting Corporate
Propaganda's Vulnerabilities

Canadians who believe that government—flaws and all—has a vital role to play in their lives, need to realize they are engaged in a war of ideas and they're losing. The preceding chapters have dissected the techniques used by corporate-sponsored propaganda to undermine public confidence in government institutions. The case studies document attacks on government involvement in areas that would constrain corporate profits and rising incomes for the wealthy. The ultimate goal of the propaganda is to break the trust people hold in their governments; to weaken government to the point where it can offer only token resistance to corporate power. As U.S. anti-tax activist Grover Norquist so colourfully exclaimed, "My goal is to cut government in half in twenty-five years, to get it down to the size where we can drown it in the bathtub."[1]

Corporate power is in the driver's seat. It has the money, organization and access to the media. It has polarized and oversimplified the workings of the economy: market good, government bad, it says incessantly. The mantra of the market has been mouthed so often we hardly notice any more. When *Globe and Mail* columnist Jeffrey Simpson wrote about the Conservatives' climate-change policy, that "Mr. Harper signalled the shift toward market-based policies—the only ones that really work," no one seemed to object.[2] The proposition that market-based policies are the only ones that really work has been uttered so frequently it has become our common sense. The economy works best, we are told incessantly, when government leaves business alone. Of course, that's not true, because business requires government support at almost every turn, as this chapter will argue.

Many progressives and liberals are frustrated and dispirited by the successes of corporate propaganda. But it took thirty years of effort to shift public discourse far enough to the right so that a Hayekian-inspired Stephen Harper could be elected prime minister and a Straussian-trained Ted Morton considered a serious candidate for Alberta premier. In the United States, and increasingly in Canada, the corporate-sponsored propaganda infrastructure is a smoothly operating machine in which copious corporate and foundation dollars are transformed into a never-ending stream of propaganda aimed at society's opinion leaders and the general public. From the foundations and corporate funders who are increasing their support as they see the efficacy of their dollars at work—although with a downturn during the economic recession—to the think-tanks distributed from coast to coast and around the world, to the cadres of libertarian academics and media pundits, to the sophisticated student-recruitment and -training programs that ensure the movement will continue into the next generations, to the welcoming embrace of the corporate media, the system has the momentum. And even with the election of the centrist Democrat Barack Obama, the system didn't miss a beat, mobilizing against Obama's spending-stimulus package and proposed tax hikes.

Perhaps the most important development in turning back social and economic rights is the degree of cooperation practiced by conservative special interest groups. In the United States, they were able to meld their various ideologies into three words that can fit on a bumper sticker: "Leave Us Alone." Grover Norquist uses the motto to bring together anti-tax taxpayers, property owners against regulations that reduce property values, small business owners who want less regulation and lower taxes, gun owners who don't want limitations on their ownership and use of weapons, religious conservatives who don't want foreign values imposed on them by government, parents who send their children to private schools, and the most "venal," anti-regulation, anti-union, anti-minority stream of corporate America.[3] The political principle that holds them all together is that government should be limited, and the people—and business—free. Every Wednesday, Norquist heads a meeting in the Washington office of his Americans for Tax Reform, to ensure the leaders of a hundred conservative groups, congressional aides, conservative reporters and editors and lobbyists are on the same page. By the end of the meeting, participants usually agree on the next week's agenda.

Norquist's organizational genius went even further. He built "a solid working alliance with the Fortune 500 corporate elite and its K Street lobbyists," investigative journalist Robert Dreyfuss wrote just months after the controversial 2000 election. (K Street is the Washington, D.C., street where many lobbyists and think-tanks have their offices.) Norquist chained "the ideological conservatives together with the business guys, who have the money, and ... put that money to work in the service of the conservative movement," Dreyfuss wrote, quoting the Campaign for America's Future, a long-time Norquist foe.[4] Leading Norquist funders are the "taxophobic sin industries," tobacco, gambling and liquor. This is ironic, Dreyfuss claimed, given that many Christian fundamentalist groups are in Norquist's coalition. Tobacco giant Phillip Morris was the largest contributor, followed by Indian bands with gambling casinos, the liquor industry, Microsoft, Pfizer, Time Warner and UPS. Corporate lobbyists pay Americans for Tax Reform between $10,000 and $25,000 for the privilege of attending several intimate dinners at Norquist's home.[5]

Canada doesn't have a Grover Norquist, yet. Nor is there a Wednesday meeting to discuss strategy. Those will likely come, since everything that happens in the U.S. of benefit to the wealthy is eventually replicated in Canada. In the meantime, the right in Canada coalesces in the Civitas Society. As mentioned on page 186, classical liberals, conservatives and libertarians formed this society after they failed to create a unified right-wing party at the "Winds of Change" conference in Calgary in 1996. Civitas has no charismatic leader like Norquist; the presidency rotates among leading conservatives and libertarians such as Atlantic Institute for Market Studies president Brian Lee Crowley, *National Post* editorial board member Lorne Gunter, Calgary School leader and Stephen Harper adviser Tom Flanagan and C.D. Howe Institute president Bill Robson. Nor is Civitas an organization devising strategy and tactics, as Norquist's group does; it is an ideas organization, a "speakers' club," as founder William Gairdner envisioned it.[6] Civitas members are individuals, while the individuals in Norquist's group represent member organizations. Instead of weekly meetings to move forward an agenda, Civitas holds annual conferences to discuss and debate issues. The 2007 conference in Halifax, for instance, featured panels on how to turn Aboriginals into free-marketers, how to beat down Islam and how science has been polluted by politics (not religion).[7] Like

Americans for Tax Reform, Civitas does have the right political connections: Stephen Harper is a long-time member—he made a surprise visit to the 2006 conference just after becoming prime minister—and his former chief of staff, Ian Brodie, was a Civitas director. Norquist has high hopes for Civitas. He was an invited speaker at the 2006 conference and reminded attendees that they were "on the same team," fighting "the same opponents: envy, sloth, and a quasi-religious faith in the power of the state."[8] Whew!

Lewis Powell would surely be amazed at the changes that have occurred in the thirty-five years since he submitted his memorandum, "Attack of American Free Enterprise System," to the U.S. Chamber of Commerce. Then, the fifteen-year-old Norquist was already a confirmed anti-communist, after reading tracts such as *Masters of Deceit*, by J. Edgar Hoover, and *Witness*, by Whittaker Chambers. On the home front, Powell and Norquist believed, the communists were behind the attack on business. Powell was not surprised that "extremists of the left" were leading the attack. But he was disturbed that the "voices joining the chorus of criticism [were coming] from perfectly respectable elements of society: from the college campus, the pulpit, the media, the intellectual and literary journals, the arts and sciences, and from politicians."[9] He urged business to "confront this problem as a primary responsibility of corporate management," as Chapter 3 described.

Powell recommended action on four fronts: the courts, the media, academia and politics. Much of today's success is a consequence of business hewing closely to Powell's recommendations. Reversing the direction of the liberal U.S. Supreme Court led by Earl Warren was a top priority for business, as well as for Powell, who would soon find himself sitting on that court. "American business and the enterprise system have been affected as much by the courts as by the executive and legislative branches of government," he wrote. "Under our constitutional system, especially with an activist-minded Supreme Court, the judiciary may be the most important instrument for social, economic and political change.

"Other organizations . . . have been far more astute in exploiting judicial action than American business. Perhaps the most active exploiters of the judicial system have been groups ranging in political orientation from 'liberal' to the far left." Powell cited the American Civil Liberties Union (ACLU) as a prime example. "It initiates or intervenes in scores of cases each year." Labour unions, civil rights groups and public interest law firms were active in the courts. "Their success, often at business' expense, has not been inconsequential," he warned.

What should business do? Powell recommended that the U.S. Chamber of Commerce should recruit "a highly competent staff of lawyers" and also engage "lawyers of national standing and reputation" to appear in carefully selected Supreme Court cases. Business must not flinch from this task, he cautioned. "There should be no hesitation to attack the Naders ... and others who openly seek destruction of the system."[10]

Powell's recommendation for court action inspired "a powerful coalition of business groups and ideologically-compatible foundations" to engage "in a multi-faceted, comprehensive, and integrated campaign to elevate corporate profits and private wealth over social justice and individual rights as the cornerstones of [the American] legal process," Alliance for Justice, an opposition group, commented.[11] It didn't take long for the California chamber, backed by then governor Ronald Reagan, to propose a non-profit legal foundation to counter the liberal public interest legal groups pressing for stronger environmental regulation and social programs. Reagan connected the chamber with Pittsburgh billionaire Richard Mellon Scaife, who funded the initial office of the Pacific Legal Foundation (PLF) in Sacramento. According to the Alliance for Justice, the centre's founding mission was to "stem the rampage" of environmentalists and "clever poverty lawyers suing to obtain welfare checks for people regardless of need at the taxpayer's expense." Other early critical support came from local developers and the chamber itself. One long-time secret backer was the Philip Morris Tobacco Co., which used the law firm in its fight against laws regulating second-hand tobacco smoke.

Over the next two decades, more than $20 million from Scaife, plus millions from other foundations and corporations, helped the PLF spawn a half-dozen additional conservative public interest law firms across the country. As the media watchdog group SourceWatch observed, the PLF "is the key right-wing litigation-happy, public interest law firm in a network of similar organisations funded initially by Scaife Foundation money across the USA in support of un-restrained capitalism, and opposed to environmental and health activism and government agency regulations."[12]

A second attack was launched on the progressive legal system in the early 1980s. Spurred by their conservative professors, notably Antonin Scalia, who became a Reagan-nominated Supreme Court judge, students at Chicago and

Yale law schools formed a new organization called the Federalist Society, to bring the war of ideas into their classrooms. Seed money for this venture came from Irving Kristol and William Simon through their Institute for Educational Affairs, which supported promising conservative students. With the backing of Olin, Scaife, Bradley, Lambe, Earhart and Koch foundations,[13] the society quickly grew into a burgeoning network of law students, lawyers and judges who espouse libertarian or socially conservative values. The society claims chapters at 180 law schools and 40,000 members and associates. The collective goal is to re-order priorities within the legal system, "to place a premium on individual liberty, traditional values and the rule of law."[14] American University law professor Jamin Raskin believes the society's political agenda is "to completely undo the landmark civil rights and civil liberties decisions of the last half of the 20th century."[15] The society serves a valuable networking function. Recent law school graduates anxious to gain a prestigious clerkship can link up with prominent radical-conservative judges at national and local functions. For more established lawyers, a speech before the society denouncing some liberal idea could be a way to be noticed by the society's "judicial scouting machine," notes Neil Lewis in the *New York Times*.[16]

The Federalist Society remained below the public radar until George W. Bush turned to it for nominations for the federal bench when he took office in 2001. Four years later, the *Times* reported that "15 of the 41 appeals court judges confirmed under Mr. Bush have identified themselves as member of the group."[17] Bush's two Supreme Court nominations, Samuel Alito and John G. Roberts for chief justice, were both associated with the Federalists. Guest speakers at the society's twenty-fifth anniversary celebration included Bush and Justices Roberts, Scalia and Clarence Thomas. The mood at the black-tie gala held in Washington's vast Union Station could have been sombre. Democrats had regained control of the Senate and could block further Federalist nominations. But the 1,800 guests were not downcast.[18] As Powell predicted, consistent funding over the long term, decades of organizing and aggressive efforts to promote a conservative, business-oriented view of law and public policy, resulted in federal courts shifted dramatically to the right. It wouldn't make much difference if a Democratic president slowed the flow of Federalist lawyers onto the bench for a few years, as happened during the Clinton administration.

According to most corporate media reports, the battles fought over confirming Federalist-connected judges are always about social "hot-button" issues, such as abortion and gay marriage. But the business press tells a different story, one about the pro-business slant of the new judges. In the year after Roberts assumed leadership of the court, the U.S. Chamber of Commerce filed friend-of-the-court briefs in fifteen cases in which the chamber presented the views of its corporate members. The chamber won thirteen, *BusinessWeek* reports, the "highest winning percentage" in its history.[19] Many of the decisions narrowed the ability of customers or shareholders harmed by corporate actions to sue the corporation or win substantial damage awards. It was "our best Supreme Court term ever," commented Robin S. Conrad, executive vice-president of the chamber's legal arm.[20]

Canadian conservatives came late to the project to transform the courts into a more conservative, business-friendly institution. They never developed a parallel organization to the Federalist Society and they took thirty years to create a public interest law firm similar to the Pacific Legal Foundation to challenge progressive laws. They did have Civitas, though, and within its private confines they spoke often about moving the legal system in a more conservative direction. They certainly knew about the Federalists. Civitas founder David Frum was president of Harvard Law School's Federalist chapter in the mid-eighties. And they followed the Federalists in making "judicial activism" their *bête noire*; this is the charge that liberal judges, instead of basing their decisions on strictly limited interpretations of the U.S. Constitution, impose their own political ideologies on their decisions. Judicial activism was imported into Canada by Straussian political scientists such as Ted Morton and Rainer Knopff at the University of Calgary.

Morton, who nearly became premier of Alberta, ranted in one newspaper column that "[i]ntoxicated by the power and status of their new self-made roles as Platonic philosopher-kings and social reformers, our judicial elites have abandoned any pretense of neutrality between competing social interests in Canadian society."[21] The rulings of these drunken deciders, that gay marriage is constitutional, for instance, was anathema to social conservatives. Endorsing gay marriage, Morton warned, would lead to the "decline of democracy."

Chapter 5 explains the Straussian deception behind the strategy to attack "special interests" such as gays, feminists and prisoner-rights activists who, Straussians claim, try to get their rights entrenched in law through the decisions of liberal judges, rather than through the statutes of Parliament. This is deceptive because Straussians like Morton, Rainer Knopff and Harper chief of staff Ian Brodie (both ex-Civitas directors) ignore the special interest with the most influence on the judicial system—business. In fact, the radical-conservative judges appointed by Reagan and Bush were the ultimate judicial activists because they applied their libertarian and social conservative ideologies to cases where they found in favour of business, an institution largely absent from the U.S. Constitution. Fred Nace, in *Gangs of America*, documents how conservative judicial activism over two centuries helped corporations, which were intended by the constitutional framers to be subservient to the state, accumulate the legal and political power they enjoy today.[22] Like the Federalist Society, Civitas members worry about interest groups with little influence and the supposedly activist judges doling out rights and privileges to them, but seem to be little concerned about the significant rights and privileges enjoyed by business.

At the 2003 Civitas conference in Toronto, Alberta lawyer Dallas Miller, a Civitas director, chaired a panel titled "Judicial activism: What's the cure?"[23] Thanks to Civitas member Stephen Harper, the answer became clear three years later: appoint socially conservative lawyers like Miller to the bench. In January 2007, the Harper government elevated Miller to the Alberta Court of Queen's Bench. Miller's conservative credentials were compelling. As executive director of the Home School Legal Defence Association of Canada, he defended home-schooling families who want to preserve their religious freedom and parental right to educate their children at home, away from the (corrupting?) influence of teachers and teacher unions. Miller represented the Christian Legal Fellowship in a case before the Supreme Court and served on the Religious Liberty Commission of the Evangelical Fellowship of Canada, the national association of evangelical churches. For his radical-conservative work, Miller received REAL Women's National Defender of the Family award in 1998.[24] (REAL Women's Gwen Landolt is a Civitas founder.) "Special interests" like women's or gay and lesbian groups might have a more difficult time in Miller's court, but what about Christian—or business—special interests?

The second front in the attack on a progressive court was launched with $200,000 from the Donner Canadian Foundation. The money enabled the Canadian Constitution Foundation (CCF) to set up shop as Canada's first conservative public interest law firm. The CCF is headed by lawyer John Carpay, former Alberta director of the Canadian Taxpayers Federation, unsuccessful Reform Party candidate and one-time assistant to Conservative federal fisheries minister Tom Siddon. The CCF would promote a conservative property-rights agenda by challenging the Charter of Rights and Freedoms. "Conservatives must reclaim [the Charter] for conservative values," CCF founder John Weston, who was elected as a Conservative MP in 2008, told a sympathetic *Calgary Herald* columnist.[25] The CCF's advisory board includes David Brown, another socially conservative lawyer appointed by Harper to a provincial supreme court. Brown represented REAL Women of Canada, the Association for Marriage and the Family, and Focus on the Family in opposing an appeal to allow gay and lesbians to receive survivor benefits from pension plans. He also defended anti-choice radicals demonstrating illegally outside abortion clinics.[26] Was he another antidote to special interests?

Carpay says his organization is modelled after the Institute for Justice, like the Pacific Legal Foundation, a libertarian public interest law firm that "represents individuals in their fight for private property rights, economic liberty, freedom of speech, commercial freedom, racial equality, and the right of parents to raise their children free from state interference."[27] The CCF kicked off its crusade to save property rights, individual freedom and economic liberty from the clutches of government bureaucrats and ideologically driven judges, with a challenge to the Nisga'a Treaty. This agreement was approved by the Nisga'a Nation and the governments of British Columbia and Canada in 2000, settling land claims after a hundred years of failed negotiation. A handful of Nisga'a and non-Aboriginals, backed by the CCF, challenged the agreement, claiming it establishes an unconstitutional third order of government and gives special rights to members of the Nisga'a Nation.[28]

The CCF's funding expanded in 2005, thanks to donations from Fraser Institute trustees, including Michael Walker, as well as *National Post* editorial board member Marni Soupcoff and a clutch of Canadian foundations.[29] With this new money, the CCF set up student chapters at law schools at York University, the University of Toronto and the University of Alberta. It also launched court actions based on the Supreme Court decision in the Chaoulli case, which opened the door to two-tier health care in Quebec. These cases challenged health care legislation in Alberta, Ontario and British Columbia. Interestingly, two of the cases were started by clients of Rick Baker, president of Timely Medical Alternatives, a Vancouver company that finds appointments at private clinics in Canada and the United States for people prepared to pay extra for treatment. Baker and Carpay appeared together on a panel at a Fraser Institute soiree attacking medicare. Ideology and business had found each other once again.[30]

With courts being politicized by the Federalists, Canadian Constitution Foundation and Civitas members, Harper could appoint conservatives without too much controversy. *Globe and Mail* columnist Jeffrey Simpson, perhaps unwittingly, validated the Harper approach by claiming judicial activism was alive and well in Canada and, as a result, became the subject of legitimate attack: "Supporters of judicial activism ... who cheered on [the courts] said it couldn't and wouldn't happen, but they were wrong," Simpson wrote. Harper was simply fixing "a judicial imbalance in the land," Simpson continued, masking the Federalist-inspired campaign to construct an imbalance.[31] Harper was able to appoint Marshall Rothstein, who was seen as centre-right, to the Supreme Court. Rothstein agreed with Harper's requirement for a Supreme Court judge: someone who would interpret the law, not be "inventive" with it.[32]

But are some judges "inventive" with the law? Do they actually engage in activism, creating rights for special interests not contained in the Canadian Charter of Rights and Freedoms? A study of Supreme Court decisions by University of Toronto law professor Sujit Choudhry concluded it's a myth the court was becoming more activist by finding in favour of special interests. The study found that governments won their cases in nearly two-thirds of decisions,[33] suggesting the Supreme Court was not knocking down laws passed by Parliament. Nor was there an upward trend to strike down laws in recent years, the study discovered. But Choudhry's work was lost in a steady drumbeat of full-frontal-attack rhetoric. He was lambasted by another Civitas director, Chris Manfredi, who is dean of arts at McGill University and, along with Morton and Knopff, a creator of the Canadian judicial activism charge.[34] Judicial activism was moving from myth to common sense, thanks to the Federalist-inspired conservatives in academia and the media.

George Lakoff, a professor of cognitive linguistics at the University of California, Berkeley, studies how conservatives frame political debates. Progressives lose the debate, he argues, every time they try to negate a conservative frame. This merely reinforces their frame, he says. The phrase "judicial activism" invokes a frame, Lakoff writes, in which judges are fair if they apply the Constitution to the cases before them in an impersonal, mechanical manner, and not be "inventive" with the law, as Marshall Rothstein warns. Activists, on the other hand, are "emotional, irrational, and outside the mainstream." Meanwhile, "liberal judges illegitimately impose their personal left-wing agendas from the bench and harm the country," Lakoff proposes. The frame's conclusion is that "we must appoint conservative judges, who will stick to what is in the Constitution, not impose their own views, and that will be good for the country."[35]

"Every part of the frame is false," Lakoff argues, "[b]ut if the public accepts the frame, the public will insist on radical conservative judges." Progressives cannot counter the frame by denying it. They must create their own frame, their own story about justice and the courts. He proposes that progressives need to adopt a "freedom judges" frame. Cases reach higher courts, he offers, because they don't fit neatly within the established categories of the law. High-court judges are always extending or narrowing the established categories of law in their decisions. So each decision inevitably changes the law in one direction or the other. Lakoff's question is: Do judges change the law for "greater or lesser freedom?" Are they "expanding—or narrowing—voting rights, civil rights, fairness principles, public protections, privacy rights, education of the public, [and] scientific knowledge . . . ?" Are they taking us back to the era of limited freedom that existed in the nineteenth century, or forward to an expansion of our freedoms?[36] If progressives hope to counter the conservative "judicial activism" frame, they must be prepared to develop and refine their own "freedom judge" frame and promote it for many years. And, Lakoff cautions, they must never use the phrase "judicial activism."

Progressives need to develop their own frames, too, in the other arenas of attack outlined by Lewis Powell. Corporate interests, in collaboration with radical conservatives, utilized similar strategies, funding priorities and propaganda techniques to shift media, universities and political parties to the right. In 1971, Powell was concerned the media were too liberal, a condition that no longer applies. The success of business and conservatives in pushing commercial media to the right is documented in David Brock's 2004 best-seller, *The Republican Noise Machine: Right-Wing Media and How it Corrupts Democracy*. Today, talk radio is dominated by conservatives; Fox News pulled all cable news programming to the right; experts from libertarian and neoconservative think-tanks dominate the airwaves; and flak organizations push all media reporting rightward. Canada is replicating the American situation, thanks to Conrad Black, who created a socially conservative–libertarian newspaper, and pushed the Southam chain to the right. And despite the centre-right positioning of most commercial media, they are still frequently depicted with a "liberal media" frame because is it useful to business propaganda to do so. A "commercial media" frame—which is already being applied—may be helpful to the progressive cause.

Powell devoted much of his memorandum to the situation in the universities. He worried they were under the influence of socialists, communists and liberals. But the ideological composition of universities was already changing. The libertarians clustered in the Mont Pèlerin Society were obtaining positions in economics departments, and Straussians were moving into political science, philosophy and history departments and law schools. Regarding the political parties, three decades of effective propaganda have pushed all parties—including social-democratic ones—to the right. They are all more business friendly than they were in the seventies.

Given the decades of effort and hundreds of millions of dollars of support, it's not surprising that business achieved success in the three issues discussed in this book—continental integration, global warming and medicare. But that success was not as all-encompassing as might have been expected. In the case of global warming, corporate propaganda delayed action for twenty years and created a sizable minority of know-nothings who write letters to the *National Post*, decrying the "junk science" of the Intergovernmental Panel on Climate Change. They claim Kyoto is nothing more than a heavy-handed attempt by government to waste billions of taxpayers' dollars and impose costly, ineffective regulations on industry. Even when the IPCC's "Fourth Consensus Report" was released in February 2007, libertarian ideologue and former Civitas president Lorne Gunter was still writing in the *National Post* that "the IPCC summary is a prospectus for big government written by big government's sales department."[37] But the libertarian frame is becoming threadbare and the message is falling off the public radar. By 2007, critics were tallying successes in exposing corporate propaganda efforts and moving policy towards the necessity of cutting CO_2 emissions, even if industry would continue to resist these initiatives and the think-tanks continue to apply the alarmist label to anyone who expressed concern.

In the case of medicare, intensive propaganda led to a fraying of support, but the public still backs the public system. A 2006 Ipsos-Reid poll found that only 15 percent of Canadians want a fully parallel public–private health care system of the kind promoted by Robert Duncan in the documentary *Medicare Schmedicare*. Twenty-five percent of Canadians support the medicare "status quo," while the remaining 60 percent favours medicare "reform," either as "enhanced medicare" or "medicare with complementary private insurance."[38] While these results seem to suggest that respondents don't support medicare, it's important to note the survey was sponsored by the Canadian Medical Association. The doctors' organization, with its ambivalent attitude towards medicare, seems to have spun the questions to encourage results supporting an increased role for profit-making enterprise in health care. By associating profit with positive words like "enhanced" and "complementary," the doctors may have ensured the results they wanted. Why would anyone support the "status quo," a negative term in most policy areas? That a quarter of respondents did so indicates medicare still enjoys strong support. But, survey aside, many actions are being taken to improve the effectiveness of medicare without the need for "enhanced" or "complementary" activities. One action, as outlined by Michael Rachlis, is to duplicate the efficiencies of small, private clinics with public clinics operating at lower cost because of lower administrative charges and without building in profits for doctors and investors.

In the case of deep integration, the strategy is to undermine government's ability to govern in the public interest and turn control of the economy and large swaths of social life over to a business council with narrow profit goals. The corporate agenda is advancing, but only because it is occurring below the public radar. The initiatives pursued are those that can proceed without the need for legislative changes because of the expected public backlash that would occur.

Corporate propaganda successes in areas not discussed in this book have also been modest. Despite thirty years of C.D. Howe and Fraser institute propaganda for tax cuts, people still want spending on social programs. Three polls released in advance of the Harper government's 2009 budget reported similar findings, that government spending was preferred to tax cuts. "They want a budget that deals with the needs of the average Canadian and the rejection for tax cuts for businesses was really, really big," reported Mario Canseco of polling company Angus Reid Strategies.[39] Nor was the focus on spending simply a consequence of the 2008 economic downturn. A poll released the day the Harper government brought down its 2007 budget indicated that 50 percent of Canadians thought that increasing spending on social programs was the most important issue for the new budget to address, while only 19 percent said that cutting taxes was most important.[40]

In fact, most Canadians suspect corporate power. The 2005 Canadian Values Study was a joint project of the *National Post*, Dominion Institute and

Innovative Research Group, so its conservative, pro-business orientation should be obvious. Nonetheless, the findings indicate that Canadians are not endorsing business control of the economy. When asked about government regulation of business, a majority of respondents (53 percent) said regulation "is necessary to keep industry from becoming too powerful," while 38 percent believed government regulation "usually does more harm than good." And this result occurred after decades of anti-regulatory propaganda. Nor were Canadians buying corporate messaging about trickle-down economics. Only 36 percent of respondents agreed with the statement that "when businesses make a lot of money, everyone benefits, including the poor," while 63 percent disagreed.[41] The *National Post* downplayed these findings.[42]

There's good reason for Canadians to be suspicious of corporate power. For one thing, a gap separates the views of the corporate elite from the rest of Canadians, as Chapter 1 indicates. On the question of climate change, for instance, 77 percent of Canadians believe Canada should meet or exceed its binding Kyoto targets for cutting CO_2 emissions, a 2006 poll suggests.[43] But a poll of chief executives the following year found that only 24 percent of them say that Canada should support the Kyoto agreement, while 52 percent say Canada should support the Asia-Pacific Partnership (APP) sponsored by the United States and the oil companies.[44] Unlike Kyoto, the APP has voluntary targets. Nor does it require countries that fail to meet their targets to compensate those that do. It is not enforceable and has little likelihood of success, but will ensure that shares in fossil-fuel companies will sustain their value.

As these surveys indicate, Canadians are not totally vulnerable to corporate propaganda. They can do more and inoculate themselves against corporate messages by becoming defensive news consumers. Corporate propagandists understand that for a message to be communicated successfully, "source credibility" is critical. As British economist John Burton told the 1983 regional meeting of the Mont Pèlerin Society in Vancouver, "Our effectiveness in communicating the case for a system of liberty . . . is, and will be, highly dependent on the authority and standing of the individuals arguing the case."[45] That's why seemingly independent academics, and not the president of Imperial Oil, are chosen to deliver the message that global warming is not occurring, and if it is, efforts to slow it down will destroy the economy. The defensive news consumer should ask: Who is this source and who might be supporting him?

Sociologist Herbert Gans argues that sources make the news. In his classic 1980 study, *Deciding What's News*, Gans defined news as "information which is transmitted from sources to audiences, with journalists . . . summarizing, refining and altering what becomes available to them from sources in order to make the information suitable for their audiences."[46] Studying who a news organization selects to be its sources can help defensive news consumers discern the propagandist's intent.

Sources are not just disinterested experts sought out by enterprising reporters. Rather, they, and the organizations they represent, work hard to get their interpretations of events into the news. By acting as sources, representatives of propaganda organizations can disseminate their messages without necessarily revealing the propaganda intent. The success of propaganda often depends on the relationship between sources and the sponsor organizations being obscured. The defensive news consumer attempts to unmask these relationships.

Sometimes looking at sources over a prolonged period can open the door to greater understanding. During the first three months of 2005, missile defence was the nation's top story. Would Canada join with the George Bush missile defence plan or not? What would Paul Martin do? At the end of February, Martin decided that Canada would not join. The fallout from this decision took up much newspaper space during March and continued until the end of the month, when Martin met with Bush and Mexican president Vicente Fox in Waco, Texas. Did Canadians get the straight goods on this coverage, or was a propaganda agenda at work?

A frequent media source for missile-defence stories was a person named Joseph Jockel, who was quoted by newspapers as diverse as the *Globe and Mail*, *National Post* and *Toronto Star*. The day Frank McKenna took over his position as Canada's ambassador to the United States, the *Post* ran a front-page story titled "Canadians accused of missile freeloading." Washington bureau chief Sheldon Alberts quoted Jockel: "The whole thing was handled by an ill-prepared Prime Minister making unfortunate statements, rushing out and contradicting his ambassador. This is no way to conduct a mature relationship with the United States," Jockel admonished the Canadians.[47] During the 2005 election campaign, Jockel was a source in the *Globe and Mail*: "More civility, more dignity . . . not what occurred under Chrétien and Martin." In the Bush administration, "there's no goodwill left towards Canada," he informed *Globe* readers, in a statement that was clearly supportive of Harper and dismissive of Martin.[48] And in the *Toronto Star*, Jockel applauded NORAD as being "absolutely essential" to the protection of the continent. The article questioned whether NORAD would survive the fallout from Martin's decision not to join Bush's missile defence program.[49] These, and other articles which quoted Jockel—over a hundred in total—framed Canada negatively because it chose not to join Bush.

In most stories, Jockel was identified simply as an academic, head (or a professor) of Canadian Studies at St. Lawrence University in Canton, New York. A reader might conclude that there must be scholarly studies indicating Canada was wrong not to join Bush's missile defence plan. But a simple Internet search would reveal connections that may be more relevant than Jockel's recent academic activities. He was, most notably, acting secretary of the U.S. section of the Canada–U.S. Permanent Joint Board on Defence in the 1980s. Later, he was a senior fellow and director of the Canada Project at the Center for Strategic and International Studies (CSIS). Clearly, there's more to this story than purported academic expertise. Researching the Permanent Joint Board on Defence provides the information that it is the senior advisory body on continental security, consisting of military and diplomatic representatives from both Canada and the United States. According to a policy statement from the Department of National Defence, Canada is encouraging "the board to consider North American defence in the context of the new security environment."[50] This statement can be interpreted to mean that the board is working to deepen cooperation and integration with little public knowledge. So a former member of an organization working secretly to deepen Canada's integration into North American defence arrangements is critical of Canada's decision not to join the missile defence plan. Big surprise! Instead of his relationship to the board being explained, the media portray Jockel as an "academic."

Jockel's link to the Center for Strategic and International Studies is also revealing. This organization is a neoconservative think-tank based in Washington, D.C. Its role is to assist the United States in advancing its global interests, making the world safe for American capital. The CSIS was a favourite of the Reagan administration and continued to enjoy influence during the Clinton and Bush years. The organization is dominated by former government officials and industry executives. Under its regional-transformation program area, the CSIS runs an Americas Program, which it describes as "integrating governance, development and security agendas in the Americas." And under this program is the Canada Project, which Jockel headed. This project is "dedicated to ... analyzing the process of deepening North American integration that is transforming them both and establishing the new dynamics of a continental economy," according to the organization's web page.[51] Jockel's work here, too, was to assist the process of integration.

Another often-quoted expert on Canada–U.S. relations is Christopher Sands. In a *Globe and Mail* article published just after Harper's 2006 election victory, Sands cautioned Harper not to be "too chummy with Bush," even though they are ideological fellow travellers, because Harper could "face another election before Bush is gone." Canadians don't like Bush, so they would punish Harper at the polls if he appeared too close to the American president.[52] In a *National Post* article written just after Harper appointed Michael Wilson as Canada's ambassador to the United States, Sands said "this could be a match made in heaven," if Wilson can develop strong relationships in Washington.[53] Sands, who was quoted in nearly three hundred articles, is usually identified as a leading expert on Canada–U.S. relations at the CSIS, the same organization where Jockel worked.

It takes only a few searches to conclude that the sources in missile defence stories were drawn from a very narrow range of hawks from the military-corporate establishment. Without further research it's impossible to ascertain why only these perspectives were privileged in the corporate media, why the media selected only hawks to shape the news about missile defence. Some experts were clearly missing. One logical voice would be a peace advocate. What should Canada do to promote world peace in light of escalating missile defence rhetoric? is a question enterprising reporters might want to ask. Another missing voice is that of the Canadian nationalist. What should Canada do to protect its remaining sovereignty? These perspectives were largely missing from news accounts, with one exception. The *Toronto Star* did provide the voices of those opposed to Canada joining the United States. It also quoted more Canadian experts. *Star* columnists Linda McQuaig, Thomas Walkom and David Crane opposed the deal, while *Star* editorials noted that Martin's refusal to join the U.S. was in tune with the public mood. But in most papers, what the public thought seemed of little interest.

Canadians who want a more effective role for government must go beyond individual defensive action. To engage in the war of ideas, they need to adopt a new name. The terms "liberal" and "left" must be dropped because they've been thoroughly demonized by conservative storm troopers. Ralph Nader is correct when he says that "conservatives of all denominations want to crush, smash and vaporize liberals and liberalism in America. They can't even say the words without a snarl."[54] In Canada, the right's common enemy is a work in progress. It is variously lefties, leftists, collectivists, socialists, Marxists, small-l and big-l liberals, environmentalists and feminists. But another name is available and already in use. When Stephen Harper dropped the word "progressive" from the name of the party of John Diefenbaker and Robert Stanfield, he created an opening for a democratic rights movement to adopt the name "progressive," throwing into stark relief the two camps: business and conservatives looking to the past and restricted freedoms, democracy and progressives looking to the future and greater freedom and justice.

As well as a common name, progressives need a common enemy if they are to rally their diverse groupings to a common cause. Historically, the enemies of the left have been poverty, homelessness, inequality, poor health care, racism and sexism. The enemy of the right, in contrast, is the left. Progressives need to make the right—the radical conservatives—the enemy. Of course, progressives must continue working to eradicate inequality and promote justice. But they must engage the enemy, who they consider the source of most injustice.

As this book has demonstrated, the progressive advances of the first two-thirds of the twentieth century have been challenged by those who profess unqualified support for the market and big business. They have been called, variously, classical liberals, neoliberals and libertarians. A better term is offered by the scholars at the progressive Berkeley, California–based Longview Institute. Proponents of unfettered free markets, they claim, are market fundamentalists, people who hold "the exaggerated and quite irrational belief in the ability of markets to solve all problems."[55] Market fundamentalists are described in earlier chapters. They are like Christian, Jewish and Islamic fundamentalists. They see everything in black and white: the market is good (god?), government is bad or evil (the devil?). The comparison with radical religion is not accidental. Their god is the free market with its invisible hand and they want the hand to smite the non-believers. They appear to believe that individual freedom and liberty are the highest achievements of civilization, higher even than the collective accomplishments of civilization itself. Market fundamentalism's canonical texts proclaim that freedom and liberty are to be achieved and protected by a system of strong private-property rights, free markets and free trade. The state should not be involved in the economy except to use its power to preserve private-property rights and market institutions.

But market-fundamentalist theology is based on a myth, economist

Duncan Foley argues, that each person's pursuit of his or her own self-interest will somehow serve the common good. Foley, who teaches at the New School for Social Research in New York, says it is a fallacy to believe, as market fundamentalists do, that the economic sphere of life constitutes a separate realm "in which the pursuit of self interest is guided by objective laws to a socially beneficent outcome." The rest of social life, in contrast, he writes, "is morally problematic and has to be weighed against . . . ends" other than self-interest.[56] Foley calls this Adam's fallacy, drawing on the work of Adam Smith. It is the belief that you can hive off one chunk of social life and say, "OK, guys, be as greedy and ruthless as you want and do bad things to other people. You don't have to worry though." Because of the invisible hand, or "capitalist social relations," as Foley calls it, everything will turn out for the good of all.[57]

At its best, Foley argues, economics is a "speculative philosophical discourse," and not a "deductive or inductive science," market-fundamentalist assertions to the contrary. The economics study of capitalist ventures "are discussions above all of faith and belief, not of fact, and hence theological," he writes. From the "fallacy that the pursuit of private self-interest will ultimately benefit the whole society stems a willingness to abide harsh economic measures and consequences, ranging from large-scale unemployment to the destruction of traditional cultures," Foley writes.[58]

One corporate propaganda triumph has been business's ability to convince the public that progressives and the left, more so than business, turn to government for financial favours, such as unemployment insurance, social welfare, housing subsidies and legal aid. Almost everyone accepts this framing of modern democratic society. The frame may be successful, but it is based on a falsehood. Business relies as much, or even more, on government for its success than environmental, social justice or anti-poverty groups. These latter groups turn to government for a variety of reasons: expanded programs, financial support or strengthened regulations. But corporations depend on government for their very existence. In a free market, corporations do not exist. Individuals are free to form partnerships and engage in any kind of trade or commercial activity they wish. But, claims Dean Baker in his compelling report "The Conservative Nanny State," individuals cannot establish a corporation, which is a legal entity that exists independently of the individuals who own it. Only governments can create corporations, with their own rights and privileges.[59]

Further, think-tanks that argue the best government is the smallest possible government ignore the fact that think-tanks themselves are a creation of government. Like for-profit corporations, think-tanks depend on government for their very existence. Governments have passed laws and regulations allowing for the creation of charitable organizations that can receive tax-free donations. Market fundamentalists seek and accept privileges and immunities conferred by government on corporations, thus legitimizing one "tentacle of Leviathan," the epithet they hurl at government. In fact, their allegiance seems to be directed more to corporate than to individual freedom. Libertarian think-tanks should oppose big business as vigorously as they do big government, but perhaps they have been compromised by the dollars they receive.

Market fundamentalists who rail about special interests and activist judges seem to have a blind spot when it comes to the fact that corporations were allowed to become large and powerful because of activist judges and legislatures. Adam Smith didn't have corporations in mind in *The Wealth of Nations*. His ideal was a market comprising small buyers and sellers. There was little room for corporations.[60] In fact, Smith opposed large corporations, which could exercise monopoly power, and maintain prices above their natural levels, for an indefinite period. He saw the corporation as a "decrepit and ill-conceived institution, a remnant of medieval privilege that was too prone to mismanagement to be useful for any but a handful of contingencies."[61]

Corporations had been banned in England for more than fifty years when Smith wrote *The Wealth of Nations* in 1776, a result of the collapse of the South Sea Company, which left many investors ruined. The legislation was repealed in 1825 and incorporation was once again legally permitted.[62] In the Canadian colonies, the first company was incorporated in 1801, but corporations were not favoured at the time. The Americans were just as suspicious. Until 1850, corporations were kept in check by their charters, which were issued by state legislatures. These charters imposed strict limits on the activities in which a corporation could engage and required that the company renew its charter every twenty years.[63] After the Civil War, Tom Scott, a northern railway promoter, in 1870 created the holding company, an entity designed to bypass legislative control. This type of corporation had only one purpose, to hold stock in other companies. Working quietly through the Pennsylvania legislature, Scott incorporated a holding company to secretly buy up a string of railway companies across the southern U.S., without having to secure charters from potentially hostile southern legislatures. This development liberated corporations from state control.[64]

Twenty years later, a clever New York lawyer named William Nelson Cromwell succeeded in transforming Scott's invention into a universal option for corporations. In 1889, his law firm lobbied the New Jersey legislature to loosen incorporation statutes so that any corporation chartered in the state could hold stock in any other corporation in America.[65] By 1901, three-quarters of all large U.S. corporations were using New Jersey as their home base. And another decade later, after New Jersey had retightened its incorporation statute in 1913, the state of Delaware grabbed the lead in granting wide-open corporate charters, a position it holds to the present.[66]

A second gift bestowed by government on investors and promoters was limited liability, meaning that shareholders in a corporation could not personally be held liable for the corporation's debts beyond the amount of their initial investment. Before the era of limited liability, a person who invested in a company was liable personally for the company's debts. "Investors' homes, savings, and other personal assets would be exposed to claims by creditors if a company failed, meaning that a person risked financial ruin simply by owning shares in a company," writes Joel Bakan in his best-selling book *The Corporation*.[67] Limited liability was introduced in England in 1850 and the Canadian colonies five years later, against significant opposition. In the United States, it was successfully sold by railway promoters who needed to raise immense pools of money to build the railroads criss-crossing the continent. They argued that average citizens would invest if they were not personally liable if the venture failed. Of course, neither would the promoters, which is how they became wealthy railroad barons.

If an oil tanker runs aground and spews its noxious cargo over hundreds of miles of pristine beach, the penalties assessed against the corporate owner of the vessel cannot exceed the assets owned by the company, including the invested capital. If these assets are not enough to pay all claims against the company, no one can collect any additional money from individual shareholders, including the billionaire shipping tycoon, who owns the majority of the shares.

As Dean Baker points out, if the shipping company had been merely a partnership between the tycoon and his allies, and not a corporation with shareholders, the individuals would have been "personally liable for making good on contractual commitments they had made and the damage they had caused."[68] The tycoon might be forced to surrender his mansion, his racehorses and yachts, and his bank accounts—if they could be located—to pay off the debts resulting from his business operations. It takes a "conservative nanny state," Baker charges, "to create an institution like a corporation, that allows investors to cause harm and not be held accountable."

But the greatest corporate coup was the co-opting of the Fourteenth Amendment to the U.S. Constitution. This amendment was enacted after the Civil War and adopted in 1868 to guarantee all persons "due process" and "equal protection of law." It was intended to protect the rights of newly freed field slaves, but ended up empowering corporations. Real persons had to pay taxes only on the residual value of their property, after mortgages were deducted. Railroad companies, in contrast, had to pay taxes on the fully assessed value of their holdings. If they could be treated the same as real persons, they could deduct the value of bonds issued by the company. These bonds often exceeded the company's assets, so the railroad company would end up paying little or no tax.

Fourteenth Amendment protection for their corporations was the Holy Grail sought by the railroad barons. They found their Sir Galahad in the unlikely guise of Stephen J. Field, a California railroad lawyer. Field was elected to the California Supreme Court thanks to their efforts. Later, they convinced Abraham Lincoln to nominate Field to the U.S. Supreme Court. Field proposed a new interpretation of the Fourteenth Amendment, not as a protective shield for freed slaves but as one for corporate and property interests. This doctrine was first applied in the famous 1886 case *Santa Clara County v. Southern Railroad Company*, which allowed the railway company to be treated as a person for tax purposes. The decision quickly became a precedent used by activist conservative judges to promote the startling proposition that corporations are persons, guaranteed equal protection of law and due process.

Fourteenth Amendment protection, limited liability and general charters of incorporation opened the floodgates to a wave of acquisitions at the turn of the twentieth century and the emergence of a handful of large, politically powerful corporations. Today, corporations are huge and immensely powerful, not because of free market magic, but because activist legislators and judges allowed corporations to become huge and immensely powerful. And with their power and money, corporations have lavishly funded the market fundamentalists to ensure they, the corporations, stay huge and powerful.

Business and its market-fundamentalist supporters may have the upper hand, but progressives are mounting many successful challenges in the war of ideas.[69] In Canada, fragments of a progressive counter-structure already exist. They include a handful of foundations that support organizations fighting the war of ideas, multi-issue and single-issue think-tanks and advocacy organizations advancing their issues, networks of progressive scholars in academic institutions across the country who are producing dozens of useful books and studies, strategies for ensuring progressive studies receive at least some attention in the corporate media, plus an ever-widening reach through progressive and critical Internet web sites.

All of this is to the good, but it is important to recognize that the progressive world is inhabited mainly by identity-based and single-issue organizations with narrowly focused, often short-term, goals. To challenge market fundamentalism, progressives need to create a single movement, or at least come together on common campaigns, as Grover Norquist was able to achieve with a plethora of conservative organizations. Acting together occurs, but rarely. How can there be a unified voice for a progressive future when not even specific sectors can speak with one voice? The environmental sector, for instance, comprises scores of environmental NGOs across Canada. Then there are other organizations and individuals working to improve, enhance or protect the environment, such as the occupational health and environmental committees of trade unions. These might someday comprise an environmental movement, but today they don't speak with one voice to counter the anti-regulation, pro–property rights messages of big business. And that's only the environmental sector. Other movements, such as women's, social justice and Aboriginal rights, have similar problems in speaking with one voice or forging broad strategies. They are often at odds with one another.

Progressives can learn from Norquist's success in balancing the distinct parts of the "center-right coalition," as he calls it. "Conservatives love to fight with each other," says Richard Lessner, executive director of American Renewal, the lobbying arm of the Family Research Council and a regular attendee at Norquist's Wednesday meetings. "What Grover's brought to the movement is to say, 'Let's find the things we can work on.'"[70] Progressives need to emulate Norquist. "If we help you fight the Trade, Investment and Labour Mobility Agreement between B.C. and Alberta, then you will need to pitch in with our toxins campaign," might be one conversation among progressive organizations.

Two values can help bring these widely disparate groups, sectors and movements together: a hostility to unbridled corporate power and a desire for justice. They are the opposite of the values espoused by market fundamentalists: a hostility to government and a desire for corporate freedom. Progressive values fit well together, coalescing around a desire to progress towards a more just society, one in which corporate power is reined in to serve the public good.

Business has become too powerful and out of control. Even *BusinessWeek* asked in a major feature in 2000, "Too much corporate power?" as business forces its way into more corners of social life.[71] A poll commissioned by the magazine found that 72 percent of Americans said business "has gained too much power over too many aspects of their lives." Surprisingly to the *BusinessWeek* editors, respondents seemed to agree with the sentiment expressed at the 2000 Democratic convention, when presidential nominee Al Gore declared that Americans must "stand up and say no" to "Big Tobacco, Big Oil, the big polluters, the pharmaceutical companies, the HMOs."[72]

Opposition to corporate power can draw many progressive sectors together. Anti-poverty organizations focus much of their attention on governments and their meagre welfare rates, inadequate health and immigration policies and social services, but they also confront private sector employers, the corporate-controlled food production and distribution system and the corporate-controlled housing market. Environmental groups fight corporate-controlled resource exploitation and the ability of corporations to offload their costs onto the environment. When the enemy is government, it is usually a government unduly influenced by corporate power. Progressive trade unions need to be brought into this conversation. They have a proven track record over many decades of resisting corporate power and promoting the interests of their members and the communities in which their members live and work.

In Canada and the United States, corporate power and the free market were reined in after the Second World War by the dictates of the mixed economy. Market forces can do some things well, but not everything, writes Robert Kuttner, author of *Everything for Sale*. "Government intervened to promote development, to temper the market's distributive extremes, to counteract its unfortunate tendency to boom-and-bust, to remedy its myopic failure to invest too little in public goods, and to invest too much in processes that harmed the human and natural environment," Kuttner explains.[73] The mixed economy that operated between the end of the Second World War and the early 1970s produced unprecedented growth and prosperity. Business, perhaps reluctantly, agreed to participate in this large-scale experiment in worker–capital–citizen cooperation. But when profits eroded, business sought to regain the upper hand, particularly through the propaganda system documented in this book. The democratic state and the trade union movement were the prime counter-weights to business domination, which is the reason that corporate propaganda attacked government so relentlessly and ferociously. It attacked unions with the same ferocity and turned its guns on environmentalists, feminists and other so-called special interests as well. The weaker government becomes, the less it is able to achieve and the more powerful corporate rule becomes.

One goal for progressives is to restore the credibility and reputation of government and the mixed economy. Reduce corporate power and replace it with a market-based system that operates in areas of the economy where markets have produced positive outcomes, such as supermarkets, consumer goods and services and raw materials. Regulate industries like banking that cannot act as pure markets. Add social and non-profit enterprise and reinforce government enterprise in areas of society and the economy where it has proven to produce socially beneficial results, such as health care, social housing and public infrastructure.

Along with a belief in the mixed economy and a suspicion of corporate power, a desire for justice—economic, social, environmental—unites progressives. The idea of justice can be simple or so complex that only highly trained philosophers can comprehend its intricacies. But the basic outline is easy to understand. In common usage, justice means "fair or impartial treatment and due reward based on honour, standards and law."[74]

American philosopher John Rawls, who died in 2002, provides a rationale for why justice is the most important value in society. His complex theory has been summarized in three words: "justice as fairness." Rawls favoured a society that is designed to help the less fortunate. His concern was with the rules of the game: the ways in which society is organized around a set of fair rules. Once the rules are established, people can then set about freely playing the game, without interference.[75] "Rawls's view is that justice demands 'maximum equal liberty' and a distribution of economic benefits which makes the least favoured person as well off as possible."[76] This is the "maximin" conception of justice, which concentrates on maximizing the minimum benefit.

As might be expected, Rawls was attacked by libertarians such as Robert Nozick and Friedrich Hayek. They argued that justice is not a matter of how benefits are distributed, but of protecting individual rights to resources. Hayek called social justice a "chimera." Appeals to social justice imply that the state has the right and duty to distribute goods and opportunities as it sees fit. This, Hayek claims, is incompatible with individual liberty, which requires that we should be able to use what is ours as we want.[77] Hayek sets up a straw man and proceeds to tear him down. Claiming that justice as fairness is nothing more than an effort by faceless bureaucrats to dole out favours to (probably) friends and supporters is a gross distortion of notions of community and public good. Can the society described by Hayek be considered just when "some people control the potential of others, control how that potential develops over time, privately appropriate[s] the surplus created in social production, and appl[ies] that surplus to restructure work, communities and future opportunities?" asks academic and former union researcher Sam Gindin. He describes the absolute lack of justice in the libertarian-neoliberal ideology: ". . . the economic freedom capitalism embodies involves guaranteeing *different* kinds of freedom for *different* people."[78] The libertarian concept of (non-) justice should be odious to progressives and should help them unite around a positive ideal, assisting in the creation of a progressive movement. Each sector—environmental, social justice, health care, women, Aboriginals—has its own way of seeing the world. But each holds a concept of justice as a defining value or goal.

There's one final requirement for a unified, effective progressive movement: such a goal cannot be achieved unless the logic changes about how progressive ventures are funded. Few Canadian foundations engage in the war of ideas. In 2003, private foundations in Canada—those controlled by a family that contributed the bulk of the funds—accounted for only $12 billion in assets, while private foundations in the United States were worth more than $400 billion, far more than the usual 10-to-1 ratio between the two countries. Worse, six of the ten largest Canadian foundations are public or community-based foundations, such as the Vancouver, with $565 million, and Sick Kids, with $470 million. These, and others like the Winnipeg, Calgary, Montreal Jewish and Edmonton foundations, make few, if any, grants to policy organizations of any political stripe. And of the family foundations, many are controlled by members of the corporate elite, so they are likely to be ambivalent towards progressive causes and unreliable supporters of political and social change. Few foundations in Canada provide the long-term strategic support for progressive policy change the way the Donner Foundation funded conservative organizations for more than a decade.

Just as Canadian conservatives learned from their American allies, Canadian progressives can benefit by understanding the problems facing progressive funding in the United States. In 1998, American activist Michael Shuman wrote a provocative article titled "Why do progressive foundations give too little to too many?"[79] The problem, he saw, wasn't that progressives were starved for funding. In fact, foundations that support progressive causes have more money than their conservative counterparts. In 1997, when Shuman wrote his lament, the leading progressive foundation, MacArthur, held assets of $3.3 billion, while the leading conservative foundation, Lynde and Harry Bradley, held just over one-tenth that amount, $460 million. Progressive foundations, Shuman charged, were spending too much of their money "foolishly." Shuman knew of what he was talking. He had completed six years as a director and chief fundraiser for the Institute for Policy Studies (IPS), the oldest and largest progressive multi-issue think-tank. His budget was $1.5 million, while that of the leading conservative think-tank, the Heritage Foundation, was $28 million, resulting in a ratio of about 19 to 1. (In 2006, the IPS brought in $3.3 million, while the Heritage's revenues were $53.8 million, lowering the ratio to 16 to 1.)

Since many foundations were run by members of the corporate elite, Shuman allowed, he wasn't surprised that most didn't open their wallets wide for progressive causes. The MacArthur Foundation was hardly as consistently progressive as Bradley was conservative. Corporations and financiers, it seems, will always be more attracted to conservative causes. Some funders did openly embrace progressives as friends, but they didn't seem to understand they were at war, or didn't care to join the struggle. Instead, they spent their money "on thousands of grassroots groups disconnected from one another and from national politics," Shuman argued. Conservative foundations gave general-support grants to a smaller number of well-chosen think-tanks and advocacy organizations, while progressive ones gave small grants to a large number of specific projects with little public policy impact. This trend has continued since Shuman wrote his article. A 2005 report by the National Committee for Responsive Philanthropy found that the ten best-funded conservative think-tanks received 90 percent of their foundation funding as general operating support, allowing them to use the money as they saw fit. The top ten progressive think-tanks, in contrast, received just 16 percent of their foundation grants as general operating support.[80] And the conservative funders supported their institutions over many years, to allow policy positions to be developed. In contrast, progressive funders gave one-year grants for specific projects and required their grantees to jump through the same hoops year after year.

Shuman complained that progressive foundations specialized in funding organizations engaged in one or few issues, such as the environment or poverty. In contrast, conservatives demonstrated that a successful political movement required building multi-issue organizations. Conservative funders invested heavily in serious intellectual exploration—in books, journals, magazine articles and conferences—without expecting an instant return. Supporting conservative public scholars over the long term enabled them to develop and hone new ideas. Supporting the institutions where the scholars set up shop allowed them to build large, effective marketing departments to promote and disseminate the scholars' work. Such funding enabled radical conservatives "to present a coherent, compelling story about the supposed horribles of Big Government, which most of the American public has now accepted," Shuman wrote.[81] Instead of moving to the centre, as the liberals did, conservatives opted to build institutions big and powerful enough to drag political debate to the right. The result is a battlefield occupied by only one army. The corporate-sponsored blitzkrieg won an easy victory.

Partly as a result of these criticisms, and partly because of the dismal showing by Democrats in the 2004 election, some funders of progressive organizations rethought their strategies. Former Clinton Commerce Department chief of staff Rob Stein developed a PowerPoint presentation dissecting radical-conservative success in building its infrastructure of multi-issue think-tanks, single-issue advocacy organizations, student-recruitment programs, training and support initiatives and media platforms. He showed this to wealthy liberals across the United States and convinced enough of them to start an organization called the Democracy Alliance (DA).[82] In 2005, eighty wealthy donors agreed to contribute one million or more dollars each to fund a network of organizations to challenge conservative domination of the public policy agenda. Funders include billionaires George Soros and Peter Lewis. Taco Bell heir Rob McKay is chair and Anna Burger of the Service Employees International Union (SEIU), co-chair. SEIU, obviously, is not a wealthy liberal, but a union that represents many of the lowest-paid workers in America. Its willingness to join the funding effort indicates the potential broad sweep of the initiative and the role progressive unions could play in turning back the conservative tide. The Democracy Alliance's mission, as outlined by *In These Times* senior editor

Christopher Hayes, is "to build a countervailing force on the left,"[83] thirty years later, to finally engage the enemy. Rob Stein told Hayes that "if we're going to build a movement, there has got to be sustained financial security for our organizations." DA would provide primarily general operating support. And it would fund for the long term, allowing organizations to build their base, which may require a long gestation period. Such grassroots organizing does not produce the immediate short-term results that most funders expect.[84]

But how realistic is it to expect wealthy families to fund the progressive movement? The DA has a difficult and ongoing problem in deciding the purpose of its funding: elect Democrats—usually of the centrist variety—or work for fundamental social and political change. The radical-conservative movement was motivated, in contrast, by class self-interest, as well as ideology. When Richard Mellon Scaife and Joseph Coors began pumping their millions into the first conservative think-tanks, they were assuring their own continued wealth accumulation. These organizations propagandized for reduced taxes, weakened unions and deregulation, all of which put more money in their funders' pockets. Ideology and class interest were one. But when wealthy individuals fund progressives, they must put ideology ahead of self-interest. "Trying to fund an economically progressive movement from a bunch of rich people is a tough sell," Jeff Krehely, research director at the National Committee on Responsive Philanthropy, admitted to Hayes.[85] Big Money can be only part of the solution. Organizations must rely on a diversity of funding sources and, in particular, their members.

Even conservatives have learned to diversify their funding. Many organizations, in fact, are funded largely by their members. Such funding serves a dual purpose: keeping the organization going financially and recruiting new members to expand the funding base. The Heritage Foundation's budget is around $53 million. Only $9.5 million comes from foundations. The bulk of the money—$25.5 million—comes from Heritage's 275,000 individual and corporate members,[86] although the portion provided by corporations is not disclosed.

Progressives in Canada and the United States are reclaiming their grassroots fundraising heritage, but there's a lot of catching up to do: in funding, in framing, in organizing and in creating the necessary broad vision. Canadian progressives could do worse than listen to Dick Martin, a popular Canadian labour leader who died in 2001. Martin started his career as a nickel miner, working under "appalling conditions" for Inco in Thompson, Manitoba. Martin rose through the ranks of the United Steelworkers Union and became head of his local, president of the Manitoba Federation of Labour, and eventually was elected secretary-treasurer of the 2.5-million-member Canadian Labour Congress (CLC), the second-highest position in Canadian labour. Having seen his fellow workers killed on the job too often, Martin's priority was worker health and safety. His efforts resulted in the first union-run occupational health clinic in the country. Reducing the effects of pollution was part of the job. Pollution poisoned workers and communities. Martin came to believe that unions had to work with environmental groups to protect the environment. Social and workplace action were both necessary.

Martin was a realist. From his position in organized labour he could see that corporate executives, the members of the Canadian Council of Chief Executives (then known as the Business Council on National Issues), "have learned about collective action. . . . They have learned to speak with one voice and to back up their demands with corporate action." But Martin bemoaned the fact that "the environment movement . . . does not have a national . . . collective lobby group. That must change," he wrote in 1993, "if . . . [we] want to be truly effective in making positive environmental changes." For Martin, the situation was "environmental anarchy," when what was needed was "one big environmental movement." Martin could have been calling for one big progressive movement: "bringing organization where much chaos exists, revenue where poverty exists, and real political punch where fly-swatting exists."[87] It's not a blueprint on the grand scale of Lewis Powell's 1971 memorandum, but it's a start.

ENDNOTES

Chapter 1

Integration . . . Even Though We Don't Want It

1   "Since Sept. 11: The responses show how terrorism and war have left their mark," *Maclean's*, 31 Dec 2001, 38

2   "Integrate economies, CNR chief advises," *Edmonton Journal*, 15 Dec 2001, H1. See also Paul Tellier, "Integration calls for debate on tough questions facing Canada," speech to the Canadian Railway Club, Montreal, 14 Dec 2001, *Canadian Speeches*, Jan/Feb 2002

3   Tom d'Aquino, "Security and prosperity, the dynamics of a new Canada-United States partnership in North America," presentation to the annual general meeting of the CCCE, Toronto, 14 Jan 2003. Retrieved 15 Dec 2007 from http://www.ceocouncil.ca/publications/pdf/b10f11 c9777f6bcf34fa14e57a594c3c/presentations_2003_01_14.pdf

4   d'Aquino, "Security and prosperity . . ."

5   Charles Davies, "The end of Bay Street," *National Post Business*, May 2002, 46

6   Lawrence Martin, *Pledge of Allegiance*. Toronto: McClelland & Stewart, 1993, 150

7   George Grant, *Lament for a Nation*. Montreal and Kingston: Carleton Library Series, McGill-Queens University Press (1971) 1997, 32

8   Steven Chase, "Deepening recession overshadows stimulus budget," *Globe and Mail*, 6 Mar 2009, A7

9   Alex Carey, *Taking the Risk Out of Democracy*. Urbana, IL: University of Illinois Press, 1997, 18

10   Carey, 20

11   Carey, 21

12   David Laidler and William Robson, "The great Canadian disinflation: The economics and politics of monetary policy in Canada, 1988–1993," C.D. Howe Institute, 1993, 34-35

13   Laidler and Robson, 16

14   "agitprop," Encyclopedia Britannica, 2007. Retrieved 31 Jul 2007 from *Encyclopedia Britannica Online* http://search.eb.com.proxy.lib.sfu.ca/eb/article-9004041

15   Carey, 90

16   Eric Boehlert and Jamison Foser, "Asymmetrical class warfare," Media Matters for America, 27 Feb 2009. Retrieved 24 Mar 2009 from http://mediamatters.org/items/200902270020

17   Boehlert and Foser, "In CNBC host Cramer's 'U.S.S.A:' 'Comrade' Obama is a 'Bolshevik' who is 'taking cues from Lenin,'" Media Matters for America, 4 Mar 2009. Retrieved 24 Mar 2009 from http://mediamatters.org/items/200903040026

18   Linda McQuaig, "Dollarization? Not here, please," *National Post*, 21 Jan 2002, FP 14

19   Martin, 122

20   David Crane, "Threat to independence demands reflection," *Toronto Star*, 5 Sep 2001, BU02

21   Chris Sorensen, "CN to hold annual meeting in U.S. this year," *National Post*, 12 Jan 2006, FP1

22   Patrick White, "A patriotic protest simmers at CN facility," *Globe and Mail*, 9 Jan 2009, A3

23   Canadian National Railway Co., "Management proxy circular," 9 Mar 2001, 11; Paul Kaihla, "Back of the rails," *Maclean's*, 13 Jan 1997, 36-38

24 Sean Silicoff, "Corporate elite takes home a 43% pay rise," *National Post*, 22 May 2001, C1

25 Emmanuel Saez and Michael Veall, "The evolution of high incomes in North America: Lessons from Canadian evidence," *American Economic Review*, Vol 39, Iss 3, June 2005, 841, fn. 16

26 Saez and Veall, 832

27 Jack Mintz, "Government policy and the Canadian advantage," *Canadian Business Economics*. Aug 2000, 6-9; François Vaillancourt and Robert Gagné, "Personal income taxes in Canada: Dissimilarities, redistributive impacts and social policy." *Canadian Tax Journal*, 1999, 927-944

28 Saez and Veall, 836, fig. 2

29 Michael Wolfson and Brian Murphy, "Income taxes in Canada and the United States," *Perspectives*, Summer 2000, 28-31. Statistics Canada, Catalogue no. 75-001-XPE

30 Saez and Veall, 840

31 Jeffrey Simpson, "With Wall Street exposed, will Bay Street get the message?" *Globe and Mail*, 20 Mar 2009, A13

32 Hemispheric Social Alliance, "Lessons from NAFTA: The High Cost of 'Free Trade,'" Ottawa, Canadian Centre for Policy Alternatives, 2003. Retrieved 22 Apr 2005 from http://www.policy-alternatives.ca/documents/National_Office_Pubs/lessons_from_NAFTA.pdf

33 Statistics Canada, "Average total income by economic family types, 1983–2002." 22 Apr 2005. Retrieved 22 Apr 2005 from http://www.statcan.ca/english/Pgdb/famil05a.htm

34 Patrice Martineau, "Federal personal income tax: Slicing the pie," Statistics Canada Publication No. 11-621-MIE No. 24, Apr 2005

35 Alan Alexandroff and Don Guy, "What Canadians have to say about relations with the United States," *CD Howe Backgrounder*, No 73, Jul 2003, 1

36 Alexandroff and Guy, 1

37 Garth Jowett and Victoria O'Donnell, *Propaganda and Persuasion*, 3rd ed. Thousand Oaks, CA: Sage, 1999, 27

38 Victoria O'Donnell and Garth Jowett, "Propaganda as a form of communication," in Ted J. Smith (ed.), *Propaganda: A Pluralistic Perspective.* New York: Praeger, 1989, 61-63

39 Anthony Pratkanis and Elliot Aronson, *Age of Propaganda: The Everyday Use and Abuse of Persuasion.* New York: W.H. Freeman, 1991, 9

40 Carey, 20

41 Terence Qualter, *Opinion Control in the Democracies.* London: Macmillan, 1985, 120-121, 123

42 Linda McQuaig, *Shooting the Hippo*, Toronto: Viking, 1995, 7

43 David Zussman, "What's after NAFTA," Industry Canada Conference on Policy Challenges of North American linkages, Calgary, 21 Jun 2001. Public Policy Forum. Retrieved 19 Dec 2007 from http://www.ppforum.ca/common/assets/speeches/en/whats_after_nafta.pdf

44 Alan Toulin, "Union with U.S. on table: PM's advisor," *National Post*, 29 Jun 2001, A1

45 Drew Fagan, "It's the year 2025. There is no border. Has Canada become the 51st state?" *Globe and Mail*, 16 Mar 2002, F1

46 Prospectus Associates et al., "Canada-U.S. Executive Summit: Economic and Political Relations Under a Bush Administration," Toronto, 5-6 Sep 2001. Retrieved 19 Dec 2007 from http://www.weareyourtype.com/Canada2FUSProgram.pdf

47 Stephen Clarkson, "What's in it for us?" *Globe and Mail*, 6 May 2002, A15

48 Murray Dobbin, *The Myth of the Good Corporate Citizen.* Toronto: Stoddart, 1998, 168-175

49 Martin, 100

50 David Langille, "The Business Council on National Issues and the Canadian state," *Studies in Political Economy*, Autumn 1987, 54

51 Martin, 247

52 Tony Clarke, *Silent Coup: Confronting the Big Business Takeover of Canada.* Canadian Centre for Policy Alternatives, 1997, 21-22

53   George Haynal, in Michael Hart, "Round table on Canada-US free trade: Is it time for round two?" *Canadian Foreign Policy*, Spring 2000, 6

54   Canada. Office of the Registrar of Lobbyists, Lobbyists Registration System, "George Haynal," updated 19 Dec 2007. Retrieved 19 Dec 2007 from https://strategis.ic.gc.ca/

55   Canadian Council of Chief Executives, "Security and prosperity: Toward a new Canada-United States partnership in North America," Jan 2003. Retrieved 19 Dec 2007 from http://www.ceo-council.ca/publications/pdf/716af13644402901250657d4c418a12e/presentations_2003_01_01.pdf; See also Canadian Council of Chief Executives, "The North American Security and Prosperity Initiative: Background, questions and answers," Mar 2003. Retrieved 19 Dec 2007 from http://www.ceocouncil.ca/publications/pdf/326ad94a31327c6a014ddf7347808918/presenta-tions_2003_03_01.pdf

56   Sarah Staples, "Health Canada eases rules on fortified foods," *Ottawa Citizen*, 14 Apr 2004, A4

57   Canada. Parliament. Senate Standing Committee on Foreign Affairs. "Issue 3—Evidence," 12 Feb 2003. Retrieved, 10 Aug 2004 from http://www.parl.gc.ca/37/2/parlbus/commbus/senate/Com-e/fore-e/03evb-e.htm

58   Jack Mintz, "Government policy and the Canadian advantage," *Canadian Business Economics*, Aug 2000, 6-9

59   C.D. Howe Institute, "2002 Annual Report," 1

60   C.D. Howe Institute, "Canada's decision to avoid joining U.S., others in invading Iraq sends 'bizarre' and self-defeating signals: C.D. Howe Institute study," Communiqué, 25 Mar 2003, 2. Retrieved 19 Dec 2006 from http://www.cdhowe.org/pdf/PressReleases/english/commentary _180pr.pdf

61   Wendy Dobson, "Shaping the future of the North American economic space: A framework for action," C.D. Howe Institute Commentary 162, Apr 2002

62   Emily Gilbert, "The inevitability of integration? Neoliberal discourse and the proposals for a new North American economic space after September 11," *Annals of the Association of American Geographers*, Mar 2005, 206. In a later paper, Howe Institute policy analyst Danielle Goldfarb recommends a step-by-step or incremental approach to a customs union. See Danielle Goldfarb, "The road to a Canada-U.S. customs union: Step-by-step or in a single bound?" C.D. Howe Institute Commentary 184, Jun 2003, 23

63   Dobson, 3

64   Samuel Huntington, "The United States," in Michel Crozier, Samuel Huntington and Joji Watanuki, *The Crisis of Democracy: Report on the Governability of Democracies to the Trilateral Commission.* New York: New York University Press, 1975, 113

65   Allan Gotlieb, "Foremost partner: The conduct of Canada-US relations," in D. Carment, F.O. Hampson and N. Hillmer (eds.), *Canada Among Nations 2003: Coping With the American Colossus.* Toronto: Oxford University Press, 2003, 28

66   Wendy Dobson, "What's the big idea, Canada?" *Globe and Mail*, 16 Apr 2002, A15; Shawn McCarthy, "New study proposes 'strategic bargain' with U.S.," *Globe and Mail*, 16 Apr 2002, A11; Drew Fagan, "Big Bang approach to U.S. ties gives each the security they need," *Globe and Mail*, 16 Apr 2002, B16; Wendy Dobson, "Canada must be a continental leader," *National Post*, 16 Apr 2002, A19; Alan Toulin, "'Big ideas' needed to safeguard U.S. trade relations," *National Post*, 16 Apr 2002, A1

67   Michael Bliss, "The end of Canadian nationalism," *National Post*, 29 Sep 2001, A1

68   Grant, 31, 43, 49

69   Michael Bliss, "Is Canada a country in decline?" *National Post*, 30 Nov 2001, A18

70   Stephen Clarkson, "Time to break free (trade)," *Globe and Mail*, 27 Sep 2002, A15

71   Stephen Clarkson, "What Uncle Sam wants," *Globe and Mail*, 2 Dec 2002, A17

72   Drew Fagan, "Is it time for Canadians to think the unthinkable?" *Globe and Mail*, 8 Dec 2000, A19

73 Drew Fagan, "It's time Canada moved ahead of the U.S. tax curve," *Globe and Mail*, 12 Feb 2002, B17

74 Drew Fagan, "Age-old disputes show flaws in current free-trade pact," *Globe and Mail*, 20 Feb 2002, B13

75 Drew Fagan, "It's the year 2025. There is no border. Has Canada become the 51st state?" *Globe and Mail*, 16 Mar 2002, F1

76 Drew Fagan, "Big Bang approach to U.S. ties gives each the security they need," *Globe and Mail*, 16 Apr 2002, B16

77 Drew Fagan, "U.S. learning value of open border," *Globe and Mail*, 23 Apr 2002, B20

78 Don Martin, "From media hack to ministry flack," *National Post*, 19 Oct 2004, A16

79 Terence Corcoran, "Barlow's back, and it feels like 1988," *National Post*, 17 Jun 2004, FP15

80 Canadian Council of Chief Executives, "New frontiers: Building a 21st century Canada-United States partnership in North America," Apr 2004, 4-5. Retrieved 20 Dec 2007 from http://www.ceocouncil.ca/publications/pdf/8502a13cf417d09eab13468e2a7c9f65/New_Frontiers_NASPI_Discussion_Paper_April_2004.pdf

81 Canadian Council of Chief Executives, "New frontiers . . . ," ii

82 Diane Francis, "Business makes up for Ottawa's neglect: CEOs head to Washington to mend fences," *National Post*, 20 Apr 2004, FP3; Barrie McKenna, "Canada-U.S. relations seen getting worse," *Globe and Mail*, 20 Apr 2004, B3

83 Canadian Council of Chief Executives, "Creating a North American community: Chairmen's statement," Independent Task Force on the Future of North America, 14 Mar 2005. Retrieved 20 Dec 2007 from http://www.ceocouncil.ca/en/view/?area_id=1&document_id=396

84 Canadian Council of Chief Executives, "Trilateral security and prosperity partnership will boost jobs and investment, say Canada's CEOs," 23 Mar 2005. Retrieved 20 Dec 2007 from http://www.ceocouncil.ca/en/view/?document_id=402&area_id=7

85 "Harper dresses strategically," *Montreal Gazette*, 1 Apr 2006, B6; Margaret Wente, "In praise of ill-dressed men," *Globe and Mail*, 1 Apr 2006, A23

86 Council of the Americas, "Security and Prosperity Partnership: Meeting with Hon. Carlos Gutierrez, U.S. Secretary of Commerce," Washington, D.C., 15 Mar 2006. Retrieved 20 Dec 2007 from http://www.spp.gov/pdf/SPPSummaryCounciloftheAmericas.pdf

87 Office of the Prime Minister, "The Security and Prosperity Partnership of North America: Next steps," Cancún, Mexico, 31 Mar 2006. Retrieved 20 Dec 2007 from http://news.gc.ca/web/view/en/index.jsp?articleid=204499&keyword=security+and+prosperity&keyword=security+and+prosperity&

88 Canadian Council of Chief Executives, 2

89 Luiza Ch. Savage, "Meet NAFTA 2.0," Macleans.ca, 13 Sep 2006. Retrieved 20 Dec 2007 from http://www.macleans.ca/article.jsp?content=20060911_133202_133202

90 Council of Canadians, "Not counting Canadians: The Security and Prosperity Partnership and public opinion," Ottawa, Apr 2008. Retrieved 23 Apr 2009 from http://www.canadians.org/integratethis/backgrounders/notcounting/Not CountingCanadians.pdf

91 Emily Gilbert, "The inevitability of integration? Neoliberal discourse and the proposals for a new North American economic space after September 11," *Annals of the Association of American Geographers*, Mar 2005, Vol 95, Iss 1, 202-222

92 Gilbert, 208

93 Gilbert, 207

94 Gilbert, 213

95 Michael Hart, "Steer or drift? Taking charge of Canada-US regulatory convergence," C.D. Howe Institute Commentary 229, Mar 2006

96 Michael Livermore, "Should environmentalists fear Cass Sunstein?" *The New Republic*, 12 Jan

2009. Retrieved 23 Apr 2009 from http://blogs.tnr.com/tnr/blogs/environmentandenergy/archive/2009/01/12/should-environmentalists-fear-cass-sunstein.aspx; Jonathan Weisman and Jess Bravin, "Obama's regulatory czar likely to set a new tone," *Wall Street Journal*, 7 Jan 2009. Retrieved 23 Apr 2009 from http://online.wsj.com/article/SB123138051682263203.html

.97　Kelly Patterson, "Canada lowers standards on pesticide use on fruits, vegetables to match U.S. limits," *Ottawa Citizen*, 8 May 2007, A1

98　Frances Russell, "Lumber deal with U.S. cuts our sovereignty," *Winnipeg Free Press*, 4 May 2006, A14

99　Robert Pastor, "The future of North America," *Foreign Affairs*, Jul 2008, Vol 87, No 4, 84-98

100　Canadian Council of Chief Executives, "Economy, Environment and Security: Taking the Canada-United States relationship to a new level," Ottawa, 19 Feb 2009. Retrieved 25 Mar 2009 from http://www.ceocouncil.ca/en/view/?document_id=1319&area_id=7

101　Canada. House of Commons. Standing Committee on Foreign Affairs and International Development, Evidence, 40th Parliament, 2nd Session, 25 Feb 2009. Retrieved 23 Apr 2009 from http://www2.parl.gc.ca/HousePublications/Publication.aspx?DocId=3697038&Language=E&Mode=1&Parl=40&Ses=2

102　Canadian Council of Chief Executives, "Canada and the United States must work together to boost free trade and economic recovery, Washington CEO summit participants agree," Washington, D.C., 24 Mar 2009. Retrieved 23 Apr 2009 from http://www.ceocouncil.ca/en/view/?document_id=1336&type_id=1

Chapter 1A
Analyzing the Deep-Integration Campaign

1　Garth Jowett and Victoria O'Donnell, *Propaganda and Persuasion*, 4th ed. Thousand Oaks, CA: Sage, 2006, Chapter 6: "How to analyze propaganda."

2　Philip Resnick, *The European Roots of Canadian Identity*. Peterborough, ON: Broadview Press, 2005, 51

3　Clifford Krauss, "Canada's view on social issues is opening rifts with the U.S.," *New York Times*, 2 Dec 2003, 1

4　Jowett and O'Donnell, 276

5　John Burton, "Communicating the idea of a free society—Overview: The nature of the message," Mont Pèlerin Society Regional Meeting, 28 Aug–1 Sep 1983, Vancouver. *Fraser Institute Focus*, No. 10, 17

6　Burton, 18

7　Bruce Campbell and Ed Finn, eds., *Living With Uncle: Canada-US Relations in an Age of Empire*. Toronto: James Lorimer, 2006

8　Barbara Yaffe, "Who's afraid of the big, bad, bilateral bogeyman?" *Vancouver Sun*, 31 Oct 2006, A13

9　Brian Laghi, "Canadians turning more sour on U.S.," *Globe and Mail*, 29 Mar 2006, A1

Chapter 2
The Propaganda Century

1　T.H. Marshall, "Citizenship and social class," in *Class, Citizenship and Social Development*. New York: Doubleday, 1965, 78-79

2　Albert O. Hirschman, *The Rhetoric of Reaction*. Cambridge, MA: Belknap Press of Harvard University Press, 1991, 3; See also Albert Hirschman, "Reactionary rhetoric," *Atlantic Monthly*, May 1989, 63; Albert O. Hirschman, "Two hundred years of reactionary rhetoric: The case of the perverse effect," The Tanner Lecture on Human Values, University of Michigan, 8 Apr 1988. Retrieved 21 Oct 2007 from http://www.tannerlectures.utah.edu/lectures/documents/hirschman89.pdf

3   Paul Johnson, *Napoleon*. New York: Viking Penguin, 2002, 46

4   Michael Kennedy, "The 'last stand' of the Jacobin clubs," *French Historical Studies*, Fall 1989, Vol 16, No. 2, 309

5   Harvey Chisick, "Pamphlets and journalism in the early French Revolution," *French Historical Studies*, Fall 1988, Vol 15, No 4, 624

6   Andy McDonald and Lene Palmer, "Propaganda: The invention of printing and its aftermath," George Mason University, 15 Dec 2003. Retrieved 29 March 2009 from http://mason.gmu.edu/~amcdonal/Printing%20and%20Its%20Aftermath.html

7   Wayne Hanley, *The Genesis of Napoleonic Propaganda, 1796–1799*. New York: Columbia University Press, 2005, xiv; see also Robert Holtman, *Napoleonic Propaganda*. Louisiana State University Press, 1950

8   Hirschman, 20

9   Alex Carey, *Taking the Risk Out of Democracy*. Urbana, IL: University of Illinois Press, 1997, 29

10 Carey, 31

11 David Vogel, *Fluctuating Fortunes*, New York: Basic Books, 1989, 114

12 Carey, 89

13 Lewis Powell, "Attack of American free-enterprise system," Confidential memorandum, 23 Aug 1971. Retrieved 23 Oct 2007 from http://www.mediatransparency.org/story.php?storyID=22

14 Stanley Cunningham, *The Idea of Propaganda*. New York: Praeger, 2002, 13

15 Carey, 20

16 Garth Jowett and Victoria O'Donnell, *Propaganda and Persuasion*, 4th ed. Thousand Oaks, CA: Sage, 2006, 7

17 Terence H. Qualter, *Opinion Control in the Democracies*. London: Macmillan, 1985, 124

18 George Lakoff, *Don't Think of an Elephant*. White River Junction, VT: Chelsea Green, 2004, 100

19 Jowett and O'Donnell, 2; Anthony R. Pratkanis and Elliot Aronson, *Age of Propaganda: The Everyday Use and Abuse of Persuasion*. New York: Freeman & Co., 1992, 9; Cunningham, 15

20 Andy McDonald and Lene Palmer, "Propaganda: Roots of propaganda," George Mason University, 15 Dec 2003. Retrieved 29 Mar 2009 from http://mason.gmu.edu/~amcdonal/Roots%20of%20Propaganda.html

21 Niccolò Machiavelli, *The Prince*, (G. Bull, trans.). Harmondsworth, UK: Penguin, 1961, 55-56 (original work published 1513), quoted in Jowett and O'Donnell, 42

22 Machiavelli, 19, quoted in Jowett and O'Donnell, 41

23 Cunningham, 17-18

24 Kevin Robins, Frank Webster and Michael Pickering, "Propaganda, information and social control," in Jeremy Hawthorn (ed.), *Propaganda, Persuasion and Polemic*. London: Edward Arnold, 1987, 6

25 Robins, Webster and Pickering, 5

26 Hirschman, 23

27 Hirschman, 24

28 Quoted in Stuart Ewen, *PR!: A Social History of Spin*. New York: Basic Books, 1996, 66

29 Ewen, 64

30 Ewen, 68

31 Ewen, 69

32 Ewen, 34

33 Simon Singh, "The Zimmermann telegram," *The Independent*, 21 Apr 2007. Retrieved 30 Mar 2009 from http://www.simonsingh.com/Zimmermann_Telegram.html

34 See Ewen, 108-127

35 Stewart Halsey Ross, *Propaganda for War*, McFarland, 1996, 225-227; George Creel, *How We Advertised America*. New York: Arno Press, 1972

36   Walter Lippmann, *The Phantom Public*. New York: Harcourt Brace, 1925, 189-190, quoted in Robins, Webster and Pickering, 14

37   Robins, Webster and Pickering, 14

38   Ewen, 77-78

39   Andrew Lohrey, "Introduction," in Alex Carey, *Taking the Risk Out of Democracy*, 1; Antony Sutton, *Wall Street and the Rise of Hitler*. Sudbury, UK: Bloomfield Books, 1975, 29-30

40   Edward Bernays, "The theory and practice of public relations: A resume," in Edward Bernays, (ed.), *The Engineering of Consent*. Norman, OK: University of Oklahoma Press, 1955, 5

41   Edward Bernays, *Propaganda*, 37, 93-94, 112, 159, cited in Cunningham, *The Idea of Propaganda*, 22

42   Ewen, 167

43   John Stauber and Sheldon Rampton, *Toxic Sludge is Good for You*. Monroe, ME: Common Courage Press, 1995, 25

44   Ewen, 34

45   Ewen, 166

46   Carey, 81-82

47   Quoted in Carey, 82

48   Margaret Duffy, "There is no two-way symmetric about it: A postmodern examination of public relations textbooks," *Critical Studies in Media Communication*, Sep 2000, 294

49   Duffy, 302

50   Duffy, 296

51   Ewen, 358-359

52   Ewen, 366-368

53   Quoted in Cunningham, 110

54   Cunningham, 110

55   Stanley Cunningham, "Smoke and mirrors: A confirmation of Jacques Ellul's theory of information use in propaganda," in Ted J. Smith (ed.), *Propaganda: A Pluralistic Perspective*. New York: Praeger, 1989, 152

56   Jowett and O'Donnell, 16

57   Jowett and O'Donnell, 17-19

58   Jowett and O'Donnell, 20

59   "Hey, a health debate!" *Globe and Mail*, 15 Apr 2005, A12

60   For a description of the ads see Cunningham, "Smoke and mirrors," 155

61   Cunningham, "Smoke and mirrors," 156

62   Cunningham, "Smoke and mirrors," 162

63   James Shanahan, *Propaganda Without Propagandists?* Cresskill, NJ: Hampton Press, 2001, 8, quoting C. Simpson, *Science of Coercion*. New York: Oxford University Press, 1994, 25

64   J. Michael Sproule, "Propaganda studies in American social science," *Quarterly Journal of Speech*, Vol. 73, 1987, 70

65   Shanahan, 8-9

66   Larry Tye, *The Father of Spin*. Crown, 1998

67   Marilyn Harris, "The high priest of hype," *BusinessWeek*, 17 Aug 1998, 13

68   Jowett and O'Donnell, 3

69   J. Michael Sproule, *Propaganda and Democracy*. Cambridge University Press, 1997, 267

70   Sproule, 265-266

71   Edward Herman, "The propaganda model revisited," *Monthly Review*, Jul/Aug 1996, 116-117

72   Oliver Boyd-Barrett, "Judith Miller, *The New York Times* and the propaganda model," *Journalism Studies*, Vol. 5, No. 4, 2004, 436

73   Stuart Allan, *News Culture*. Buckingham, UK: Open University Press, 1999, 60

74 Colin Sparks, "Extending and refining the Propaganda Model," *Westminster Papers in Communication and Culture*, 2007, Vol 4, No 2, 68-84

75 Howard Kurtz, "When the press outclasses the public," *Columbia Journalism Review*, May/Jun 1994, 31

76 Sparks, 82

77 Herman, 126

78 Byron Dorgan, "The NAFTA debate that never was," *Columbia Journalism Review*, Jan/Feb 1994, 47

79 Kurtz, 34

80 Brian Goss, "'All our kids get better jobs tomorrow': The North American Free Trade Agreement in *The New York Times*," *Journalism & Communication Monographs*, Spring 2001, Vol 3, Iss 1, 5

81 Adrian Zupp, "Who runs America: Forty minutes with Noam Chomsky," The Boston Phoenix, 5 Apr 1999. Retrieved 30 Aug 2006 from http://weeklywire.com/ww/04-05-99/boston_feature_3.html

82 Sut Jhally, "Advertising at the edge of the apocalypse," Department of Communication, University of Massachusetts at Amherst, 2001. Retrieved 7 Nov 2007 from http://www.sutjhally.com/articles/advertisingattheed/

83 See Chevron U.S.A., "Caring about the environment," 2007. Retrieved 8 Nov 2007 from http://www.chevron.com/products/learning_center/history/topic/advertising/pg4.asp; ExxonMobil, "Save the Tiger Fund conservation timeline," 2007. Retrieved 8 Nov 2007 from http://www.savethetigerfund.org/Content/NavigationMenu2/WhoWeAre/Timeline/default.htm

84 Kenny Bruno, "Shell: clouding the issue," CorpWatch, 15 Nov 2000. Retrieved 8 Nov 2007 from http://www.corpwatch.org/article.php?id=218

85 CorpWatch, "Greenwash fact sheet," 22 Mar 2001. Retrieved 8 Nov 2007 from http://www.corpwatch.org/article.php?id=242

86 Stanley Reed, "BP to Washington: Time's up," *BusinessWeek*, 11 Jun 2001, 62

87 Carey, 21

88 Toby Harnden, "Israel sends bus blown up by suicide bomber to Hague," *National Post*, 10 Feb 2004, A15

89 Terence Corcoran, "An epic struggle of good and evil," *National Post*, 6 Aug 2004, FP13

90 Peter Foster, "Khadrs at the gate," *National Post*, 14 Apr 2004, FP19

91 Terence Corcoran, "Big screen lies," *National Post*, 27 Jan 2004, FP11

92 Mark Achbar and Terence Corcoran, "Achbar v. Corcoran over *The Corporation*," *National Post*, 16 Feb 2004, FP15

93 Jonathan Kay, "An anti-corporate snuff film," *National Post*, 6 Feb 2004, A16

94 Gillian Cosgrove, "Nancy called Mulroney before Reagan's death," *National Post*, 11 Jun 2004, A12

95 Gillian Cosgrove, "ROBTv man gets Liberal ad job," *National Post*, 20 Feb 2004, A7

96 Terence Corcoran, "Climate gurus," *National Post*, 15 Apr 2004, FP11

97 Terence Corcoran, "The Reducers—scary!" *National Post*, 8 May 2004, FP11

98 Terence Corcoran, "The broken stick," *National Post*, 13 July 2004, FP11

99 Terence Corcoran, "Schindler's delist," *National Post*, 23 Nov 2004, FP17

100 Terence Corcoran, "A tonne of baloney," *National Post*, 9 Dec 2004, FP15

101 Peter Foster, "Green Adscam," *National Post*, 23 Jun 2004, FP15

102 Peter Foster, "TransAlta's latest deal is hog manure," *National Post*, 28 Aug 2004, FP11

103 Ross Gelbspan, *Boiling Point: How Politicians, Big Oil and Coal, Journalists, and Activists are Fueling the Climate Crisis—and What We Can Do to Avert Disaster*. New York: Basic Books, 2004

104 *Fontana Dictionary of Modern Thought*, 2nd ed., London: Fontana Press, 1988, 807

105 Terence Corcoran, "The Alcan Manifesto," *National Post*, 18 Nov 2005, FP15

106 Terence Corcoran, "How to farm in a police state," *National Post*, 5 Aug 2006, FP15

107   Terence Corcoran, "Wal-Mart's winners," *National Post*, 10 Mar 2005, FP23

108   Terence Corcoran, "Praise God and pass the propaganda," *National Post*, 8 Mar 2005, FP23

109   Peter Foster, "Capitalism is a liberator," *National Post*, 15 Dec 2006, FP17

110   Peter Foster, "Private water: only in the U.K.?—Pity," *National Post*, 4 Oct 2006, FP19

111   Peter Foster, "Hurricane Hugo," *National Post*, 30 May 2007, FP19

112   Alfred Hirschman, *The Rhetoric of Reaction*, 11

113   Hirschman, 11-12

114   Hirschman, 12

115   Hirschman, 12-13

116   Hirschman, 26

117   Margaret Somers and Fred Block, "From poverty to perversity: Ideas, markets and institutions over 200 years of welfare debate," *American Sociological Review*, 2005, Vol 70, 261

118   Fraser Institute, "2007 Annual Report," 4-5. Italics added.

119   John Donohue III and Steven Levitt, "The impact of legalized abortion on crime," *Quarterly Journal of Economics*, May 2001, Vol 116, Iss 2, 379-420. For a response to their critics, see John Donohue III and Steven Levitt, "Measurement error, legalized abortion, the decline in crime: A response to Foote and Goetz (2005)." Jan 2006. Retrieved 1 Apr 2009 from http://pricetheory.uchicago.edu/levitt/Papers/ResponseToFooteGoetz2006.pdf

120   Hirschman, 28

121   Stuart Murray and Hugh Mackenzie, "Bringing minimum wages above the poverty line," Canadian Centre for Policy Alternatives, Mar 2007, 35-6. Retrieved 2 Mar 2008 from http://www.policyalternatives.ca/documents/National_Office_Pubs/2007/minimum_wage_above_poverty_line.pdf

122   Wikipedia, "Minimum wage," 30 Mar 2009. Retrieved 1 Apr 2009 from http://en.wikipedia.org/wiki/Minimum_wage

123   Keith Godin and Neils Veldhuis, "The economic effects of increasing British Columbia's minimum wage," Fraser Institute, 7 Jan 2009, 22. Retrieved 1 Apr 2009 from http://www.fraserinstitute.org/Commerce.Web/product_files/EconomicEffectsBCMinimumWage.pdf

124   Somers and Block, 277

125   Charles Murray, *Losing Ground: America's Social Policy, 1950–1980*. New York: Basic Books, 1984, 9, quoted in Hirschman, 29

126   Somers and Block, 265

127   Quoted in Somers and Block, 279

128   John Woolley and Gerhard Peters, "William J. Clinton, The President's radio address—30 November 1996," The American Presidency Project, University of California at Santa Barbara. Retrieved 1 Apr 2009 from http://www.presidency.ucsb.edu/ws/index.php?pid=52294

129   U.S. Department of Health and Human Services, Administration for Children and Families, "Caseload data," 21 Jan 2009. Retrieved 31 Mar 2009 from http://www.acf.hhs.gov/programs/ofa/data-reports/caseload/caseload_recent.html

130   U.S. Census Bureau, "Historical poverty tables," 28 Aug 2008. Retrieved 31 Mar 2009 from http://www.census.gov/hhes/www/poverty/histpov/histpovtb.html

131   James Mulvale, "Review of Jamie Peck, Workfare States," Guildford Press, 2001, *Canadian Journal of Sociology Online*, Jan-Feb 2002. Retrieved 1 Apr 2009 from http://www.cjsonline.ca/reviews/workfare.html

132   Arthur Kennickell, "Currents and undercurrents: Changes in the distribution of wealth, 1989–2004," Federal Reserve Board, Washington, D.C., 30 Jan 2006. Retrieved 31 Mar 2009 from http://www.federalreserve.gov/Pubs/FEDS/2006/200613/200613pap.pdf

133   Congressional Budget Office, U.S. Congress, "Historical effective tax rates, 1979 to 2005: Supplement with additional data on sources of income and high-income households,"

Washington, D.C., Dec 2008. Retrieved 31 Mar 2009 from http://www.cbo.gov/doc.cfm?index=9884

Chapter 3
American Roots: The Rise of the Corporate Propaganda System

1 Bill Moyers, "The Public Mind: Illusions of News." Princeton NJ: Films for the Humanities and Sciences, 1994

2 Gerard De Groot, "Reagan's Rise," *History Today*, Sep 1995, 34

3 Stuart Ewen, *PR! A Social History of Spin*. New York: Basic Books, 1996, 395

4 Reported in James E. Coombs and Dan Nimmo, *The New Propaganda*. New York: Longman, 1993, 79

5 Ewen, 395-396

6 Bill Boyarsky, *Ronald Reagan: His Life and Rise to the Presidency*. New York: Random House, 1981, 77; Lou Cannon, *Reagan*. New York: G.B. Putnam's Sons, 1982, 93

7 Ewen, 395

8 Anne Edwards, *Early Reagan: The Rise to Power*. New York: Morrow, 1987, 460, 475; Michael Schaller, *Reckoning with Reagan: America and its President in the 1980s*. New York: Oxford University Press, 1992, 10

9 Edwards, 485; Ronald Reagan, *An American Life*. New York: Simon & Schuster, 1990, 139; Schaller, 13-14

10 David Vogel, *Fluctuating Fortunes: The Political Power of Business in America*. New York: Basic Books, 1989, 35

11 Vogel, 38

12 Vogel, 59

13 Vogel, 43-44

14 Richard Armstrong, "The passion that rules Ralph Nader," *Fortune*, May 1971, 145

15 Matthew N. Lyons, "Business conflict and right-wing movements," in Amy E. Ansell (ed.), *Unraveling the Right: The New Conservatism in American Thought and Politics*. Boulder, CO: Westview Press, 1998, 87-88

16 Lyons, 88

17 Alex Carey, *Taking the Risk out of Democracy: Corporate Propaganda Versus Freedom and Liberty*. Urbana, IL: University of Illinois Press, 1997, 29

18 A.S. Cleveland, "Some political aspects of organized industry," Harvard University Thesis Collection, Harvard College Library, 1947, quoted in Carey, 28

19 Carey, 30

20 *Harper's Weekly*, Aug 1956, 18-19, italics in original, cited in Peter B. Levy, (ed.), *America in the Sixties—Right, Left and Center*. Westport, CN: Greenwood Press, 1998, 7-8

21 Vogel, 10-11; Sharon Beder, *Global Spin: The Corporate Assault on Environmentalism*. White River Junction, VT: Chelsea Green Publishing, 1998, 16-17

22 Carey, 89

23 Murray Dobbin, *The Myth of the Good Corporate Citizen: Democracy Under the Rule of Big Business*. Toronto: Stoddart, 1998, 166

24 Vogel, 198; Carey, 92-3

25 Brian Friel, "Trust in government on the decline again," *Government Executive*, 13 Jul 1999. Retrieved 18 Feb 2008 from http://www.govexec.com/dailyfed/0799/071399b1.htm

26 Lewis F. Powell, Jr., "Confidential memorandum: Attack of American free enterprise system," 23 Aug 1971. Retrieved 21 Aug 2007 from http://www.mediatransparency.org/story.php?storyID=22

27 Jerry Landay, "The Powell Manifesto: How a prominent lawyer's attack memo changed

America," Mediatransparency.org, 20 Aug 2002. Retrieved 21 Aug 2007 from http://www.mediatransparency.org/story.php?storyID=21

28   Vogel, 101-103

29   Carey, 89

30   Amy Wilentz, "On the intellectual ramparts," *Time*, 1 Sep 1986. Retrieved 20 Aug 2007 from http://www.time.com/magazine/article/0,9171,962189,00.html

31   Robert G. Kaiser and Ira Chinoy, "Scaife: Funding father of the right," *Washington Post*, 2 May 1999, A1

32   Jerry Landay, "Simon said: The neocon hothouse that William Simon built," Mediatransparency.org. Posted 23 June 2004. Retrieved 21 Aug 2007 from http://www.mediatransparency.org/story.php?storyID=19

33   Eric Alterman, "Fighting smart," *Mother Jones*, Jul/Aug 1994, 59-61

34   Ruth Rosen, "Challenge market fundamentalism," TomPaine.com, 5 Feb 2007. Retrieved 5 Feb 2007 from http://www.tompaine.com/print/challenge_market_fundamentalism.php

35   Sasha Lilley, "On neoliberalism: an interview with David Harvey," *Monthly Review*, 19 Jun 2006. Retrieved 21 Aug 2007 from http://mrzine.monthlyreview.org/lilley190606.html

36   Sharon Beder, *Free Market Missionaries: The Corporate Manipulation of Community Values.* London: Earthscan, 2006, 94

37   Greg Grandin, "Milton Friedman and the economics of empire," *Counterpunch*, 17 Nov 2006. Retrieved 22 Aug 2007 from http://www.counterpunch.org/grandin11172006.html

38   Grandin

39   Bill Van Auken, "Mourning for Pinochet—US establishment shows its affinity for fascism," Global Research, 12 Dec 2006. Retrieved 28 Dec 2007 from http://www.globalresearch.ca/index.php?context=va&aid=4145

40   James Gwartney and Robert Lawson, *Economic Freedom of the World: 2007 Annual Report,* Fraser Institute, 4 Sep 2007. Retrieved 28 Dec 2007 from http://www.fraserinstitute.org/commerce.web/publication_details.aspx?pubID=4872

41   John Ranelagh, *Thatcher's People: An Insider's Account of the Politics, the Power, and the Personalities.* London: HarperCollins, 1991, ix.

42   Grandin

43   Grandin

44   Grandin

45   Atlas Economic Research Foundation, "How did Atlas start?" 2006. Retrieved 22 Aug 2007 from http://www.atlasusa.org/V2/main/page.php?page_id=319

46   Jean Stefancic and Richard Delgado, *No Mercy: How Conservative Think Tanks and Foundations Changed America's Social Agenda.* Philadelphia: Temple University Press, 1996, 68

47   Shadia Drury, *The Political Ideas of Leo Strauss*, updated ed. Palgrave Macmillan, 2005, xi

48   Earl Shorris, "Ignoble liars: Leo Strauss, George Bush and the philosophy of mass deception," *Harper's Magazine*, Jun 2004, 68

49   Drury, xiii

50   Shadia Drury, *Leo Strauss and the American Right*, New York: St. Martin's Press, 1999, 12

51   Shadia Drury, quoted in Jim Lobe, "Strong must rule the weak, said neo-cons' muse," CommonDreams.org News Center, 8 May 2003. Retrieved 22 Aug 2007 from http://www.commondreams.org/headlines03/0508-02.htm

52   Anne Norton, *Leo Strauss and the Politics of American Empire.* New Haven, CN: Yale University Press, 2004, 178-179. See also Drury, *Leo Strauss*, 27-28

53   Norton, 178

54   Quoted in Gary Dorrien, *The Neoconservative Mind: Politics, Culture and the War of Ideology,* Philadelphia: Temple University Press, 1993, 102

55 Dorrien, 68

56 Dorrien, 69

57 Dorrien, 8

58 Eric Alterman, "Neoconning the media: A very short history of neoconservatism," Media Transparency, 22 Apr 2005. Retrieved 16 Feb 2006 from http://www.mediatransparency.org/story/printerfriendly.php?storyID=2. See also Dorrien, *The Neoconservative Mind*, 100

59 Dorrien, 101

60 Dorrien, 101, fn.103

61 American Enterprise Institute, "2008 Annual Report," 5 Dec 2008, 45. Retrieved 2 Apr 2009 from http://www.aei.org/docLib/20081205_2008AnnualReportweb.pdf

62 David Weigel, "Conservative think tank adjusts to tough times," *Washington Independent*, 13 Mar 2009. Retrieved 2 Apr 2009 from http://washingtonindependent.com/33697/conservative-think-tank-adjusts-to-tough-times

63 George W. Bush, "President discusses the future of Iraq," The White House, 26 Feb 2003. Retrieved 27 May 2009 from http://georgewbushwhitehouse.archives.gov/news/releases/2003/02/20030226-11.html

64 Taken from Media Transparency, "Conservative movement moves in," mediatransparency.org, n.d. Retrieved 2 Sep 2007 from http://www.mediatransparency.org/story.php?storyID=20

65 Oliver Boyd-Barrett, "Judith Miller, the *New York Times*, and the propaganda model," *Journalism Studies*, Vol 5, No 4, 2004, 435-449; Jude Wanniski, "Judith Miller, warhawk reporter," wanniski.com, 23 Jul 2003. Retrieved 30 Dec 2007 from http://www.wanniski.com/showarticle.asp?articleid=2776; Ahmed Amr, "Judith Miller's dirty little secret," Media Monitors Network, 7 Aug 2005. Retrieved 30 Dec 2007 from http://usa.mediamonitors.net/content/view/full/17512

66 Think Progress, "The architects of war: Where are they now?" Retrieved 2 Sep 2007 from http://thinkprogress.org/the-architects-where-are-they-now/

67 Leon Hadar, "The surge scam: getting rid of the goat," IRC Right Web, 12 Sep 2007. Retrieved 16 Sep 2007 from http://rightweb.irc-online.org/rw/4541

68 National Committee for Responsive Philanthropy, "Axis of ideology: Conservative foundations and public policy," Mar 2004, 19

69 Stefancic and Delgado, 53

70 Jane Mayer, "Politics 84—Heritage Foundation: right-wing thinkers push ideas," *Wall Street Journal*, 7 Dec 1984, 1

71 Stefancic and Delgado, 53

72 Stefancic and Delgado, 53

73 Heritage Foundation, "2006 Annual Report," 22. Retrieved 18 Aug, 2007 from http://www.heritage.org/About/upload/AnnualReport06.pdf

74 James Allen Smith, *The Idea Brokers: Think Tanks and the Rise of the New Policy Elite*. New York: Free Press, 1991, 19

75 Deroy Murdock, "William Simon: hero of the revolution," *National Review Online*, 5 Jun 2000. Retrieved 19 Aug 2007 from http://article.nationalreview.com/?q=MzU4OWUxYjg1OTk3ZTFmMjI5NjhjNjQ1NWJjMjJjYTE=

76 John Miller, "The very foundation of conservatism," *New York Times*, 28 Nov 2005, A19

77 People for the American Way, "Buying a movement: Right-wing foundations and American politics," 1996, 14. Retrieved 16 Sep 2007 from http://www.pfaw.org/pfaw/dfiles/file_33.pdf

78 Lawrence Soley, "Heritage clones in the heartland," *Extra*, Sep-Oct 1998. Retrieved 7 Sep 2007 from http://www.fair.org/index.php?page=1430

79 Soley, 92

80 National Committee for Responsive Philanthropy, 14, table 3

81 Norton, 11-12

82   Ira Chinoy and Robert Kaiser, "Decades of contributions to conservatism," *Washington Post*, 2 May 1999, A25

83   Karen Rothmyer, "Unindicted co-conspirator?" *The Nation*, 23 Feb. 1998, 19-20

84   Rothmyer, 19

85   Eric Alterman, "The 'right' books and big ideas," *The Nation*, 22 Nov. 1999, 17

86   James Allen Smith, 182

87   Media Transparency, "John M. Olin Foundation, Inc. grant recipients," n.d. Retrieved 17 Sep 2007 from http://www.mediatransparency.org/recipientsoffunder.php?funderID=7

88   William Harms, "Olin Center offers last conference on 'Empire and Liberty,'" *Chicago Chronicle*, 28 Apr 2005. Retrieved 19 Aug 2007 from http://chronicle.uchicago.edu/050428/olin.shtml; John M. Olin Center for Inquiry into the Theory and Practice of Democracy, "About the Olin Center," 2 Jan 2000. Retrieved 19 Aug 2007 from http://olincenter.uchicago.edu/about_olin.html

89   National Committee for Responsive Philanthropy, 44-45

90   Sally Covington, "How conservative philanthropies and think tanks transform US policy," *Covert Action Quarterly*, Winter 1998, 7-8

91   Ari Berman, "The social security sham," *The Nation*, 18 Nov 2004. Retrieved 7 Apr 2009 from http://www.thenation.com/blogs/outrage/2015/the_social_security_sham

92   Media Transparency, "Cato Institute," n.d. Retrieved 3 Apr 2009 from http://mediatransparency.org/recipientprofile.php?recipientID=51'; Cato Institute, "Cato Social Security Choice Papers," n.d. Retrieved 3 Apr 2009 from http://www.cato.org/pubs/ssps/sspstudies.html

Chapter 4
Building the Infrastructure: The 1970s and the 1980s

1   Lorne Gunter, "An evening with premiers, past, present and future," *National Post*, 16 Oct 2004, A13

2   Tom Olsen, "Take up health battle, Harris tells Klein," *Calgary Herald*, 14 Oct 2004, A6

3   CBC News, "Klein leads tribute to Fraser Institute," Calgary, updated 13 Oct 2004. Retrieved 19 Sep 2007 from http://www.cbc.ca/canada/calgary/story/2004/10/13/ca_fraser20041013.html

4   CBC News

5   Fraser Institute, "A salute to the Fraser Institute: 30 years of influential ideas," 12 Oct 2004. Retrieved 19 Sep 2007 from http://www.fraserinstitute.ca/admin/events/files/Invitation.pdf

6   "Yesterday's 'right wing' is today's norm," *The Province*, 14 Oct 2004, A20; reprinted as "Daring to dissent," *Ottawa Citizen*, 14 Oct 2004, A16; "Fraser Institute was right for 30 years," *Windsor Star*, 25 Oct 2004, A7

7   Gunter

8   Bruce Foster, "Rural Calgary," *Globe and Mail*, 10 May 2002, A16. See also Trevor Harrison, *Of Passionate Intensity: Right-Wing Populism and the Reform Party of Canada*. Toronto: University of Toronto Press, 1995, 30-31

9   This section is based partially on Donald Gutstein, "Corporate advocacy: The Fraser Institute," *City Magazine*, Sep 1978, 32-39

10   Murray Dobbin, quoted in Brooke Jeffery, *Hard Right Turn*. Toronto: HarperCollins, 1999, 420

11   Fraser Institute, "Challenging perceptions: Twenty-five years of influential ideas," 1999, 2

12   Jeffery, 421

13   Fraser Institute, "The Fraser Institute at 30: a retrospective," 2004, 2. Retrieved 3 Jan 2008 from http://www.fraserinstitute.org/files/PDFs/About_Us/30th_Retrospective.pdf; Fraser Institute, "Income and Expenditure," "Annual Report 1978," 13

14   Patrick Durrant, "Thinking is his business," *The Province*, 23 Jul 1975, 9

15   Fraser Institute, "Annual report 1978," ii

16   Fraser Institute, "The Fraser Institute membership list," 6 Mar 1979, addendum to 1978 Annual Report

17 Murray Dobbin, *The Myth of the Good Corporate Citizen.* Toronto: Stoddart, 1998, 166

18 See, for instance, "George Froehlich Business Editor," *Vancouver Sun,* 5 Jul 1975

19 Herbert Grubel and Michael Walker (eds.), *Unemployment Insurance: Global Evidence of its Effects on Unemployment.* Vancouver: Fraser Institute, 1978, 34

20 Grubel and Walker, 2

21 United States Fire Administration, National Fire Data Center, "Restaurant fires," Oct 2004. Retrieved 19 Sep 2007 from http://www.usfa.dhs.gov/downloads/pdf/tfrs/v4i3.pdf

22 Grubel and Walker, 24

23 John Schreiner, "Getting government out of the marketplace," *Financial Post,* 17 Mar 1979

24 James Dean, "The case for continued controls (and other heresies)," in Michael Walker (ed.), *Which Way Ahead? Canada After Wage and Price Controls.* Vancouver: Fraser Institute, 1977, 227, 226

25 Walker, *Which Way Ahead?,* 233

26 Walter Heller et al., "Economy: Toward a 'carrots' and/or 'sticks' approach." *New York Times,* 12 Mar 1978

27 Albert Hirschman, *The Rhetoric of Reaction.* Cambridge, MA: Belknap Press of Harvard University Press, 1991, 11

28 Walter Block and Michael Walker (eds.), *Discrimination, Affirmative Action, and Equal Opportunity.* Fraser Institute, 1982, xv

29 Block and Walker, xvi

30 Harry Rankin, "Fraser Institute calls shots," *Pacific Tribune,* 14 Sep 1983

31 "Study claims anti-bias laws actually hurt minority groups," *Vancouver Sun,* 21 Jan 1982, A12

32 Richard Gwyn, "Put ideas in the stew and stir up the pot," *Vancouver Sun,* 13 Mar 1982, A7

33 See, for instance, Walter Block and Michael Walker, "Marriage key to gap in wages," *Globe and Mail,* 22 Oct 1985, A7

34 Marianne Tefft, "More freedom through less government," *Globe and Mail,* 21 Jul 1984, 28

35 Harrison, 49; see also Jeffery, 407-408

36 Arthur Drache, "Tax law mutes individual, not corporate voices," *Financial Post,* 6 Jun 1995, 31; Jeffery, 414

37 Harrison, 49

38 Harrison, 50

39 "Alberta Report turns 25," *Alberta Report,* 1 Nov 1999, 3

40 Harrison, 51

41 Paula Simons, "A distinctive Alberta voice is silenced," *National Post,* 24 Jun 2003, A18; "A magazine mourned," *Globe and Mail,* 25 Jun 2003, A16; "Byfield's magazine provided a unique Western voice," *Vancouver Sun,* 26 Jun 2003. A10; "Alberta Report falls silent after 30 years," *Edmonton Journal,* 28 Jun 2003, A18

42 Harrison, 52

43 Sid Tafler, "Pushing the 'right' ideas," *Globe and Mail,* 10 Dec 1983, 8

44 "And that was the beginning of restraint . . ." *New Directions,* Jun/Jul 1985, 10

45 "And that was . . . ," 12-13

46 Tafler

47 Barbara McLintock, "B.C. now home to radical right," *The Province,* 10 Jul 1983, A1

48 Warren Magnusson, "Introduction," in Warren Magnusson et al., *The New Reality: The Politics of Restraint in British Columbia.* Vancouver: New Star Books, 1984, 12

49 Harrison, 54

50 "Walker says fiscal restraint eludes B.C.; intentions right," *Vancouver Sun,* 7 Dec 1983, C9

51 Sandra Christensen, *Unions and the Public Interest.* Vancouver: Fraser Institute, 1980, 56

52 Michael Walker, "The budget by the economist who advised the British Columbia government," *The Province,* 12 Jul 1983, B3

53   "Fraser Institute to be quizzed on rent controls," *Vancouver Sun*, 18 Oct 1983, A18
54   James Pitsula and Kenneth Rasmussen, *Privatizing a Province: The New Right in Saskatchewan*. Vancouver: New Star Books, 1990, 31
55   Pitsula and Rasmussen, 34
56   Pitsula and Rasmussen, 116-117
57   Pitsula and Rasmussen, 120
58   Pitsula and Rasmussen, 118
59   Pitsula and Rasmussen, 139; Mark Stobbe, *The Selling of Saskatchewan*, in Lesley Biggs and Mark Stobbe, (eds.), *Devine Rule in Saskatchewan*. Saskatoon: Fifth House Publishers, 1991, 86
60   Stobbe, 87
61   Pitsula and Rasmussen, 140
62   Stobbe, 88; Pitsula and Rasmussen, 140
63   Pitsula and Rasmussen, 140
64   Stobbe, 88-89; Pitsula and Rasmussen, 142
65   Pitsula and Rasmussen, 142
66   Pitsula and Rasmussen, 177
67   Stobbe, 90; Institute for Saskatchewan Enterprise, *International Privatization: Global Trends, Policies, Processes, Experiences*. Saskatoon, 1990
68   John Schreiner, "Don't bet on Devine rule ending yet," *Financial Post*, 21 Sep 1991, 9
69   Harrison, 34; Murray Dobbin, *Preston Manning and the Reform Party*. Toronto: James Lorimer, 1991, 29-30
70   Harrison, 35-6
71   Dobbin, 49
72   Dobbin, 50
73   Dobbin, 75
74   Frank Dabbs, "Calgary's new right-wing cabal," *Alberta Report*, 24 Sep 1984, 8-9; Harrison, 94-5
75   Harrison, 104
76   *Alberta Report*, 4 Aug 1984
77   Dobbin, 50-51
78   Dobbin, 75
79   Peter C. Newman, *Titans: How the New Canadian Establishment Seized Power*. Toronto: Viking, 1998, 461
80   Newman, 446; Harrison, 107-8; Dobbin, 75
81   Harrison, 108-109; Dobbin, 75-76; Ian Pearson, "Thou shall not ignore the West," *Saturday Night*, Dec 1990, 42
82   Harrison, 111
83   David Laycock, *The New Right and Democracy in Canada*. Don Mills, ON: Oxford University Press, 2001, 10
84   Pearson, 37
85   Laycock, 56
86   Laycock, 57
87   Laycock, 10
88   Dobbin, 91-95, 97-98
89   Jeffery, 413
90   Harrison, 108
91   Maude Barlow, "The NCC: Not national, not citizens and not a coalition," Canada News Wire, 12 Jun 1997
92   Nick Fillmore, "Right stuff: An inside look at the National Citizens Coalition," *This Magazine*, July 1986, 8
93   Jeffery, 409-411; Dobbin, *The Myth . . .*, 202-203

Chapter 5

The Propaganda Machine in Action: The 1990s and Beyond

1   David Rovinsky, "The ascendancy of western Canada in Canadian policymaking," Center for Strategic and International Studies, Washington, D.C., 16 Feb 1998, 2; see also Brian Mulawka, "Go west, young intellectual," *Alberta Report*, 30 Mar 1998, 8

2   Fraser Institute, "Annual Report 2005," 40

3   Rovinsky, 1

4   John Ibbotson, "Educating Stephen: What does the Conservative party's enigmatic leader really stand for?" *Globe and Mail*, 26 Jun 2004, F4

5   Jeet Heer, "Philosopher king," *National Post*, 17 May 2003, A18

6   Ibbotson

7   Marci McDonald, "The man behind Stephen Harper," *The Walrus*, Oct 2004, 36

8   McDonald, 38

9   Austin Bramwell, "Review of Eric Voegelin: The Restoration of Order," *National Review*, 1 Jul 2002, 45-6

10 McDonald, 40

11 Anne Norton, *Leo Strauss and the Politics of American Empire*. New Haven, CN: Yale University Press, 2004, 58

12 Clifford Orwin, "Remembering Allan Bloom," *American Scholar*, Summer 1993, Vol 62, Iss 3, 423-430

13 Bramwell; see also Jonah Goldberg, "Immanent corrections," *National Review Online*, 16 Jan 2002. Retrieved 29 May 2009 from http://article.nationalreview.com/?q=ODQ5Y2ZiNjAzMjdl NDAwMTk2MTgxNGVlYTE1Nzc5YjQ=#more

14 McDonald, 41

15 McDonald, 42

16 McDonald, 42; Suzanne Methot, "Controversial author nabs Donner prize," *Windspeaker*, Jul 2001, 24, 34; see also *Canadian Directory to Foundations and Grants*, 16th ed., 2002, 288

17 Peter Verberg, "Judicial power under scrutiny," *Alberta Report*, 21 Oct 1996, 31

18 Paul Mitchinson, "Calgary neo-cons hunt controversy," *National Post*, 22 Jul 2000, B1

19 American Enterprise Institute, "Walter Berns, resident scholar," 2005. Retrieved 8 Jan 2008 from http://www.aei.org/scholars/scholarID.4/scholar.asp

20 Media Transparency, "Grant search results Walter Berns," 2005. Retrieved 8 Jan 2008 from http://www.mediatransparency.org/

21 Jeremy Rabkin, "Cornell's Public Law Tradition in Political Science," Cornell University College of Arts and Sciences Newsletter, Spring 1995, Vol, 16, No 2. Retrieved 8 Jan 2008 from http://www.arts.cornell.edu/newsletr/spring95/rabkin.htm

22 F.L. Morton and Rainer Knopff, *The Charter Revolution and the Court Party*. Peterborough, ON: Broadview Press, 2000, 152-153

23 Morton and Knopff, 13

24 Morton and Knopff, 25

25 Morton and Knopff, 152

26 Ibbotson

27 McDonald, 43

28 Stephen Harper and Tom Flanagan, "Our benign dictatorship," *Next City*, Winter 1996/97, 34-40, 54-56

29 See Kevin Michael Grace, "Alberta first," *The Report*, 19 Feb 2001, 10-13

30 Morton and Knopff, 10

31 Krishna Rau, "A million for your thoughts," *Canadian Forum*, Jul/Aug 1996, 12

32 Rau, 14

33   Rau, 11; Miro Cernetig, "Neocons: young bucks of the new right," *Globe and Mail*, 5 Feb 1994, D1

34   Sources for these figures are: Rau, 16; Thomas Walkom, "Right-wing causes find a rich and ready paymaster," *Toronto Star*, 25 Oct 1997, E1, and various editions of the *Canadian Directory to Foundations and Grants*

35   Tasha Kheiriddin and Adam Daifallah, "Rescuing Canada's right," *Western Standard*, 8 Nov 2004, 29

36   The mission changed between 1998 and 1999. Compare *Canadian Directory to Foundations and Grants*, 13th ed., 1999, 38 and 12th ed., 1998, 27

37   "A fistful of secret power—and an arms business to prop it up," *The Province*, 4 Feb 1994, A30. The foundation held assets of $78 million in 2005

38   Canadian Revenue Agency, "Qualified Donees—The Garfield Weston Foundation," Charities Listings, Modified 6 Sep 2005. Retrieved 2 Oct 2007 from http://www.cra-arc.gc.ca/ebci/haip/srch/sec/SrchLogin-e?login=true&searchType=Registered; Children First School Choice Trust, "Staff," 2007. Retrieved 2 Oct 2007 from http://www.childrenfirstgrants.ca/main/index.php?pid=2&page_id=166

39   Atlantic Institute for Market Studies, "Board of directors," 2007. Retrieved 1 May 2007 from http://www.aims.ca/aboutaims.asp?cmPageID=90

40   Sherry Stein, "Letter to Martin Broughton regarding research program in emulation of the Social Affairs Unit," British American Tobacco, 28 Jan 2000. Retrieved 6 Jan 2009 from http://legacy.library.ucsf.edu/tid/lbc53a99

41   Michael Walker, "Letter to Adrian Payne regarding centre for studies in risk and regulation," British American Tobacco, 19 June 2000. Retrieved 6 Jan 2009 from http://legacy.library.ucsf.edu/tid/mbc53a99

42   Walker

43   Atlantic Institute for Market Studies, "Brian Lee Crowley," 2007. Retrieved 1 May 2007 from http://www.aims.ca/aboutaims.asp?cmPageID=125

44   Frontier Centre for Public Policy, "FCPP staff," 2007. Retrieved 2 Oct 2007 from http://www.fcpp.org/main/people.php?CategoryID=6

45   Montreal Economic Institute, "Staff," 2005. Retrieved 3 Feb 2006 from http://www.iedm.org/main/authors_en.php?authors_type=2

46   Atlantic Institute for Market Studies, "1997–98 Annual Report," 30 Sep 1998, 22. Retrieved 2 Oct 2007 from http://www.aims.ca/media/documents/ar1998.pdf

47   Gillian Cosgrove, "Laurier Club membership has its privileges," *National Post*, 11 Dec 1999, B11

48   Frontier Centre for Public Policy, "Board of research advisors," 2007. Retrieved 19 Oct 2007 from http://www.fcpp.org/main/people.php?CategoryID=%202

49   Fraser Institute, "2006 Annual Report," 34, 35

50   Kelvin Ogilvie, "From public U to private U," Atlantic Institute for Market Studies, Sep 2005. Retrieved 1 May 2007 from http://www.aims.ca/aimslibrary.asp?ft=1&fd=0&fi=1&id=1195&p=1

51   Jay Bryan, "Is Quebec ready for laissez-faire economics?" *Montreal Gazette*, 30 Mar 1999, D1; Atlantic Institute for Market Studies, "AIMS: About AIMS: Jean-Luc Migue," 19 Oct 2007. Retrieved 19 Oct 2007 from http://www.aims.ca/cm_Print.asp?cmPageID=252

52   Atlantic Institute for Market Studies, "Annual Report, 1996-97," Retrieved 1 May 2007 from http://www.aims.ca/media/documents/ar1997.pdf

53   Fraser Institute, "2007 Annual Report," 38

54   Fraser Institute, "2007 Annual Report," 38

55   Kevin Taft and Gillian Steward, *Clear Answers: The Economics and Politics of For-Profit Medicine*. Edmonton: Duval House Publishers, 2000, 27-33

56 Lynn Spink, "Editor's note," in Lynn Spink (ed.), "Bad work: A review of papers from a Fraser Institute conference on 'right-to-work' laws," York University, Centre for Research on Work and Society, Working paper No. 16, Toronto, 1997, 2. See also, Michael Valpy, "Take that, and that," *Globe and Mail,* 22 Jul 1997, A13

57 Martha MacDonald, "Alberta weighs the evidence," in Spink (ed.), 10

58 David Coates, "Ruling mythologies," in Spink (ed.), 15

59 Sheena Starky, "Tax Freedom Day: a cause for celebration or consternation?" Canada, Library of Parliament, 18 Sep 2006. Retrieved 27 May 2007 from http://www.parl.gc.ca/information/library/PRBpubs/prb0632-e.htm

60 Statistics Canada, "Income tax . . . by the numbers," Statistics Canada, 27 Apr 2009. Retrieved 11 May 2009 from http://www42.statcan.ca/smr08/smr08_129-eng.htm

61 Jeremy Brown, Kenneth Green, Steven Hansen and Liv Fredricksen, "Environmental Indicators," (Sixth Edition). Vancouver: Fraser Institute, Apr 2004, 7

62 Hilda McKenzie and William Rees, "An analysis of a brownlash report," *Ecological Economics,* Mar 2007, Vol 61, Iss 2/3, 506

63 "The great divide," *Economist,* 4 Mar 2004, 38

64 Joe Woodard, "Tax the rich and damn the deficit," *Alberta Report,* 14 Feb 1994, 15-18

65 Lauri Friesen, "The social contract rewritten," *Alberta Report,* 18 Aug 1997, 10

66 Shafer Parker, Jr., "Ottawa, the last obstacle to national unity," *Alberta Report,* 24 Aug 1998, 10

67 Canada West Foundation, "2004 Annual Report," 4

68 Dominion Institute, "About," modified 29 Jun 2007. Retrieved 20 Oct 2007 from http://www.dominion.ca/about.htm

69 John Fraser, ". . . and the rest is history," *National Post,* 6 Jun 2001, B3

70 "The death of history," *Globe and Mail,* 23 Sep 2000, A12

71 Dan Gardner, "Ignorance wrapped in a flag on Canada Day," *Ottawa Citizen,* 3 Jul 1998, A9

72 Dominion Institute, "Passages to Canada: Teachers resource booklet," 2001. Retrieved 20 Oct 2007 from http://www.passagestoCanada.com/PTCeng.pdf

73 National Citizens Coalition, *Consensus,* special edition, 1994. Quoted in Murray Dobbin, *The Myth of the Good Corporate Citizen.* Toronto: Stoddart, 1998, 206

74 Janice Tibbetts, "Supreme Court maintains cap on election spending," *CanWest News,* 18 May 2004, 1

75 Les Sillars, "Somebody get him a white hat," *Alberta Report,* 26 Sep 1994, 10

76 Nick Fillmore, "Right stuff," *This Magazine,* July 1986, 10

77 "NCC refuses to disclose its finances," *Hamilton Spectator,* 17 Aug 1996, A7

78 Colin T. Brown, "Doesn't like NDP," *The Record, Kitchener-Waterloo,* 1 Aug 1991, A4

79 Maude Barlow, "The NCC: Not national, not citizens and not a coalition," Canada News Wire, 12 Jun 1997

80 Fraser Institute, *Frontline,* Sep 2004, 3

81 Fraser Institute, *Frontline,* Feb 2005, 4; See also, Marjorie Cohen, "Neo-cons on campus," *This Magazine,* Jul 1995, 30

82 Fraser Institute, *Fraser Forum,* Jun 1996. Retrieved 21 Oct 2007 from http://oldfraser.lexi.net/publications/forum/1996/june/FF-06-96.html; See also Institute for Humane Studies, "Craig Yirush," no date. Retrieved 1 Mar 2008 from http://www.theihs.org/people/id.762/people.asp

83 Patti Edgar, "A date with the Fraser Institute," *The Martlett,* UVic, 17 Jan 2000. Retrieved 28 Jul 2005 from http://www.peak.sfu.ca/the-peak/2000-1/issue2/fraserinstitute.html

84 See, for instance, "Student essay contest: How can property rights protect the environment? Free-market environmentalism resource guide," Fraser Institute, 2005. Retrieved 15 Jun 2005 from http://www.fraserinstitute.ca/studentcentre/essay.asp?tnav=1&scnav=4

85 Fraser Institute, *Fraser Forum,* Jun 2008, 28

86   Fraser Institute, "Summer internship program 2005: Research projects, 2005." No longer available online

87   Fraser Institute, *Frontline*, Sep 2004, 3

88   Michael Valpy, "The journalist as political player," *Globe and Mail*, 11 Apr 1996, A19; see also James Winter, *Democracy's Oxygen*. Montreal: Black Rose Books, 1997, 79; Doug Saunders, "A party to crash," *This Magazine*, Mar/Apr 1996, 32-3

89   Civitas Society, "Eleventh annual national conference," 4-6 May 2007, Halifax. Retrieved 21 Oct 2007 from http://www.civitassociety.ca/docs/2007_programme_(2_May_07).pdf

90   David Kirkpatrick, "Club of the most powerful gathers in strictest privacy," *New York Times*, 28 Aug 2004, 10

91   Robert Dreyfuss, "Reverend Doomsday," *Rolling Stone*, 28 Jan 2004. Retrieved 10 Apr 2007 from http://www.rollingstone.com/politics/story/5939999/reverend_doomsday/

92   "Full text of Stephen Harper's 1997 speech," Canadian Press, 14 Dec 2005. Retrieved 10 Apr 2007 from http://www.ctv.ca/servlet/ArticleNews/story/CTVNews/20051213/elxn_harper_speech_text_051214/20051214

93   Sheldon Alberts, "Klein backs unite-the-right movement," *National Post*, 27 Oct 1998, A1

94   Elections Canada, "Political Parties Financial Report (Database)," Search by top contributors, fiscal period 2002. Retrieved 9 Jan 2008 from http://www.elections.ca/ecFiscals/fiscalmain.asp?ran=55054.59&objectType=static&action=display&ul=1&year=2000

95   "Stephen Harper: Taking Canada by stealth," *Canada Newswire*, Ottawa, 9 Jun 2004, 1

96   Stephen Harper, "Rediscovering the right agenda," *Citizens Centre Report*, Jun 2003, 73

Chapter 6
Gateway to the Public Mind

1   World Health Organization, "World malaria report 2008: Summary and key points," Geneva, Switzerland, 2008, vii. Retrieved 13 Apr 2009 from http://www.who.int/malaria/wmr2008

2   Elizabeth Nickson, "Green power, black death," *National Post*, 9 Jan 2004, A12

3   Deroy Murdock, "Green imperialists are killing millions," *National Post*, 26 Jan 2004, A12

4   Robert Sopuck, "Eco-imperialism won't save the environment," *National Post*, 28 Dec 2004, A19. See also Paul Driessen, "Eco-imperialism: The greatest threat to Africa's future," 21 Jan 2004. Retrieved 17 Nov 2007 from http://www.eco-imperialism.com/content/article.php3?id=1

5   Margaret Wente, "Bring back DDT: Eco-imperialism is killing African children," *Globe and Mail*, 27 Apr 2004, A19

6   Richard Tren, "EU pesticide ban threatens millions," *Ottawa Citizen*, 19 Jan 2009, A11

7   Knowlton Nash, "This imperfect necessity," *content* magazine, Jan/Feb 1988, 11

8   Sheila Watt-Cloutier, Robert Charlie and John Crump, "We can all win," *Globe and Mail*, 11 Dec 2000, A14

9   United Nations Environment Programme, "Stockholm Convention on POPS to become international law, launching a global campaign to eliminate 12 hazardous chemicals," 14 May 2004. Retrieved 17 Nov 2007 from http://www.pops.int/documents/press/EIF/pr5-04POPsEIF-E.pdf. See also "Governments take decisive action to rid the world of persistent organic pollutants (POPs) through the Stockholm Convention," 6 May 2005. Retrieved 17 Nov 2007 from http://www.pops.int/documents/meetings/cop_1/press/pr5-05POPsCOP1.doc

10   "International public health strategy," Sep 1998. Retrieved 13 Apr 2009 from http://legacy.library.ucsf.edu/tid/xvp83c00

11   Aaron Swartz, "Rachel Carson, mass murderer?" *Extra*, Sep/Oct 2007. Retrieved 13 Apr 2009 from http://www.fair.org/index.php?page=3186

12   GMWatch, "Congress of Racial Equality—CORE," n.d. Retrieved 17 Nov 2007 from http://www.gmwatch.org/profile1.asp?PrId=174&page=C

13 SourceWatch, "Center for the Defense of Free Enterprise," modified 12 Nov 2007. Retrieved 17 Nov 2007 from http://www.sourcewatch.org/index.php?title=Center_for_the_Defense_of_Free_Enterprise

14 Center for the Defense of Free Enterprise, "Economic Human Rights Project," n.d. Retrieved 17 Nov 2007 from http://www.cdfe.org/EHRP.htm

15 SourceWatch, "Committee for a Constructive Tomorrow," modified 6 Oct 2007. Retrieved 17 Nov 2007 from http://www.sourcewatch.org/index.php?title=Committee_for_a_Constructive_Tomorrow

16 Exxonsecrets.org, "Factsheet: Committee for a Constructive Tomorrow," n.d. Retrieved 17 Nov 2007 from http://www.exxonsecrets.org/html/orgfactsheet.php?id=25

17 Kirsten Weir, "Rachel Carson's birthday bashing," Salon.com, 29 June 2007. Retrieved 13 Apr 2009 from http://www.salon.com/news/feature/2007/06/29/rachel_carson

18 Philip Knightley, quoted in Philip Taylor, *War and the Media: Propaganda and Persuasion in the Gulf War.* Manchester, UK: Manchester University Press, 1992, 24

19 James Winter, *Democracy's Oxygen: How Corporations Control the News.* Montreal: Black Rose Books, 1997, 71

20 Quoted in Noam Chomsky, *Necessary Illusions: Thought Control in Democratic Societies.* Toronto: Anansi Press, 2003, 13

21 Canadian Newspaper Association, "Statement of principles," adopted 1977, revised 1995. Retrieved 17 Nov 2007 from http://www.cna-acj.ca/client/cna/cna.nsf/web/StatementofPrinciples?OpenDocument&nLoc=3.6

22 *Abrams v. United States, 1919,* cited in Noam Chomsky, *Necessary Illusions,* 7

23 Canadian Business, "Rich 100," 23 Nov 2008. Retrieved 13 Apr 2009 from http://list.canadian-business.com/rankings/rich100/2008/ranking/Default.aspx?sp2=1&d1=a&sc1=0; John Gray, "Rich 100" Fallen giants," *Canadian Business,* 22 Dec 2008. Retrieved 13 Apr 2009 from http://www.canadianbusiness.com/after_hours/lifestyle_activities/article.jsp?content=20081222_10011_10011

24 Quoted in David Hayes, *Power and Influence: The Globe and Mail and the News Revolution.* Toronto: Key Porter Books, 1992, 52

25 Quoted in James Winter, *Mediathink.* Montreal: Black Rose Books, 2002, xxvi

26 Linda McQuaig, *Shooting the Hippo.* Toronto: Viking, 1995, 12

27 Media members of CCCE, 2007: Michael Sabia (Bell Canada Enterprises: owned CTV, *Globe and Mail*); Leonard Asper (CanWest Global); John M. Cassady (Corus Entertainment); Andre and Paul Desmarais (Power Corp.); Ted Rogers (Rogers Communications); Richard Harrington (Thomson Corp.); Geoffrey Beatty (Woodbridge Co.—Thomson family holding company), Ian Greenberg (Astral Media)

28 Keith Jones, "Big business blasts Canada's Liberal government," World Socialist Web Site 11 Apr 2000. Retrieved 20 Feb 2008 from http://www.wsws.org/articles/2000/apr2000/chre-a11.shtml; see also Joan Walters and April Lindgren, "CEOs blame Canada: Ireland cited as a model for economic growth," *Montreal Gazette,* 6 Apr 2000, A1, Jonathon Gatehouse, "Passion emerges from sea of blue suits," *National Post,* 6 Apr 2000, A8

29 Global TV, "Is equalization equal?" *Global Sunday,* 20 Feb 2005. Retrieved 19 Nov 2007 from CBCA Complete database

30 Steve Rendall, "An aggressive conservative vs. a 'liberal to be determined,'" *Extra,* Nov/Dec 2003. Retrieved 17 Nov 2007 from http://www.fair.org/extra/0311/hannity-colmes.html

31 Danielle Smith, "Holes poked in environmental claims," *Calgary Herald,* 21 Nov 1999, A15

32 Danielle Smith, "Jobs flourish when businesses earn big profits," *Calgary Herald,* 8 Feb 2000, A22

33 Global TV, "The nanny state," *Global Sunday,* 12 Dec 2004. Retrieved 19 Nov 2007 from CBCA Complete database

34   Global TV, "State of the union—gay OK?" *Global Sunday*, 5 Dec 2004. Retrieved 19 Nov 2007 from CBCA Complete database

35   Global TV, "Political pandemonium," *Global Sunday*, 30 Jan 2005. Retrieved 19 Nov 2007 from CBCA Complete database

36   "The Left," *Fontana Dictionary of Modern Thought*, 2nd ed., Fontana Press, 1988, 470

37   Global TV, "Should Ottawa sign on to missile defence?" *Global Sunday*, 5 Dec 2004. Retrieved 19 Nov 2007 from CBCA Complete database

38   Global TV, "Does the state have any place in the cribs of the nation?" *Global Sunday*, 20 Feb 2005. Retrieved 19 Nov 2007 from CBCA Complete database

39   See, for instance, Scott Piatkowski, "Zero degrees of separation," Rabble News, 19 Nov 2003. Retrieved 19 Nov 2007 from http://www.rabble.ca/columnists_full.shtml?x=28439

40   Bernard Cohen, *The Press and Foreign Policy*. Princeton, NJ: Princeton University Press, 1963, 13, emphasis added; quoted in Maxwell McCombs, *Setting the Agenda*. Cambridge: Polity Press, 2004, 2-3

41   McCombs, 2

42   Everett Rogers, William Hait and James Dearing, "A paradigmatic history of agenda-setting research," in Shanto Iyengar and Richard Reeves, (eds.), *Do the Media Govern?* Thousand Oaks, CA: Sage Publications, 1997, 227-228

43   Leonard Pitts, "No such thing as objective media," *Charleston Gazette*, 17 Dec 2001, 4A

44   Robert Hackett and Richard Gruneau, *The Missing News*. Ottawa: Canadian Centre for Policy Alternatives, 2000

45   Project Censored, "Top 25 stories of 2008," modified 14 Oct 2007. Retrieved 22 Nov 2007 from http://www.projectcensored.org/censored_2008/index.htm

46   McCombs, 102

47   McCombs, 103

48   Fraser Institute, "Toward the new millennium—A five year plan for the Fraser Institute—draft," n.d. See also Linda Goyette, "Fraser Institute revealed: Right-wing think tank brags about its media manipulation," *Edmonton Journal*, 17 Jan 1997, A16; Clive Thompson, "Ever wonder what think-tanks think about? Here's a glimpse," *Catholic New Times*, 7 Sep 1997, 10-11

49   Fraser Institute, "2002 Annual Report," 4. Retrieved 22 Nov 2007 from http://www.fraserinstitute.org/files/PDFs/annual_reports/2002_Annual_Report.pdf

50   Fraser Institute, "2002 Annual Report," 25

51   "Day of decision faces B.C. voters," *Vancouver Sun*, 16 Oct 1991, A20

52   Donald Gutstein, "Budget coverage out of balance," The Tyee, 21 Feb 2005. Retrieved 17 Apr 2009 from http://thetyee.ca/Mediacheck/2005/02/21/BudgetCoverageOutofBalance/

53   "Foreign policy reviews should not be conducted," *Maclean's*, 2 May 2005, 17

54   John Geddes, "Meet the real Stephen Harper," *Maclean's*, 9 May 2005, 23-27

55   Brian Bergman, "The European fix," *Maclean's*, 16 May 2005, 24-25

56   James Winter, *Democracy's Oxygen: How Corporations Control the News*. Montreal: Black Rose Books, 1997, 32-33

57   "Left-wing shtick: the Vancouver Province is criticized for removing a professor's comments from a story," *Media Magazine*, Spring 2000, 15

58   Casey Mahood, "Second Southam editor resigns over Black," *Globe and Mail*, 8 Oct 1996, A6

59   Stanley Tromp, "Last word," *Media Magazine*, Summer 2001. Retrieved 22 Nov 2007 from http://www.caj.ca/mediamag/summer2001/lastword.html

60   "Who 'we' is," *Ottawa Citizen*, 8 Mar 1997, B6

61   Chris Cobb, "*Montreal Gazette* editor quits over new 'approach,'" *Ottawa Citizen*, 27 Aug 1996, A2

62   "Harassing calls drive Toronto correspondent from Quebec City home," *Montreal Gazette*, 8 Feb 1990, A6; Tu Thanh Ha, "Montreal Gazette hires editor-in-chief," *Globe and Mail*, 25 Jul 2000, A7

63   See for instance, Conrad Black, "Conrad Black's response to the CBC," *Ottawa Citizen*, 26 Oct 1996, B7

64   Neil Seeman, "He was a conservative to call our own," *Globe and Mail*, 25 Aug 2001, A13

65   Winter, *Democracy's Oxygen*, 78

66   Sheldon Alberts, "Klein backs unite-the-right movement," *National Post*, 27 Oct 1998, A1; Scott Feschuk, "Klein's entrance bursts Clark's bubble," *National Post*, 27 Oct 1998, A7; Giles Gherson, "Clark urged to help create new right wing," *National Post*, 27 Oct 1997, A7; "Forward into the past," *National Post*, 27 Oct 1998, A19

67   Sheldon Alberts and John Ibbotson, "Tories reject call for new leader to unite parties," *National Post*, 28 Oct 1998, A1; Sheldon Alberts, "Activists ponder creation of new right-wing party," *National Post*, 28 Oct 1998, A7; Stephen Harper, "United Alternative an offer Joe Clark can't afford to refuse," *National Post*, 28 Oct 1998, A18

68   Edison Stewart, "Letterhead of Black firm used to solicit Tory funds," *Toronto Star*, 18 Mar 1997, A11; Rosemary Speirs, "The Right resurfaces in Ontario Tories," *Toronto Star*, 11 Jun 1986, A19; Richard Brennan, "Long uses *Post*'s reader list," *Toronto Star*, 19 May 2000, A1; Robert Fife, "Black denies funding Long leadership bid," *National Post*, 20 May 2000, A2

69   Quoted in *Frank Magazine* 14, Jun 2000, 18

70   Elections Canada, "Financial Reports," 24 Nov 2007. Retrieved 24 Nov 2007 from http://www.elections.ca/scripts/webpep/fin/welcome.aspx?lang=e

71   Atlantic Institute for Market Studies, "Outgoing president's message," Annual Report 1998–99, 11

72   Don Cayo columns in the *Vancouver Sun*, 23 Dec 2003, 7 May 2004, 4 Mar 2005, 25 Jun 2005, 15 Sep 2005, 25 Nov 2005, 28 Apr 2006, 17 Apr 2007, 19 Jun 2007, 15 Sep 2007

73   Fazil Mihlar, "A creative solution for our untenable EI system," *Vancouver Sun*, 12 Oct 2004, A13

74   Media Transparency, "Mackinac Center for Public Policy," n.d. Retrieved 23 Nov 2007 from http://www.mediatransparency.org/recipientprofile.php?recipientID=197

75   Lawrence Brunner and Stephen Colarelli, "Individual unemployment accounts," *Independent Review*, Spring 2004. Retrieved 23 Nov 2007 from http://www.independent.org/publications/tir/article.asp?issueID=13&articleID=40

76   Media Transparency, "Independent Institute," n.d. Retrieved 23 Nov 2007 from http://www.mediatransparency.org/recipientgrants.php?recipientID=1119

77   Media Transparency, "Heartland Institute," n.d. Retrieved 23 Nov 2007 from http://www.mediatransparency.org/recipientgrants.php?recipientID=152

78   Media Transparency, "National Bureau of Economic Research," n.d. Retrieved 24 Nov 2007 from http://www.mediatransparency.org/recipientprofile.php?recipientID=243

79   Media Transparency, "Grants to National Bureau of Economic Research from Smith Richardson Foundation," n.d. Retrieved 24 Nov 2007 from http://www.mediatransparency.org/recipient-fundergrants.php?funderID=6&recipientID=243

80   Fazil Mihlar, "Capitalism is in fact culture's friend," *Vancouver Sun*, 26 Apr 2004, A6

81   Media Transparency, "George Mason University," n.d. Retrieved 23 Nov 2007 from http://www.mediatransparency.org/recipientgrants.php?recipientID=413

82   Fazil Mihlar, "Out of the semi-dark age," *Vancouver Sun*, 29 Sep 2007, C4

83   Ezra Levant, "A legacy of liberty," *Western Standard*, 16 May 2005. Retrieved 23 Nov 2007 from http://westernstandard.ca/website/article.php?id=772

84   Edward Herman and Noam Chomsky, *Manufacturing Consent*. New York: Pantheon Books, 1988, 26

85   Trudy Lieberman, *Slanting the Story*. New York: New Press, 2000, 24

86   Lieberman, 25

87   "Reed Irvine takes AIM at the media," *Human Events*, 21 Jan 1994, 10

88   Accuracy in Media, "Mission statement," 2007. Retrieved 24 Nov 2007 from http://www.aim.org/static/21_0_7_0_C

89   Herman and Chomsky, 27

90   Herman and Chomsky, 28; David Brock, *The Republican Noise Machine*. New York: Crown, 2004, 75-80

91   Brock, 84-5; SourceWatch, "Center for Media and Public Affairs," modified 22 Sep 2007. Retrieved 24 Nov 2007 from http://www.sourcewatch.org/index.php?title=Center_for_Media_ and_Public_Affairs

92   Brock, 85-86

93   Brock, 87

94   David Croteau, "Examining the 'liberal media' claim," FAIR, Jun 1998. Retrieved 24 Nov 2007 from http://www.fair.org/index.php?page=2447

95   Jim Hartz and Rick Chappell, "Worlds apart: How the distance between science and journalism threatens America's future," First Amendment Center, Nashville, TN, 1997. Retrieved 28 Apr 2009 from http://www.firstamendmentcenter.org/PDF/worldsapart.PDF

96   David Appell, "Review of *It Ain't Necessarily So*," by David Murray et al., Salon.com, 2 Jul 2001. Retrieved 24 Nov 2007 from http://archive.salon.com/books/review/2001/07/02/murray/index. html

97   Canadian Statistical Assessment Service, "Why CanStats?" 2002. Retrieved 13 Nov 2002 from http://www.canstats.ca/about_canstats.asp. The CanStats web site has been retired.

98   Jeremy Brown, "Media distorts sea-lice findings," *CanStats Bulletin*, 29 Apr 2004. Retrieved 2 Nov 2004 from http://canstats.org/readmore.asp?sNav=pb&id=655

99   CBC News British Columbia, "Sea lice threatens salmon run, says researcher," 28 Apr 2004. Retrieved 24 Nov 2007 from http://www.cbc.ca/canada/british-columbia/story/2004/04/28/ bc_lice20040428.html

100   Jeremy Brown and Kenneth Green, "Good news is no news: Media failure to cover salmon study skews public perception," *CanStats Bulletin*, 25 Oct 2004. Retrieved 2 Nov 2004 from http://canstats.org/print_readdetail.asp?id=710

101   AquaNet—Canada's Research Network in Aquaculture, "Partners and collaborations," n.d. Retrieved 2 Nov 2004 from http://www.aquanet.ca/English/partner/index.php

102   Ronald A. Hites et al., "Global assessment of organic contaminants in farmed salmon," *Science*, 9 Jan 2004, 226-229

103   Derrick Penner, "Studies clash over levels of PCBs in farmed salmon," *Vancouver Sun*, 22 Oct 2004, H5

104   Salmon of the Americas, "New studies show PCB levels in farmed salmon comparable to wild: Here's the new data," 21 Oct 2004. Retrieved 2 Nov 2004 from http://www.salmonoftheameri- cas.com/topic_10_04_pcbsalmon.html

105   Alexandra Morton, "A salmon sleuth's disturbing find," *TheTyee*, 21 Nov 2004. Retrieved 13 Jan 2005 from http://www.thetyee.ca

106   Jeremy Brown, "A stain upon the science," *CanStats Bulletin*, 7 Dec 2004. Retrieved 13 Jan 2005 from http://canstats.org/readdetail.asp?id=719

107   Margaret Wente, "The collapse of climate 'consensus,'" *Globe and Mail*, 16 Aug 2005, A13

108   Naomi Oreskes, "Beyond the Ivory Tower: The scientific consensus on climate change," *Science*, 3 Dec 2004, 1686. Retrieved 29 Dec 2006, from http://www.sciencemag.org/cgi/content/ full/306/5702/1686

Chapter 7
Delaying Action on Climate Change

1   Patrick Brethour, "Support for Kyoto plunges," *Globe and Mail*, 2 Nov 2002, A1

2   Andrew Chung, "Alberta's Kyoto poll 'fraudulent': Anderson," *Toronto Star*, 5 Nov 2002, A7

3   Darrell Bricker, "The Kyoto numbers," *Globe and Mail*, 7 Nov 2002, A24; see also Jill Maloney, "Ipsos-Reid defends Kyoto-poll questions," *Globe and Mail*, 7 Nov 2002, A9

4 Hugh Winsor, "Poll questions on Kyoto carry different weights," *Globe and Mail*, 8 Nov 2002, A4

5 Alex Carey, *Taking the Risk Out of Democracy*, Urbana, IL: University of Illinois Press, 1995, 20

6 Josh Matlow, "Big Oil's Kyoto party," *NOW Online*, 24 Oct 2002. Retrieved 28 Nov 2007 from http://www.nowtoronto.com/issues/2002-10-24/news_story4_p.html

7 Carol Howes, "Canada won't sign Kyoto: Peterson," *National Post*, 13 Mar 2002, FP5; Brent Jang, "Imperial Oil executives mince no words on Kyoto or anything else," *Globe and Mail*, 13 Mar 2002, B9

8 Madhavi Acharya, "Imperial unrepentant over 'dirty' gasoline," *Toronto Star*, 21 Aug 2000, 1

9 Alan Toulin, "Alberta offers Kyoto alternative," *National Post*, 28 Mar 2002, FP1

10 Eva Ferguson, "Klein cools off on Kyoto challenge," *Calgary Herald*, 19 Apr 2002, A1

11 Canadian Coalition for Responsible Environmental Solutions, "Coalition formed to advance 'Made in Canada' strategy on climate change," Canada NewsWire, 26 Sep 2002. Retrieved 13 Nov 2002 from http://www.newswire.ca/releases/September2002/26/c5088.html; Steven Chase, "Business groups opposed to Kyoto," *Globe and Mail*, 27 Sep 2002, B3; O'Dwyer's PR Daily, "'Made in Canada' pollution plan," 26 Sep 2002. Retrieved 13 Nov 2002 from http://www.odwyerpr.com/0925national.htm

12 Paul Haavardsrud, "Buckee criticizes oil lobby on Kyoto," *National Post*, 1 Feb 2003, FP3

13 Canadian Coalition for Responsible Environmental Solutions

14 Hugh Winsor, "Oil patch candour needed on ad campaign," *Globe and Mail*, 13 Nov 2002, A4

15 Corporate Watch UK, "Burson-Marsteller: A corporate profile," Jul 2002. Retrieved 27 Nov 2007 from http://www.corporatewatch.org.uk/?lid=395

16 Ann Reilly Dowd and Suneel Ratan, "How to get things done in Washington," *Fortune*, 9 Aug 1993, 60

17 Michael Duffy and Ann Blackman, "I hear you, I hear you," *Time*, 21 Jun 1993, 20; Sheldon Rampton and John Stauber, "Correction: Burson-Marsteller and the Global Climate Coalition," PR Watch, Fall 2001. Retrieved 27 Nov 2007 from http://www.prwatch.org/prissues/2001Q3/cx.html

18 Steven Chase, "Liberal MPs want details on Kyoto," *Globe and Mail*, 10 Oct 2002, A7

19 Robert Benzie, "E-mail offers Eves Tories' a strategy," *National Post*, 18 Oct 2002, A4; Josh Matlow; Center for Media and Democracy, "Canadian Coalition for Responsible Environmental Solutions," SourceWatch, modified 6 Nov 2006. Retrieved 27 Nov 2007 from http://www.sourcewatch.org/index.php?title=Canadian_Coalition_for_Responsible_Environmental_Solutions

20 Robert Benzie, Alan Toulin and Ian Bailey, "Ontario joins Alberta, B.C. in Kyoto fight," *National Post*, 24 Oct 2002, A1

21 Hugh Winsor, "Poll questions ..."

22 Kate Jaimet, "Kyoto's cost $2,700 per family: study," *Ottawa Citizen*, 13 Nov 2002, D1; Ross McKitrick, "Counting the costs." Prepared for the Canadian Taxpayers Federation, Nov 2002. Retrieved 27 Nov 2007 from http://www.taxpayer.com/pdf/Kyoto_Protocol_Report_(November_12_2002).pdf

23 Center for Media and Democracy, "The Advancement of Sound Science Coalition," SourceWatch, modified 1 July 2007. Retrieved 27 Nov 2007 from http://www.sourcewatch.org/index.php?title=The_Advancement_of_Sound_Science_Coalition

24 Steven Chase, "Foes of Kyoto Protocol aim to stir up doubts," *Globe and Mail*, 13 Nov 2002, A4; Darren Yourk, "Climate experts call for Kyoto delay," *Globe and Mail* Update, 13 Nov 2002. Retrieved 17 Nov 2006 from http://www.theglobeandmail.com/servlet/ArticleNews/front/RTGAM/20021113/wkyot1113/Front/homeBN/breakingnews; APCO Worldwide (Canada), "Kyoto's fatal flaws revealed," Climate Search, 12 Nov 2002. Retrieved 14 Nov 2002 from http://www.climatesearch.com/newsDetail.cfm?newsId=54

25 John Cushman Jr., "Industrial group plans to battle climate treaty," *New York Times*, 26 Apr 1998, 1

26   Sharon Beder, *Global Spin: The Corporate Assault on Environmentalism*. White River Junction, VT: Chelsea Green Publishing, 1997, 216

27   Kris M. Wilson, "Communicating climate change through the media," in Stuart Allen, Barbara Adam and Cynthia Carter (eds.), *Environmental Risks and the Media*. London: Routledge, 1999, 202

28   Center for Media and Democracy, "Patrick J. Michaels," SourceWatch, modified 1 Oct 2007. Retrieved 27 Nov 2007 from http://www.sourcewatch.org/index.php?title=Patrick_Michaels; "Pat Michaels: scientist, energy industry lackey, *Washington Post* contributor," Media Matters for America, 20 May 2004. Retrieved 21 April 2006 from http://mediamatters.org/items/printable/200405200001

29   Timothy Gardner, "US: Power group promoting global warming skeptic," Reuters, 27 Jul 2006. Retrieved 27 Nov 2007 from http://www.corpwatch.org/article.php?id=13978&printsafe=1

30   Aaron Kessler, "State: Climatologist appointed by university," *Charlottetown Daily Progress*, 19 Aug 2006. Retrieved 27 Nov 2007 from http://www.dailyprogress.com/servlet/Satellite?pagename=CDP/MGArticle/CDP_BasicArticle&c=MGArticle&cid=1149190060797

31   Sharon Beder, *Global Spin*, 94; Peter Montague, "Ignorance is strength," *Rachel's Environment and Health Weekly*, 8 Nov 1995. Retrieved 27 Nov 2007 from http://www.rachel.org/bulletin/pdf/Rachels_Environment_Health_News_656.pdf; The Heat is Online, "ExxonMobil: the sceptics new partner," n.d. Retrieved 27 Nov 2007 from http://www.heatisonline.org/contentserver/objecthandlers/index.cfm?id=3645&method=full;

32   Richard Littlemore, "Tim Ball: the first Canadian PhD in climatology," deSmogBlog, 15 Jun 2006. Retrieved 14 Aug 2006 from http://www.desmogblog.com/tim-ball-the-first-canadian-phd-in-climatology?print_version=true; Charles Montgomery, "Meet Mr. Cool: Nurturing doubt about climate change is big business," *Globe and Mail*, 12 Aug 2006, F4

33   *Calgary Herald* et al., "Statement of Defence," Court of Queen's Bench of Alberta, Judicial District of Calgary, Dr. Timothy Ball and *Calgary Herald* et al., 7 Dec 2006, 12. Retrieved 17 Apr 2009 from http://www.desmogblog.com/sites/beta.desmogblog.com/files/Calgary Herald Statement of Defence.pdf

34   *Calgary Herald* et al., 2

35   Montgomery

36   Jane Taber, "Chrétien gives unruly caucus a directive," *Globe and Mail*, 22 Nov 2002, A4

37   Frank Graves, "Kyoto support stable," *Globe and Mail*, 6 Nov 2002, A16

38   Bruce Campion-Smith, "Harper would reopen missile defence debate," *Toronto Star*, 13 Jan 2006, A1

39   Brian Laghi, "Harper not bound by Liberal initiatives," *Globe and Mail*, 13 Jan 2006, A6. See also Joe Boughner, "Harper coverage a family affair," *Mediascout*, 13 Jan 2006. Retrieved 26 Nov 2007 from http://maisonneuve.org/index.php?&page_id=12&article_id=2007

40   Canada, Office of the Registrar of Lobbyists, Lobbyists Registration System, "Public registry search," 29 Nov 2007. Retrieved 29 Nov 2007 from https://strategis.ic.gc.ca/app/secure/ec/lrrs/displaySearchReg.do;jsessionid=0000oRGrCf5sf8phzpVERu64pBj:12edujrta?lang=eng

41   Friends of the Earth, "Fourth survey of climate change disclosure in SEC filings," Sept 2005. Retrieved 29 Nov 2007 from http://www.foe.org/camps/intl/corpacct/wallstreet/secsurvey2005.pdf

42   Wilson, "Communicating climate change . . . ," 204

43   Sir Robert May and Richard Pitts, "Communicating the science behind global environmental change issues," in Joe Smith, (ed.), *The Daily Globe: Environmental Change, the Public and the Media*. London: Earthscan Publications, 2000, 18

44   Kenny Bruno, Joshua Karliner and China Brotsky, "Greenhouse gangsters vs. climate justice," Transnational Resource and Action Center, Nov 1999, 1-2, 8. Retrieved 29 Nov 2007 from

http://s3.amazonaws.com/corpwatch.org/downloads/greenhousegangsters.pdf

45 Kenny Bruno, Joshua Karliner and China Brotsky, "Greenhouse gangsters . . . ," 11-19

46 Bill McKibben, "The coming meltdown," *New York Review of Books*, 12 Jan 2006. Retrieved 29 Nov 2007 from http://www.nybooks.com/articles/18616

47 David Helvarg, *The War Against the Greens*. San Francisco: Sierra Club Books, 1994, 31

48 John Stauber and Sheldon Rampton, *Toxic Sludge Is Good For You*. Monroe ME: Common Courage Press, 1995, 124-125

49 Bruno, Karliner and Brotsky, 12

50 Helvarg, 31

51 Bruno, Karliner and Brotsky, 12

52 Bruno, Karliner and Brotsky, 8

53 Bruno, Karliner and Brotsky, 13

54 WEFA, "Global warming: the high cost of the Kyoto Protocol," 1998, 1. Retrieved 29 Nov 2007 from http://downloads.heartland.org/11399.pdf

55 "Put a tiger in your think tank," *Mother Jones*, May/Jun 2005. Retrieved 21 Dec 2005 from http://www.motherjones.com/news/featurex/2005/05/exxon_chart.html

56 David Adam, "Oil industry targets EU climate policy," *The Guardian*, 8 Dec 2005, 6

57 See various web pages on Hoover Institution web site, http://www-hoover.stanford.edu/. These pages were retrieved between 2001 and 2004.

58 Marshall Institute, "William O'Keefe," n.d. Retrieved 2 Dec 2007 from http://www.marshall.org/experts.php?id=83

59 Harvard-Smithsonian Center for Astrophysics, "Twentieth-century climate not so hot," 31 Mar 2003. Retrieved 30 Nov 2007 from http://cfa-www.harvard.edu/press/archive/pr0310.html; Ross Gelbspan, *Boiling Point*. New York: Basic Books, 2004, 54-55

60 Gelbspan, *Boiling Point*, 56; Antonio Regalado, "Warming's skeptics face storm clouds," *Wall Street Journal*, 31 Jul 2003, A3; Clare Goodess, "Stormy times for climate research," Scientists for Global Responsibility, *SGR Newsletter 28*, Nov 2003. Retrieved 30 Jun 2006 from http://www.sgr.org.uk/climate/Stormy_Times_NL28.htm

61 Geoffrey Lean, "Global warming approaching point of 'no return,' warns leading climate expert," *Independent on Sunday*, 23 Jan 2005, 7; Gelbspan, *Boiling Point*, 47-49;

62 Juliet Eilperin, "Climate official's work is questioned," *Washington Post*, 5 Dec 2005, A19

63 Chris Mooney, "Some like it hot," MotherJones.com, May 2005. Retrieved 30 Nov 2007 from http://www.motherjones.com/news/feature/2005/05/some_like_it_hot.html; Joe Truini, "Bush to unveil voluntary program," *Waste News*, 3 Feb 2003, 4

64 John Carey, "Global warming: Suddenly the climate in Washington is changing," *BusinessWeek*, 27 Jun 2005, 91

65 Laura Jones, (ed.), *Global Warming: The Science and the Politics*. Vancouver: Fraser Institute, 1997, 17

66 Laura Jones, "Let's talk about the weather," *Fraser Forum*, Feb 1998, 39-40

67 Glenn Spencer, "The Four Kings of Carbon," Citizens for a Sound Economy, 26 Mar 2001. Retrieved 1 Dec 2007 from http://www.freedomworks.org/informed/issues_template.php?issue_id=398

68 United Nations Conference on Environment and Development, "Rio Declaration on Environment and Development," Rio de Janeiro, Jun 1992. Retrieved 17 Apr 2009 from http://www.unep.org/Documents.Multilingual/Default.asp?documentid=78&articleid=1163

69 Laura Jones, "The precautionary principle is reckless," *Fraser Forum*, Mar 1999, 15-16

70 Frank Cross, *Could Kyoto Kill?* Washington, D.C.: Competitive Enterprise Institute, Oct 1998. Retrieved 1 Dec 2007 from http://www.cei.org/pdf/1186.pdf

71 Quoted by ExxonSecrets, "Factsheet: Reason Foundation," n.d. Retrieved 1 Dec 2007 from http://www.exxonsecrets.org/html/orgfactsheet.php?id=63

72   ExxonSecrets, "Factsheet . . ."

73   Fraser Institute, "The Politics, Science and Economics of Kyoto," *Fraser Forum*, Jan 2003

74   Kenneth Green, "Kyoto Krazy," *Fraser Forum*, Jan 2003, 6

75   Barry Cooper, "Like lipstick on a pig . . .: The politics of Kyoto," *Fraser Forum*, Jan 2003, 4-5

76   Environmental Literacy Council, "Funders," 25 Sep 2007. Retrieved 2 Dec 2007 from http://www.enviroliteracy.org/article.php/701.html

77   American Enterprise Institute, "National Research Initiative: Scholars, Fellows and Projects," 2005. Retrieved 19 Nov 2006 from http://www.aei.org/research/nri/subjectareas/projectID.22/default.asp

78   Ian Sample, "Scientists offered cash to dispute climate study," *The Guardian*, 2 Feb 2007. Retrieved 18 Apr 2009 from http://www.guardian.co.uk/environment/2007/feb/02/frontpagenews.climatechange

79   Center for Media and Democracy, "Ross McKitrick," SourceWatch, 19 Aug 2005. Retrieved 18 Aug 2006 from http://www.sourcewatch.org/index.php?title=Ross_McKitrick

80   Ross McKitrick, "Thin-air syndrome," *National Post*, 13 Nov 2001, FP13

81   Paul Thacker, "Congressman unmoved by peer review, asks to see raw data," American Chemical Society: *ES&T Online News*, 6 July 2005. Retrieved 19 Nov 2006 from http://pubs.acs.org/subscribe/journals/esthag-w/2005/jul/policy/pt_congress.html

82   Paul Thacker, "How the *Wall Street Journal* and Rep. Barton celebrated a global-warming skeptic," American Chemical Society: *ES&T Online News*, 31 Aug 2005. Retrieved 15 May 2006 from http://pubs.acs.org/subscribe/journals/esthag-w/2005/aug/business/pt_wsj.html

83   Gavin Schmidt and Caspar Ammann, "Dummies guide to the latest 'Hockey Stick' controversy," Real Climate: Climate Science from Climate Scientists, 18 Feb 2005. Retrieved 30 Jun 2006 from http://www.realclimate.org/index.php?p=121

84   Paul Thacker, "Skeptics get a journal," American Chemical Society: *ES&T Online News*, 31 Aug 2005. Retrieved 15 May 2006 from http://pubs.acs.org/subscribe/journals/esthag-w/2005/aug/policy/pt_skeptics.html

85   Thacker, "How the *Wall Street Journal* . . ."

86   Center for Responsive Politics, "James M. Inhofe (R-OK): Top Industries," 2007. Retrieved 2 Dec 2007 from http://www.opensecrets.org/politicians/indus.asp?CID=N00005582&cycle=2006; Ross Gelbspan, *Boiling Point*, 55

87   Kenneth Green "Questioning Kyoto," *Calgary Herald*, 6 Nov 2003, A19; Michael Campbell, "Expect more attacks on anti-Kyoto conclusions," *Vancouver Sun*, 1 Nov 2003, H3; Lorne Gunter, "Research debunks greenhouse theory," *Edmonton Journal*, 12 Nov 2003, A16; Tim Patterson, "Incorrect data flaws Kyoto agreement," *Windsor Star*, 8 Nov 2003, A10

88   Antonio Regalado, "In climate debate, the 'Hockey Stick' leads to a face-off," *Wall Street Journal*, 14 Feb 2005, A1

89   Thacker, "How the *Wall Street Journal* . . ."

90   Thacker, "How the *Wall Street Journal* . . ."

91   National Center for Atmospheric Research, "Media advisory: the hockey stick controversy," 11 May 2005. Retrieved 2 Jul 2006 from http://www.ucar.edu/news/releases/2005/ammann.shtml

92   Marcel Crok, "Breaking the hockey stick," *National Post*, 27 Jan 2005, FP11

93   Harvey Leifert, "The hockey-stick face-off," *National Post*, 31 Jan 2005, FP15

94   Mark Milke, "Climate science goes on trial," *Calgary Herald*, 30 Jan 2005, A14; Barry Cooper, "Bent data, bent hockey stick," *Calgary Herald*, 2 Feb 2005, A12; Danielle Smith, "One-tonne bunkum: The figures just don't make sense," *Calgary Herald*, 12 Feb 2005, A22; *Global Sunday*, "The Kyoto plan, Interview with Ross McKitrick," 13 Feb 2005; Sean Myers, "Canada to meet Kyoto targets, Dion says," *Ottawa Citizen*, 14 Feb 2005, A4

95   Center for Responsive Politics, "Joe Barton (R-TX): Top Industries," 2007. Retrieved 2 Dec 2007 from http://www.opensecrets.org/politicians/indus.asp?CID=N00005656&cycle=2006

96 Thacker, "Congressman unmoved . . ."
97 National Academies, "Surface temperature reconstructions for the last 2,000 years," *Report in Brief*, June 2006. Retrieved 2 Dec 2007 from http://www.dels.nas.edu/dels/rpt_briefs/Surface_Temps_final.pdf
98 Terence Corcoran, "Last days of the hockey stick," *National Post*, 23 Jun 2006, FP15
99 Ross McKitrick and Steve McIntyre, "Misled again," *National Post*, 12 Jul 2006, FP19
100 Based on Wilson, "Communicating climate change . . . ," 201; see also Kris Wilson, "Mass media as sources of global warming knowledge," *Mass Communication Review*, Vol 22 no 1, 1995, 75-89
101 Ian Clark et al., "Open Kyoto to debate," *National Post*, 6 Apr 2006, FP19
102 Philip Austin et al., "We want more action," *National Post*, 20 Apr 2006, FP19
103 Terence Corcoran, "Review the science," *National Post*, 20 Apr 2006, FP19
104 Reuven Brenner, "Climate 90 miss the point of debate," *National Post*, 28 Apr 2006, FP19
105 Charles Montgomery, "Nurturing doubt about climate change is big business," *Globe and Mail* 12 Aug 2006, F4
106 "Friends of Science critiques the evidence for man-made climate change," *Daily Oil Bulletin*, 12 Jun 2006. Retrieved 2 Dec 2007 from http://www.dobmagazine.nickles.com/columns/pulse.asp?article=magazine%2Fcolumns%2F060612%2FMAG_COL2006_UC0000.html
107 Mike De Souza, "Elections Canada asked to investigate anti-Kyoto Protocol group," *Ottawa Citizen*, 18 Feb 2008, A6
108 Mike De Souza, "Kyoto sceptics cleared of vote violations," *Calgary Herald*, 24 Sep 2008, A1
109 Mike De Souza, "Tory worked for anti-Kyoto lobby," *Calgary Herald*, 22 Feb 2008, A6
110 Terence Corcoran, "Hockey sticks and hatchets," *National Post*, 23 Aug 2006, FP18
111 Ben Berkowitz, "Most powerful energy boss stepping down," *National Post*, 5 Aug 2005, FP3
112 Ross Gelbspan, *Boiling Point*, New York: Basic Books, 2004

Chapter 8
Killing Medicare . . . To Save It?

1 Robert Duncan, *Medicare Schmedicare*, International Documentary Television, in association with the CBC, 2005. Broadcast 8 Dec 2005 on CBC TV and repeated 12 Dec 2005 on *CBC Newsworld*
2 Through the Canadian Television Fund ($135,000), Knowledge Network (unknown amount), Canadian Film or Video Production Tax Credit, and Film Incentive B.C. (substantial federal and provincial tax credits)
3 Personal e-mail
4 Aaron Delwiche, "Propaganda," modified 2 Jan 2006. Retrieved 4 Dec 2007 from http://www.propagandacritic.com/
5 *Fontana Dictionary of Modern Thought*, "Revolution," Fontana Press, 1988, 745
6 Fraser Institute, "Canada's common sense revolution in medicare reform," a Fraser Institute Round Table Luncheon with Dr. Brian Day, Toronto, 20 Apr 2006. Retrieved 20 Mar 2009 from http://www.fraserinstitute.org/commerce.web/product_files/Day Toronto Flyer.pdf
7 CBC-Radio Canada, Office of the Ombudsman, "Review of complaints about 'Medicare Schmedicare,'" Jun 2006. Retrieved 4 Dec 2007 from http://www.cbc.ca/ombudsman/page/medicarereview.pdf
8 British Columbia, Ministry of Health Services, "Amendments strengthen legislation, protect patients," 17 Nov 2003. Retrieved 4 Dec 2007 from http://www2.news.gov.bc.ca/nrm_news_releases/2003HSER0049-001017.htm
9 Amy O'Brian, "Premier backs off bill limiting private clinics," *Vancouver Sun*, 18 Dec 2003, A1
10 Ian Bailey and Lena Sin, "Bill curbing private clinics put on hold," *The Province*, 18 Dec 2003, A6
11 Amy O'Brian, "Medical system 'failed' board of trade official," *Vancouver Sun*, 6 Dec 2003, B1
12 Terry Bell, "Private surgery ban will kill Olympic careers: Athlete," *The Province*, 7 Dec 2003, A6

13   Pete McMartin, "Medical broker reopens cross-border health care," *Vancouver Sun*, 8 Dec 2003, B1

14   John Stauber and Sheldon Rampton, *Toxic Sludge Is Good For You*. Monroe, ME: Common Courage Press, 1995, 173

15   Lyle Stewart, "Good PR is growing," *This Magazine*, May/Jun 2002, 29

16   Sonia Verma, "Not in my backyard," *This Magazine*, Nov/Dec 1998, 32; Mining Association of Canada, "Study finds primary metals sector has highest overall ranking in Canada for use of advanced technologies," 20 Nov 2001. Retrieved 6 Dec 2007 from http://www.mining.ca/www/_news/news_264.php

17   Charlie Gillis, "Talisman airstrip used by military, CEO discloses," *National Post*, 14 Jan 2000, A4

18   Jenefer Curtis, "Now cross my other palm," *Canadian Business*, Nov 1996, 20; Glen McGregor, "Senior Martin advisors still paid lobbyists," *National Post*, 22 Nov 2003, A12

19   Canada, Lobbyists Registration System, "Search and browse public registry: Hill and Knowlton," 4 Dec 2007. Retrieved 4 Dec 2007 from https://strategis.ic.gc.ca/app/secure/ec/lrrs/search.do;jsessionid=0000foB7kYx8t6H-XZbeBi2DVYv:12edujrta

20   British Columbia, Public Registry, Lobbyists Reports, "Activity by Lobbyist: Bruce Young," 4 Dec 2007. Retrieved 4 Dec 2007 from https://eservice.ag.gov.bc.ca/lra/public_reports.jsp

21   Hill and Knowlton, "Sandra Stoddart-Hansen promoted to vice-president and general manager," Press release, 4 Dec 2003. Retrieved 6 Dec 2007 from http://www.hillandknowlton.ca/newsroom/2003/sshansen_Dec4_2003.htm

22   Jim Beatty, "Clinics stop surgeries, fear for their survival," *Vancouver Sun*, 5 Dec 2003, A1

23   Ambulatory Surgical Centres Canada, "Planning your practice, building your future," 2003, Retrieved 27 Feb 2006 from http://www.asc-canada.ca/services/index.html

24   Gillian Cosgrove, "Laurier Club membership has its privileges," *National Post*, 11 Dec 1999, B11

25   Tom Blackwell, "Canadians want 2-tier health," *National Post*, 1 Jun 2004, A1; Joseph Brean, "52% back private care: Quebec, B.C., Prairies favour a user-pay alternative: poll," *National Post*, 26 Apr 2005, A1; Valentin Petkantchin, "Canadians want choice in health care," *Ottawa Citizen*, 23 Jan 2006, A15

26   Medical Services Commission, "Financial statement," 2001 to 2007. Retrieved 23 Feb 2008 from http://www.health.gov.bc.ca/msp/financial_statement.html

27   Canadian Health Services Research Foundation, "Myth: A parallel system would reduce waiting times in the public system," *Mythbusters*, Mar 2005. Retrieved 6 Dec 2007 from http://www.chsrf.ca/mythbusters/pdf/myth17_e.pdf

28   Patrick Sullivan, "Working group considers major changes as CMA develops new policy on health financing," *Canadian Medical Association Journal*, July 1993, 87

29   Edwin Coffey, "The way is not Clair," *Montreal Gazette*, 24 Jan 2001, B3

30   Tom Blackwell, "From Beatles and Castro to the CMA," *National Post*, 18 Feb 2006, A4

31   Edwin Coffey, "Too much rhetoric in health-care debate," *Montreal Gazette*, 9 Mar 2002, B5

32   Edwin Coffey, "Impaired freedom," *Montreal Gazette*, 22 May 2004, A31

33   For example, Edwin Coffey, "The case for increased privatization of Canadian health care," *McGill Journal of Medicine*, 2008, Vol 11 no 1, 75-76

34   Montreal Economic Institute, "Using private insurance to finance health care," *Economic Note*, Nov 2005. Retrieved 6 Dec 2007 from http://www.iedm.org/uploaded/pdf/nov05_en.pdf

35   Valentin Petkantchin, "A made-in-Canada prescription," *National Post*, 10 Nov 2005, FP19

36   Gillian Cosgrove, "Laurier Club membership . . ."

37   Josee Legault, "Patients come second in CHUM version," *Montreal Gazette*, 26 Nov 2004, A23

38   Louise Gagnon, "Private health care urged to end long waiting lists," *Medical Post*, 5 May 1998, 52

39   "Physician vows to take parallel-system to Supreme Court," *Canadian Medical Association Journal*, 2 Jun 1998, 1509

40 Aaron Derfel, "Medicare board okays brokering plan," *Montreal Gazette*, 2 Feb 2008, A8
41 Montreal Economic Institute, "Supreme Court ruling in the Chaoulli case—private health-care can now benefit Canadians," Media release, 9 Jun 2005. Retrieved 6 Dec 2007 from http://www.iedm.org/main/print_mediareleases_en.php?mediareleases_id=81
42 Andre Picard, "Doctors back private health insurance," *Globe and Mail*, 18 Aug 2005, A1
43 "The CMA's message," *Globe and Mail*, 19 Aug 2005, A12
44 Pamela Fayerman, "Doctors pick private-care pioneer," *Vancouver Sun*, 15 Feb 2006, A2
45 Norma Greenaway, "Doctors signal dismay, pick private-care chief," *National Post*, 23 Aug 2006, A1
46 Antonia Maioni, *Parting at the Crossroads: The Emergence of Health Insurance in the United States and Canada*. Princeton, NJ: Princeton University Press, 1998, 61; See also Colleen Fuller, *Caring for Profit*. Vancouver: New Star Books, 1998, 25
47 Maioni, 62
48 Maioni, 93
49 Fuller, 40
50 Fuller, 41, Maioni, 98
51 Fuller, 21, Maioni, 104
52 Fuller, 42, Maioni, 120
53 Fuller, 44, Maioni, 122
54 Maioni, 132
55 Fuller, 63
56 Fuller, 63-64
57 Fuller, 75
58 Fuller, 51
59 Murray Dobbin, "The white cat and black cat of medicare," *Winnipeg Free Press*, 23 May 2004
60 Brian Laghi, "Harper advocates private hospitals," *Globe and Mail*, 26 Sep 2002, A4
61 Kevin Taft and Gillian Steward, *Clear Answers: The Economics and Politics of For-Profit Medicine*. Edmonton: Duval House Publishers, 2000, 34
62 Taft and Steward, 36; Steve Mertl, "Pressure to spend mounting, Klein says," *Edmonton Journal*, 11 May 1999, A7
63 Taft and Steward, 37
64 Taft and Steward, 38, 39
65 Taft and Steward, 67
66 Dawn Walton, "At Alberta clinic, profit seen in positive light," *Globe and Mail*, 15 Oct 2002, A6
67 Karen van Kampen, "Surgical strike," *National Post Business*, Feb 2002, 47
68 Fuller, 85-86
69 "Health-care heresies: welcome and overdue," *Globe and Mail*, 15 Feb 2006, A16
70 "Private healthcare. Let's talk about it," *Globe and Mail*, 7 Dec 2005, A22
71 "The tough questions for public medicare," *Globe and Mail*, 23 Aug 2005, A12
72 "Ontario's dismissal of privately provided care," *Globe and Mail*, 17 Mar 2007, A14
73 "When a public payer employs private care," *Globe and Mail*, 26 Mar 2007, A16
74 "The CMA errs on private payment," *Globe and Mail*, 1 Aug 2007, A14
75 "Cautious on private care," *Globe and Mail*, 22 Feb 2008, A20
76 "Chaoulli comes to Ontario," *National Post*, 3 May 2007, A18
77 "Destroying medicare's myths," *National Post*, 10 Jun 2005, A15
78 "Give private insurance a chance," *National Post*, 19 Sep 2005, A11
79 "A welcome health care revolution," *National Post*, 2 Mar 2006, A14
80 Michael Goldbloom and Jim Carter, "Language is a vital part of health, social services," *Montreal Gazette*. 19 Nov 1986, B3

81   Anne Kershaw, Jack Rafter, Murray Hogben and Allison Dawe, "A second look at the race from a local perspective," *Kingston Whig-Standard*, 22 Nov 1988, 40

82   "Medicare's future: Listening to the CMA," *Windsor Star*, 22 Aug 1995, A6

83   Victor Dirnfeld, "An ill wind is blowing through health-care system," *Vancouver Sun*, 15 Apr 1996, A11

84   Shaune MacKinlay, "Dingwall backs one-tier health," *Daily News*, 19 Aug 96, 3

85   Ake Blomqvist, *The Health Care Business: International Evidence on Private Versus Public Health Care Systems*. Vancouver: Fraser Institute, 1979

86   Martin Zelder, "Will Alberta's health care reforms succeed?" *Fraser Forum*, Jan 2000, 14

87   Taft and Steward, 27-33

88   Lawrence Solomon, "Rise of a zombie," *National Post*, 31 Jul 2002, FP15

89   Don Cayo, "Heart attack strikes in Haiti," *Vancouver Sun*, 18 Apr 2001, A16

90   Cynthia Ramsay and David Gratzer, "Crucial debate clouded by political expediency," *Fraser Forum*, June 1997. Retrieved 1 June 2009 from http://oldfraser.lexi.net/publications/forum/1997/june/FF-06-97.html

91   Consumer Policy Institute, "Health care campaign," 1997. Retrieved 11 Mar 2006 from http://www.c-p-i.org/cpi/print.cfm?ContentID=11122

92   David Gratzer, "Mediocre results for medicare," *National Post*, 1 Aug 2001, A14

93   Evelyn Forget, Raisa Deber and Leslie Ross, "Medical Savings Accounts: Will they reduce costs?" *Canadian Medical Association Journal*, 23 July 2002, 143-147

94   Forget et al., "Medical Savings Accounts," 146

95   Solomon

96   William C. Hsiao, "Behind the ideology and theory: What is the empirical evidence for Medical Savings Accounts?" *Journal of Health Politics, Policy and Law*, Aug 2001, 734

97   Samuel Shortt, "Medical Savings Accounts in publicly funded health care systems: enthusiasm versus evidence," *Canadian Medical Association Journal*, 23 Jul 2002, 160

98   David Gratzer, "It's time to consider Medical Savings Accounts," *Canadian Medical Association Journal*, 23 Jul 2002, 151

99   Shortt, 160-161

100   Hsiao, 734

101   "The trouble with MSAs," *Globe and Mail*, 27 Jul 2002, A16

102   Michael Rachlis, "Public solutions to health care wait lists," Canadian Centre for Policy Alternatives, Dec 2005. Retrieved 1 Feb 2006 from http://www.policyalternatives.ca/documents/National_Office_Pubs/2005/Health_Care_Waitlists.pdf; Andre Picard, "Public clinics can thrive on methods privately honed," *Globe and Mail*, 15 Dec 2005, A17

103   Rachlis, 31

104   Rachlis, 30

105   Rachlis, 5

106   Rachlis, 21

107   Angus Reid, "Healthcare in Canada," Press release, 2 Feb 2000. Retrieved 14 Dec 2007 from http://www.ipsos-na.com/news/pressrelease.cfm?id=978; Lisa Priest, "Gloom about health care widespread," *Globe and Mail*, 3 Feb 2000, A4

108   Ipsos-Reid, "Seven in ten Canadians think that the overall quality of the health care system in Canada will be the same (39%) or worse (32%) in ten years," Press release, 21 Oct 2008. Retrieved 22 Mar 2009 from http://www.ipsos-na.com/news/pressrelease.cfm?id=4134

109   Kathleen Wilson and Mark W. Rosenberg, "The geographies of crisis: Exploring accessibility to health care in Canada," *Canadian Geographer*, Fall 2002, 227, 228

110   Wilson and Rosenberg, 233

Chapter 9

Targeting Corporate Propaganda's Vulnerabilities

1 Robert Dreyfuss, "Grover Norquist: 'Field Marshall' of the Bush plan," *The Nation*, 14 May 2001. Retrieved 22 Jan 2008 from http://www.thenation.com/doc/20010514/dreyfuss

2 Jeffrey Simpson, "Pulling a climate-change rabbit out of a Tory hat," *Globe and Mail*, 12 Jan 2007, A15

3 Micah Sifrey, "Bumpersticker banner," TomPaine.com, 16 Jun 2003. Retrieved 25 Jan 2007 from http://www.tompaine.com/Archive/scontent/8098.html

4 Dreyfuss

5 Peter Stone, "Grover and Jack's long adventure," nationaljournal.com, 10 Jan 2005. Retrieved 22 Jan 2008 from http://nationaljournal.com/about/njweekly/stories/2005/1001nj1.htm

6 William Gairdner, "The history of Civitas," *The Civil Conversation*, Jan 2007, 3

7 Civitas, "Eleventh annual national conference, programme" Halifax, 4-6 May 2007

8 Grover Norquist, "The international reach of Civitas," *The Civil Conversation*, Mar 2007, 6

9 Lewis Powell, "Confidential memorandum: Attack of American free enterprise system," 23 Aug 1971. Retrieved 21 Aug 2007 from http://www.mediatransparency.org/story.php?storyID=22

10 Powell

11 Alliance for Justice, "Justice for sale: Shortchanging the public interest for private gain," 1993, 1. Retrieved 21 Jan 2008 from http://www.afj.org/assets/resources/resources2/Justice-for-Sale.pdf

12 Center for Media and Democracy, "Pacific Legal Foundation," SourceWatch, modified 28 Aug 2007. Retrieved 21 Jan 2008 from http://www.sourcewatch.org/index.php?title=Pacific_Legal_Foundation

13 Media Transparency, "Recipient grants: Federalist Society for Law and Public Policy Studies," 2006. Retrieved 22 Jan 2008 from http://www.mediatransparency.org/recipientgrants.php?recipientID=112

14 Federalist Society, "About us," n.d. Retrieved 22 Jan 2008 from http://www.fed-soc.org/aboutus/css.print/default.asp

15 Thomas Edsall, "Federalist Society becomes a force in Washington," *Washington Post*, 18 Apr 2001, A4

16 Neil Lewis, "A somber annual meeting for conservative lawyers," *New York Times*, 19 Nov 2006, 26

17 Jason DeParle, "Nomination for Supreme Court stirs debate on influence of Federalist Society," *New York Times*, 1 Aug 2005, 12

18 Jeff Jacoby, "A 'shadowy' society," *Boston Globe*, 21 Nov 2007, A19

19 Michael Orey, "The Supreme Court: Open for business," *BusinessWeek*, 9 Jul 2007, 30

20 Robert Barnes and Carrie Johnson, "Pro-business decision hews to pattern of Roberts court," *Washington Post*, 22 Jun 2007, D1

21 Ted Morton, "Gay marriage and the decline of democracy in Canada," *Winnipeg Free Press*, 3 Jul 2003, A9

22 Fred Nace, *Gangs of America: The Rise of Corporate Power and the Disabling of Democracy*. San Francisco: Berrett-Koehler, 2003

23 Civitas, "Seventh annual national conference, programme," Toronto, 25-27 Apr 2003

24 Home School Legal Defence Association, "HSLDA of Canada announces the departure of Dallas K. Miller, Q.C.," News release, 19 Nov 2004. Retrieved 3 Feb 2008 from http://www.hslda.ca/news_release.pdf; Christian Legal Fellowship, "Conference speakers and leaders," Conference 2002, Banff, Alta. Retrieved 3 Feb 2008 from http://www.christianlegalfellowship.org/Conference/2002%20featured_speakers.htm

25 Nigel Hannaford, "Take back the Charter," *Calgary Herald*, 13 Aug 2005, A20

26 "All rise for David Brown," *National Post*, 2 Oct 2006, A14; Kirk Makin, "PM's pick for bench draws fire," *Globe and Mail*, 21 Sep 2006, A5; Jim Rankin, "Court limits abortion pickets," *Toronto Star*, 31 Aug 1994, A1

27   John Carpay, "Activists should turn to courts to protect individual freedoms," *Montreal Gazette*, 6 Mar 2006

28   John Carpay, "The case against the Nisga'a Nation," *National Post*, 14 Dec 2005, A22

29   Canadian Constitution Foundation, "2006 Annual Report," 5. Retrieved 3 Feb 2008 from http://www.canadianconstitutionfoundation.ca/files/pdf/Annual_Report_2006_FINAL.pdf

30   Fraser Institute, "Media advisory: Fraser Institute cocktail series hosts discussion on Canada's ailing health care system," 22 Oct 2007. Retrieved 30 Jan 2008 from http://www.marketwire.com/mw/release.do?id=783394

31   Jeffrey Simpson, "Harper's counter-attack on the activists," *Globe and Mail*, 13 Feb 2007, A17

32   Andrew Chung, "Stacked court: Could it happen here?" *Toronto Star*, 1 Jul 2007, A10

33   Sujit Choudhry and Claire E. Hunter, "Measuring judicial activism on the Supreme Court of Canada," *McGill Law Journal*, Aug 2003, 525-562

34   Christopher Manfredi and James B. Kelly, "Misrepresenting the Supreme Court's record?" *McGill Law Journal*, Aug 2004, 741-765

35   George Lakoff, *Whose Freedom?* New York: Farrar, Straus and Giroux, 2006, 245

36   Lakoff, 246

37   Lorne Gunter, "A prospectus for big government," *National Post*, 5 Feb 2007, A13

38   Ipsos Reid, "Canadian views on health care scenarios," 7 Jun 2006. Retrieved 4 Feb 2008 from http://www.ipsos-na.com/news/pressrelease.cfm?id=3102

39   Joanna Smith, "Canadians open to deficit: Poll," *Toronto Star*, 24 Jan 2009

40   Campbell Clark, "Social programs trump tax cuts: poll," *Globe and Mail*, 19 Mar 2007, A4

41   Innovative Research Group, "Canadian values similar to other advanced democracies," Canadian Values Study: Day Five Release, 29 Sep 2005. Retrieved 24 May 2007 from http://www.innovativeresearch.ca/Canadian%20Values%20Study_Factum%20280905.pdf

42   Scott Stinson, "Canadians' views are not unique, poll finds," *National Post*, 29 Sep 2005, A22

43   Dennis Bueckert, "Canadians want Kyoto targets met," *The Province*, 6 Sep 2006, A8

44   Compas, Inc., "Asia-Pacific Partnership embraced 2:1 over Kyoto," 29 May 2006. Retrieved 29 May 2007 from http://www.compas.ca/data/060529-KyotoAndAsia-PacificPartnership-EPCB.pdf

45   John Burton, "Communicating the idea of a free society—Overview: The nature of the message," Mont Pèlerin Society Regional Meeting, 28 Aug–1 Sep 1983, Vancouver. *Fraser Institute Focus*, No 10, 17

46   Herbert Gans, *Deciding What's News*. New York: Vintage Books, 1980, 80

47   Sheldon Alberts, "Canadians accused of missile freeloading," *National Post*, 1 Mar 2005, A1

48   Paul Koring, "Canadian vote chance to end 'petty rancour' with Bush team," *Globe and Mail*, 28 Dec 2005, A15

49   Bruce Campion-Smith, "Canada's decision to stay out of the U.S. missile defence program has some worried it will hurt the NORAD alliance," *Toronto Star*, 5 Mar 2005, F01

50   Canada, Department of National Defence, "Defence policy statement," 10 Sep 2006. Retrieved 29 Dec 2006, from http://www.dnd.ca/site/Reports/dps/main/04_e.asp

51   Center for Strategic and International Studies, "Canada: overview," 2008. Retrieved 4 Feb 2008 from http://www.csis.org/americas/canada/

52   Paul Koring, "Tread lightly with Bush, observers warn," *Globe and Mail*, 25 Jan 2006, A4

53   Allan Woods and Mike Blanchfield, "Could be a match made in heaven," *National Post*, 16 Feb 2006, A4

54   "Liberalism regained: Building the next progressive majority," *Harper's Magazine*, Aug 2004, 35

55   Ruth Rosen, "Challenge market fundamentalism" TomPaine.com, 5 Feb 2007. Retrieved 5 Feb 2007 from http://www.tompaine.com/print/challenge_market_fundamentalism.php

56   Duncan Foley, *Adam's Fallacy: A Guide to Economic Theology*. Cambridge, MA: Belknap Press of Harvard University Press, 2006, xiii; see also Peter Steinfels, "Economics: the invisible hand of the market," *New York Times*, 25 Nov 2006, 5

57 Foley, 43

58 Foley, xv

59 Dean Baker, "The conservative nanny state," Washington, DC: Center for Economic and Policy Research, 2006, 7

60 David C. Korten, "The Betrayal of Adam Smith," in *When Corporations Rule the World.* West Hartford, CT: Kumarian Press, 1995. Retrieved 5 Jan 2007 from http://deoxy.org/korten_betrayal.htm

61 Nace, *Gangs of America*, 57

62 Joel Bakan, *The Corporation: The Pathological Pursuit of Profit and Power.* New York: Free Press, 2004, 9

63 Nace, 57

64 Nace, 62

65 Nace, 67

66 Nace, 68

67 Bakan, 11

68 Baker, 40

69 See Andrew Rich, "War of ideas," *Stanford Social Innovation Review*, Spring 2005, 18-25

70 Quoted in Robert Dreyfuss, "Grover Norquist: 'Field Marshall' of the Bush plan," *The Nation*, 14 May 2001. Retrieved 22 Jan 2008 from http://www.thenation.com/doc/20010514/dreyfuss

71 Aaron Bernstein, "Too much corporate power?" *BusinessWeek*, 11 Sep 2000, 145-158

72 Bernstein, 145

73 Robert Kuttner, *Everything for Sale.* Chicago: University of Chicago Press, 1999, 3

74 *Webster's New Collegiate Dictionary.* Springfield, MA: G & C. Merriam Co., 1981, 623

75 See: Henry Richardson, "John Rawls," Internet Encyclopedia of Philosophy, 2006. Retrieved 22 May 2007 from http://www.iep.utm.edu/r/rawls.htm; Peter Jedicke, "Notes on John Rawls, A Theory of Justice, 1971," 1997. Retrieved 22 May 2007 from http://infotech.fanshawec.on.ca/faculty/jedicke/rawls.htm

76 *Fontana Dictionary of Modern Thought*, 2nd ed., London: Fontana Press, 1988, 450

77 *Fontana Dictionary*

78 Sam Gindin, "Anti-capitalism and the terrain of social justice," *Monthly Review*, 1 Nov 2002, 4; italics in original

79 Michael Shuman, "Why do progressive foundations give too little to too many?" *The Nation*, 12 Jan 1998, 11-16

80 Christopher Hayes, "The new funding heresies," *In These Times*, 26 Jun 2006. Retrieved 17 Aug 2006 from http://www.inthesetimes.com/site/main/print/2697

81 Shuman

82 Hayes

83 Hayes

84 Hayes

85 Hayes

86 Heritage Foundation, 2005 Annual Report, 1 Mar 2006. Retrieved 26 Jan 2007 from http://www.heritage.org/About/upload/96065_1.pdf

87 Dick Martin, "The need for a collective voice," *National Round Table Review*, Spring 1993, 12.

SELECTED BIBLIOGRAPHY

Accuracy in Media. "Mission statement." 2008. http://www.aim.org/static/21_0_7_0_C.

"Alberta Report turns 25." *Alberta Report*, November 1, 1999, 3.

Alexandroff, Alan and Don Guy. "What Canadians have to say about relations with the United States." *CD Howe Institute Backgrounder* no 73, July 2003. http://www.cdhowe.org/pdf/backgrounder_73.pdf.

Allan, Stuart. *News Culture.* Buckingham, UK: Open University Press, 1999.

Alliance for Justice. "Justice for sale: Shortchanging the public interest for private gain." 1993. http://www.afj.org/assets/resources/resources2/Justice-for-Sale.pdf.

Alterman, Eric. "Fighting smart." *Mother Jones*, July/August 1994, 59-61.

———. "Neoconning the media: A very short history of neoconservatism." Media Transparency, April 22, 2005. http://www.mediatransparency.org/story/printerfriendly.php?storyID=2 (accessed February 16, 2006; site now discontinued).

———. "The 'right' books and big ideas." *The Nation*, November 22, 1999, 16-21.

Ambulatory Surgical Centres Canada. "Planning your practice, building your future." 2003. http://www.asc-canada.ca/services/index.html.

American Enterprise Institute. "2008 Annual Report." December 5, 2008. http://www.aei.org/docLib/20081205_2008AnnualReportweb.pdf.

———. "National Research Initiative: Scholars, Fellows and Projects." 2005. http://www.aei.org/research/nri/subjectareas/projectID.22/default.asp.

———. "Walter Berns, resident scholar." 2005. http://www.aei.org/scholars/scholarID.4/scholar.asp.

Amr, Ahmed. "Judith Miller's dirty little secret." Media Monitors Network, August 7, 2005. http://usa.mediamonitors.net/content/view/full/17512.

"And that was the beginning of restraint…" *New Directions*, June/July 1985, 10-16.

Angus Reid. "Healthcare in Canada." Press Release, February 2, 2000. http://www.ipsos-na.com/news/pressrelease.cfm?id=978.

Appell, David et al. "Review of It Ain't Necessarily So,'" Salon.com, July 2, 2001. http://archive.salon.com/books/review/2001/07/02/murray/index.html.

AquaNet—Canada's Research Network in Aquaculture. "Partners and collaborations." n.d. http://www.aquanet.ca/English/partner/index.php.

Armstrong, Richard. "The passion that rules Ralph Nader." *Fortune*, May 1971, 144-147.

Atlantic Institute for Market Studies. "AIMS: About AIMS: Jean-Luc Migue." October 19, 2007. http://www.aims.ca/cm_Print.asp?cmPageID=252.

———. Annual Report 1997-98. September 30, 1998. http://www.aims.ca/media/documents/ar1998.pdf.

———. Annual Report 1996-97. November 7, 1997. http://www.aims.ca/media/documents/ar1997. pdf.

———. "Brian Lee Crowley." 2007. http://www.aims.ca/aboutaims.asp?cmPageID=125.

———. "Board of directors." 2007. http://www.aims.ca/aboutaims.asp?cmPageID=90.

———. "Outgoing president's message." Annual Report 1998-99. October 22, 1999, 10-12. http://www.aims.ca/media/documents/ar1999.pdf.

Atlas Economic Research Foundation. "Atlas, year in review." Fall 2006. http://www.atlasusa.org/V2/files/pdfs/2006_Fall_YIR.pdf.

Bakan, Joel. *The Corporation: The Pathological Pursuit of Profit and Power.* New York: Free Press, 2004.

Barlow, Maude. "The NCC: Not national, not citizens and not a coalition." Canada News Wire, June 12, 1997.

Batc, Roger. "International public health strategy." September 1998. http://legacy.library.ucsf.edu/tid/xvp83c00.

Beder, Sharon. *Free Market Missionaries: The Corporate Manipulation of Community Values.* London: Earthscan, 2006.

———. *Global Spin: The Corporate Assault on Environmentalism.* White River Junction, VT: Chelsea Green Publishing, 1998.

Bergman, Brian. "The European fix." *Maclean's*, May 16, 2005, 24-25.

Berman, Ari. "The social security sham." *The Nation*, November 18, 2004. http://www.thenation.com/blogs/outrage/2015/the_social_security_sham.

Bernays, Edward. *Propaganda.* Brooklyn, NY: Ig Publishing, 2005.

———. "The theory and practice of public relations: A resume." In *The Engineering of Consent*, edited by Edward Bernays, 3-25. Norman, OK: University of Oklahoma Press, 1955.

Block, Walter and Michael Walker, eds. *Discrimination, Affirmative Action, and Equal Opportunity.* Vancouver: Fraser Institute, 1982.

Blomqvist, Ake. *The Health Care Business: International Evidence on Private Versus Public Health Care Systems.* Vancouver: Fraser Institute, 1979.

Boehlert, Eric and Jamison Foser. "Asymmetrical class warfare." Media Matters for America, February 27, 2009. http://mediamatters.org/items/200902270020.

———. "In CNBC host Cramer's 'U.S.S.A.:' 'Comrade' Obama is a 'Bolshevik' who is 'taking cues from Lenin.'" Media Matters for America, March 4, 2009. http://mediamatters.org/items/200903040026.

Boughner, Joe. "Harper coverage a family affair." *Mediascout*, January 13, 2006. http://maisonneuve.org/index.php?&page_id=12&article_id=2007 (accessed November 26, 2007; site now discontinued).

Boyarsky, Bill. *Ronald Reagan: His Life and Rise to the Presidency.* New York: Random House, 1981.

Boyd-Barrett, Oliver. "Judith Miller, the *New York Times* and the propaganda model." *Journalism Studies* (2004): 435-449.

Bramwell, Austin. "Review of Eric Voegelin: The Restoration of Order." *National Review*, July 1, 2002, 45-46.

British Columbia. Ministry of Health Services. "Amendments strengthen legislation, protect patients."

November 17, 2003. http://www2.news.gov.bc.ca/nrm_news_releases/2003HSER0049-001017. htm.

———. "MSC Financial Statement ('Blue Book')." 2001 to 2008." http://www.health.gov.bc.ca/msp/ financial_statement.html.

British Columbia. Public Registry. "Lobbyists Reports." n.d. https://eservice.ag.gov.bc.ca/lra/public_ reports.jsp.

Brock, David. *The Republican Noise Machine.* New York: Crown, 2004.

Brown, Jeremy. "Media distorts sea-lice findings." Fraser Institute, *CanStats Bulletin*, April 29, 2004. http://canstats.org/ (accessed November 2, 2004; site now discontinued).

———. "A stain upon the science." Fraser Institute, *CanStats Bulletin*, December 7, 2004. http:// canstats.org/ (accessed January 13, 2005; site now discontinued)

Brown, Jeremy, Kenneth Green, Steven Hansen and Liv Fredricksen. "Environmental Indicators," 6th ed. Vancouver: Fraser Institute, April 2004. http://www.fraserinstitute.org/Commerce.Web/ product_files/EnvironmentalIndicators2004.pdf.

Brown, Jeremy and Kenneth Green. "Good news is no news: Media failure to cover salmon study skews public perception." Fraser Institute, *CanStats Bulletin*, October 25, 2004. http://canstats. org/ (accessed November 2, 2004; site now discontinued).

Brunner, Lawrence and Stephen Colarelli. "Individual unemployment accounts." *Independent Review*, Spring 2004. http://www.independent.org/publications/tir/article. asp?issueID=13&articleID=40.

Bruno, Kenny. "Shell: clouding the issue." CorpWatch, November 15, 2000. http://www.corpwatch. org/article.php?id=218.

Bruno, Kenny, Joshua Karliner and China Brotsky. Greenhouse gangsters vs. climate justice. Transnational Resource and Action Center, November 1999. http://s3.amazonaws.com/ corpwatch.org/downloads/greenhousegangsters.pdf.

Bueckert, Dennis. "Business group slams Kyoto, offers 'made-in-Canada' alternative." Canadian Press NewsWire, September 26, 2002.

Bulloch, Alan, Oliver Stallybrass and Stephen Tombley, eds. *Fontana Dictionary of Modern Thought.* 2nd ed. London: Fontana Press, 1988.

Burton, John. "Communicating the idea of a free society—Overview: The nature of the message." Mont Pèlerin Society Regional Meeting, August 28—September 1, 1983, Vancouver. *Fraser Institute Focus*, No. 10.

Bush, George W. "President discusses the future of Iraq." The White House, February 26, 2003. http:// georgewbush-whitehouse.archives.gov/news/releases/2003/02/20030226-11.html.

Calgary Herald, et al. "Statement of Defence." Court of Queen's Bench of Alberta, Judicial District of Calgary, Dr. Timothy Ball and the *Calgary Herald* et al. December 7, 2006, http://www. desmogblog.com/sites/beta.desmogblog.com/files/Calgary Herald Statement of Defence.pdf.

Campbell, Bruce and Ed Finn, eds. *Living With Uncle: Canada-US Relations in an Age of Empire.* Toronto: James Lorimer, 2006.

Canada. Department of National Defence. "Defence policy statement." September 10, 2006. http:// www.dnd.ca/site/Reports/dps/main/04_e.asp.

Canada. Elections Canada. "Financial Reports Home Page." June 16, 2009. http://www.elections.ca/ scripts/webpep/fin/welcome.aspx?lang=e

Canada. Office of the Commissioner of Lobbying of Canada. "Registry Search." February 10, 2009. http://www.ocl-cal.gc.ca/eic/site/lobbyist-lobbyiste1.nsf/eng/h_nx00274.html.

Canada. Office of the Prime Minister. "Leaders' joint statement." Cancún, Mexico, March 31, 2006. http://news.gc.ca/web/

Canada. Parliament. House of Commons. Standing Committee on Foreign Affairs and International Development. "Evidence." Meeting 5, 40th Parliament, 2nd Session, February 25, 2009. http://www2.parl.gc.ca/HousePublications/Publication.aspx?DocId=3697038&Language=E&Mode=1&Parl=40&Ses=2.

Canada. Parliament. Senate Standing Committee on Foreign Affairs. "Issue 3—Evidence." 37th Parliament, 2nd Session, February 12, 2003. http://www.parl.gc.ca/37/2/parlbus/commbus/senate/Com-e/fore-e/03evb-e.htm.

Canada Revenue Agency. "Charities and Giving." February 20, 2009. http://www.cra-arc.gc.ca/tx/chrts/menu-eng.html.

Canada West Foundation. "2004 Annual Report." April 26, 2005. http://www.cwf.ca/V2/files/2004+Annual+Report.pdf.

Canadian Business, "Rich 100." *Canadian Business*, November 23, 2008. http://list.canadianbusiness.com/rankings/rich100/2008/ranking/Default.aspx?sp2=1&d1=a&sc1=0.

Canadian Constitution Foundation. "2006 Annual Report." http://www.canadianconstitutionfoundation.ca/files/pdf/Annual_Report_2006_FINAL.pdf.

Canadian Council of Chief Executives. "Canada and the United States must work together to boost free trade and economic recovery, Washington CEO summit participants agree." Washington, DC, March 24, 2009. http://www.ceocouncil.ca/en/view/?document_id=1336&type_id=1.

———. "Economy, Environment and Security: Taking the Canada-United States relationship to a new level." Ottawa, February 19, 2009. http://www.ceocouncil.ca/en/view/?document_id=1319&area_id=7.

———. "Trilateral security and prosperity partnership will boost jobs and investment, say Canada's CEOs." Ottawa, March 23, 2005. http://www.ceocouncil.ca/en/view/?document_id=402&area_id=7.

——— "Creating a North American community: Chairmen's statement." Independent Task Force on the Future of North America, March 14, 2005. http://www.ceocouncil.ca/en/view/?area_id=1&document_id=396.

———. "New frontiers: Building a 21st century Canada-United States partnership in North America." April 2004. http://www.ceocouncil.ca/publications/pdf/8502a13cf417d09eab13468e2a7c9f65/New_Frontiers_NASPI_Discussion_Paper_April_2004.pdf.

———. "The North American Security and Prosperity Initiative: Background, questions and answers." March 2003. http://www.ceocouncil.ca/publications/pdf/326ad94a31327c6a014ddf7347808918/presentations_2003_03_01.pdf.

———. "Security and prosperity: Toward a new Canada-United States partnership in North America." January 2003. http://www.ceocouncil.ca/publications/pdf/716af13644402901250657d4c418a12e/presentations_2003_01_01.pdf.

Canadian Newspaper Association. "Statement of principles." adopted 1977, revised 1995. http://www.cna-acj.ca/en/about/principles.

Canadian Statistical Assessment Service. "Why CanStats?" 2002. http://www.canstats.org/ (accessed November 13, 2002; site now discontinued).

Canadian Health Services Research Foundation. "Myth: A parallel system would reduce waiting times in the public system." *Mythbusters*, March 2005. http://www.chsrf.ca/mythbusters/pdf/myth17_e.pdf.

Canadian National Railway Co. "Management proxy/information circular." Montreal, March 9, 2001.

Cannon, Lou. *Reagan.* New York: G.B. Putnam's Sons, 1982.

Carey, Alex. *Taking the Risk Out of Democracy.* Urbana, IL: University of Illinois Press, 1997.

Carey, John. "Global warming: Suddenly the climate in Washington is changing." *BusinessWeek*, June 27, 2005, 91.

Cato Institute. "Cato Project on Social Security Choice." n.d. http://www.cato.org/pubs/ssps/sspstudies.html.

CBC News British Columbia. "Sea lice threatens salmon run, says researcher." April 28, 2004. http://www.cbc.ca/canada/british-columbia/story/2004/04/28/bc_lice20040428.html.

CBC-Radio Canada, Office of the Ombudsman. "Review of complaints about 'Medicare Schmedicare.'" June 2006. http://www.cbc.ca/ombudsman/page/medicarereview.pdf.

C.D. Howe Institute. "2002 Annual Report." Toronto, 2002.

———. "Canada's decision to avoid joining U.S., others in invading Iraq sends 'bizarre' and self-defeating signals: C.D. Howe Institute study." *Communiqué*, March 25, 2003. http://www.cdhowe.org/pdf/PressReleases/english/commentary_180pr.pdf.

Center for Media and Democracy. "The Advancement of Sound Science Coalition." SourceWatch, July 1, 2007. http://www.sourcewatch.org/index.php?title=The_Advancement_of_Sound_Science_Coalition.

———. "Canadian Coalition for Responsible Environmental Solutions." SourceWatch, November 6, 2006. http://www.sourcewatch.org/index.php?title=Canadian_Coalition_for_Responsible_Environmental_Solutions.

———. "Pacific Legal Foundation." SourceWatch, August 28, 2007. http://www.sourcewatch.org/index.php?title=Pacific_Legal_Foundation.

———. "Patrick J. Michaels." SourceWatch, October 1, 2007. http://www.sourcewatch.org/index.php?title=Patrick_Michaels.

———. "Ross McKitrick." SourceWatch, August 19, 2005. http://www.sourcewatch.org/index.php?title=Ross_McKitrick.

———. "Tom Harris (Canadian engineer/PR specialist)." SourceWatch, March 31, 2009. http://www.sourcewatch.org/index.php?title=Tom_Harris_(Canadian_engineer/PR_specialist).

Center for Responsive Politics. "James M. Inhofe (R-OK): Top Industries." 2007. http://www.opensecrets.org/politicians/summary.php?cid=N00005582&cycle=2006.

———. "Joe Barton (R-TX): Top Industries," 2007. http://www.opensecrets.org/politicians/summary.php?cid=N00005656&cycle=2006.

Center for Strategic and International Studies. "Canada: overview." 2008. http://www.csis.org/americas/canada/.

Center for the Defense of Free Enterprise. "Economic Human Rights Project." n.d. http://www.cdfe.org/EHRP.htm (accessed November 17, 2007; site now discontinued).

Children First School Choice Trust. "Staff." 2007. http://www.childrenfirstgrants.ca/main/index.php?pid=2&page_id=166.

Chisick, Harvey. "Pamphlets and journalism in the early French Revolution." *French Historical Studies* (Fall 1988): 623-645.

Chomsky, Noam. *Necessary Illusions: Thought Control in Democratic Societies.* Toronto: Anansi Press, 2003.

Choudhry, Sujit and Claire E. Hunter. "Measuring judicial activism on the Supreme Court of Canada." *McGill Law Journal* (August 2003): 525-562.

Christensen, Sandra. *Unions and the Public Interest.* Vancouver: Fraser Institute, 1980.

Christian Legal Fellowship. "Conference speakers and leaders." Conference 2002, Banff, Alta. http://www.christianlegalfellowship.org/Conference/2002%20featured_speakers.htm (accessed February 3, 2008; site now discontinued).

Civitas Society. "Eleventh annual national conference, programme." Halifax, May 4-6, 2007. http://www.civitascanada.ca/docs/2007_programme_(2_May_07).pdf.

———. "Seventh annual national conference, programme," Toronto, April 25-27, 2003. http://www.civitascanada.ca/docs/2003PreliminaryProgram15March03(2).pdf.

Clarke, Tony. *Silent Coup: Confronting the Big Business Takeover of Canada.* Toronto: James Lorimer, 1997.

Coates, David. "Ruling mythologies." In *Bad Work: A Review of Papers from a Fraser Institute Conference on 'Right-to-Work' Laws,* edited by Lynn Spink, 15-18. Toronto: York University, Centre for Research on Work and Society, 1997.

Coffey, Edwin. "The case for increased privatization of Canadian health care." *McGill Journal of Medicine* (2008): 75-76.

Cohen, Bernard. *The Press and Foreign Policy.* Princeton, NJ: Princeton University Press, 1963.

Cohen, Marjorie. "Neo-cons on campus." *This Magazine,* July 1995, 30-32.

Compas, Inc. "Asia-Pacific Partnership embraced 2:1 over Kyoto." May 29, 2006. http://www.compas.ca/data/060529-KyotoAndAsia-PacificPartnership-EPCB.pdf.

Consumer Policy Institute. "Health care campaign." 1997. http://www.c-p-i.org/cpi/print.cfm?ContentID=11122.

Coombs, James and Dan Nimmo. *The New Propaganda.* New York: Longman, 1993.

Cooper, Barry. "Like lipstick on a pig …: The politics of Kyoto." *Fraser Forum,* January 2003, 4-5. http://www.fraserinstitute.org/Commerce.Web/product_files/FraserForum_January2003.pdf.

Corporate Watch. "Burson-Marsteller: A corporate profile." July 2002. http://www.corporatewatch.org.uk/?lid=395.

Corporate Watch. "Greenwash fact sheet." March 22, 2001. http://www.corpwatch.org/article.php?id=242.

Council of the Americas. "Security and Prosperity Partnership: Meeting with Hon. Carlos Gutierrez, U.S. Secretary of Commerce." Washington, DC, March 15, 2006. http://www.spp.gov/pdf/SPPSummaryCounciloftheAmericas.pdf.

Council of Canadians. "Not counting Canadians: The Security and Prosperity Partnership and public opinion." Ottawa, April 2008. http://www.canadians.org/integratethis/backgrounders/notcounting/index.html.

Covington, Sally. "How conservative philanthropies and think tanks transform US policy." *Covert Action Quarterly,* Winter 1998, 6-16.

Creel, George. *How We Advertised America.* New York: Arno Press, 1972.

Cross, Frank. "Could Kyoto Kill?" Washington, DC: Competitive Enterprise Institute, October 1, 1998. http://cei.org/gencon/025,01186.cfm.

Croteau, David. "Examining the 'liberal media' claim." *Fairness and Accuracy in Reporting,* June 1, 1998. http://www.fair.org/index.php?page=2447.

Cunningham, Stanley. *The Idea of Propaganda.* New York: Praeger, 2002.

———. "Smoke and mirrors: A confirmation of Jacques Ellul's theory of information use in propaganda." In *Propaganda: A Pluralistic Perspective* , edited by Ted J. Smith, 151-163. New York: Praeger, 1989.

Curtis, Jenefer. "Now cross my other palm." *Canadian Business,* November 1996, 20.

Dabbs, Frank. "Calgary's new right-wing cabal." *Alberta Report,* September 24, 1984, 8-9.

d'Aquino, Tom. "Security and prosperity, the dynamics of a new Canada-United States partnership in North America." Presentation to the annual general meeting of the Canadian Council of Chief Executives, Toronto, January 14, 2003. http://www.ceocouncil.ca/publications/pdf/b10f11c9777f6bcf34fa14e57a594c3c/presentations_2003_01_14.pdf.

Davies, Charles. "The end of Bay Street." *National Post Business,* May 2002, 38-46.

Dean, James. "The case for continued controls (and other heresies)," in *Which Way Ahead? Canada After Wage and Price Controls,* edited by Michael Walker, 225-237. Vancouver: Fraser Institute, 1977.

De Groot, Gerard. "Reagan's Rise." *History Today* (September 1995): 31-36.

Delwiche, Aaron. "Propaganda." January 2, 2006. http://www.propagandacritic.com/.

DeSmogBlog.com. "Congress of Racial Equality." n.d. http://www.desmogblog.com/congress-on-racial-equality-core.

Dobbin, Murray. *The Myth of the Good Corporate Citizen: Democracy Under the Rule of Big Business.* Toronto, Stoddart, 1998.

———. *Preston Manning and the Reform Party.* Toronto: James Lorimer, 1991.

Dobson, Wendy. "Shaping the future of the North American economic space: A framework for action." *C.D. Howe Institute Commentary* 162, April 2002. http://www.cdhowe.org/pdf/commentary_162.pdf.

Dominion Institute, "About." n.d. http://www.dominion.ca/about.htm.

———. "Passages to Canada: Teachers resource booklet." 2001. http://www.passagestoCanada.com/PTCeng.pdf.

Donohue, John III and Steven Levitt. "The impact of legalized abortion on crime." *Quarterly Journal of Economics* (May 2001): 379-420.

Dorgan, Byron. "The NAFTA debate that never was." *Columbia Journalism Review,* January/February 1994, 47-49.

Dorrien, Gary. *The Neoconservative Mind: Politics, Culture and the War of Ideology.* Philadelphia: Temple University Press, 1993.

Dowd, Ann Reilly and Suneel Ratan. "How to get things done in Washington." *Fortune,* August 9, 1993, 60-62.

Dreyfuss, Robert. "Grover Norquist: Field Marshall' of the Bush plan." *The Nation,* May 14, 2001. http://www.thenation.com/doc/20010514/dreyfuss.

————. "Reverend Doomsday." *Rolling Stone*. January 28, 2004. http://www.rollingstone.com/politics/story/5939999/reverend_doomsday/.

Drury, Shadia. *Leo Strauss and the American Right*. New York: St. Martin's Press, 1999.

————. *The Political Ideas of Leo Strauss*, updated ed. New York: Palgrave Macmillan, 2005.

Duffy, Margaret. "There's no two-way symmetric about it: A postmodern examination of public relations textbooks." *Critical Studies in Media Communication* (September 2000): 294-315.

Duffy, Michael and Ann Blackman. "I hear you, I hear you." *Time*, June 21, 1993, 20-23.

Edwards, Anne. *Early Reagan: The Rise to Power*. New York: Morrow, 1987.

Ewen, Stuart. *PR!: A Social History of Spin*. New York: Basic Books, 1996.

ExxonSecrets. "Factsheet: Committee for a Constructive Tomorrow." n.d. http://www.exxonsecrets.org/html/orgfactsheet.php?id=25.

————. "Factsheet: Reason Foundation." n.d. http://www.exxonsecrets.org/html/orgfactsheet.php?id=63.

Fairness and Accuracy in Reporting. "An Aggressive Conservative vs. a 'Liberal to be Determined.'" *Extra*, November-December 2003. http://www.fair.org/extra/0311/hannity-colmes.html.

Federalist Society. "About us." n.d. http://www.fed-soc.org/aboutus/.

Fillmore, Nick. "Right stuff: An inside look at the National Citizens Coalition." *This Magazine*, July 1986, 4-11, 19.

Foley, Duncan. *Adam's Fallacy: A Guide to Economic Theology*. Cambridge, MA: Belknap Press, 2006.

Forget, Evelyn, Raisa Deber and Leslie Ross. "Medical Savings Accounts: Will they reduce costs?" *Canadian Medical Association Journal* (July 23, 2002): 143-147.

"Foreign policy reviews should not be conducted." *Maclean's*, May 2, 2005, 17.

Fraser Institute, "Annual Report, 1978."

————. "Canada's common sense revolution in medicare reform." A Fraser Institute Round Table Luncheon with Dr. Brian Day, Toronto, April 20, 2006. http://www.fraserinstitute.org/commerce.web/product_files/Day Toronto Flyer.pdf.

————. "Challenging perceptions: Twenty-five years of influential ideas." 1999. http://www.fraserinstitute.org/Commerce.Web/product_files/challenging_perceptions.pdf.

————, "The cost of justice in Canada." *Fraser Forum*, June 1996. http://oldfraser.lexi.net/publications/forum/1996/june/FF-06-96.html.

————, "The Fraser Institute at 30: A retrospective." 2004. http://www.fraserinstitute.org/files/PDFs/About_Us/30th_Retrospective.pdf.

————. "The Fraser Institute membership list." Addendum to 1978 annual report, March 6, 1979.

————. *Frontline* 3 no. 2, September 2004.

————. *Frontline* 4 no. 1, February 2005.

————. "Media advisory: Fraser Institute cocktail series hosts discussion on Canada's ailing health care system." October 22, 2007. http://www.marketwire.com/mw/release.do?id=783394.

————. "On liberty and public choice: The Fraser Institute and Liberty Fund, Inc. host student colloquium." *Fraser Forum*, June 2008, 28. http://www.fraserinstitute.org/Commerce.Web/product_files/FraserForum_June2008.pdf.

————. "The politics, science and economics of Kyoto." *Fraser Forum,* January 2003. http://www. fraserinstitute.org/commerce.web/product_files/FraserForum_January2003.pdf.

————. "A salute to the Fraser Institute: 30 years of influential ideas." October 12, 2004. http://www. fraserinstitute.org/commerce.web/product_files/Invitation.pdf.

————. "Student essay contest: How can property rights protect the environment? Free-market environmentalism resource guide." Fraser Institute, 2005. http://www.fraserinstitute.ca/ studentcentre/intern.asp (accessed June 15, 2005; site now discontinued).

————. "Summer internship program 2005: Research projects, 2005." http://www.fraserinstitute.ca/ studentcentre/essay.asp (accessed June 15, 2005; site now discontinued).

————. "Toward the new millennium—A five year plan for the Fraser Institute—draft." n.d.

————. "2007 Annual Report: Changing the World." http://www.fraserinstitute.org/files/PDFs/ annual_reports/2007_Annual_Report.pdf.

————. "2006 Annual Report: 'If it matters, measure it.'" http://www.fraserinstitute.org/files/PDFs/ annual_reports/2006_Annual_Report.pdf.

————. "2005 Annual Report: 'If it matters, measure it.'" http://www.fraserinstitute.org/files/PDFs/ annual_reports/2005_Annual_Report.pdf.

————. "2002 Annual Report." http://www.fraserinstitute.org/files/PDFs/annual_reports/2002_ Annual_Report.pdf.

Friel, Brian. "Trust in government on the decline again." *Government Executive,* July 13, 1999. http:// www.govexec.com/dailyfed/0799/071399b1.htm.

"Friends of Science critiques the evidence for man-made climate change." *Daily Oil Bulletin,* June 12, 2006. http://www.dobmagazine.nickles.com/columns/pulse.asp?article=magazine%2Fcolum ns%2F060612%2FMAG_COL2006_UC0000.html

Friends of the Earth. "Fifth survey of climate change disclosure in SEC filings." October 2006. http:// www.foe.org/pdf/SECFinalReportandAppendices.pdf.

Friesen, Lauri. "The social contract rewritten." *Alberta Report,* August 18, 1997 10-11.

Frontier Centre for Public Policy. "FCPP staff." 2007. http://www.fcpp.org/main/people. php?CategoryID=6.

————. "Expert advisory panel." 2007. http://www.fcpp.org/main/people.php?CategoryID=%202.

Fuller, Colleen. *Caring for Profit.* Vancouver: New Star Books, 1998.

"Full text of Stephen Harper's 1997 speech," Canadian Press, December 14, 2005. http://www.ctv.ca/ servlet/ArticleNews/story/CTVNews/20051213/elxn_harper_speech_text_051214/20051214.

Gagnon, Louise. "Private health care urged to end long waiting lists." *Medical Post* (May 5, 1998): 52.

Gairdner, William. "The history of Civitas." *The Civil Conversation,* January 2007. http://www. civitascanada.ca/docs/Civitas_newsletter_Vol_2_No_1_(January_2007).pdf.

Gans, Herbert. *Deciding What's News.* New York: Vintage Books, 1980.

Gardner, Timothy. "US: Power group promoting global warming skeptic." Reuters, July 27, 2006. http://www.corpwatch.org/article.php?id=13978&printsafe=1.

Geddes, John. "Meet the real Stephen Harper." *Maclean's,* May 9, 2005, 23-27.

Gelbspan, Ross. *Boiling Point: How Politicians, Big Oil and Coal, Journalists, and Activists are Fueling the Climate Crisis—and What We Can Do to Avert Disaster.* New York: Basic Books, 2004.

Gilbert, Emily. "The inevitability of integration? Neoliberal discourse and the proposals for a new North American economic space after September 11." *Annals of the Association of American Geographers* (Mar 2005): 202-222.

Gindin, Sam. "Anti-capitalism and the terrain of social justice." *Monthly Review,* November 1, 2002, 1-14.

Global TV. "Does the state have any place in the cribs of the nation?" *Global Sunday,* February 20, 2005. CBCA Complete database.

———. "Is equalization equal?" *Global Sunday,* February 20, 2005. CBCA Complete database.

———. "State of the union—gay OK?" *Global Sunday,* December 5, 2004. CBCA Complete database.

———. "The nanny state." *Global Sunday,* December 12, 2004. CBCA Complete database.

———. "Political pandemonium." *Global Sunday,* January 30, 2005. CBCA Complete database.

———. "Should Ottawa sign on to missile defence?" *Global Sunday,* December 5, 2004. CBCA Complete database.

Godin, Keith and Neils Veldhuis. "The economic effects of increasing British Columbia's minimum wage." Fraser Institute, January 7, 2009. http://www.fraserinstitute.org/Commerce.Web/product_files/EconomicEffectsBCMinimumWage.pdf.

Goldberg, Jonah. "Immanent corrections." *National Review Online,* January 16, 2002. http://article.nationalreview.com/?q=ODQ5Y2ZiNjAzMjdlNDAwMTk2MTgxNGVlYTE1Nzc5YjQ=#more.

Goldfarb, Danielle. "The road to a Canada-U.S. customs union: Step-by-step or in a single bound?" *C.D. Howe Institute Commentary* 184, June 2003. http://www.cdhowe.org/pdf/commentary_184.pdf.

Goodess, Clare. "Stormy times for climate research." Scientists for Global Responsibility, *SGR Newsletter.* November 2003. http://www.sgr.org.uk/climate/Stormy_Times_NL28.htm.

Goss, Brian. "'All our kids get better jobs tomorrow': The North American Free Trade Agreement in The *New York Times.*" *Journalism & Communication Monographs* (Spring 2001): 3-47.

Gotlieb, Allan. "Foremost partner: The conduct of Canada-US relations." In *Canada Among Nations 2003: Coping With the American Colossus,* edited by D. Carment, F.O. Hampson and N. Hillmer, 19-31.Toronto: Oxford University Press, 2003.

Grace, Kevin Michael. "Alberta first." *The Report,* February 19, 2001, 10-13.

Grandin, Greg. "Milton Friedman and the economics of empire." *Counterpunch,* November 17, 2006. http://www.counterpunch.org/grandin11172006.html.

Grant, George. *Lament for a Nation.* Montreal and Kingston: McGill-Queens University Press, (1971) 1997.

Gratzer, David. "It's time to consider Medical Savings Accounts." *Canadian Medical Association Journal* (July 23, 2002): 151-152.

Gray, John. "Rich 100: Fallen giants," *Canadian Business,* December 22, 2008. http://www.canadianbusiness.com/after_hours/lifestyle_activities/article.jsp?content=20081222_10011_10011.

Green, Kenneth. "Kyoto Krazy." *Fraser Forum,* January 2003, 6-7. http://www.fraserinstitute.org/Commerce.Web/product_files/FraserForum_January2003.pdf.

Grubel, Herbert and Michael Walker, eds. *Unemployment Insurance: Global Evidence of its Effects on Unemployment.* Vancouver: Fraser Institute, 1978.

Gutstein, Donald. "Budget coverage out of balance." The Tyee, February 21, 2005. http://thetyee.ca/Mediacheck/2005/02/21/BudgetCoverageOutofBalance/.

————. "Corporate advocacy: The Fraser Institute." City Magazine, September 1978, 32-39.

Gwartney, James and Robert Lawson. "Economic Freedom of the World: 2007 Annual Report." Economic Freedom Network, 2007. http://www.fraserinstitute.org/commerce.web/product_files/EconomicFreedomoftheWorld2007.pdf.

Hackett, Robert and Richard Gruneau. The Missing News. Ottawa: Canadian Centre for Policy Alternatives, 1999.

Hadar, Leon. "The surge scam: getting rid of the goat." IRC Right Web, September 11, 2007. http://www.rightweb.irc-online.org/beta/articles/display/The_Surge_Scam_Getting_Rid_of_the_Goat/.

Hanley, Wayne. The Genesis of Napoleonic Propaganda, 1796-1799. New York: Columbia University Press, 2005.

Harms, William. "Olin Center offers last conference on 'Empire and Liberty.'" Chicago Chronicle, April 28, 2005. http://chronicle.uchicago.edu/050428/olin.shtml.

Harper, Stephen. "Rediscovering the right agenda." Citizens Centre Report, June 2003, 72-77.

Harper, Stephen and Tom Flanagan. "Our benign dictatorship." Next City, Winter 1996/1997, 34-40, 54-56.

Harris, Marilyn. "The high priest of hype." BusinessWeek, August 17, 1998, 13.

Harrison, Trevor. Of Passionate Intensity: Right-Wing Populism and the Reform Party of Canada. Toronto: University of Toronto Press, 1995.

Hart, Michael. "Round table on Canada-US free trade: Is it time for round two?" Canadian Foreign Policy (Spring 2000): 1-14.

————. "Steer or drift? Taking charge of Canada-US regulatory convergence." C.D. Howe Institute Commentary 229, March 2006. http://www.cdhowe.org/pdf/commentary_229.pdf.

Hartz, Jim and Rick Chappell. "Worlds apart: How the distance between science and journalism threatens America's future." First Amendment Center, Nashville, TN, 1997. http://www.firstamendmentcenter.org/PDF/worldsapart.pdf.

Harvard-Smithsonian Center for Astrophysics. "20th century climate not so hot." March 31, 2003. http://cfa-www.harvard.edu/press/archive/pr0310.html.

Hayes, Christopher. "The new funding heresies." In These Times, June 26, 2006. http://www.inthesetimes.com/main/article/2697/.

Hayes, David. Power and Influence: The Globe and Mail and the News Revolution. Toronto: Key Porter Books, 1992.

Helvarg, David. The War Against the Greens. San Francisco: Sierra Club Books, 1994.

Hemispheric Social Alliance. "Lessons from NAFTA: The High Cost of 'Free Trade.'" Ottawa, Canadian Centre for Policy Alternatives, 2003. http://www.policyalternatives.ca/documents/National_Office_Pubs/lessons_from_NAFTA.pdf.

Heritage Foundation. "2006 Annual Report." 2006. http://www.heritage.org/About/upload/AnnualReport06.pdf.

————. "2005 Annual Report." March 1, 2006. http://www.heritage.org/About/upload/96065_1.pdf.

Herman, Edward. "The propaganda model revisited." Monthly Review (July/August 1996): 115-128.

Herman, Edward and Noam Chomsky. Manufacturing Consent. New York: Pantheon Books, 1988.

Hirschman, Albert O. "Reactionary rhetoric." *Atlantic Monthly,* May 1989, 63-69.

——. *The Rhetoric of Reaction.* Cambridge, MA: Belknap Press, 1991.

——. "Two hundred years of reactionary rhetoric: The case of the perverse effect." The Tanner Lecture on Human Values, University of Michigan, April 8, 1988. http://www.tannerlectures.utah. edu/lectures/documents/hirschman89.pdf.

Hites, Ronald A. et al. "Global assessment of organic contaminants in farmed salmon." *Science* (January 9, 2004): 226-9.

Holtman, Robert. *Napoleonic Propaganda.* Baton Rouge, LA: Louisiana State University Press, 1950.

Home School Legal Defence Association. "HSLDA of Canada announces the departure of Dallas K. Miller, Q.C." News Release, November 19, 2004. http://www.hslda.ca/news_release.pdf (accessed February 10, 2008; site now discontinued).

Hsiao, William C. "Behind the ideology and theory: What is the empirical evidence for Medical Savings Accounts?" *Journal of Health Politics, Policy and Law* (August 2001): 733-737.

Huntington, Samuel. "The United States." In *The Crisis of Democracy: Report on the Governability of Democracies to the Trilateral Commission,* edited by Michel Crozier, Samuel Huntington and Joji Watanuki, 59-118. New York: New York University Press, 1975.

Ipsos Reid. "Canadian views on health care scenarios." June 7, 2006. http://www.ipsos-na.com/news/ pressrelease.cfm?id=3102.

——. "Seven in ten Canadians think that the overall quality of the health care system in Canada will be the same (39%) or worse (32%)in ten years." October 21, 2008. http://www.ipsos-na.com/ news/pressrelease.cfm?id=4134.

Innovative Research Group. "Canadian values similar to other advanced democracies." The Canadian Values Study: Day Five Release, September 29, 2005. http://www.innovativeresearch. ca/Canadian%20Values%20Study_Factum%20280905.pdf.

Institute for Humane Studies. "Craig Yirush," n.d. http://www.theihs.org/people/id.762/people.asp.

Jedicke, Peter. "Notes on John Rawls, A Theory of Justice, 1971." 1996. http://gs.fanshawec.ca/ pjedicke/Rawls.htm.

Jeffery, Brooke. *Hard Right Turn.* Toronto: HarperCollins, 1999.

Jhally, Sut. "Advertising at the edge of the apocalypse." Department of Communication, University of Massachusetts at Amherst, 2001. http://www.sutjhally.com/articles/advertisingattheed/.

John M. Olin Center for Inquiry into the Theory and Practice of Democracy. "About the Olin Center." January 2, 2000. http://olincenter.uchicago.edu/about_olin.html.

Johnson, Paul. *Napoleon.* New York: Viking Penguin, 2002.

Jones, Keith. "Big business blasts Canada's Liberal government." World Socialist Web Site, April 11, 2000. http://www.wsws.org/articles/2000/apr2000/chre-a11.shtml.

Jones, Laura, ed. *Global Warming: The Science and the Politics.* Vancouver: Fraser Institute, 1997.

——. "Let's talk about the weather." *Fraser Forum,* February 1998, 39-40. http://oldfraser.lexi.net/ publications/forum/1998/february/environment.html.

——. "The precautionary principle is reckless." *Fraser Forum,* March 1999, 15-16. http://oldfraser. lexi.net/publications/forum/1999/03/precautionary.html.

Jowett, Garth and Victoria O'Donnell. *Propaganda and Persuasion,* 4th ed. Thousand Oaks, CA: Sage, 2006.

————. *Propaganda and Persuasion*, 3rd ed. Thousand Oaks CA: Sage, 1999.

Kaihla, Paul. "Back on the rails." *Maclean's*, January 13, 1997, 36-38.

Kennedy, Michael. "The 'last stand' of the Jacobin clubs." *French Historical Studies* (Fall 1989): 309-344.

Kennickell, Arthur. "Currents and undercurrents: Changes in the distribution of wealth, 1989-2004." Federal Reserve Board, Washington, DC, January 30, 2006. http://www.federalreserve.gov/Pubs/FEDS/2006/200613/200613pap.pdf.

Kheiriddin, Tasha and Adam Daifallah. "Rescuing Canada's right." *Western Standard*, November 8, 2004, 29-33.

Korten, David C. *When Corporations Rule the World.* West Hartford, CT: Kumarian Press, 1995.

Krehely, Jeff, Meaghan House and Emily Kernan. *Axis of Ideology: Conservative Foundations and Public Policy.* National Committee for Responsive Philanthropy, March 2004.

Kurtz, Howard. "When the press outclasses the public." *Columbia Journalism Review*, May/June 1994, 31-34.

Kuttner, Robert. *Everything for Sale.* Chicago: University of Chicago Press, 1999.

Laidler, David and William Robson. "The great Canadian disinflation: The economics and politics of monetary policy in Canada, 1988-1993." C.D. Howe Institute, January 1994.

Lakoff, George. *Don't Think of an Elephant.* White River Junction, VT: Chelsea Green, 2004.

————*Whose Freedom?* New York: Farrar, Straus and Giroux, 2006.

Landay, Jerry. "The Powell Manifesto: How a prominent lawyer's attack memo changed America." Mediatransparency.org, August 20, 2002. http://www.mediatransparency.org/story.php?storyID=21 (accessed August 21, 2007; site now discontinued).

————. "Simon said: The neocon hothouse that William Simon built." Mediatransparency.org. June 23, 2004. http://www.mediatransparency.org/story.php?storyID=19 (accessed August 21, 2007; site now discontinued).

Langille, David. "The Business Council on National Issues and the Canadian state." *Studies in Political Economy* (Autumn 1987): 41-85.

Laycock, David. *The New Right and Democracy in Canada.* Don Mills, ON: Oxford University Press, 2001.

"Left-wing shtick: the Vancouver Province is criticized for removing a professor's comments from a story." *Media*, Spring 2000, 15.

Levant, Ezra. "A legacy of liberty." *Western Standard*, May 16, 2005. http://westernstandard.ca/website/article.php?id=772.

"Liberalism regained: Building the next progressive majority." *Harper's Magazine*, August 2004, 31-38.

Lieberman, Trudy. *Slanting the Story.* New York: New Press, 2000.

Lilley, Sasha. "On neoliberalism: an interview with David Harvey." *Monthly Review*, June 19, 2006. http://mrzine.monthlyreview.org/lilley190606.html.

Lippmann, Walter. *The Phantom Public.* New York: Harcourt Brace, 1925.

Littlemore, Richard. "Tim Ball: the first Canadian PhD in climatology." deSmogBlog, June 15, 2006. http://www.desmogblog.com/tim-ball-the-first-canadian-phd-in-climatology?print_version=true.

Livermore, Michael. "Should environmentalists fear Cass Sunstein?" *The New Republic*, January 12, 2009. http://blogs.tnr.com/tnr/blogs/environmentandenergy/archive/2009/01/12/should-environmentalists-fear-cass-sunstein.aspx.

Lobe, Jim. "Strong must rule the weak, said neo-cons' muse." CommonDreams.org News Center, May 8, 2003. http://www.commondreams.org/headlines03/0508-02.htm.

Lohrey, Andrew. "Introduction." In Alex Carey, *Taking the Risk Out of Democracy*, 1-8. Urbana, IL: University of Illinois Press, 1997.

Lyons, Matthew N. "Business conflict and right-wing movements." In *Unraveling the Right: The New Conservatism in American Thought and Politics*, edited by Amy E. Ansell, 80-102. Boulder, CO: Westview Press, 1998.

MacDonald, Martha. "Alberta weighs the evidence." In *Bad Work: A Review of Papers from a Fraser Institute Conference on 'Right-to-Work' Laws*, edited by Lynn Spink, York University, Centre for Research on Work and Society, Toronto, 1997, 15-18.

Magnusson, Warren. "Introduction." In *The New Reality: The Politics of Restraint in British Columbia*, edited by Warren Magnusson et al., 11 15. Vancouver: New Star Books, 1984.

Maioni, Antonia. *Parting at the Crossroads: The Emergence of Health Insurance in the United States and Canada*. Princeton, NJ: Princeton University Press, 1998.

Manfredi, Christopher and James B. Kelly. ""Misrepresenting the Supreme Court's record?" *McGill Law Journal* (August 2004): 741-765.

Marshall, T.H. *Class, Citizenship and Social Development*. New York: Doubleday, 1965.

Marshall Institute. "William O'Keefe." n.d. http://www.marshall.org/experts.php?id=83.

Martin, Dick. "The need for a collective voice." *National Round Table Review*, Spring 1993, 12.

Martin, Lawrence. *Pledge of Allegiance*. Toronto: McClelland & Stewart, 1993.

Martineau, Patrice. "Federal personal income tax: Slicing the pie." Statistics Canada Publication No. 11-621-MIE No. 24, April 2005. http://www.statcan.gc.ca/pub/11-621-m/11-621-m2005024-eng.pdf.

Matlow, Josh. "Big Oil's Kyoto party." *NOW Online*. October 24, 2002. http://www.nowtoronto.com/news/story.cfm?content=134108&archive=22,8,2002.

May, Sir Robert and Richard Pitts. "Communicating the science behind global environmental change issues." In *The Daily Globe: Environmental Change, the Public and the Media*, edited by Joe Smith, 15-25. London: Earthscan Publications, 2000.

McCombs, Maxwell. *Setting the Agenda*. Cambridge: Polity Press, 2004.

McDonald, Andy and Lene Palmer. "Propaganda: The invention of printing and its aftermath." George Mason University, December 15, 2003. http://mason.gmu.edu/~amcdonal/Printing%20and%20Its%20Aftermath.html.

———. "Propaganda: Roots of propaganda." George Mason University, December 15, 2003. http://mason.gmu.edu/~amcdonal/Roots%20of%20Propaganda.html.

McDonald, Marci. "The man behind Stephen Harper." *The Walrus*, October 2004, 34-49.

McKenzie, Hilda and William Rees. "An analysis of a brownlash report." *Ecological Economics*, (March 2007): 505-515.

McKibben, Bill. "The coming meltdown." *New York Review of Books*, January 12, 2006. http://www.nybooks.com/articles/18616.

McKitrick, Ross. "Counting the costs: Effects of the federal Kyoto strategy on Canadian households." Prepared for the Canadian Taxpayers Federation, November 2002. http://www.taxpayer.com/pdf/Kyoto_Protocol_Report_(November_12_2002).pdf.

McQuaig, Linda. *Shooting the Hippo*. Toronto: Viking, 1995.

Media Transparency. http://www.mediatransparency.org (accessed various dates; site now discontinued).

Medicare Schmedicare. DVD. Directed by Robert Duncan. International Documentary Television Corporation/CBC/Filmwest Associates, 2005.

Methot, Suzanne. "Controversial author nabs Donner prize." *Windspeaker,* July 2001, 24, 34.

Mining Association of Canada. "Study finds primary metals sector has highest overall ranking in Canada for use of advanced technologies." November 20, 2001. http://www.mining.ca/www/_news/news_264.php.

Mintz, Jack. "Government policy and the Canadian advantage." *Canadian Business Economics* (August 2000): 6-9.

Montague, Peter. "Ignorance is strength." *Rachel's Environment & Health News.* November 8, 1995. http://www.rachel.org/en/node/3974.

Montreal Economic Institute. "Staff." 2005. http://www.iedm.org/main/authors_en.php?authors_type=2.

———. "Supreme Court ruling in the Chaoulli case—private health-care can now benefit Canadians."'Media Release, June 9, 2005. http://www.iedm.org/main/print_mediareleases_en.php?mediareleases_id=81.

———. "Using private insurance to finance health care." *Economic Note,* November 2005. http://www.iedm.org/uploaded/pdf/nov05_en.pdf.

Mooney, Chris. "Some like it hot." *Mother Jones.* May 2005. http://www.motherjones.com/news/feature/2005/05/some_like_it_hot.html.

Morton, Alexandra. "A salmon sleuth's disturbing find." The Tyee, November 20, 2004. http://thetyee.ca/Views/2004/11/20/SalmonSleuth/.

Morton, F.L. and Rainer Knopff. *The Charter Revolution and the Court Party.* Peterborough, ON: Broadview Press, 2000.

Mulawka, Brian. "Go west, young intellectual." *Alberta Report,* March 30, 1998, 8-10.

Mulvale, James. "Review of Jamie Peck, Workfare States." *Canadian Journal of Sociology Online,* January-February 2002. http://www.cjsonline.ca/reviews/workfare.html.

Murdock, Deroy. "William Simon: hero of the revolution." *National Review Online,* June 5, 2000. http://article.nationalreview.com/?q=MzU4OWUxYjg1OTk3ZTFmMjI5NjhjNjQ1NWJjMjJjYTE=.

Murray, Charles. *Losing Ground: America's Social Policy, 1950-1980.* New York: Basic Books, 1984.

Murray, Stuart and Hugh Mackenzie. "Bringing minimum wages above the poverty line." Canadian Centre for Policy Alternatives, March 2007. http://www.policyalternatives.ca/documents/National_Office_Pubs/2007/minimum_wage_above_poverty_line.pdf.

Nace, Fred. *Gangs of America: The Rise of Corporate Power and the Disabling of Democracy.* San Francisco: Berrett-Koehler, 2003.

Nash, Knowlton. "This imperfect necessity." *content.* January/February 1988, 7-11.

National Academies. "Surface temperature reconstructions for the last 2,000 years." Report in Brief, June 2006. http://www.dels.nas.edu/dels/rpt_briefs/Surface_Temps_final.pdf.

National Center for Atmospheric Research. "Media advisory: the hockey stick controversy." May 11, 2005. http://www.ucar.edu/news/releases/2005/ammann.shtml.

Newman, Peter C. *Titans: How the New Canadian Establishment Seized Power.* Toronto: Viking,

1998.

Norquist, Grover. "The international reach of Civitas." *The Civil Conversation*, March 2007. http://www.civitascanada.ca/docs/Civitas_Newsletter_Vol_II_No_3_(Sept_07).pdf.

Norton, Anne. *Leo Strauss and the Politics of American Empire.* New Haven, CN: Yale University Press, 2004.

O'Donnell, Victoria and Garth Jowett. "Propaganda as a form of communication." In *Propaganda: A Pluralistic Perspective*, edited by Ted J. Smith, 49-63. New York: Praeger, 1989.

Ogilvie, Kelvin. "From public U to private U." Atlantic Institute for Market Studies, September 2005. http://www.aims.ca/aimslibrary.asp?ft=1&fd=0&fi=1&id=1195&p=1.

Oreskes, Naomi. "Beyond the Ivory Tower: The scientific consensus on climate change." *Science*, December 3, 2004, 1686. http://www.sciencemag.org/cgi/content/full/306/5702/1686.

Orey, Michael. "The Supreme Court: Open for business." *BusinessWeek*, July 9, 2007, 30.

Orwin, Clifford. "Remembering Allan Bloom." *American Scholar* (Summer 1993): 423-430.

Parker, Shafer Jr. "Ottawa, the last obstacle to national unity." *Alberta Report*, August 24, 1998, 10.

Pastor, Robert. "The future of North America." *Foreign Affairs* (Jul/Aug 2008): 84-98.

"Pat Michaels: scientist, energy industry lackey, Washington Post contributor." Media Matters for America, May 20, 2004. http://mediamatters.org/items/printable/200405200001.

Pearson, Ian. "Thou shall not ignore the West." *Saturday Night*, December 1990, 34-45.

People for the American Way. "Buying a movement: Right-wing foundations and American politics." 1996. http://67.192.238.59/multimedia/pdf/Reports/buyingamovement.pdf.

"Physician vows to take parallel-system to Supreme Court." *Canadian Medical Association Journal* (June 2, 1998): 1509.

Piatkowski, Scott. "Zero degrees of separation." Rabble News, November 19, 2003. http://www.rabble.ca/columnists/zero-degrees-separation.

Pitsula, James and Kenneth Rasmussen. *Privatizing a Province: The New Right in Saskatchewan.* Vancouver: New Star Books, 1990.

Powell, Lewis. "Confidential memorandum: Attack of American free enterprise system." August 23, 1971. http://www.mediatransparency.org/story.php?storyID=22.

Pratkanis. Anthony and Elliot Aronson. *Age of Propaganda: The Everyday Use and Abuse of Persuasion.* New York: W.H. Freeman, 1992.

Project Censored. "Top 25 stories of 2008." October 14, 2007. http://www.projectcensored.org/censored_2008/index.htm.

Prospectus Associates et al. "Canada-U.S. Executive Summit: Economic and Political Relations Under a Bush Administration." Toronto, September 5-6, 2001. http://www.weareyourtype.com/Canada2FUSProgram.pdf.

"Put a tiger in your think tank." *Mother Jones.* May/June 2005. http://www.motherjones.com/politics/2005/05/put-tiger-your-think-tank.

Qualter, Terence. *Opinion Control in the Democracies.* London: Macmillan, 1985.

Rabkin, Jeremy. "Cornell's Public Law Tradition in Political Science." *Cornell University College of Arts and Sciences Newsletter*, Spring 1995. http://www.arts.cornell.edu/newsletr/spring95/rabkin.htm.

Rachlis, Michael. "Public solutions to health care wait lists." Canadian Centre for Policy. Alternatives, December 2005. http://www.policyalternatives.ca/documents/National_Office_Pubs/2005/Health_Care_Waitlists.pdf.

Rampton, Sheldon and John Stauber. "Correction: Burson-Marsteller and the Global Climate Coalition." PR Watch, Fall 2001. http://www.prwatch.org/prwissues/2001Q3/cx.html.

Ramsay, Cynthia and David Gratzer. "Crucial debate clouded by political expediency." Fraser Forum, June 1997. http://oldfraser.lexi.net/publications/forum/1997/june/FF-06-97.html.

Ranelagh, John. Thatcher's People: An Insider's Account of the Politics, the Power, and the Personalities. London: HarperCollins, 1991.

Rau, Krishna. "A million for your thoughts." Canadian Forum, July/August 1996, 11-17.

Reagan, Ronald. An American Life. New York: Simon & Schuster, 1990.

"Reed Irvine takes AIM at the media." Human Events, January 21, 1994, 10.

Reed, Stanley. "BP to Washington: Time's up." BusinessWeek, June 11, 2001, 62.

Rendall, Steve. "An aggressive conservative vs. a 'liberal to be determined.'" Extra, November/December 2003. http://www.fair.org/extra/0311/hannity-colmes.html.

Resnick, Philip. The European Roots of Canadian Identity. Peterborough, ON: Broadview Press, 2005.

Rich, Andrew. "War of ideas." Stanford Social Innovation Review (Spring 2005): 18-25.

Richardson, Henry. "John Rawls." Internet Encyclopedia of Philosophy, 2006. http://www.iep.utm.edu/r/rawls.htm.

Robins, Kevin, Frank Webster and Michael Pickering. "Propaganda, information and social control." In Propaganda, Persuasion and Polemic, edited by Jeremy Hawthorn, 1-17. London: Edward Arnold, 1987.

Rogers, Everett, William Hait and James Dearing. "A paradigmatic history of agenda-setting research." In Do the Media Govern? edited by Shanto Iyengar and Richard Reeves, 225-236. Thousand Oaks, CA: Sage Publications, 1997.

Rosen, Ruth. "Challenge market fundamentalism." TomPaine.com, February 5, 2007. http://www.tompaine.com/print/challenge_market_fundamentalism.php.

Ross, Stewart Halsey. Propaganda for War. Jefferson, NC: McFarland, 1996.

Rothmyer, Karen. "Unindicted co-conspirator?" The Nation. February 23, 1998, 19-24.

Rovinsky, David. "The ascendancy of western Canada in Canadian policymaking." Center for Strategic and International Studies, Washington, DC, February 16, 1998. http://www.csis.org/media/csis/pubs/pp0902.pdf.

Saez, Emmanuel and Michael Veall. "The evolution of high incomes in North America: Lessons from Canadian evidence." American Economic Review (June 2005): 831-849.

Salmon of the Americas. "New studies show PCB levels in farmed salmon comparable to wild: Here's the new data." October 21, 2004. http://www.prnewswire.com/cgi-bin/stories.pl?ACCT=109&STORY=/www/story/10-21-2004/0002291312&EDATE.

Saunders, Doug. "A party to crash." This Magazine, March/April 1996, 32-33.

Savage, Luiza Ch. "Meet NAFTA 2.0." MACLEANS.CA, September 13, 2006. http://www.macleans.ca/article.jsp?content=20060911_133202_133202.

Schaller, Michael. Reckoning with Reagan: America and its President in the 1980s. New York: Oxford University Press, 1992.

Schmidt, Gavin and Caspar Ammann. "Dummies guide to the latest 'Hockey Stick' controversy." Real Climate: Climate Science from Climate Scientists, February 18 2005. http://www.realclimate.org/index.php?p=121.

Shanahan, James. *Propaganda Without Propagandists?* Cresskill, NJ: Hampton Press, 2001.

Shorris, Earl. "Ignoble liars: Leo Strauss, George Bush and the philosophy of mass deception." *Harper's Magazine*, June 2004, 65-71.

Shortt, Samuel. "Medical Savings Accounts in publicly funded health care systems: enthusiasm versus evidence." *Canadian Medical Association Journal* (July 23, 2002): 159-162.

Shuman, Michael. "Why do progressive foundations give too little to too many?" *The Nation*, January 12, 1998, 11-16.

Sifrey, Micah. "Bumpersticker banner." TomPaine.com, June 16, 2003. http://www.tompaine.com/Archive/scontent/8098.html.

Sillars, Les. "Somebody get him a white hat." *Alberta Report,* September 26, 1994, 10.

Simpson, Christopher. *Science of Coercion.* New York: Oxford University Press, 1994.

"Since Sept. 11: The responses show how terrorism and war have left their mark," *Maclean's*, December 31, 2001.

Smith, James Allen. *The Idea Brokers: Think Tanks and the Rise of the New Policy Elite.* New York: Free Press, 1991.

Soley, Lawrence. "Heritage clones in the heartland." *Extra*, September-October 1998. http://www.fair.org/index.php?page=1430.

Somers, Margaret and Fred Block. "From poverty to perversity: Ideas, markets and institutions over 200 years of welfare debate." *American Sociological Review* (February 2005): 260-287.

SourceWatch. Center for Media and Democracy. http://www.sourcewatch.org/.

Sparks, Colin. "Extending and refining the Propaganda Model." *Westminster Papers in Communication and Culture* (July 2007): 68-84.

Spencer, Glenn. "The Four Kings of Carbon." *Citizens for a Sound Economy*, March 26, 2001. http://www.freedomworks.org/informed/issues_template.php?issue_id=398.

Spink, Lynn. "Editor's note." In *Bad Work: A Review of Papers from a Fraser Institute Conference on 'Right-to-Work' Laws*, edited by Lynn Spink, York University, Centre for Research on Work and Society, Toronto, 1997, 2.

Sproule, J. Michael. *Propaganda and Democracy.* Cambridge University Press, 1997.

———. "Propaganda studies in American social science." *Quarterly Journal of Speech* (February 1987): 60-78.

Starky, Sheena. "Tax Freedom Day: a cause for celebration or consternation?" Library of Parliament, September 18, 2006. http://www.parl.gc.ca/information/library/PRBpubs/prb0632-e.htm.

Statistics Canada. "Income tax ... by the numbers." April 27, 2009. http://www42.statcan.ca/smr08/smr08_129-eng.htm.

———. "Average total income by economic family types, 1983-2002." April 22, 2005. http://www.statcan.ca/english/Pgdb/famil05a.htm.

Stauber, John and Sheldon Rampton. *Toxic Sludge is Good for You.* Monroe, ME: Common Courage Press, 1995.

Stefancic, Jean and Richard Delgado. *No Mercy: How Conservative Think Tanks and Foundations Changed America's Social Agenda.* Philadelphia: Temple University Press, 1996.

Stein, Sherry. "Letter to Martin Broughton regarding research program in emulation of the Social Affairs Unit." *British American Tobacco*, January 28, 2000. http://legacy.library.ucsf.edu/tid/lbc53a99.

Stewart, Lyle. "Good PR is growing." *This Magazine*, May/June 2002, 29-33.

Stobbe, Mark. "The Selling of Saskatchewan." In *Devine Rule in Saskatchewan*, edited by Lesley Biggs and Mark Stobbe, 81-109. Saskatoon: Fifth House Publishers, 1991.

Stone, Peter. "Grover and Jack's long adventure." Nationaljournal.com, January 10, 2005. http://nationaljournal.com/about/njweekly/stories/2005/1001nj1.htm.

Sullivan, Patrick. "Working group considers major changes as CMA develops new policy on health financing." *Canadian Medical Association Journal* (July 1993): 86-88.

Sutton, Antony. *Wall Street and the Rise of Hitler*. Sudbury, UK: Bloomfield Books, 1975.

Swartz, Aaron. "Rachel Carson, mass murderer?" *Extra*, September/October 2007. http://www.fair.org/index.php?page=3186.

Taft, Kevin and Gillian Steward. *Clear Answers: The Economics and Politics of For-Profit Medicine*. Edmonton: Duval House Publishers, 2000.

Taylor, Philip. *War and the Media: Propaganda and Persuasion in the Gulf War*. Manchester, UK: Manchester University Press, 1992.

Tellier, Paul. "Integration calls for debate on tough questions facing Canada." Speech to the Canadian Railway Club, Montreal, December 14, 2001, *Canadian Speeches*, January/February 2002.

Thacker, Paul. "Congressman unmoved by peer review, asks to see raw data." American Chemical Society: ES&T Online News, July 6, 2005. http://pubs.acs.org/subscribe/journals/esthag-w/2005/jul/policy/pt_congress.html (accessed May 15, 2006; site now discontinued).

———. "How the Wall Street Journal and Rep. Barton celebrated a global-warming skeptic." American Chemical Society: ES&T Online News, August 31, 2005. http://pubs.acs.org/subscribe/journals/esthag-w/2005/aug/business/pt_wsj.html (accessed May 15, 2006; site now discontinued).

———. "Skeptics get a journal." American Chemical Society: ES&T Online News, August 31, 2005. http://pubs.acs.org/subscribe/journals/esthag-w/2005/aug/policy/pt_skeptics.html (accessed May 15, 2006; site now discontinued).

"The great divide," *The Economist*, March 4, 2004, 38-39.

The Heat is Online. "ExxonMobil: the sceptics new partner." n.d. http://www.heatisonline.org/contentserver/objecthandlers/index.cfm?id=3645&method=full.

Think Progress. "The architects of war: Where are they now?" http://thinkprogress.org/the-architects-where-are-they-now/.

Thompson, Clive. "Ever wonder what think-tanks think about? Here's a glimpse." *Catholic New Times*, September 7, 1997, 10-11.

Tromp, Stanley. "Last word." Media, Summer 2001. http://www.caj.ca/mediamag/summer2001/lastword.html.

Truini, Joe. "Bush to unveil voluntary program." *Waste News*. February 3, 2003, 4.

Tye, Larry. *The Father of Spin*. New York: Crown Publishers, 1998.

United Nations Environment Programme. "Governments take decisive action to rid the world of persistent organic pollutants (POPs) through the Stockholm Convention." May 6, 2005. http://www.pops.int/documents/meetings/cop_1/press/pr5-05POPsCOP1.doc.

————. "Stockholm Convention on POPS to become international law, launching a global campaign to eliminate 12 hazardous chemicals." May 14, 2004. from http://www.pops.int/documents/press/EIF/pr5-04POPsEIF-E.pdf.

United Nations Conference on Environment and Development. "Rio Declaration on Environment and Development." Rio de Janeiro, June 1992. http://www.unep.org/Documents.Multilingual/Default.asp?documentid=78&articleid=1163.

U.S. Census Bureau. "Historical poverty tables." August 28, 2008. http://www.census.gov/hhes/www/poverty/histpov/histpovtb.html.

U.S. Congress. Congressional Budget Office. "Historical effective tax rates, 1979 to 2005: Supplement with additional data on sources of income and high-income households." Washington, DC, December 2008. http://www.cbo.gov/doc.cfm?index=9884.

U.S. Department of Health and Human Services, Administration for Children and Families. "Caseload data." January 21, 2009. http://www.acf.hhs.gov/programs/ofa/data-reports/caseload/caseload_recent.html.

Vaillancourt, François and Robert Gagné. "Personal income taxes in Canada: Dissimilarities, redistributive impacts and social policy." *Canadian Tax Journal* (1999): 927-944.

Van Auken, Bill. "Mourning for Pinochet—US establishment shows its affinity for fascism." *Global Research*, December 14, 2006. http://www.globalresearch.ca/index.php?context=va&aid=4145.

van Kampen, Karen. "Surgical strike." *National Post Business*, February 2002, 38-49.

Verberg, Peter. "Judicial power under scrutiny." *Alberta Report*, October 21, 1996, 31.

Verma, Sonia. "Not in my backyard." *This Magazine*, November/December 1998, 32-38.

Vogel, David. *Fluctuating Fortunes*, New York: Basic Books, 1989.

Walker, Michael. "Letter to Adrian Payne regarding centre for studies in risk and regulation." *British American Tobacco*, June 19, 2000. http://legacy.library.ucsf.edu/tid/mbc53a99.

Wanniski, Jude. "Judith Miller, warhawk reporter." wanniski.com, July 23, 2003. http://www.wanniski.com/showarticle.asp?articleid=2776.

Weigel, David. "Conservative think tank adjusts to tough times." *Washington Independent*, March 13, 2009. http://washingtonindependent.com/33697/conservative-think-tank-adjusts-to-tough-times.

Weir, Kirsten. "Rachel Carson's birthday bashing." Salon.com, June 29, 2007, http://www.salon.com/news/feature/2007/06/29/rachel_carson.

Wharton Economic Forecasting Associates. "Global warming: the high cost of the Kyoto Protocol." 1998. http://www.heartland.org/policybot/results/11399/Global_Warming_The_High_Cost_of_The_Kyoto_Protocol.html.

Wilentz, Amy. "On the intellectual ramparts." *Time*, September 1, 1986. http://www.time.com/magazine/article/0,9171,962189,00.html.

Wilson, Kathleen and Mark W. Rosenberg. "The geographies of crisis: Exploring accessibility to health care in Canada." *Canadian Geographer* (Fall 2002): 223-234.

Wilson, Kris M. "Communicating climate change through the media." In *Environmental Risks and the Media*, edited by Stuart Allen, Barbara Adam and Cynthia Carter, 201-217. London: Routledge, 1999.

Winter, James. *Democracy's Oxygen: How Corporations Control the News*. Montreal: Black Rose Books, 1997.

————. *Mediathink*. Montreal: Black Rose Books, 2002.

Wolfson, Michael and Brian Murphy. "Income taxes in Canada and the United States." *Perspectives, Statistics Canada*, Catalogue no. 75-001-XPE, Summer 2000, 28-31.

Woodard, Joe. "Tax the rich and damn the deficit." *Alberta Report*, February 14, 1994, 15-18.

Woolley, John and Gerhard Peters. "William J. Clinton, The President's radio address—30 November 1996." The American Presidency Project, University of California at Santa Barbara. http://www.presidency.ucsb.edu/ws/index.php?pid=52294.

World Health Organization. "World malaria report 2008: Summary and key points." Geneva, Switzerland, 2008. http://www.who.int/malaria/wmr2008.

Zelder, Martin. "Will Alberta's health care reforms succeed?" *Fraser Forum*, January 2000. http://oldfraser.lexi.net/publications/forum/2000/01/section_03.html

Zupp, Adrian. "Who runs America: Forty minutes with Noam Chomsky." *Boston Phoenix*, April 5, 1999. http://weeklywire.com/ww/04-05-99/boston_feature_3.html.

Zussman, David. "What's after NAFTA." Industry Canada Conference on Policy Challenges of North American linkages, Calgary, June 21, 2001, Public Policy Forum. http://www.ppforum.ca/common/assets/speeches/en/whats_after_nafta.pdf (accessed December 19, 2007; site now discontinued).